Enterprise Storage Systems

Guide to

- Understanding storage system capabilities
- Understanding vendor tactics
- Developing system and vendor requirements
- Making informed acquisition decisions

David J. Sacks

Chicago, Illinois, U.S.A.

To Robin

Abstract

Enterprise storage systems are designed for and acquired by customers such as businesses and governments.

Customers should understand the capabilities of these storage systems, understand the capabilities vendors can offer and how they market and sell to customers, understand how to identify their particular storage and vendor requirements, and understand how to evaluate and compare systems and vendors.

However, these objectives are not easily achieved due to the sophistication and complexity of today's advanced storage technologies and due to a highly competitive market where vendors try to outdo each other to gain customers' limited time and attention.

This guide helps customers navigate this environment to have a successful, satisfying system acquisition and ownership experience. It provides numerous insights to help customers view these systems and vendors with a knowledgeable and critical eye.

Readers who should benefit from this guide include chief information officers, data center managers, storage administrators, and any organization personnel involved with making or influencing enterprise storage system acquisition decisions. Others who may benefit include industry participants such as consultants, analysts, and vendors.

Preface

I wrote this book at the culmination of a long career in Information Technology (IT). It captures insights I've gained and lessons I've learned that I believe are of significant value to anyone in the IT industry who acquires, administers, supports, or writes about computer storage systems.

My IT career leading to this book has been quite an adventure. When I started working with computers in the late 1960s storage was just a peripheral attached to mainframes. Today, computer storage is an indispensable element of any computing infrastructure. It has capabilities, complexities, and sophistication that make it a major area of specialization in its own right, alongside servers and networks. Customers can choose from many different storage systems sold by many different vendors. The high degree of competition and ongoing investment in research and development in the industry drive what appear to be nonstop advances in storage technology.

This book is a guide to help readers understand the capabilities of enterprise storage systems and evaluate different storage systems and the vendors who sell them. Reflecting on my decades of experience in IT, I believe my credentials make me well-qualified to write this guide. My career began as a part-time mainframe application programmer for an automotive fleet leasing firm while working towards a Bachelor of Science in Mathematics at the Illinois Institute of Technology with a minor in Computer Science. Upon graduation I joined the IBM Corporation's mainframe operating system development team. After nearly a decade in development I transferred to IBM's Sales organization as a Systems Engineer assisting sales representatives with selling, installing, and supporting mainframe computers and storage. During that time I wrote the *MVS Answer Book*[1], providing a unique perspective on the capabilities of mainframe computers.

When storage evolved to a level of sophistication requiring dedicated specialists, I chose to take that path. I became an expert on high-end IBM storage, talking with customers from the U.S. and other countries about their storage needs. I subsequently took on marketing responsibilities, focusing on high-end storage systems from IBM and how they compared to systems from competitors. I wrote numerous papers and gave numerous presentations to help customers and co-workers better understand these systems. I spoke with industry analysts to represent IBM's views about storage. I provided advice-and-counsel to sales teams in competitive situations. I shared my knowledge with the high-end storage development team. These experiences taught me quite a lot about the storage system industry from many different perspectives.

---

[1] Published by John Wiley & Sons, Inc., 1994.

The variety of roles I've taken on, the extensive research I've done, my time spent with so many industry participants – and especially the time spent with customers who willingly shared with me their experiences with storage from multiple vendors – provided me the knowledge and insights I've captured in this Guide.

Acknowledgments

I want to thank reviewers of the draft of this Guide. In alphabetical order:

Barrett Sweet, based on his years of experience in direct sales and sales management at multiple IT companies, provided helpful perspectives on sales topics.

Bill Cochran, drawing on his many years selling and supporting storage hardware and software, helped clarify many technical points.

Linda Evans, whose IT career has included managing systems engineers, selling storage, and more, has always paid impressive attention to detail; her suggestions helped add clarity throughout the Guide.

Mike Stanek, who has worked for multiple storage vendors, provided extensive and thoughtful input covering both technical topics and readability.

It has been my privilege to work with each of these storage and IT business experts. Their feedback has helped make the Guide better than it otherwise would have been. Any errors or omissions herein are my responsibility.

Contents

Introduction

This Guide provides insights and recommendations to help organizations have a productive and satisfying experience when acquiring enterprise storage systems. It addresses the kinds of fundamental questions customers, vendors, and industry watchers ask about the storage acquisition process:

- What benefits can enterprise storage systems provide to customers?

- What benefits can storage vendors provide to customers?

- How can customers determine their particular storage and vendor requirements?

- What messages and tactics do vendors use to help make a sale?

- How can customers determine the system and vendor best able to meet their storage requirements?

If the answers were few and simple, there would be little need for this Guide. But that's not the case. The IT storage system marketplace is bursting with an almost overwhelming variety of offerings. Customer-vendor relationships range from friendly to adversarial. And, customers can take varied paths to arrive at a decision.

Insights into the acquisition process have immense value to all parties involved. That is the main focus of this Guide. Let's begin.

The term *enterprise storage system* refers to computer storage systems designed for organizations such as businesses and governments. *Enterprise* storage is distinguished from *consumer* storage in personal computers and other personal devices. The focus in this Guide is on enterprise storage systems (aka enterprise storage arrays) that support accessing data both randomly and sequentially; these systems are historically based on disk technology (in contrast to tape technology best used for accessing data sequentially).

Different enterprise storage systems can significantly differ in attributes such as capacity, availability, performance, function, and cost.

Enterprise storage systems are manufactured by many well-known IT companies such as Dell, EMC, Fujitsu, Hitachi, HP, Huawei, IBM, NetApp, and Oracle. Many less well-known enterprise storage system manufacturers also exist. New (startup) enterprise storage companies frequently enter the market.

Sellers of storage systems include the manufacturers and associated companies called *business partners* and *value-added resellers (VARs)*. Collectively, these sellers are the storage system *vendors*.

Competition among vendors is nothing less than fierce. Before discussing the important implications for customers it is insightful, if only for historical perspective, to review why this is so.

High market opportunity for vendors. The worldwide market opportunity for enterprise storage system revenue is generally measured in tens of billions of U.S. dollars per year.[2] There is additional potential revenue for associated offerings such as storage network equipment, host software-based storage management offerings, and professional services. Due to the widespread acceptance of industry-standard hardware components and methods for connecting hosts (aka servers) and storage systems, most enterprise storage systems can attach to most types of hosts, promoting a large market.[3]

High customer demand. The demand for enterprise storage systems continues with no end in sight. These systems sometimes take new forms (such as virtualized storage, discussed later), but customers' requirements for enterprise storage (such as high levels of capacity, availability, and performance) are expected to persist. Reasons behind continuing demand include increases in the amount of data supporting legacy applications such as inventory and purchasing, increased computer management of unstructured data such as email and audio and video files, and data generated by new applications. Another contributor to demand is advances in storage technology often supported only by newer models of storage systems. While the increasing use of public cloud storage (i.e., storage capacity rented over the Internet) may slow the growth of storage capacity in customers' on-premises data centers, overall demand for enterprise storage systems is expected to remain very healthy for the foreseeable future.[4]

Easier entry into the industry than ever before. When enterprise storage systems first emerged decades ago each manufacturer was largely vertically integrated, meaning they

---

[2] Reference: http://www.idc.com/getdoc.jsp?containerId=prUS25666715.

[3] There are exceptions. IBM z Systems z/OS mainframes require special types of connections to storage supported by only a few storage system models in the marketplace. Some hosts support storage located inside the same cabinet as the host and that storage normally cannot be accessed by other hosts. (This is sometimes called *internal storage* or *integrated storage* and is generally available only from the host's manufacturer. However external storage systems are often preferred by customers due to advantages such as their ability to be shared by multiple hosts and the ability for customers to choose among a variety of such systems in the marketplace.)

[4] Demand for enterprise storage will continue because organizations need storage whether it resides in an organizations' data center or in the cloud. While some in the storage industry have speculated that organizations will increasingly replace on-site enterprise storage systems with public cloud storage, this is unlikely to widely occur in the near future. Reasons include the increased time it takes for applications to access data over long distances using shared networks, concerns about the availability and security of storage systems not under an organization's direct control (and containing data often called "the family jewels"), functional requirements not satisfied by cloud storage offerings, and the challenges of migrating existing data to or from the cloud or among different cloud offerings.

built the components they integrated into computer and storage systems. Today, enterprise storage systems of various types can be assembled to a great extent using commodity parts available from multiple manufacturers. Examples of such parts include hard disk drives (HDDs) and solid-state drives (SSDs), host connections via Fibre Channel[5] and Ethernet components, and processor chips. Software that runs on internal processors and is useful as a foundation for the manufacturers' programming that runs enterprise storage systems is generally available (e.g., open source Linux operating systems). Efficient designs for many software-based storage functions are widely known. What differentiates enterprise storage system models from each other is mainly the particular combination of hardware components used, how they are connected together, and the software that drives the system, providing the particular functions it supports.

The emergence of niche markets. The earliest years in the enterprise storage industry saw a one-size-fits-all approach that was good enough to address the relatively simple storage needs of most customers. Today's advanced hardware and software storage technologies and different ways those technologies can be used provides opportunities for both new and established manufacturers to design storage systems optimized for particular use cases, helping those manufacturers differentiate themselves from their competitors. Examples of such use cases include systems optimized for one or more of the following: accessing data as blocks, accessing data as files, managing backups (through emulating tape storage), and managing archived data. Other optimizations that can distinguish different system models include low cost, high capacity, a high level of management function, and a high level of performance.

Extensive competition among enterprise storage system vendors has both good and bad consequences for customers.

The good news is that customers now have more options than ever when it comes to acquiring enterprise storage systems. Significant competition for each customer's business keeps prices relatively low while also motivating manufacturers to deliver increased product capabilities at an ever faster pace.

The bad news is that customers must deal with vendors often trying to outdo each other to gain customers' limited time and attention, often resorting to ever more compelling claims about their own products and ever increasing attacks, justified or not, on competitors' products. This can be an unwanted distraction, even annoyance, when many organizations are confronted with significant day-to-day demands in managing their data centers. Consider: Shortages in administrative personnel and skills, frequent upgrades to and replacement of IT equipment, support for new applications required by the enterprise, increased demands for system availability and performance – all to be handled within budget constraints.

Related developments bring both good and bad news. Customers today have access to a massive amount of information from vendors and other sources to help them make informed storage system decisions. On the other hand, it can take a good deal of time and patience to

---

[5] The British spelling (of U.S. "fiber") was adopted for this technology. Fibre Channel cables need not use fiber optic technology.

cope with all that information which can range from vendor publications to industry analysts' reports and commentators' blogs.

Given the complexity and variety of state-of-the-art enterprise storage systems, the variety of vendors selling these systems, as well as the abundance of information to sort through, customers are challenged (to put it mildly) when it comes to answering questions such as: What can storage systems and vendors potentially do? What do I need them to do for my organization? How do I sort through valid, grandiose, and conflicting claims? What system and vendor should I choose? These questions must often be answered without the benefit of hands-on experience with all the systems and vendors under consideration. Vendors often use this situation to their advantage in their selling tactics to help sway buying decisions their way. (The situation is similar to the complexities of consumers choosing among today's wide assortment of automobile models, manufacturers and dealers, and numerous options at-extra-cost. Deciding among enterprise storage systems and vendors can be far more complex.)

Is there anything enterprise storage customers can do to make the best decisions under the circumstances?

The answer, fortunately, is yes. Broadly, there are a few steps that can go a long way towards addressing the challenges. These steps follow a simple model of decision making: state the problem to be addressed, gather information, determine requirements, evaluate and compare options, then make the decision. In more detail:

State the problem to be addressed: In this case, the problem is a need for computer storage to hold and help manage data for a relatively long time.

Gather information on what storage systems can do: This step identifies the capabilities of enterprise storage systems. It might seem that this step should follow a step to determine requirements. However, it makes sense to first gather information about what storage systems currently available in the marketplace can actually do because many customers are not aware of all the capabilities of today's sophisticated storage systems. Knowing about those capabilities can help shape requirements. (If, for example, a customer did not know some storage systems can encrypt data on drives to help protect data security, they wouldn't make that a requirement.) Equally important, the learning process reveals what today's storage systems *cannot* do. (As an analogy: if you know you need personal transportation you might desire a flying car, but at this time it is useless to require one.) While this step calls for some understanding of storage technology, the task is simplified by focusing on *what* these systems can do rather than on the deep technology of *how* they do it "under the covers," as fascinating as that can be.

Gather information on what vendors can do: It is important to gather information about the values vendors can offer. Vendors' offerings, such as professional services, can help lighten many customers' burdens. It is also important to understand how vendors market and sell their storage systems to customers. Like vendors in any industry, every storage vendor can be expected to convey a message that what they are selling is terrific. Knowing how to discern what information and claims vendors provide are useful, and what may be only distractions, has significant practical value.

Determine requirements: Armed with the gathered information, customers can identify their particular storage system requirements based on available system and vendor capabilities.[6] This step also identifies a customer's requirements for the vendor they want to do business with. If a customer does not know what they need and want in an enterprise storage system and vendor, any system from any vendor would theoretically do.

Evaluate and compare alternatives: While many storage systems and vendors may appear to support similar capabilities, the overall capabilities of different systems and vendors often vary significantly. Customers can benefit from an objective process to evaluate and compare systems and vendors to determine which combination best addresses their requirements.

Make the decision: If the above steps were executed well, the storage system and vendor best able to address a given customer's requirements may be apparent. However, the overall decision process is not a machine that necessarily works in only one way with one unambiguous answer as output. Subjective considerations may apply as is the case in many acquisition decisions.

To briefly summarize this introduction, this Guide provides practical information to help organizations optimize their enterprise storage procurement decisions. The goal is to help ensure customers have a successful, satisfying acquisition and ownership experience.

Not that long ago storage was "just a peripheral." All focus was on the host. The length of this Guide alone is an indicator of how far storage has come from those days.

Notes

1. To get the most out of this Guide, the reader should preferably be familiar with basic storage concepts and terminology (e.g., hardware, software, I/O, host, drive, volume, cache, and performance). *Part I, Storage Fundamentals - Concepts and Terminology,* provides an introduction to storage technology for readers with limited background in storage or desiring a review of that subject. The other parts of this Guide attempt to provide sufficient information and examples to make topics understandable even to readers with a limited familiarity with storage technology. (The author isn't fond of books that seem to assume the reader already knows a lot about the subject matter.) Nevertheless, to better understand some technical considerations, in some cases a reader may find it helpful to consult with (in-house or industry) storage experts, or perhaps do some background reading using the extensive information found on the Web.

2. This Guide is divided into parts that align with the decision steps described earlier. Part I provides an overview of storage system concepts and terminology intended as an introduction or refresher for readers with limited storage experience. Part II provides

---

[6] A customer may occasionally determine they could use a capability in a storage system or a vendor not currently offered. The customer might ask the vendor whether the capability could be offered in the future.

insights into the capabilities of enterprise storage systems: *what* these systems can do (with minimal time spent on the underlying technologies of *how* they do it).   Part III provides insights into the capabilities of vendors: what value they potentially offer and how they announce, market, and sell enterprise storage systems to customers.   Part IV provides insights to help customers determine their particular storage and vendor requirements plus insights to help customers evaluate and compare the capabilities of storage systems and vendors against those requirements.

Parts are divided into chapters. Some discussions could reasonably be included in more than one chapter. For example, the discussion of vendors' capacity guarantees is in the *Marketing Tactics* chapter though it potentially could have been in the *Capacity* chapter or the *Prices and Costs* chapter. In most cases, such discussions are included in only one chapter.

Except for Part I, most chapters in each part have three sections: A chapter begins with a short introduction. That is followed by bulleted topics providing insights into the chapter's subject such as definitions, examples, and supporting topics; clearly marked *Tips* are embedded into selected discussions. Ending a chapter is an *Additional Tips* section. Tips provide commentary on factual points, suggest actions customers can take, and suggest questions customers can ask vendors. (It is not intended that a given customer would necessarily act on every tip suggested in this Guide.   Rather, tips are there for consideration so that readers might determine which ones are most pertinent to their situation.)

Finally, while this Guide strives to explain storage system capabilities at a practical level without delving too deeply into the underlying technology, a few topics struck the author as ones where some readers may want a bit more technical background. Accordingly, a few short appendices are included and referenced in the main text.   One appendix, for example, addresses the question: Why is the ability for multiple computers to share data not as simple as just connecting them to the same storage system?

3. This Guide is intended to apply mainly to general purpose enterprise storage systems independently of various forms they can take.[7]   Such systems include block-access storage, file-access storage, and software-defined storage (e.g., virtual storage appliances). Object-access storage is also mentioned. Many storage system attributes (such as availability, performance, and data replication functions) have numerous common considerations regardless of the enterprise storage system variation supporting them.

4. Specific vendors and products are rarely mentioned in this Guide. One reason is to arm the reader with insights that are product-independent and expected to continue to apply over time; this avoids the long, dense (and often boring) tables frequently used to compare the detailed specifications of different storage system models, information that can quickly become out-of-date. Another reason is to arm the reader with insights into marketing and

---

[7] Considerations that apply to only very specialized storage systems, such as deduplication appliances, virtual tape libraries, and public cloud storage, are not covered in this Guide.

sales tactics customers commonly confront from storage system vendors, but to do so without pointing fingers at particular vendors who may employ these tactics.

5. About some terms used throughout this Guide:

The terms "host" and "server" are used interchangeably.

The term "user," common in the IT world, is employed in a generic sense of a user of storage. A user can be a host or an application or an administrator. The meaning is hopefully clear from the context.

The abbreviation *aka* (also known as) is used frequently in this Guide when defining terms. Many aspects of storage are described equivalently by more than one term. One reason is that various vendors and analysts have assigned different terms to comparable hardware components and comparable software-based functions, and more than one such term has sometimes become widely used.

Following industry convention, in abbreviations "B" stands for bytes and "b" stands for bits. For example, 100GB means one hundred gigabytes and 10Gb/s means ten gigabits per second. (Among many in the industry, a rate such as 10Gb/s is stated as simply "10Gb," though that can be confusing.)

"Risk" and "business risk" are occasionally mentioned. There are two basic aspects to risk customers should consider: the probability an undesired situation will occur and the severity (e.g., harm) of the situation if it does occur.

Some technical terms (such as "architecture" and "software-defined storage") lack definitions used consistently in the industry. Sometimes, definitions from standards organizations are cited. Sometimes, a discussion indicates the lack of a precisely agreed upon definition and does its best to describe the meaning of a term.

6. A storage system's capacity to hold data can be partitioned in different ways. Volumes are one way that is very common. To simplify this Guide, discussions that refer to capacity often mention volumes but not other types of partitions such as file systems and object containers (both of which are discussed in the *Data Access Protocols* chapter in *Part I, Storage Fundamentals - Concepts and Terminology*).

7. Storage management topics covered in this Guide are generally limited to facilities integrated in and directly supported by enterprise storage systems. Host-based management facilities – including storage resource management, hierarchical storage management (hsm), backup management, and more – are very important topics to be sure, but deserve as in-depth a discussion as this Guide provides for the storage systems themselves and that is beyond the scope of this Guide.

8. This Guide includes references to various websites to augment discussions. When this Guide was written, the referenced sites appeared to be virus-free. However, as is true in general when accessing the Web, readers are advised to use means such as anti-virus software to help protect against the possibility of malicious websites.

Part I.

Storage Fundamentals - Concepts and Terminology

The first part of this Guide provides an introduction to enterprise storage systems, especially useful to readers with limited familiarity with storage system concepts, facilities, and terminology. (It's interesting to observe that in the computer storage industry, and probably others, many terms and concepts "catch on" rather than being invented by some official organization.) Additional concepts, facilities, and terms are introduced in later parts of the Guide where they are most relevant. Here, the goal is to provide sufficient (and hopefully interesting) background information to make the other parts of the Guide more meaningful; this is not a comprehensive storage tutorial.

Why is this information important? It covers concepts and defines terms commonly used by storage administrators and storage vendors, and these concepts and terms may arise during a storage acquisition process. If a decision-maker, whether an individual or a committee, is in a meeting where their organization's storage requirements are being discussed or a vendor is giving a presentation, having the background presented in this part of the Guide will help make many points understandable.

This material is more technical than the subsequent parts of the Guide that focus on acquisition topics. In particular, it does not contain the tips presented later. If a reader knowledgeable in the basics of storage technology scans this part of the Guide and concludes "I already know this stuff," they may reasonably choose to skip this section.

Accessing Storage

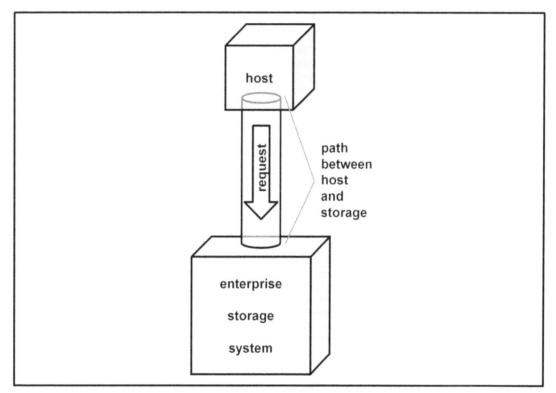

A host communicates with an enterprise storage system by sending requests to read or write data over a path that connects the host and storage system together.

A *host* or *server* is a general purpose computer used mainly by enterprises such as businesses and governments to run programs, including operating systems and applications.

An *enterprise storage system* (simply *storage system* for brevity) is a repository that stores (writes) data received from hosts and retrieves (reads) that data to hosts on request. Many enterprise storage systems include internal processors running software that helps manage data; such storage systems can be thought of as computers that specialize in storage.[8]

To request access to data in storage, an application program may include statements like:

---

[8] The term *compute* is sometimes used in the industry as a noun to mean the processing capability of hosts or storage systems to run software, distinguishing that from a capability to store data, as in "My storage system's design lets customers separately grow compute and storage capabilities."

```
OPEN Myfile
READ record from Myfile
. . .program instructions to do something with the data just read. . .
CLOSE Myfile
```

Such requests may go directly to a host's operating system or may go to *middleware* like a database management system that in turn forwards the requests to the operating system. The operating system translates such high-level requests from applications into lower-level (i.e., more detailed) requests known as *I/O (Input/Output) commands*, or *I/O requests*, or *I/O operations*, or simply *I/Os*. An I/O command is a message sent by a host to a storage system telling the storage system what the host wants it to do. For example, an I/O command may request a storage system to read 1,000 bytes of data at a certain location in the storage system and return that data to the host.

A host sends I/O commands over a *path* to a storage system. A path may be as simple as a cable directly connecting a host and storage system. Or, a path may be a network that includes intermediate devices such as switches. A network may even carry other types of messages in addition to I/O commands.

An observation about the relationship between host computers and storage systems: A storage system is generally unaware of the meaning of the data it receives from hosts, e.g., how that data is used by applications or how some data may be related to other data. Although, as we'll see, storage system internal software can help manage data in useful ways, the data itself is generally treated as just bits and bytes. It is host software and, ultimately, human users that are aware of what data means, e.g., that some data is a text document, or is a set of slides in a presentation, or is a photograph, or is a video, or is the layout of a Web page, or contains references to other stored data.

Storage Devices

The fundamental storage system component supporting storage of digital data is a storage device. Storage devices, and storage systems in general, are sometimes called *secondary storage* or *auxiliary storage*, in contrast to internal computer memory being called *primary storage* or *main storage* or *main memory*.[9]

The following images are examples of the main types of storage devices used in storage systems. The devices are shown without covers. Each device is roughly the size of a deck of playing cards.[10]

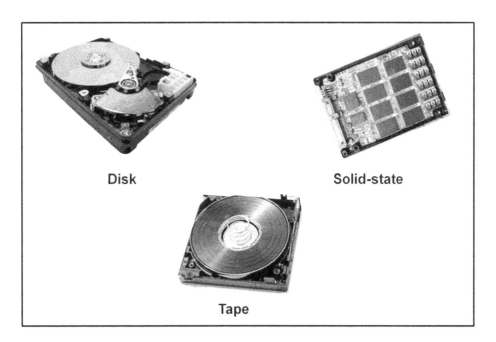

Disk   Solid-state

Tape

[9] In this Guide, as in most of the IT industry, the terms "memory" and "storage" are often used interchangeably. However, one of the two terms may be the one most commonly used in a particular context. For example, enterprise storage systems are called just that, not "enterprise memory systems." And, because internal computer electronic memory to hold programs and data is usually based on DRAM (Dynamic Random Access Memory) technology, it is commonly called "memory," not "storage."

[10] Image sources:
Disk: https://commons.wikimedia.org/wiki/File:Hdd_od_srodka.jpg.
Solid-state: https://commons.wikimedia.org/wiki/File:Embedded_World_2014_SSD.jpg.
Tape: https://commons.wikimedia.org/wiki/File:LTO2-cart-wo-top-shell.jpg.

Disk Devices

Currently, most enterprise storage systems are based on disk devices. Videos demonstrating how disk devices work can be found at http://www.youtube.com by searching for *how a disk drive works*.

A disk device is similar to a phonograph record and player packaged together, with a few significant differences.

o Unlike the single platter of a phonograph record, a disk device has one or several platters connected to a common axis (aka spindle, a term sometimes used as a synecdoche for a disk drive.

o Unlike the single spiral groove on a record, each disk device's platter typically has thousands of separate concentric *tracks*.

o Unlike the arm-and-needle in a record player that follows a record's spiral groove from beginning to end, the *arm* in a disk device is a comb-like structure where the teeth of the comb are interleaved with the platters. The end of each "tooth" has a *read/write head*. The entire arm moves to position the appropriate head over the appropriate track; that operation is called *seeking*.[11] (To position one head over one track on one side of a platter, the single arm necessarily moves all heads together. That's less expensive and simpler than having an independent arm and head for each side of each platter.) The following diagram shows a close-up view of the arm with its comb-like heads interleaved with a disk device's platters.[12]

o Unlike a record's groove permanently inscribed in the surface at the factory, disk device platters are coated with a material called a *medium* that records data magnetically as 0 and 1 bits and allows changing data in place. For a write I/O request, a head causes appropriate track locations to be set to 0 and 1 bits to match the data in the request. For a

---

[11] Some radio receivers support a "seek" button. Pressing the seek button causes the radio to jump to the next detected station, skipping over intermediate frequencies from the listener's perspective.

[12] Image source: https://commons.wikimedia.org/wiki/File:HDD_Heads.JPG.

read I/O request, the head recognizes the magnetic orientation of the data in the location it is requested to read and the disk device transmits the data to the requestor.

The ability to directly move a read/write head to a desired track on the device without accessing all data on intermediate tracks and to read or write data starting at a location on that track (as soon as that location rotates under the appropriate head), allows disk technology to efficiently support accessing data both randomly and sequentially. This is an incredibly important advantage over tape technology which, based on a ribbon of magnetizable material, is optimized for sequential access.

Disk storage devices are typically packaged in *modules* known as *hard disk drives (HDDs)* or *disk drive modules (DDMs)*. The module package helps keep out dust and prevent damage.[13] These modules generally come in industry-standard sizes and shapes (aka *form factors*). The most common form factors are 2.5-inches (aka small form factor, SFF) and 3.5-inches (aka large form factor, LFF); these sizes refer to the diameter of the disk platters.

It is important to understand that applications do not need to be aware of how a disk device works. The program that implements an application needs only a high-level view of storage; for example, the program simply requests the host's operating system to read or write a particular record in a particular file. The operating system maintains tables that let it translate the application's request to an I/O request it sends to a particular device and relative location in that device, e.g., disk device 112 / location 9,036. The disk device internally translates the relative location to the physical location (i.e., platter, track, position on track) in the device. These layers of translation allow applications to be programmed in a device-independent way. This enables the underlying data to be moved to different devices and for the underlying storage technology to change – it doesn't have to be a disk – without applications needing to be modified.

Solid-State Devices

While disk technology has served the IT industry well for decades and is expected to continue to be widely used for years to come, disk storage is being supplemented and gradually supplanted by solid-state storage. Locations in solid-state storage are accessed

---

[13] "Hard" refers to the rigidity of the platters, in contrast to "floppy disks" available in the early days of personal computers. "Drive" refers to the fact that the earliest disk devices in the 20th century (comparable to records) had to be manually mounted on another device (comparable to a record player) that contained a motor and movable arm to "drive" the disk. Today, disk modules contain their own motors to manage rotation and arm movement and are typically always online to hosts, enabling fast access to data.

In contrast, tape modules, called *cartridges*, contain only media. When a cartridge is needed it must be "mounted on" or "loaded into" or "inserted into" a tape drive that contains a motor to move the tape media over fixed read/write heads in the drive. That generally makes the cost of tape storage lower than the cost of disk storage for similar capacities to hold data because a single tape drive can be used to support many cartridges, though only one cartridge at a time. Despite their higher cost, the fast random access capability of disk (and certain other) devices makes them indispensable to most applications.

electronically. Because it has no moving parts, solid-state storage is generally faster – often much faster – than mechanical disk storage; it is also more reliable. (Cost considerations are discussed in the *Prices and Costs* chapter.)

Solid-state storage is generally packaged on *cards*. A single card may be packaged in the same-size module as an HDD. Alternatively, multiple cards may be packaged together in a larger enclosure. Potential benefits of an enclosure for multiple cards include saving physical space compared to multiple HDD modules and supporting controllers designed specifically for those enclosures (e.g., to connect to higher speed paths than HDDs and to preserve data in case a card fails).

However it is packaged, solid-state storage is often designed to support accessing data as if it was disk storage. In that case, the device is often called a *solid-state drive* (*SSD*) , a *solid-state disk* (*SSD*) , or, sometimes, an *enterprise flash drive* (*EFD*). An HDD-sized SSD module generally emulates one HDD; an enclosure of multiple cards may emulate multiple HDDs. An SSD responds to the same I/O requests to read and write data as an HDD. When SSDs are packaged in modules that have the same form factor as HDDs, SSDs can readily be used in a storage system originally designed only for HDDs. (In Information Technology (IT), it is common for a new technology to emulate aspects of an older technology to make it easier to use the new technology.)

More about HDDs and SSDs

The data capacity of an individual drive, whether an HDD or an SSD, is typically measured as a number of 8-bit bytes ranging from hundreds of gigabytes to several terabytes. By convention, drive capacity is measured as a decimal value (e.g., 1 terabyte = 1 TB = 1,000,000,000,000 bytes). Enterprise storage systems contain multiple drives.

HDDs are often categorized based on performance (i.e., speed) and on data capacity. Some HDDs are designed for relatively high performance. Others are optimized for relatively high capacity. (Higher drive capacity generally reduces the cost per unit of capacity and requires fewer total drives to support a given amount of capacity.) HDDs optimized for high capacity are sometimes called *capacity-optimized* or *nearline* drives. HDDs optimized for high performance are sometimes called *performance-optimized* drives. At the time this is being written, HDDs that rotate at 15,000 RPM (revolutions per minute) are the fastest HDDs while nearline drives typically rotate at 7,200 RPM.[14] Because of the increasing use of SSDs, HDDs with higher RPMs are unlikely to ever be manufactured.

---

[14] In recent years, a new type of drive is being offered by some drive manufacturers that combines HDD and solid state technology in the same drive module to form a *solid state hybrid drive (SSHD)*. An SSHD keeps the busiest (aka *hottest*) data in solid-state memory to boost performance compared to HDDs. SSHDs would provide limited value in enterprise storage systems because those systems generally have large shared solid-state caches, discussed later, which can be more efficient than a small cache inside each SSHD.

SSDs are also commonly categorized based on whether they are optimized for performance or capacity. SSDs are generally based on *flash memory* technology where data is stored in *cells*. *Single-level cell (SLC)* drives have one bit per cell and support the highest performance while *multi-level cell (MLC)* drives support two (or more) bits per cell for higher capacity per device but lower performance compared to SLC drives, though MLC SSDs are still much faster than HDDs. (Sometimes, the term "flash drive" is used instead of "SSD," but "flash" refers to a particular technology and over time other solid-state technologies may be used in SSDs.)[15]

Drives are sometimes categorized into *tiers* (i.e., tier 0, tier 1, and so on) where the lowest tier number supports the highest speed. Beyond being ordered by relative performance, however, which drives are in which tiers can vary by storage system or by user designation. There is no industry standard for this.

Important Attributes

HDDs and SSDs are designed to support two critically important attributes storage systems rely on: *persistence* and *nonvolatility*.

Persistence means that data stored in the media is preserved for a relatively long time (measured in years). One way persistence is supported is by a physical property of the media called nonvolatility. A storage medium is said to be *volatile* if it requires a continuous source of power to maintain its contents. It is important that media used for long-term storage of data be *non*volatile so that a temporary loss of external power does not result in loss of data stored in the media. Nonvolatility also enables storage modules to be moved from one place to another while preserving their data.

An example of nonvolatile storage media familiar to many readers is the type of solid-state media, flash memory, used in flash drives (aka "thumb drives" due to their size) for personal computers. An example of volatile storage is the type of solid-state media, Dynamic Random Access Memory (DRAM), used for computer memory: if a personal computer, for example, is unplugged from a source of electricity, once its battery is drained the contents of the computer's memory are lost. That is why a computer must be rebooted and applications restarted once power is restored. (Computer memory is much faster than secondary storage devices. That enables computers to run applications at the speeds we are familiar with, but the type of solid-state technology used to support the high speed of computer memory is volatile – and relatively expensive.)

---

[15] The form of flash memory used in SSDs is sometimes called *NAND flash memory* because it is based on microscopic components that use NOT AND logic gates. MLC flash is sometimes called TLC (triple-level cell) when each cell contains three bits.

Storage Systems

Why integrate storage devices into a storage *system* containing multiple storage devices and other components? Why not just connect individual storage devices directly to hosts?

A *system* is defined as a group of related parts that move or work together. A system can do more than the individual parts can do in isolation. So, a storage system can provide more value – more capabilities – than individual storage devices. Some examples of this value are below; later chapters include additional examples.

Enterprise storage systems typically contain multiple HDDs or multiple SSDs; a storage system containing both HDDs and SSDs is known as a *hybrid system*. Smaller storage systems may contain only a few storage devices and be roughly the size of a dresser drawer while large storage systems may consist of a few thousand devices housed in multiple refrigerator-sized cabinets.

Example of a moderately sized enterprise storage system containing multiple storage modules. It is about 18 inches (.5 meters) in height.[16]

Some hosts need to store and retrieve so much data that it takes tens or hundreds or even thousands of storage devices to provide the capacity to hold it all. A single storage device currently may hold up to several terabytes (i.e., several trillion bytes) of data, so a thousand devices can hold up to several petabytes (i.e., several thousand terabytes) of data. (A host's

---

[16] Image source: https://commons.wikimedia.org/wiki/File:HP_EVA4400-1.jpg.

internal memory is not large enough to hold that much data, in addition to being volatile and thus not useful to hold data that must persist for a long time.)

If each storage device had to be connected separately to a host, the number of connections, e.g., the number of cables, would be unmanageable. By packaging multiple storage devices and other relevant components together in a large enclosure, the resulting storage *system* can have as few as one or two connections to a given host. In essence, a host's I/O request simply tells the storage system which devices it wants to access.

A storage system can be designed to be shared by multiple hosts. In many enterprise applications multiple hosts need to access the same data. Having a storage system support multiple connections so it can be attached to different hosts is surely more practical than having individual storage device modules each support multiple connections because the cables could end up being bulkier than the module itself.[17]

Another benefit of a storage system is that it can share many internal hardware components among all its storage devices. For example, a small number of fans can be used to cool all the devices in the system rather than having a fan inside each module. Further, a system could have extra (spare) fans in case a fan fails. Sharing components in this way reduces cost and reduces the number of components that could potentially fail.

An additional benefit of a storage system is that it can contain its own internal computers, sometimes actual servers and sometimes processor chips integrated into other components. These computers run software supporting many capabilities useful for the entire system – capabilities not supported by individual storage devices. These capabilities are often called *data management, data services*, or *data management services*. For example, a data management service supported by many storage systems is the ability to make a copy of data inside the storage system. While it would be possible for a host running applications to also perform such data management services, having the storage system perform them leaves host resources freer to work on running applications.

---

[17] The ability of multiple hosts to share data can require more than just physically connecting those hosts to the same storage system. This is discussed in *Appendix A. Data Sharing*.

Storage System Hardware

A storage system is not an indivisible monolith. It consists of a set of hardware and software *components* ("building blocks") that contribute to the system's overall capabilities. The set of components that compose a particular storage system form the system's *configuration*.

The hardware components of a storage system compose its *physical configuration*, the focus of this chapter. Individual hardware components are mostly invisible to hosts and applications. In practice, the same kinds of hardware components are commonly found in storage systems from different manufacturers. Storage system models differ in the number of components, the speed of components, how components are connected together "under the covers," and the names manufacturers assign to the components. (Another important difference between storage system models, the system's software, is discussed later.)

A simple storage system

Let's begin the hardware discussion at a high level based on the following diagram:

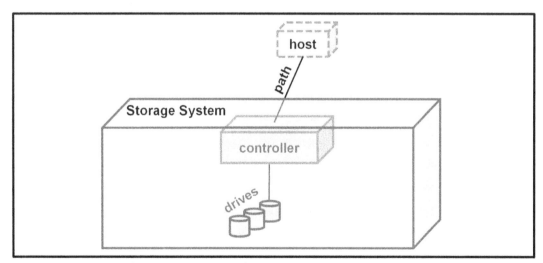

A high-level view of a host connected to a storage system showing selected internal hardware components.

A *path* (think of a cable) from the host connects to a *controller* inside the storage system. A controller is a component that contains processing capability (i.e., one or more processor chips), accepts some form of input, and generates some form of output. In the storage system shown in the diagram, the controller accepts I/O commands from the host and passes each command to the appropriate (HDD or SSD) drive based on information in the commands. The diagram depicts a simple system with a single host connecting to a single controller by a single path. Actual systems may contain one or more controllers that may be connected to one or more hosts via multiple paths; actual paths may be contiguous cables or may include intermediate devices such as switches.

Controller is a generic term and the controllers in a given storage system may have names assigned by the manufacturer (e.g., "adapters"). In some storage systems, components that might be thought of as separate controllers are organized into larger components for ordering purposes and those larger components may be called *controllers*, *nodes*, *servers*, *engines*, or other manufacturer-assigned names.

The drives provide capacity to hold data. Additionally, each drive has an internal controller (not shown) that acts on I/O commands sent to the drive by the controller and reads or writes data in a way appropriate for the specific technology used in the drive. For example, a controller in a disk drive manages movement of the mechanical arm.

Outside the box: host-to-storage paths

Hosts and storage communicate by sending messages over a physical connection path, typically in the form of a cable. Host-to-storage paths are important to consider for several reasons. There are different types of path technologies. Hosts and connected storage systems must support compatible technologies (or ways to manage differences). Numerous cables are often located under a data center floor and can require time and effort to manually install, remove, and change.[18]

Host-storage connectivity is part of the technology field of *networking*. Whether for host-storage connectivity or more general use, networking is a sophisticated and often complex technology specialty in its own right. Different types of storage networks differ in attributes such as the types of cables, performance, distance limitations, supported network devices such as switches, basic communication protocols (that may transport I/O requests and other types of messages), cost, and prevalence of use by IT organizations. This discussion focuses on points most relevant to storage system requirements; the term "network" is used broadly to include direct host-to-storage paths as well as paths with intermediate network devices such as switches.

Background

The following brief perspective on how host-storage connectivity evolved is useful to introduce some commonly used terms and concepts.

---

[18] Readers are likely familiar with the difficulty of managing cables just for their personal computer equipment. Imagine a data center with hundreds of cables connecting devices that may be dozens of meters apart.

Many early host-storage connections used a standard called Small Computer System Interface (SCSI, pronounced "skuh'-zee"). SCSI originally encompassed both the physical cables and the I/O commands sent between hosts and storage. A SCSI connection often provided the data path all the way from the host to the drives. A SCSI cable consisted of a ribbon of wires where the bits in one or two 8-bit bytes were sent in parallel down different wires. That parallelism improved the speed of moving data over a cable, but limited the distance between a host and a storage system to a few meters to ensure a set of bits sent together from one end of the cable arrived at the other end at nearly the same time so they could be reliably reassembled into the associated bytes.

Over time, the ways hosts connected to storage systems diverged from the ways drives were connected inside storage systems. Factors motivating this divergence include:

1) The need for growing data centers to support relatively long distances between hosts and storage systems while inside the storage system only a relatively short distance was needed to connect to its internal drives. The longer host-to-storage distance required changing from SCSI's parallel data path to a *serial* path which, because bits were transmitted one after the other, those bits could be transmitted faster and for longer distances than possible using a parallel path.

2) The emergence of types of host-storage connectivity, e.g., Fibre Channel and Ethernet, which provided more networking functions (such as switched paths) than parallel SCSI.

3) A storage system could be designed to support multiple connection types yet internally connect its drives in a single way. In practice, SCSI paths continued to be used internally in storage systems for some time because the distances between components in a cabinet were relatively short and manufacturers were experienced in producing SCSI drives.

Other technologies eventually supplanted parallel SCSI paths to drives inside storage systems. For a time, a form of Fibre Channel (called FC-AL, Fibre Channel-Arbitrated Loop) was used to connect drives. Another technology eventually supplanted Fibre Channel for drive connectivity and it remains prevalent today: SAS (serial-attached SCSI).[19] (Some drive manufacturers have introduced drives with native Ethernet interfaces, but deployment is very limited at the time this is being written.)

What is particularly interesting is that the original SCSI command set was tightly associated with the physical SCSI network. However, as host-to-storage connections diverged from the drive connections inside a storage system, the use of SCSI commands was preserved which avoided a lot of reprogramming. For example, SCSI commands can be transmitted over Fibre Channel paths or over Ethernet paths.

---

[19] Readers may have heard of another drive attachment type called SATA: Serial Advanced Technology Attachment. SATA has often been used in personal computers. SAS connections can support drives with SATA interfaces.

Overview of Path Types

The path type appropriate to a given host-storage connection depends on factors such as the types of connections the hosts and storage systems support as well as the type of data access protocol used by applications, discussed in the *Data Access Protocols* chapter. Below is an overview of path types; a comparison covering performance, cost, supported distances, management, and supported network devices is beyond the scope of this discussion.[20]

- Fibre Channel. This is a popular type of host-storage system connection that supports the SCSI command set. It is widely used in larger data centers.

- FICON. IBM z Systems mainframes support a connection standard called FICON (*Fibre Connection*, pronounced "feye'-kahn") that shares much technology with Fibre Channel. However, rather than SCSI I/O commands, FICON uses a different set of I/O commands that support the particular way z Systems communicate with storage systems.

- Ethernet. Ethernet is a popular general purpose networking technology. It is frequently used to support many types of messages (e.g., email and Web traffic) in addition to storage I/Os. Ethernet can support both local area networks (LANs) and wide area networks (WANs).

- SCSI over Ethernet (iSCSI). Similar to transporting SCSI commands over Fibre Channel, SCSI commands can be transported over Ethernet. This is called iSCSI (pronounced "eye-skuh'-zee"; the "i" refers to an underlying protocol layer called IP).

- Fibre Channel over Ethernet (FCoE). FCoE (pronounced letter by letter) is an emerging connection type. It basically preserves storage functions supported by Fibre Channel and familiar to Fibre Channel users, but employs Ethernet hardware rather than hardware designed for Fibre Channel. Because Ethernet is commonly deployed by customers for uses outside of storage, using FCoE for storage can help reduce the different types of network hardware an organization needs to support.

  Both FCoE and iSCSI support SCSI protocols over Ethernet. It is unclear whether customers needing the SCSI command set will converge onto one of these technologies over time or whether they will coexist for the foreseeable future.

- Less common network types sometimes used for host-storage paths:

  ○ InfiniBand. InfiniBand is used by a few storage systems as the host-storage path. This appears to apply mainly to environments requiring very high performance.

---

[20] Nevertheless, a few words about network devices are warranted. Examples of intermediate devices in a network are *hubs* and *switches*. One use is to allow multiple hosts to share paths to multiple storage devices without direct end-to-end cables. (To directly connect m hosts to n storage systems would require at least $m \times n$ cables.) In the case of Fibre Channel, some switches are called "switches" and some are called "directors." While directors tend to have more built-in redundancy and a higher number of ports compared to switches, there are no industry standards to definitively distinguish the two categories of switches.

- ○ PCI Express (PCIe).   PCIe (pronounced letter by letter) is primarily used to connect components inside a host or storage system. However, some storage systems support direct PCIe connections to hosts; this appears to apply mainly to environments requiring very high performance.

- ○ Serial Attached SCSI (SAS).   Some small enterprise storage systems support SAS (rhymes with "mass") for the host-storage path although it is more common to find SAS used inside a storage system for the internal paths to drives.

Note that the speed of a path is typically specified in bits per second. That is because networks in general transmit bits serially (i.e., one at a time). Moreover, most networks use 10-bit transmission characters: 8 bits (one byte) of user data plus two bits added for network synchronization purposes.   For example, a 16 gigabit/second (16Gb/s) Fibre Channel connection can transmit 1.6 gigabytes/second (1.6GB/s).

Inside the box: a tour of system components

Before looking directly inside the box, a few words about the box itself are warranted. The metal container in which a storage system is packaged may go by various manufacturer-assigned terms that can vary by system model. Common terms include: enclosures, modules, cabinets, frames, bays, and drawers. Some storage systems are housed in vendor-supplied or customer-supplied industry-standard 19-inch racks while other systems require floor-standing vendor-supplied cabinets of other sizes. The height of enclosures, especially drawer-size enclosures designed to be installed in 19-inch racks, is conventionally measured in units of U (rack Units) where 1U = 1.752 inches.   (Reference: http://en.wikipedia.org/wiki/Rack_unit.)

Major storage system hardware components inside the box are illustrated in the diagram below.

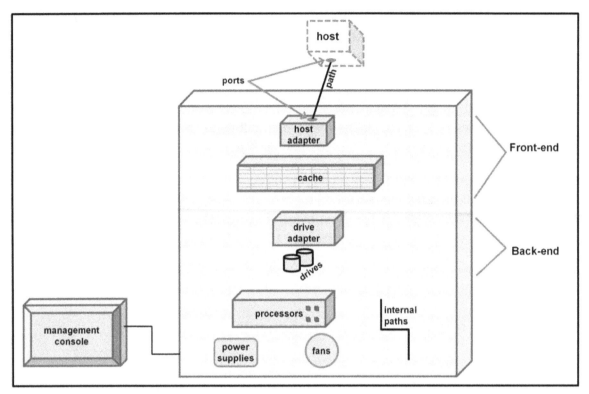

Major enterprise storage system hardware components.

Starting from the right side, then moving from top to bottom:

- <u>Front-end / Back-end</u>. As shown on the far right, a storage system is often described as having a *front-end* and a *back-end*. The components in the front-end are generally those conceptually "closest" to hosts; those components are often shown at the top of a diagram of a storage system. The components in the back-end such as the drives are often shown at the bottom of a diagram. Other components, such as power supplies, are usually not associated with the front-end or back-end. The physical location of components in a storage system's enclosure may be unrelated to their location in a diagram.

- <u>Host, path, port, and adapter</u>. One or more *hosts* connect (or attach) to a storage system over one or more *paths (aka channel paths)*. A path may be a cable that provides a direct host-to-storage connection, as shown. Or a path may consist of a cable that goes from a host to a network device such as switch (not shown) where the switch connects to the storage system; more complex networks can be used. The length of a path may range from relatively short (e.g., a few meters) to virtually unlimited lengths depending on the technology used.   Several industry-standard host-storage connection technologies are nearly universally used; Ethernet and Fibre Channel may be the most common. A given storage system model may support multiple connection technologies.

  A cable plugs into a *port* (i.e., a socket) in the host and in the storage system. The port in the host may be part of a controller component called a *host bus adapter (HBA)* or *network interface card (NIC)* (not shown). The port in the storage system is often called a *host port* that may be part of a controller component called a *host adapter, channel director, front-end adapter*, or *front-end director*.

Hosts and storage systems may each support multiple ports on one or more controllers. Smaller storage systems may have only a few host ports on one or two controllers while larger storage systems may have over one hundred host ports spread across multiple controllers.

A host may connect to a storage system via one or more paths. Using two paths is common, configured through different adapters in the host and storage system so that access to the storage system is preserved even if one port or one controller fails.

A host may connect to one or more storage systems. A storage system may connect to one or more hosts.

- Cache. Storage system *cache* is a form of electronic storage intended to boost system performance. The basic idea is to implement a cache that is much faster than the back-end drives; the storage system uses the cache to hold the most active data.[21] Users are generally unaware of cache other than its impact on performance. In some storage systems, administrators can set system parameters to control which data can reside in cache. (More is said about cache in the *Performance* chapter.)

  The technology used to implement storage system cache is typically Dynamic Random Access Memory (DRAM), the memory technology used in many hosts. Some storage systems use SSD technology as a cache. However, SSD technology is typically slower than DRAM and so is likely to be used as a cache only when the back-end drives are HDDs.

  In response to an I/O request to read data, host adapters first look for that data in cache and if it is there it can be returned to the requesting host very quickly. Else, that data is retrieved from back-end drives; that takes longer but is still quite fast by human standards, e.g., a small fraction of a second. In response to an I/O request to write data, host adapters usually place that data directly in cache and signal the host that the I/O operation is complete. The storage system later *destages* that data from cache to the appropriate drive.

  Storage system cache based on DRAM, like computer memory, is usually volatile, meaning it needs a constant supply of external power to maintain its data. In practice, however, loss of power to the storage system normally does not result in data loss. That's because for data in cache read from nonvolatile back-end drives, cache holds only a copy of that data. For data just written to a storage system and placed in cache, batteries are usually in the system to provide temporary power long enough to destage that data to nonvolatile media in case of a power outage.

- Drive adapter. *Drive adapters* are controllers also called *back-end adapters*. (In some storage systems a front-end and back-end adapter are combined into a single controller.) A

---

[21] Caching is not limited to storage systems, but is a useful principle in computing in general. The idea is to use a small fast storage to hold a frequently accessed subset of data that resides in slower storage. (Perhaps that slower storage is intrinsically slower, or perhaps its access is slowed due to network distance or speed.) For example, personal computers often use a portion of an internal drive as a cache for Web pages previously accessed by a browser so that if those pages are accessed again they can be quickly retrieved from the internal drive without having to be transmitted over a (slower) communications network.

drive adapter typically connects to and manages multiple drives. Drive adapters are often configured in pairs connecting to the same set of drives so that access to drives is preserved even if one adapter in a pair fails.

When a host adapter receives a request to read data and does not find that data in cache, it passes the request to the drive adapter that connects to the drive holding the data. That drive adapter then sends the request to the appropriate drive. When a host adapter receives a request to write data it temporarily stores that data in cache; the drive adapter that manages the drive where that data will be written later destages that data from cache to that drive.

Drive adapters may support the ability to store data in a redundant way on drives so that, if a drive fails, applications can continue to access data; a prominent technique to support this redundancy is called *RAID* (Redundant Array of Independent Drives) and is discussed in the *Availability* chapter.

Drive adapters may also manage *drive sparing* to replace a failed drive by a pre-installed spare drive or by other spare system capacity reserved for that purpose.

- Drives. Enterprise storage systems typically support multiple drives; some models support up to several thousand drives. As discussed earlier in the *Storage Devices* chapter, there are two types of drives used in contemporary enterprise storage systems: *hard disk drives (HDDs)* and *solid-state drives (SSDs)*.[22] Both types of drives, especially HDDs, are often depicted as cylinders in diagrams because of the stack of one or more circular platters in HDDs which were the only type of direct-access storage for decades; that shape also helps distinguish storage drives from other rectangles common in IT diagrams.

Other components

The following storage system components are generally not considered to be front-end or back-end components.

- Processors. Enterprise storage systems typically contain one or more *processors* (aka *microprocessors*). Processors can reside inside various storage system components such as the front-end and back-end adapters. Processors run software that supports a storage system's functions including handling I/O requests received by host adapters, accessing drives attached to the back-end adapters, managing what data resides in cache, and more. Further, every drive, whether an HDD or SSD, contains at least one processor to manage drive function, though vendors generally don't count those processors in specifications that cite the number of processors in a storage system. Some processors are general-purpose programmable processors (as found in personal computers). Others are *application-specific*

---

[22] Whether they contain HDDs, SSDs, or both, because of their history enterprise storage systems are still often called "disk systems." Ironically, the term coined decades ago by IBM for disk-based storage for mainframes was *DASD*, Direct Access Storage Device, a term that, had it persisted, would have readily accommodated the use of SSDs.

integrated circuits (ASICs, pronounced "ay'-six") optimized for specific functions and typically designed for a specific storage system model. Storage system vendors may draw attention to a system's use of ASICs as evidence of system efficiency; however, ASICs can be more costly than general-purpose commercially available processors.

- Management console. A *management console* connected to the storage system helps administrators manage the system. The console may support a graphical user interface (GUI, pronounced "goo'-ee") or a command line interface (CLI, pronounced "c-l-i"). For example, an administrator can use the console to check on system status to determine whether it is operating normally. Some storage systems support multiple consoles to maintain access to administrative functions even if one console fails. A management console may also be used by a vendor's system maintenance personnel.

- Power supplies. *Power supplies* convert electricity fed into the system into forms needed by internal components and distribute that electricity to those components. For example, a power supply may convert external AC current into internal DC current. Some storage systems have multiple power supplies designed to maintain system access even if one power supply fails.

- Fans. Storage systems are designed to operate within a certain temperature range. Hardware components can generate a significant amount of heat. Fans draw cool air into a storage system and expel heated air from the system. This helps prevent overheating that could cause component failures. Some storage systems have multiple fans to help maintain a desired internal temperature even if one fan fails.

- Internal paths. Various storage system components involved with data movement need to communicate with each other and so are connected together inside the system. Connections may be by internal cables or by plugging components into a shared circuit board called a *backplane*. For example, many storage systems use Peripheral Component Interconnect Express (PCIe, pronounced "p-c-i-e") paths to connect components to internal processors. PCIe is designed to move data at high speed over short distances. Many storage systems use Serial-attached SCSI (SAS) paths between drive adapters and drives because SAS is designed specifically for that kind of connectivity. PCIe, SAS, and another internal path type sometimes used, InfiniBand, are industry-standard connectivity technologies.

Note that the hardware in enterprise storage systems shipped from system manufacturers generally has strict limitations on how it can be modified by customers, if at all. The components are integrated and tested together at the factory. Any changes, such as hardware repairs or upgrades, must usually be authorized by the manufacturer; otherwise the system warranty may be voided. (Some organizations build their own storage systems from commodity (aka commercial off-the-shelf, COTS) components in which case they are acting as their own system manufacturer or integrator.)

Storage System Software

While storage hardware is necessary to build storage systems and is the result of years of technology advances, it is its software that brings a storage system to life, just as the software in personal computers brings those marvelous machines to life.

Today's sophisticated enterprise storage systems are essentially computers that run software designed to manage I/O requests from hosts and manage storage system hardware components. Storage system software provides the function delivered by hardware controllers and coordinates how controllers work together. Storage system software provides data management functions such as the ability to make copies of data inside a system, the ability to encrypt data in a system, the ability for administrators to customize the way a storage system operates, and much more. This software is often called an *operating environment* or *microcode* or *firmware* or *licensed machine code.* It fulfills a role in a storage system similar to operating system software in a host.

Software function inside storage systems has increased over time, as illustrated by the following diagram.

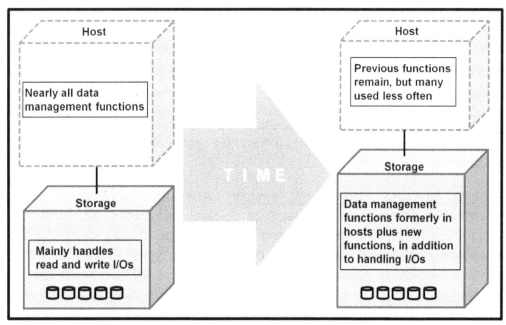

Software-based data management function has moved from hosts to storage systems over time.

In the early days of computer storage in the mid 20th century, nearly all data management functions resided in host-based software. Storage system internal function was mainly support for low level I/O requests from hosts, such as reading and writing data, and early forms of error handling. Later, more function started being added directly inside storage systems. Examples of the earliest such functions are maintaining redundant data to preserve access to that data even if a drive fails, enhancing performance through managing a hardware cache, and making copies of data for uses ranging from backup to disaster recovery. (*Part II* of this Guide discusses many data management functions supported by enterprise storage systems.)

Adding data management functions already supported by hosts to storage systems did not mean those functions were necessarily removed from hosts; not every storage system model supports every host-based function. But functions supported by storage systems offer several advantages: Storage system-based functions generally support all hosts attached to the same storage system in a consistent way. Storage systems may support functions not supported by all hosts. Using storage system-based functions rather than similar host-based functions offloads work from hosts, freeing host resources to be applied to applications.[23]

Today, the storage system operating environment provided by the system manufacturer is an essential component of most enterprise storage systems. It normally cannot be replaced by software from another party except in the case of software-defined storage (SDS, discussed later) running on a computer acquired separately by a customer. The only changes a customer can generally make to the software designed for a particular storage system are replacing older versions by newer versions, or modifying parts of the software with *fixes* (aka *patches*) from the manufacturer that repair software defects (aka *bugs*). In other words, a conventional storage *system* is a combination of hardware and software components designed and integrated by the same manufacturer, with a particular component configuration selected by the customer.

Users (i.e., applications, hosts, and administrators) interact with storage system software in the following ways.

1. Requests for data. Applications request to read or write data and hosts forward those requests to a storage system where they are ultimately handled by storage system software.

2. Requests for data management function. Authorized applications and storage administrators interact with a storage system to invoke software-based data management functions such as making copies of data. These kinds of management requests may be made via one or more of the following types of interfaces to the storage system: a host-based application programming interface (*API*), a host-based command line interface (*CLI*), or a graphical user interface (*GUI*). Depending on the storage system model, management requests originating from a host may be communicated to the storage system over the same path as I/O requests via specially formatted requests

---

[23] To be fair, it must be noted that host-based storage management functions have the potential advantage of being able to be applied against any attached storage system, providing consistency compared to inconsistent or absent support in those storage systems.

that a storage system recognizes as data management commands, or management requests may occur over a separate connection used only for such requests.

3. Requests to manage the logical configuration. Administrators interact with storage system software to control how storage system capabilities appear to users and how the system behaves in various circumstances. This is called the *logical configuration* (in contrast to the system's hardware components that make up the *physical configuration* discussed previously).[24] A system's logical configuration together with its physical configuration determines a storage system's entire configuration.

Examples of storage system logical configuration parameters include the ability to define system administrators and their authorities to manage the system, the ability to control how capacity is provisioned (i.e., allocated or assigned) to hosts, and the ability to control how the system handles various error conditions. Like requests for data management function, interfaces to manage the logical configuration of a given system may include API, CLI, and/or GUI. This topic is discussed further in the *Logical (Software) Configuration Management* chapter.

---

[24] The term *logical configuration* is widely used but has no industry-standard definition. This Guide uses the term to refer to how a storage system is customized by setting software parameters that specify how the system appears and behaves from the perspective of users.

Data Access Protocols

I/O requests from hosts to access storage capacity conform to a particular *data access protocol* (aka *access method*). That is, the messages conveying the requests are in specific formats and support a particular way of organizing and accessing data. An essential storage system requirement is that it must support the particular protocols users use to communicate with it.

Fundamental access protocol operations include the ability to create data, read data, update data, and delete data; this is sometimes (unfortunately) referred to as *CRUD*; if a search function is supported the term is *SCRUD*. In addition to these basic operations, an access protocol also indicates how storage can be partitioned into subsets that can be *provisioned* (i.e., assigned) to different hosts and applications.

The most common ways capacity is provisioned and accessed in storage systems is by a *block-access* protocol, a *file-access* protocol, or an *object-access* protocol. Every storage system supports at least one protocol and some storage systems support multiple protocols.

Many applications access data indirectly through *middleware* such as a database management system (DBMS). In that case, it is the middleware that more directly accesses storage and the particular access protocol used may be transparent to applications. For applications that access storage more directly, part of the application design process is selecting which data access protocol(s) to use. As is true of most alternatives in IT, the answer depends on the goals to be achieved and weighing the trade-offs between different protocols, based on both general considerations and on particular implementations.

Block-access protocol

A block-access protocol provides a very flexible way to provision and access capacity with little structure imposed on how that capacity is used.

Capacity is provisioned by storage administrators dividing system capacity into *logical volumes* (aka *virtual volumes* or *logical unit numbers (LUNs, rhymes with "runs")* or simply *volumes*). A volume is a logically contiguous set of bytes[25] similar to a physical drive. A

---

[25] "Logically contiguous" means the bytes appear to applications to be consecutive and adjacent, e.g., byte-1, byte-2…byte-n. However, the bytes may not actually be stored that way on media.

volume's capacity is determined by an administrator and can differ from the capacity of the physical drives installed in a system.[26] Hosts are assigned one or more *volumes*.

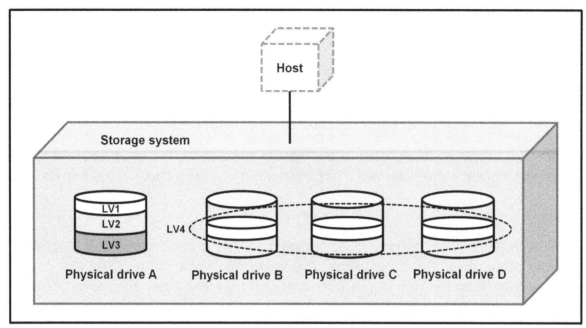

Block-access storage is partitioned into logical volumes. A given physical drive might be partitioned into multiple logical volumes; a large logical volume might span all or parts of multiple physical drives. In the diagram, physical drive A contains three logical volumes: LV1, LV2, and LV3. LV4 is distributed across three physical drives: B, C, and D.

Capacity in a volume is accessed in small chunks called *blocks*. The content and size of a block is up to the application. For example, a block might contain one or more records in a database or may contain a portion of a large digitized image; one application may organize its data as a set of 1000-byte blocks while another organizes its data as a set of 4,096-byte blocks. Hosts read and write data by making an I/O request specifying a volume ID assigned when the volume was created, and the location (as a relative offset) of a block within that volume. The simplicity of a block-access protocol means it generally has low overhead so that the speed of accessing data is limited mainly by hardware speeds.

Block-access protocol implementations in different storage systems may differ in ways such as the maximum capacity of a logical volume and the maximum number of logical volumes that can be coexist in the system.

Many types of applications use block-access protocols. One example is a host-based database management system (DBMS) where fast I/O is important and the DBMS manages how data is organized (e.g., as tables within volumes). Another example is a legacy application designed to use block-access storage before other types of data access protocols

---

[26] In the early years of storage systems, before storage evolved to allow administrators to specify the capacity of different volumes independently of the capacity of the installed drives, terms such as *disk*, *disk drive*, *physical drive*, *spindle*, *volume*, and *LUN* referred to a single hardware disk-based storage device. Note: The term *LUN* generally applies to volumes or drives accessed using the Small Computer System Interface (SCSI) block-access protocol, commonly supported by many hosts; *volume* is a more generic term than LUN.

were even available in the marketplace. Other examples are file-access and object-access protocols, described below, which are sometimes just layers of programming "on top of" software supporting a block-access protocol.

File-access protocol

A file-access protocol provides a more structured way than a block-access protocol to provision and access storage capacity. A file-access protocol lets users assign a file-name to an amount of logically contiguous capacity. The content of a file is up to the application. Files are often described as *unstructured data* such as a text document or image, in contrast to *structured data* such as a database that organizes data into fields within records within tables.[27]

File-access protocols organize files into a hierarchical (tree) structure of *directories* (aka *folders*) as shown below.

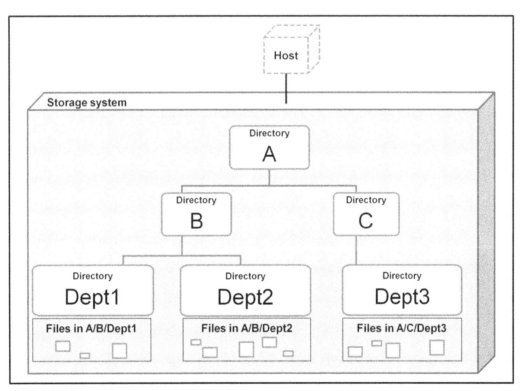

An example of files organized in a hierarchical file system. In this example, files are stored in the lowest level of directories.

Capacity is provisioned by an administrator dividing capacity into *file systems* (aka *filesystems*), the name for a hierarchy of directories. What is assigned to a host or application can be an entire file system or only specific directories (aka *shares*). Various mechanisms are

---

[27] The terms "structured" and "unstructured" are widely used in the industry, but are not precise. Even an "unstructured" file has a structure supported by the applications that create and use the file. For example, a text document may include heading information a text editor can interpret to identify the author and date of creation. An image may include information about its length and width in pixels.

employed by different file systems to limit the amount of capacity consumed by users. *Quotas* of maximum capacity may be assigned to individual users. A maximum capacity may be assigned to individual directories. Some file-access storage systems use *volumes* to hold file systems and administrators can control the size of those volumes; however, those volumes are generally invisible to applications using file-access protocols.

A file is accessed via I/O requests that specify the file name and the hierarchy of directories it resides in. Because of the overhead to manage a file system structure and because file systems are often accessed over long distance networks, performance may not be as fast as the performance of a block-access protocol.

File-access protocols may differ in ways such as performance, the maximum supported size of a file, how users requesting access to a file are authenticated, and in other ways. A given storage system or host may support none or some number of file-access protocols. Commonly used file-access protocols include *Network File System* (*NFS*, which originated in the UNIX environment), *Server Message Block* (*SMB*, which originated in the Windows environment; the name *Common Internet File System (CIFS)* is sometimes used as a synonym, but actually refers to a specific "dialect" of SMB)[28], and *File Transfer Protocol (FTP)*.

Examples of applications that are well-suited for file-access protocols include applications with files that readily fit into a hierarchical directory structure and that can benefit from file sharing mechanisms that may be supported. Another example is applications where files need to be shared over arbitrary distances via networks. The relative simplicity of installing a storage system supporting file-access protocols (e.g., because they use Ethernet rather than Fibre Channel connections) may be important to organizations with limited storage administrator resources.

Object-access protocol

An object-access protocol provides a way to provision and access capacity that is more structured than block-access protocols but less structured than file-access protocols.

An object is similar to a file (e.g., it has logically contiguous capacity), but the organization of objects is "flat" without a hierarchy of directories. Each object is treated as an indivisible whole by the storage system. An important capability of object-access protocols is that they are designed to support very large numbers of objects, e.g., billions, subject to capacity limitations of the supported storage systems.

Each object is accessed via I/O requests that specify the unique ID assigned to the object by the storage system when the object is created, not by a user-defined file name. It is up to the application to manage the IDs of objects it creates, perhaps in an index that associates a meaningful name to each object.

---

[28] See http://msdn.microsoft.com/en-us/library/windows/desktop/aa365233%28v=vs.85%29.aspx.

An important capability of an object-access protocol is that applications can assign *metadata* to an object. Metadata contains information about the object in a key:value format. For example, an object's metadata could include the name of the user who owns the object (e.g., owner:Jane Doe) and other significant data. The metadata can be used to locate desired objects via an I/O request that returns the IDs of all objects in the storage system matching the metadata search criteria.

Provisioning of capacity may be accomplished by an administrator dividing the storage system capacity into subsets sometimes called *containers* or *buckets*. In some object-access implementations the size of a container and the maximum number of objects in a container can be controlled by an administrator. Different containers may be assigned to different users who can then create and access objects they place in the assigned containers.

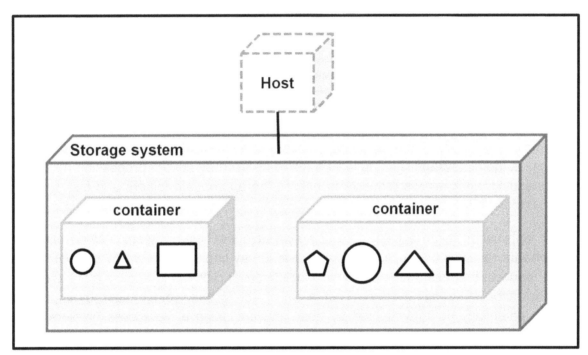

An object storage system may be partitioned into subsets of capacity. Each container can hold multiple objects depicted here as geometric figures.

There are multiple implementations of object-access protocols in the marketplace. No industry-standard object-access protocol has emerged, though some proprietary protocols are used more widely than others. These protocols differ in ways such as performance, maximum object size, and the syntax of I/O requests. Some implementations are offered as cloud-based services.

Object storage is best-suited for data that changes infrequently or not at all because a stored object's data can be modified only by replacing the entire object. An object's metadata may be updatable, however. Examples of applications well-suited for object-access storage include data archiving, backup files, and applications with large numbers (e.g., millions or billions) of files that can benefit from object storage's metadata search capabilities (e.g., images described by keywords).

Note that some vendors use the term "content storage" rather than "object storage."

Notes about Data Access Protocols

- Performance, availability, support for industry standards, and other attributes can vary among different implementations of access protocols.

- A given storage system may support one or multiple access protocols. Systems supporting multiple protocols are called *unified systems*. The most common case may be storage systems supporting both block-access and file-access protocols.

- An access protocol used by an application may vary from the protocols supported by other elements in the end-to-end application-to-drive path. Programming in a host or storage system can sometimes "translate" one protocol to another, transparently to applications. Because block-access provides a very flexible way to access data with minimum imposed structure and because most drives support a block-access protocol, other access protocols are often implemented by software that uses storage systems or drives that support block-access. Here are some examples of protocol translation:

  1) Personal computer users depend on this flexibility all the time, though many users likely do not realize it. Personal computers organize data as files stored in a hierarchical structure of folders or directories. Operating system software handles requests to access the file system (e.g., to read a file to be used by a word processing application) by issuing block-access requests to access the appropriate folders and files stored on an internal block-access drive.

  2) An application might access data using an object-access protocol. When other host software receives the application's requests it may implement them by translating them to requests that use a file-access (or block-access) protocol to access a file-access (or block-access) storage system. That is, an object-access protocol used by applications can potentially be implemented by host software using a file-access or block-access storage system.

  3) A file-access storage system may accept file-access protocol I/O requests from hosts, but internally use a block-access protocol to access the physical drives it uses to store the directory hierarchy and files.

Topology

Topology, in a storage system context, refers to how hosts, storage, and data access protocol software are arranged physically.

Historically, the industry has often cited three basic topologies known as *DAS*, *SAN*, and *NAS* (where each acronym is pronounced as a word that roughly rhymes with *mass*). These terms continue to be widely used today. The discussion first describes the meaning of this taxonomy, then points out several drawbacks.

Descriptions of DAS (Direct Attached Storage), SAN (Storage Area Network), and NAS (Network Attached Storage) in the industry typically differentiate these topologies based on two criteria: (1) whether storage is directly connected to a host or resides in a network so it can be shared by multiple hosts and (2) the location of software supporting the "file system." In this context, "file system software" is not intended to imply only software supporting a hierarchy-oriented file-access protocol; it is whatever software is used to manage how data is organized.

Below is a typical (but not the only) way the DAS/SAN/NAS taxonomy is illustrated:

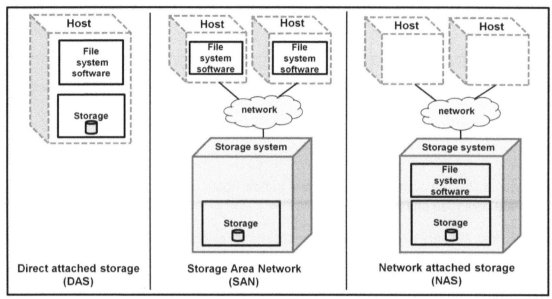

Typical diagram comparing DAS, SAN, and NAS.[29]

DAS (Direct Attached Storage): Storage is connected to only one host. The file system is managed by software in the host.

SAN (Storage Area Network): Storage is connected to hosts over a network. The file system is managed by software in the host.

NAS (Network Attached Storage): Storage is connected to hosts over a network. The file system is managed by software in the storage system. A NAS-based storage system is sometimes called a *filer*.

These three terms have been used in the storage industry for years to describe storage topologies and continue to be widely used. But the continued usefulness of this taxonomy is questionable for several reasons:

- "DAS" doesn't distinguish between storage devices housed in the server enclosure (where both the server and storage are typically from the same vendor) and storage devices in one or more external systems directly attached (i.e., cabled) to only that server (where the storage can potentially come from one or more vendors that are not the server vendor).

- "SAN" refers to a network while "NAS" refers to storage attached to a network.

- The terms don't clarify what to call a block-access storage system shared by multiple hosts via direct connections rather than via a (SAN) with its intermediate devices.

- It is unclear whether a block-access storage system connected to only one host over a network should be called DAS or SAN.

---

[29] In IT, networks are typically drawn as clouds. Networks may contain cables and devices such as hubs, switches, and satellite dishes. A cloud indicates that the particular way a host and storage are connected via a network is not essential to the point being made.

- It is unclear what to call a configuration where a storage system connects to multiple hosts over a network and the system's capacity is divided into subsets where each subset is dedicated to a different host, or some subsets are dedicated to individual hosts and other subsets are shared by multiple hosts.

- The taxonomy does not readily accommodate newer topologies such as virtualized storage systems and Server SANs, discussed in the *Architecture* chapter.

- Even a prominent storage industry standards organization, the Storage Networking Industry Association (SNIA, pronounced "snee'-uh," http://www.snia.org), offers definitions that appear less than clear. Consider SNIA's definition of DAS: "One or more dedicated storage devices connected to one or more servers."[30]

- Taxonomy diagrams and explanations place "file system software" in either a host or storage system. That does not accommodate cases where both hosts and storage systems contain portions of the software supporting a file system. For example, a storage system may contain the software to divide the capacity of a block-access storage system into volumes, while a host contains the software to manage (e.g., create, update, and delete) files inside those volumes.

- The taxonomy does not accommodate storage hardware appliances called *gateways*. Gateways perform a protocol translation, then forward the translated request to a storage system capable of handling it. Gateways may not contain any storage capacity of their own. A common type of gateway is a NAS gateway that accepts file-access protocol I/O requests and translates them to block-access I/O requests. This can be illustrated by building on the basic NAS diagram from the DAS/SAN/NAS taxonomy:

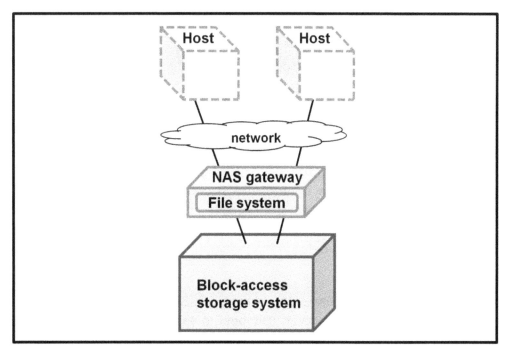

Illustration of a NAS gateway.

---

[30] Source: http://www.snia.org/education/dictionary/d.

When host software receives a request from an application to access a file that the software determines resides in a NAS-based file system, the software sends the request to a location in the network that an administrator identified as that NAS system. That location may actually be a gateway that contains the components of a NAS system (e.g., processors and software) *except* for storage devices. The gateway attaches (as a "front-end" or "NAS head") to another storage system, typically a block-access storage system that does contain storage devices; the gateway manages data in that system as a hierarchical file system. So, the gateway translates the file-access protocol I/O requests it receives from a host into block-access protocol I/O requests to read and write to the attached block-access storage system.

- The taxonomy doesn't readily accommodate *unified storage systems* that support both host-based file systems and storage system-based file systems. This is illustrated below:

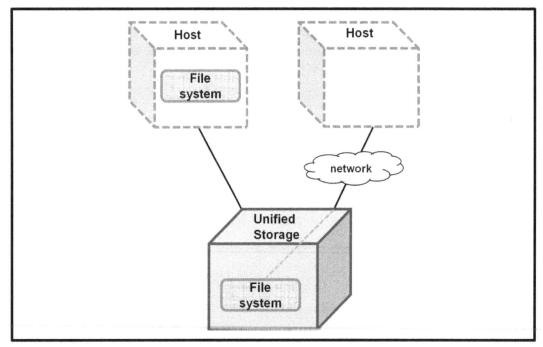

Example of a unified storage system.

In this example, the host on the left contains the software to manage the file system and communicates to the unified storage system using a block-access protocol. That host-storage connection could be via a direct (DAS) connection (shown) or via a SAN (not shown). The host on the right uses a file-access protocol to communicate to the same unified storage system, but accesses that storage system as a NAS system which contains the software to do the detailed management of the file system and maintain it on storage devices.

Despite these kinds of issues, the use of the terms DAS, SAN, and NAS remains widespread. Given the drawbacks described, however, it is best to examine the details of any particular topology under consideration and not rely on only a simplified 3-letter label. It is important to understand the particular hardware elements involved and what access protocol software resides in each hardware "box" of the total configuration. That can affect cost, performance, availability, and more.

Architecture

A storage system's *architecture* is a high-level description of its major components and how they relate to each other. It generally omits many technical details (such as the speed of internal processors) that apply to a particular system that implements the architecture. It can apply to a specific storage system model or family of similar models in the marketplace, or it could describe the structure of a hypothetical storage system. A system's architecture might informally be said to define its personality.

Although the term "architecture" is widely used in the storage industry (as well as in IT in general), it does not appear to have a standard definition identifying precisely what it should and should not describe. Sometimes, the term is used interchangeably with "design"; sometimes, a design is said to specify the details of a particular implementation of an architecture. For the purposes of this discussion the two terms are largely interchangeable.

An architectural description can apply to an entire system, to only a system's hardware components, to only a system's software components, or even to only a subset of a system such as a system's cache. A relatively comprehensive architectural description of a storage system would include: what the system's basic hardware components (sometimes called "hardware resources") are and how they relate to each other, how the system's software is structured, what functions the system's software supports including data access protocols and data management services, and what (external) storage topologies the system supports.

Storage system hardware architectures in particular are commonly highlighted by vendors and commented on in the industry, often in diagrams used for marketing purposes. Perhaps the focus on hardware is due to hardware being more tangible than software; hardware is what is most visible when a customer first installs a storage system or shows off a data center.

A few illustrative storage hardware architectures are shown and briefly discussed below. By identifying how system hardware components are organized, a system's hardware architecture might be viewed as the hardware topology *inside* a storage system. There are no industry-standard ways to draw storage architectures, no industry-standard names for these architectures, no standards for how much or how little information should be in an architectural diagram, and hosts are rarely if ever shown on such diagrams though hosts are shown here for clarity. The intent is to give the reader a taste of different hardware architectures and the kinds of diagrams they may see from storage vendors.[31]

---

[31] Some readers may expect to see the terms *scale-up* and *scale-out* in this discussion. Those terms are discussed in the *Physical Configuration Management* chapter. In brief, scale-up means more

Self-Contained Storage System Architectures

These are the most traditional/conventional storage system architectures. They have proven to work well over many years and describe many storage systems in the marketplace today.

A single, self-contained storage system can be packaged in one cabinet or a small number of cabinets directly connected to each other. If the system can contain multiple cabinets, the reason is usually to provide space to hold more components than a single, reasonably sized cabinet can hold. (The term *monolithic* is sometimes used to describe this architecture, but keep in mind the system contains multiple components.)

The following diagram shows a relatively simple self-contained system architecture illustrative of some enterprise storage systems sometimes classified as *midrange* systems. (More is said later about classifying storage systems as entry, midrange, and high-end; for now, consider midrange storage systems to support capabilities somewhere between the simplest and most complex systems.)

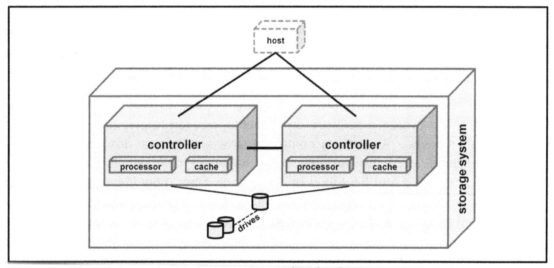

Illustration of a relatively simple single storage system hardware architecture.

The purpose of supporting two controllers is to provide redundancy in case one controller fails or needs to be taken offline for some reason (such as repair). Because, as shown, a host can be connected to both controllers and drives are connected to both controllers, this redundancy allows all data to remain accessible to hosts even if one controller is offline.

The following diagram shows a more complex self-contained system architecture illustrative of some enterprise storage systems sometimes classified as high-end systems. Most interconnections between components (e.g., how host adapters and drive adapters connect to cache) are not shown to avoid clutter. Note that each adapter has its own processor (shown as a small cube) and that there is also a pool of shared processors.

hardware components can be added to a single system (e.g., to add capacity for data), while scale-out means multiple systems can be connected together to appear as a single system to users.

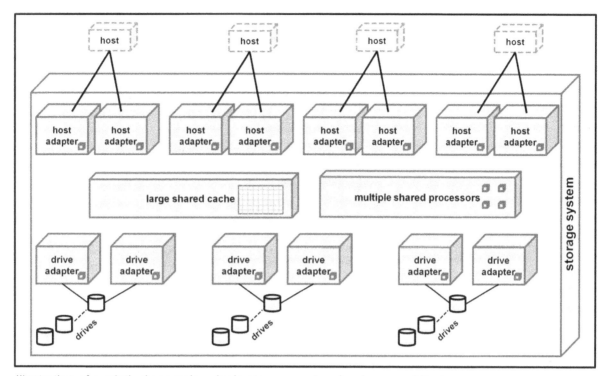

Illustration of a relatively complex single storage system hardware architecture.

The use of multiple controllers, here called adapters, supports higher scalability than would be supported if there were only one or two controllers. This allows more hosts to be connected to the system and more drives to hold data to be configured in the system. Adapters are configured in pairs to preserve access to data if a single adapter in a pair is unavailable.

Cluster (Grid) Storage System Architectures

In some storage system architectures, multiple storage systems work together to appear as a single system to users by supporting functions that "hide" their separateness.

These architectures are known as *clusters* or *grids*. (The terms "cluster" and "grid" are often used in the industry without clear distinction and are used interchangeably here.) Each element in a cluster or grid architecture that is (at least hypothetically) capable of being a stand-alone storage system is often called a *node*. The nodes are sometimes said to be "tightly coupled" to each other.

Clustered systems can increase performance and capacity by adding nodes and sometimes by adding components within a node. Scalability in terms of the maximum number of nodes is often limited to eight or fewer in practice; larger numbers may be supported if nodes can be geographically distributed and communicate over a network. (The complex self-contained storage system architecture discussed earlier is sometimes considered to be a variation of a clustered architecture, though it does not strictly consist of multiple, potentially independent systems.)

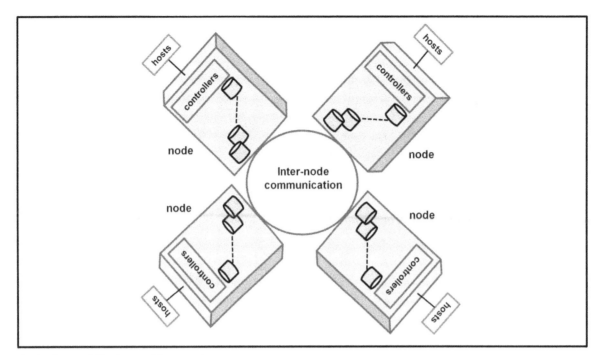

A cluster architecture of four nodes.

Federated Storage System Architectures

Some storage system architectures support functions that work across multiple systems to form a *federation* of systems. The federated systems are usually (but not always) from one or more system families from the same manufacturer. The systems in a federation communicate over a network. Typical supported functions include a single console to manage the systems and migrating data nondisruptively between systems without host involvement to balance I/O workloads. Other than the federated functions, the systems operate independently.[32] The arrangement is sometimes referred to as *loosely coupled* systems.

Federated storage systems sit conceptually between self-contained storage systems and clustered (grid) systems. There is no industry standard dictating the number or kind of functions that must be supported to warrant the "federation" label. (In particular, data replication between two storage systems (discussed later in the *Inter-System Data Replication* chapter) is arguably a form of federation. However, it is rarely if ever described that way, perhaps because support for that function preceded the concept of "storage federation" by decades.)

Federated systems are discussed further in the *Logical (Software) Configuration Management* chapter.

---

[32] An inescapable analogy is to Star Trek's United Federation of Planets. Each member planet is an independent civilization, but planets in the Federation cooperate in some ways.

Virtualized (Software-Defined) Storage System Architectures

In the context of IT, virtualization can be broadly defined as the principle of presenting capabilities to users that may differ from the supported capabilities of computer resources (such as servers and storage systems). In other words, the presented capabilities are *virtually* there. Typically, virtual capabilities are provided by software that resides somewhere between a user and computer resources that may not inherently support the capabilities.

SNIA defines storage virtualization[33] as:

1. [Storage System] The act of abstracting, hiding, or isolating the internal function of a storage (sub) system or service from applications, compute servers or general network resources for the purpose of enabling application and network independent management of storage or data.

2. [Storage System] The application of virtualization to storage services or devices for the purpose of aggregating, hiding complexity or adding new capabilities to lower level storage resources.

In some cases, virtualization is entirely internal to a storage system. A widely known example is letting administrators create logical volumes (aka virtual volumes or LUNs) that can be different capacities than the physical drives installed in a block-access storage system. (Hosts were never aware of the transition over time from directly being aware of physical drives in a storage system to only being aware of virtual volumes.)

In practice, however, the term "storage virtualization" (or "virtualized storage") most often refers to external facilities to control storage systems by treating individual systems as components of a virtual system. This came about as the storage industry and its customers increasingly realized most of the value in many storage systems really lies in its internal software, just as most of the value in a personal computer really lies in its software. While storage system software has historically been locked into the manufacturer's hardware storage cabinets, in recent years the storage industry has introduced storage software unbundled from specific storage systems so the same software can control multiple, even incompatible, storage systems.

When storage system software is an offering (e.g., product or open source software) in its own right and the storage hardware the software manages can be in separate systems (that otherwise could have operated on their own), the storage architecture is called by names such as *software-defined storage (SDS)*, a *storage hypervisor*, a *storage virtualization facility*, or *virtualized storage*.[34]

---

[33] Source: http://www.snia.org/education/dictionary/s.

[34] This Guide uses the terms "storage virtualization facility," "virtualized storage," "storage hypervisor," and "software-defined storage" interchangeably unless otherwise noted. Some in the storage industry use the terms differently. For example, SDS may sometimes be defined as using commodity servers to run the software, but this Guide does not treat that as a defining characteristic.

An SDS architecture enables customers to customize their own hardware + software storage systems to an extent previously not possible. A side benefit to the storage industry is that SDS makes it easier for software-only manufacturers to enter the industry compared to the past when hardware manufacturing facilities were also needed.

A typical SDS architecture works as follows: The software is designed to run on a server to provide hardware essential to any enterprise storage system. That includes processors to run the software, internal memory to hold the software and perhaps also serve as a data cache, and connection ports other hosts use to connect to the SDS server, just as those other hosts would connect to a conventionally integrated hardware + software storage system.[35] The main thing missing from the server as just described is storage capacity for data. That capacity can be provided by connecting the SDS server to storage; that storage could be internal drives in the server or external storage systems or both, depending on the capabilities of the SDS software.

The following diagram contrasts an environment with conventionally architected storage systems on the left to an SDS environment on the right. The SDS software provides common functions that can be applied to all the external storage systems the SDS software manages.

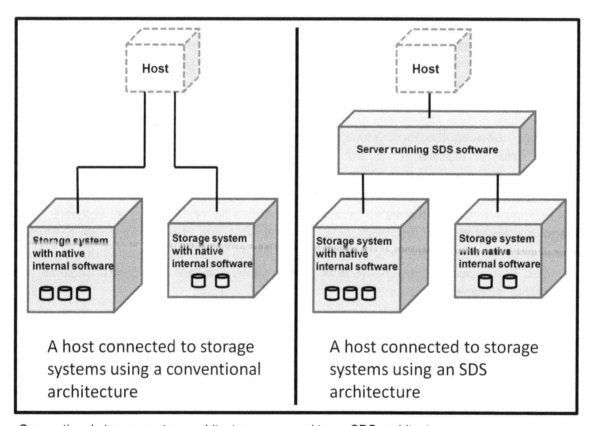

Conventional storage system architecture compared to an SDS architecture.

SDS architecture provides an optional way to help customers manage storage. Some SDS offerings have been in use by customers for many years. While most storage systems used

---

[35] In products based on this architecture, the SDS server may be based on x86 architecture because such servers are widely used, are available from multiple manufacturers, and are relatively inexpensive. (Reference: http://en.wikipedia.org/wiki/X86.)

by customers are likely still based on non-SDS architectures, SDS appears to be increasing in popularity.

Storage virtualization is discussed further in the *Logical (Software) Configuration Management* chapter.

Server SAN Storage System Architectures

A *Server SAN* is a relatively new storage system architecture.[36] A Server SAN is an alternative to conventional, built-for-purpose enterprise storage systems. It is a variation of software-defined storage that supports high levels of storage scalability. Like many new concepts, the definition of a Server SAN may still be evolving, but the following discussion covers the basics.

"Server" refers to a set of servers, each supporting direct-attached storage (e.g., internal drives) and running software to support the Server SAN. In practice, these are typically low-cost servers (e.g., commodity x86-based servers). The software provides data management services and manages communication among the servers.

"SAN" refers to the set of servers together supporting a shared pool of storage accessible over a network to application hosts.

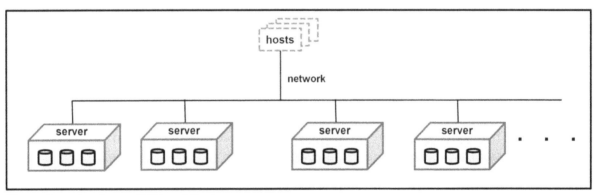

Illustration of a Server SAN architecture.

Implementations of a Server SAN architecture could differ in many ways. A given server may run production applications and also be part of a Server SAN; or, a server SAN may be a set of servers dedicated to supporting storage to facilitate separately managing (e.g., growing and migrating) host systems and storage systems. A host might submit its I/O requests to a designated server that routes the requests to the server owning the relevant storage; or, a software driver installed in the host may help manage that routing. Other differences could include the type of data access protocols supported, the data management services supported, the types of servers and operating systems supported, the type of network the servers use to communicate with each other (which could differ from the type of network a host uses to access a Server SAN), and more.

---

[36] The term "Server SAN" may have originated in an article at http://wikibon.com/server-san-market-definition/.

Very large Server SANs (typically measured in petabytes (thousands of terabytes) of capacity) are sometimes called *hyperscale storage*. Some large Web organizations such as Amazon and Google implement hyperscale storage.

Final Thoughts

As this chapter shows, there are many ways storage systems can be architected. It seems that if someone can think of an architecture, it may well be implemented somewhere.

Over time, storage engineers have developed different architectures for storage systems. To-date, there has not proven to be a single all-around best architecture. Given the widespread information about storage architectures, if there was a single best architecture all engineers would presumably use it. In practice, architectures are designed with certain goals in mind such as certain levels of performance, capacity, and function at a certain cost to address a certain segment of the market. In addition, manufacturers are motivated to provide new generations of storage systems highly compatible with previous generations of systems already successful in the market; that can often inhibit significantly deviating from a proven architecture.[37]

The success of a storage architecture depends on the creativity and technical prowess of the architectural team. It also depends on the success of the teams marketing and selling the systems based on a given architecture. It can also depend on the ability of the architecture and architectural team to accommodate future technical advances possibly not anticipated when the architecture was developed. For example, many storage systems originally designed for HDDs were able to later accommodate SSDs because system and SSD manufacturers worked together so SSDs would be compatible with HDD module sizes and interfaces.[38]

Vendors often highlight the architectures of systems they are selling, claiming superiority over the architectures of competing systems. Nevertheless, what really matters to customers – or

---

[37] Manufacturers typically use very different system architectures for lower-end and higher-end storage systems. In some cases that is for historical reasons (e.g., a storage manufacturer buys another manufacturer and inherits the architecture of acquired systems). In some cases the design/development groups for different storage systems in the same company work independently. If a manufacturer had the luxury of starting from a clean slate, it is likely they would prefer to (try to) create a single architecture where hardware can scale from entry to midrange to high-end, the same software (or at least subsets) can run on all models, and price is competitive at any scale. That ideal may not (yet) be practical.

[38] SSD manufacturers were motivated to cooperate with HDD-based storage system manufacturers because compatibility gave them immediate access to the broad, existing HDD-based storage system market. However, some entrepreneurs took advantage of native flash memory efficiencies to build flash-based storage systems from the ground up, unhindered by the constraints of systems designed for HDDs. The new all-flash systems were able to provide high capacity densities in small enclosures by not requiring SSD modules to match HDD module sizes. The rise of such all-flash systems, in turn, motivated HDD-based storage system designers to improve the capabilities of their systems; for example, some manufacturers directly integrated flash memory cards into their systems along with HDDs.

what really *should* matter, a major theme of this Guide – is whether their storage requirements are met by what a particular storage *system* (and associated vendor) can do. That includes how both hardware and software together address requirements for capacity, availability, performance, and much more, all of which are topics for Part II.

Part II.

Insights into
Storage System Capabilities

An enterprise storage system is a critical part of an organization's IT infrastructure. How well it supports that infrastructure depends on its technical capabilities: what it can (and can't) do. That includes considerations of effectiveness and efficiency. In a word: quality. Given the complexity and broad capabilities of today's storage systems, quality isn't a single "have it or don't" attribute; rather, it is a consequence of multiple factors which are discussed in this part of the Guide.

Before an organization can identify its particular storage requirements so it can pursue acquiring a system to address them, personnel responsible for identifying those requirements and for making the storage system decision must understand what these systems are capable of doing. This is part of the "gathering information" phase of the overall decision process.

Host Support

A fundamental customer requirement for enterprise storage systems is that they support the hosts and operating systems the customer uses to run their applications.

Because of the current widespread support by storage system manufacturers and server manufacturers of technology standards for connecting storage to servers (such as Fibre Channel and Ethernet), most enterprise storage systems can attach to a wide variety of servers. That is a significant benefit to customers compared to the earliest days of computing when only computers and storage from the same manufacturer worked together. However, even today not every storage system can connect to any and all models of servers and even when connectivity is supported there can be significant differences in the capabilities of that support.

Concepts and Facilities

- <u>How hosts and storage relate</u>. Hosts and their applications are the primary users of a storage system. They connect to it, write data to it, read data from it, and often manage that data in various ways. Additional relationships between hosts and storage systems include supported locations (e.g., the maximum distance over which they can be connected and whether storage is housed in a separate cabinet), supported data access protocols (e.g., file-access), and supported connection types (e.g., Ethernet).

  The choice of a new storage system may be constrained by attributes of the current or planned host environment. Constraints to consider include how host applications that would use the storage are designed (e.g., to use a particular data access protocol), recommendations or requirements imposed by the vendors of host software products that would use the storage (e.g., a recommendation to use block-access storage rather than file-access storage for performance reasons), and how a data center housing hosts is able to support storage (e.g., the size and shape of available floor space).

- <u>Host-storage physical connectivity</u>. Hosts and storage systems communicate by sending messages over physical connection paths such as Fibre Channel and Ethernet. The types of connection paths supported, the speed of those paths, the number of connection ports, and the data access types supported over a given path type can all vary by host and by storage system model. Additionally, a storage system must support (e.g., be tested by the manufacturer to work with) the types of host bus adapters (HBAs) or network interface cards (NICs) attached hosts use for path connectivity.

Tip: A given storage system model may support options for connectivity to hosts (e.g., options for multiple path types and the number of ports of each type). That can provide flexibility for both initially installed configurations and potential future upgrades.

Tip: Some network types support auto-negotiation. Auto-negotiation is an interaction between communicating network devices (e.g., a host's port and a storage system's port, or a switch's port and a storage system's port) to allow devices that support multiple speeds to operate at the highest common speed. This is useful if an organization is gradually migrating different systems to higher network speeds and not all installed systems support the same higher speed at the same time.

- Host/OS support. Customers require that a proposed enterprise storage system support the servers and operating system (OS) types and releases to which it needs to be attached. Not every storage system supports every server or every server/OS combination.

Tip: If a storage system lacks required host support, such as support for a particular host model, or a particular operating system version, or a particular network adapter, sometimes a vendor will be willing to add it, perhaps doing the testing at a customer's site. (The feasibility of adding such support and doing so in a timely manner depends on the capability needed. For example, adding support for a particular host's variation of the SCSI protocol to a storage system that already supports SCSI for other hosts can be relatively straightforward. However, adding support for InfiniBand connectivity to a storage system that does not support it can be relatively difficult and perhaps not cost-justifiable by a manufacturer if demand is low.)

Tip: A storage vendor should maintain information identifying other devices (e.g., server/OSs and SAN switches) that have been tested (or are at least expected) to connect to and work with that vendor's storage systems. That information may take the form of an "interoperability" document or online tool. Customers should consult such information, or ask vendors to do so, for all equipment the customer plans to attach to a proposed storage system.

Tip: A storage vendor may support attachment of a customer's hosts and network devices to a storage system at the time the storage system is acquired. Customers should ask the vendor whether they plan to continue support over the time frame the customer anticipates needing it.

- Storage-host functional synergy. Some functions implemented in some storage systems or in some hosts require cooperation (i.e., exchanging information or performing actions) between the storage system and host that goes beyond basic functions such as supporting simple I/O requests to read and write data. This is sometimes described as functional *synergy* between a host and a storage system.

This kind of cooperation is usually for functions that enhance, but are not required for, basic host or storage operation. The benefits of host-storage synergy functions can include enhanced performance, improved storage availability, easier system administration, and more. Synergy functions are typically implemented in host-based and storage system-based software, but could be implemented in hardware. A given storage system may support all, some, or none of the storage synergy functions a given host supports, and vice versa. Here are three examples of host-storage functional synergy:

1) Some vendors have offerings that support using SSDs inside hosts as a host-side data cache to boost performance compared to accessing data from an external storage system. In some cases, the software that manages the host cache is designed to cooperate with an external storage system to optimize which data resides in the host cache and to avoid double caching the same data in both the host cache and storage system cache.

2) The host-based VMware hypervisor supports application programming interfaces (APIs) that storage systems may optionally support for improved efficiency. This includes VAAI (vSphere Storage APIs – Array Integration) and VASA (vSphere APIs for Storage Awareness). (Reference: http://www.vmware.com.)

3) IBM z Systems z/OS (mainframe) servers support numerous functions that can improve host-storage operations.[39] An example is Extended Address Volumes (EAV) that supports very large logical volume capacities for easier volume management; EAV effectiveness is limited if a storage system does not support the maximum volume size EAV supports. Another example is information in I/O commands about the priority of the applications requesting access to data, allowing storage systems to support those priorities when multiple I/Os contend for the same storage resources. (If applications can access a particular storage system resource only one at a time and multiple applications want to use that resource, awareness of applications' priorities helps the storage system determine which application goes next.)

- ISV management products. ISV (Independent Software Vendor) host-based software products that help manage storage systems provide functions such as data archiving, logical volume management, backup management, and reporting. These products sometimes support only selected hosts and/or selected storage systems. Customers using (or planning to use) such ISV products should determine whether storage systems they are evaluating are supported.

There are other ISV-related considerations storage customers should be aware of. Some storage vendors have programs to certify that ISV offerings work with their storage. Conversely, some ISV vendors support certifications of storage systems that pass an ISV-defined test). Some ISV vendors provide recommendations for storage system performance capabilities needed to help their product operate satisfactorily.

---

[39] The z/OS operating system was previously named OS/390 and, before that, MVS.

Additional Tips

- *Just because a vendor says their storage system supports function X, customers should not assume X is supported by that storage system for all host/OSs. Sometimes, a given storage system supports functions that work with only selected server/OS hosts, not with all hosts the storage system supports. For example, some storage systems support some functions that work with "open" hosts, but not with mainframe hosts; conversely, some storage systems support functions that work with mainframe hosts but not with "open" hosts.[40] Therefore, a customer should ask their vendors whether all storage system functions the customer is interested in are supported for all required hosts without restriction.*

- *Customers should determine how responsive a storage system vendor is in providing support for new generations of hosts, network devices, and new releases of the software that drives them. Similarly, users of ISV host-based software that supports only selected storage systems should determine the ISV's responsiveness to supporting new releases and generations of those systems. Helpful information includes a vendor's history in this area as well as a vendor's claim to a customer about the vendor's objectives. This can be important because, for example, a customer will not want to install a new generation of server or OS only to learn that their storage system will not be supporting it as soon as the customer needs that support. That could delay the customer's ability to take advantage of capabilities of the new server or OS, or even require acquiring a different storage system that has the desired support.*

---

[40] *The term "open" is widely used in the industry to describe hosts running certain operating systems. The term originally referred to UNIX-based hosts (see http://www.unix.org) because UNIX operating system software was freely available and installable on many different types of hosts. Over time, however, multiple development organizations added proprietary functions to create unique versions of UNIX. Today, the term "open" is ambiguous; it is often used to mean any hosts that are not (IBM z Systems) mainframe hosts even though many such hosts also run proprietary operating systems.*

Capacity

The ability of a storage system to hold a quantity of data – referred to as a system's *capacity* (aka *space* or *size*) – is clearly one of the foremost requirements customers place on any storage system. Customers have strong preferences for the minimum amount of data a given storage system must be able to hold because that minimizes the number of storage systems to acquire and manage. It also facilitates efficient use of storage system resources; for example, a storage system's cache can be shared by all data inside the same system.

The data capacity a modern enterprise storage system can support far exceeds that of just a few years ago. In the second decade of the 2000s, some HDDs each support several terabytes of capacity (where 1 terabyte = 1,000 gigabytes). The maximum capacities of the largest enterprise storage systems, capable of supporting thousands of drives, are measured in thousands of terabytes. Still, the demand for capacity is so high that many larger customers can address their capacity needs only by installing multiple storage systems.

Concepts and Facilities

- <u>Measuring capacity</u>. Storage system capacity is typically specified as a number of bytes (i.e., 8-bit alphanumeric characters) in decimal units such as megabytes (10^6 bytes = 1 MB), gigabytes (10^9 bytes = 1 GB), terabytes (10^{12} bytes = 1 TB), and petabytes (10^{15} bytes = 1 PB). Larger capacities are measured in exabytes (10^{18} bytes = 1 EB), and beyond. The capacity names increase by a factor of 1,000 (10^3) so, for example, 1 terabyte is 1,000 gigabytes.

  Note that in acronyms such as *MB*, by convention a capital *B* means *byte* while a small *b* means *bit*. Capacities for storage and computer memory are typically measured in bytes while the speed (aka bandwidth) of a network is typically measured in bits per second.

  Historically, prefixes like *mega* and *giga* have sometimes been used ambiguously as both decimal (base 10) and binary (base 2) measures. To address the ambiguity the industry is increasingly using new units for binary quantities such as mibibyte = 1 MiB = 2^{20} bytes = 1,048,576 decimal bytes. In contrast, one megabyte = 1 MB = 10^6 bytes = 1,000,000 decimal bytes.

  Tip: While storage system and drive manufacturers conventionally use decimal measures for drive capacities, the ambiguity persists for other storage system measures. To avoid misunderstandings, measurements cited for storage system capacity (and for other system components such as cache) in customer-vendor interactions, in vendor documentation, and in storage management reports should be clearly defined. (Reference: http://en.wikipedia.org/wiki/IEC_prefix.)

- **Physical capacity vs. usable capacity.** It is important to distinguish *physical capacity* from *usable capacity.*

  Physical capacity (aka *raw capacity*) is storage system capacity calculated as the sum of the capacities of configured drives before any data is stored on them. (This definition excludes any drives permanently reserved for storage system internal use only, e.g., drives that hold only system microcode.)

  Usable capacity is storage system capacity available to users for holding data. This is the capacity of most interest to customers. The amount of usable capacity needed by a given customer is totally dependent on that customer's environment. Usable capacity is needed not only for a customer's application software and data, but also for other purposes such as holding copies the customer may make of that data, holding host operating system software and related data such as system error logs, and holding commercial middleware software and related data such as a database manager's indexes and transaction logs.

  The usable capacity in a storage system may be less (or may be even more, as explained later) than the physical capacity of that system. Reasons usable capacity can be less include: How drives are formatted by a storage system (e.g., by adding system-generated data to help recover from certain types of errors), how administrator-created volumes are formatted by hosts (e.g., with volume identification and file directory information), how much spare capacity is configured in case of drive failures, and how much capacity is used for redundancy to preserve access to data in case of drive or other failures. (Of these items, only the type of redundancy protection and/or the number of spare drives may be customer options that can impact how much physical capacity is available as usable capacity.)

  Tip: Customers should specify their storage system capacity requirements to vendors in terms of usable capacity. Vendors should then be responsible for determining the amount of physical (raw) capacity needed to support the usable capacity requirement. (Other customer requirements can also influence how much physical capacity is needed; for example, availability requirements may only be met by a particular type of redundancy which in turn requires a certain amount of physical capacity; see RAID, discussed in the *Availability* chapter.)

  Tip: It is generally a best practice to plan to use less than 100% of usable capacity, reserving some capacity for unanticipated "need it now" capacity requests. Perhaps an unanticipated copy of a large file must be made. Or, consider that even if it is planned to upgrade an installed storage system with additional capacity or to replace an installed system with a larger capacity system, production use of the upgrade or new system may be delayed for any number of unanticipated reasons (e.g., delayed shipment of the upgrade by the vendor, problems migrating to a new system, or a delay needed by the customer for financial reasons).

Tip: *Some storage systems limit maximum usable capacity regardless of how much physical capacity is configured. In particular, that kind of restriction, not necessarily highlighted by vendors, may limit the extent to which a system can benefit from the highest capacity drives (aka* nearline *drives). Customers should ask vendors whether such a restriction on maximum usable capacity applies to the vendors' storage systems being considered. This helps customers avoid making what may seem a safe, but is possibly an erroneous, assumption: that a system's usable capacity can easily be increased by installing more drives or installing higher capacity drives limited only by the maximum number of drives supported by the system.*

Tip: *Maximum usable capacity may be limited for a practical reason: As data is added to a storage system, total I/O activity to the system may increase (unless the data is idle or is accessed only when other data is idle), at some point causing I/O (and application) performance to unacceptably degrade. One example is that a system's processing power may be incapable of supporting a desired level of performance when I/O activity exceeds some threshold, regardless of the capacity used. Another example is that some storage systems have internal processes to increase the amount of contiguous unused space by actively rearranging where data is located, taking system resources away from production work. (A storage system design that can exhibit this behavior is "log-structured file.") The point is, customers need to understand the performance capabilities of a storage system so they can plan to not use more capacity than is consistent with meeting performance goals. (There's always the alternative of choosing to let performance degrade and dealing with complaints and missed schedules. That may be acceptable for low priority work or for limited periods of time.)*

- <u>Facilities to increase usable capacity</u>. Some storage systems are able to manage physical capacity so that usable capacity is larger, possibly much larger, than the physical capacity remaining after items identified above (such as formatting) are accounted for.

  This may sound like the magic of somehow putting more than one liter of water in a one liter bottle. However, it is achievable if one or more optimizations for managing physical capacity are implemented by a storage system (or by host software). The major potential benefit of capacity optimization techniques is saving money by reducing the amount of physical capacity needed to support a required amount of usable capacity. (The saved money may be to the customer's benefit (i.e., a lower price to acquire a system meeting their capacity needs), or the vendor's benefit (i.e., a reduced cost for hardware needed to provide a given amount of capacity), or may benefit both parties.) Fortunately, capacity optimizations are generally attainable without modifying applications.

  Below is a list of common capacity optimization techniques. A particular storage system model may support all, some, or none of these optimizations.

  - <u>Thin provisioning</u>. This may be the most widely supported capacity optimization. In the absence of thin provisioning, when a volume or file system or object container is created, the storage system reserves physical capacity matching the entire requested size. For example, if a storage administrator creates a 100GB volume, 100GB of unused physical capacity is reserved for (i.e., allocated or assigned to) that volume even though that capacity is initially empty from a user's perspective. Often, not all that capacity ends up being used, meaning some physical capacity is wasted.

However, when a thin provisioned volume is created little or no physical capacity is initially reserved. Only as hosts write data to the volume is unused physical capacity assigned to it, in small units of space that may be called *chunks* or *extents* or *pages* or *segments* or *tracks,* depending on the storage system model. (To contrast traditional fully allocated volumes with thin volumes, the traditional volumes are sometimes called *standard volumes* or *thick volumes*.)

o <u>Compression</u>. This optimization uses algorithms to reduce the amount of data stored on drives compared to storing uncompressed data. Data is stored in a way that allows it to be fully rebuilt to satisfy read I/O requests. An example of a simple compression algorithm is replacing a continuous group of identical characters by a single character and a count of the number of times it is repeated; actual compression algorithms are generally much more sophisticated.

o <u>Deduplication</u>. This optimization, informally called dedupe (pronounced "dee'-doop"), detects duplicate data and stores only one copy of that data. That data may be duplicate files or may be smaller, duplicate blocks of data, depending on how dedupe is implemented. An example of where dedupe is beneficial is when multiple emails have the same attachments. Another example is a virtual desktop infrastructure (VDI) environment that stores identical images of personal computer software.

The following diagram illustrates the three capacity optimization techniques discussed.

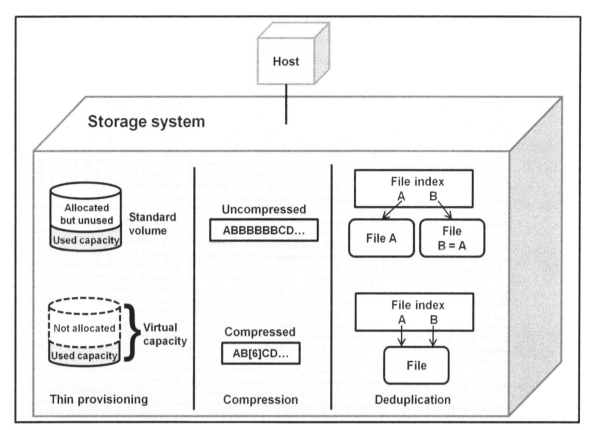

Illustration of three types of capacity optimization. The top of each column shows an unoptimized use of capacity while the bottom of each column shows the optimized capacity.

Thin provisioning, compression, and deduplication can be combined in some storage systems, potentially increasing physical capacity savings even more than systems implementing fewer or none of these optimizations. These efficiencies can often apply to internally created copies of data as well as to the original data.

Tip: *The main potential benefit of storage system capacity optimization features is usually cost savings due to needing less physical capacity to support a given amount of usable capacity. However, some vendors charge extra for capacity optimization features, reducing any cost savings.*

Tip: *A vendor proposing a storage system that does not support capacity optimizations may (need to) lower the price of their storage system to compensate when competing against systems that do support such optimizations. Customers may want to ask whether any such compensation also applies to future capacity upgrades.*

Tip: *Capacity optimization techniques can make capacity planning more difficult because the amount of usable capacity resulting from these optimizations can be difficult to predict. Administrators of storage systems employing capacity optimizations generally need to pay attention to how those facilities work, the characteristics of the data to be stored in the system, and how physical capacity is being consumed so more physical capacity can be ordered in sufficient time to meet application needs.*[41]

o *Some applications initially format volumes assigned to them with control information meaningful to the applications. In that case, the potential capacity savings of thin provisioned volumes may be reduced or nullified.*

o *The aggregate (usable) capacities of thin volumes can exceed a system's physical capacity. That could lead to a case where an application fails due to a storage system using all its physical capacity even though a volume the application is writing to still appears to have plenty of unused capacity. That situation can't happen with standard (thick) volumes where capacity is assigned when the volumes are created.*

o *Not all data written to a storage system may compress equally well. The effectiveness of a given compression algorithm can depend on the bit patterns of the data. For example, a data block containing all zero bits may compress much better than a data block containing a more random combination of zero bits and one bits. Some data, such as digital images, may be compressed by an application before being written to storage so that further compression may not be possible.*

o *Space savings due to deduplication depend on the amount of duplicate data written to the storage system and the granularity of what the system treats as duplicate data, e.g., duplicate blocks or duplicate files.*

o *A vendor may make a general marketing claim something like "my product supports up to 90% space savings due to compression or deduplication." "Up to" is a key phrase meaning "it depends." It is important that customers identify the characteristics of the data to which the claim applies and determine to what extent the claim applies to the characteristics of the data they plan to store.*

Tip: *Customers should consult their vendors to understand the performance implications of supported capacity optimization features.*

o *In some cases, capacity optimizations provide a performance benefit. For example, if the storage system compresses data not only on drives but also in cache, that could increase the amount of data that can reside in cache or could allow performance goals to be met with a smaller cache.*

o *If data in a storage system in compressed form can be transmitted as-is over communications links in remote mirroring configurations, a customer might save money by not acquiring communications equipment that supports compression at extra cost. Further, reducing the amount of data to be transmitted over communication links can improve potentially improve performance or reduce link bandwidth requirements. (Remote mirroring is discussed in the* Inter-System Data Replication *chapter.)*

---

[41] *Some capacity optimizations are designed to send messages to administrators alerting them when a certain percentage of physical space is exhausted. (While some manufacturers have at least considered it, it is not clear whether any storage systems are able to automatically order more storage capacity at such times, presumably with customer permission.)*

o *In some cases there may be a performance drawback. For example, frequently adding small capacity increments to thin provisioned volumes may add significant system overhead. As another example, data compression may add significantly to storage system processor utilization.*

Tip: *The efficiency of capacity optimization techniques can vary.*

o *Thin provisioning efficiency can vary in multiple ways. Only some thin provisioning implementations save space by not storing blocks containing only binary zeros. Only some thin provisioning implementations cooperate with hosts to release used capacity when individual files are deleted.*

o *Some compression and deduplication facilities operate* inline, *meaning the optimization applies to data as it enters the system. In contrast, some facilities operate only in a* post-processing *mode that runs periodically against data recently stored in the system, a design that can reduce, or at least delay, capacity savings. Customers will want to understand the performance implications in either case. (Deduplication was originally introduced for backup-to-disk use where performance is sometimes not a major concern. However, deduplication of production data (sometimes called dedupe of* primary storage) *has become more common.)*

Tip: *Some host operating systems, some host applications (such as database management systems), and some storage virtualization facilities support capacity optimization techniques that can be applied to any attached storage system. Potential benefits compared to capacity optimizations implemented inside individual storage systems include the following:*

o *There are potential cost savings due to not needing capacity optimization features in each storage system.*

o *System administration may be easier due to having common capacity optimization facilities that work the same way regardless of storage system.*

o *For data compression, reduced host-to-storage path utilization or reduced virtualization facility-to-storage path utilization may improve performance; or it may reduce the number or speed of paths needed.*

o *For data compression, the ability to store more data in storage system cache (an optimization not necessarily supported by storage system-based compression), potentially improves performance or reduces the amount of cache needed.*

Note that wherever the compression (and associated decompression) process is performed can increase processor utilization. Some implementations use special processor chips just for the compression process.

Additional Tips

• *Some vendors offer "capacity guarantees." See the* Marketing Tactics *chapter.*

- *It is desirable that a storage system support the ability to increase capacity by installing additional drives while access to data continues without disruption. A related desirable function is the ability to move existing data to new drives in the same system without disruption; some storage systems support ways to relocate data automatically and some support the ability for storage administrators to manually move data among drives inside the system (e.g., at the level of individual logical volumes in block-access storage systems).*

- *It is often desirable to add capacity for data to an installed storage system rather than install an additional system or replace a system by one supporting more capacity. Adding capacity to an installed system usually costs less than acquiring a new system and is an easier activity to manage. Prior to adding capacity to an installed system, customers should determine whether that system supports all the storage requirements of the new data, not only capacity, and should determine whether that system can handle any increased I/O load without hindering applications from meeting their performance objectives.*

- *There is little direct relationship between the maximum capacity a storage system supports and the performance the system is capable of. It should not be assumed that if storage system A supports a larger maximum capacity than storage system B, that means A supports better performance than B. While it is true that a system supporting more drives may support running more I/O requests in parallel, there might be bottlenecks in other system components that limit any performance benefit.*

- *Some storage systems reserve a portion of capacity ordered by customers for use by the storage system, thus making that capacity unavailable to applications. Common cases include spare drives (used to replace failed drives) and support for data redundancy. Those are reasonable uses customers are generally familiar with.*

  However, some customers may not realize that some storage systems reserve a portion of customer-ordered capacity for possibly unanticipated reasons. For example, some storage systems reserve drive capacity to enable preserving data written to cache, but not yet written to drives, in case of loss of external power. (Storage systems can include internal batteries to support that process.) If a storage system reserves customer-ordered capacity for this purpose, that can amount to an unexpected reduction in usable capacity. Some storage systems avoid this reduction in usable capacity by including dedicated internal drives to preserve the written data in cache in case of loss of external power.

  To help protect themselves from such considerations, customers should ask vendors the direct question: Does the proposed system configuration support the customer's usable capacity requirement?

Availability

Storage system *availability* refers to the ability of users (whether end users, hosts, applications, or administrators) to access a storage system's capabilities whenever they are needed (i.e., on demand). Availability is also known as *uptime* or *time online* (as opposed to *downtime* or *time offline* or *outage*).

A high level of storage system availability is usually a high priority customer requirement for the simple reason that unavailable storage system capabilities can have unwanted consequences for an organization, including lost business. A specific availability requirement can vary by user and by application. While an availability requirement is often 24 hours a day every day (aka 24 x 7, pronounced "24 by 7"), it can be less for particular applications. For example, a brick-and-mortar store may need access to storage only when the store is open for business.

Awareness of what conditions can potentially cause storage system downtime, and how storage systems can potentially be designed to remain available in spite of such conditions, helps customers evaluate a system's ability to support their availability requirements.

Concepts and Facilities

- <u>About availability</u>. Availability is not a single all-or-nothing storage system property. The situation is not as simple as being able to characterize a system at a particular time as available or unavailable. For example, a storage system may be able to correctly handle I/O requests from hosts, yet at the same time have a problem that temporarily prevents an administrative command from functioning normally.[42]

  In practice, unimpaired availability of all capabilities of a given storage system over long periods of time is difficult at best to achieve and impossible to ensure ahead of time. Causes of impaired availability range from internal system problems to human errors. This chapter focuses mainly on internal system problems and how they can be managed.

---

[42] Availability requirements often focus on the ability of a storage system to support I/O requests. But the ability to perform data management functions can be equally important. For example, if a business process requires that a storage system make a copy of data for use by an application and that copy cannot be made for some reason, the application cannot run. As another example, if storage system management interfaces are offline, preventing administrators from provisioning capacity to hosts, new or changed applications may not be put into production on schedule.

However, customers can help reduce human errors by means such as sufficient training of administrators and fostering a culture of IT professionalism.[43]

Enterprise storage systems are relatively complex machines that, while normally highly reliable, can potentially fail for many reasons. (A "failure" means a hardware or software component is not working as designed.[44]) As is often said (only partially in jest): if something can go wrong, it will, and usually at the worst time. The timing and duration of storage system failures are generally unpredictable. (Rarely, an installed storage system has been so problematic the vendor replaced it with a new system.)

Storage systems include many hardware components and many of those contain numerous subcomponents.[45] In some cases, the failure of just one hardware component or subcomponent can potentially impact access to an entire storage system. Even though many enterprise storage systems are designed with extensive hardware redundancy, even redundant components can potentially (though relatively rarely) all fail at the same time – more precisely, during overlapped periods of time.

Storage system internal software is also susceptible to failure. Contemporary enterprise storage systems are supported by software comparable in complexity to many host operating systems. Some software failures are minor such as a misspelled word in an informational message sent to a system administrator. Some software failures are major such as a program defect causing loss of data (that can hopefully be recovered from a backup copy).

Because of the importance of storage system availability to customers, the industry has spent significant effort on improving this aspect of storage systems. Today's enterprise storage systems are often so adept at recovering from some failure situations that those failures may go unnoticed by users. For example, if one component fails, another may be able to handle its work. A storage system may be able to confine the impact of some failures to a subset of the system while other parts of the system continue to function normally. For example, because a single storage system may support data belonging to hundreds of applications, a system problem preventing access to only some data impacts only the subset of applications needing that particular data.

There are practical obstacles to designing, developing, testing, and shipping storage systems capable of non-stop availability. Considering software in particular, manufacturers are generally unable to identify and fix all software defects before a storage system ships

---

[43] Examples of elements of a culture of IT professionalism that can promote high levels of availability and minimize human error are formal processes for change management and problem management. (Reference: https://en.wikipedia.org/wiki/IT_service_management)

[44] "Hardware eventually fails. Software eventually works." is a clever observation generally attributed to Michael Hartung, a storage architect and IBM Fellow. The point is that electronic and mechanical components eventually break while software can eventually be debugged.

[45] Examples of components include drives, power supplies, and adapters for host connections. Examples of subcomponents are processors on those adapters. A component that can be repaired or replaced in-place in an installed machine after the component fails is sometimes called a *Field Replaceable Unit* (FRU, rhymes with "new").

because there are so many possible paths through program code and too little time to test every possible operational scenario; thus, some bugs end up being found by customers. More broadly, manufacturers pursue conflicting goals such as: use high quality components but keep manufacturing costs low, do a good job of testing products but keep testing costs low, and get a product to market quickly to maximize revenue but ensure high availability to foster a good reputation.   Such conflicting goals are not unique to the IT industry, of course.

Tip: Availability can be in the eye of the beholder. A storage administrator might view a storage system as available because it is in perfect working condition, but if the network connecting the system to hosts is not working, the system is unavailable as far as hosts and applications are concerned.

- Terminology. There are multiple terms commonly used in the industry when discussing storage system availability. Not all vendors (or vendor representatives) may use all these terms or use them in the same way, so customers should ask vendors how they define terms they use.

The following discussions of terms provide a storage context, though these terms may also be used in other IT contexts. Terms are ordered here to help present them in a logical sequence. Some definitions are indicated to be from the Storage Networking Industry Association (SNIA) and can be found in SNIA's dictionary (http://www.snia.org/education/dictionary).

Reliability refers to the ability of an individual system component (usually a major hardware component such as a drive or adapter) to operate as designed. However, "reliability" is also sometimes used informally to describe an entire system (e.g., "This storage system is very reliable.") in which case it seems to be interchangeable with *availability*. When the failure of a single component can disable a system capability the component is called a *single point of failure (SPOF)*, defined by SNIA as "One component or path in a system, the failure of which would make the system inoperable."[46]

Fault tolerance (aka *failure tolerance*) is defined by SNIA as "The ability of a system to continue to perform its function (possibly at a reduced performance level) when one or more of its components has failed." In many storage systems, multiple, unrelated components can fail concurrently and fault tolerance of each is maintained. For example, if both a drive and a power supply happen to fail at the same time, access to data and function should continue if each component is fault tolerant. Ideally, fault tolerance is accompanied by the ability to repair or replace failed components concurrently with system operation; this is called *concurrent repair* or *hot swapping*. However, when a failed component can be repaired or replaced only by disabling a system capability the component is called a *single point of repair (SPOR)*. Fault tolerance is discussed further later in this chapter.

---

[46] SNIA's definition of SPOF applies to rendering an entire system inoperable. It is arguably more meaningful to customers for the term to apply to impairment of significant system capability, not merely loss of all capability. What is a significant capability is ultimately up to the user. This point also applies to the terms *single point of repair* and *availability*.

Availability is defined by SNIA as "The amount of time that a system is available during those time periods when it is expected to be available, often measured as a percentage of an elapsed year."

High availability (sometimes abbreviated *HA*) is defined by SNIA as "The ability of a system to perform its function continuously (without interruption) for a significantly longer period of time than the reliabilities of its individual components would suggest." This is about a storage system avoiding *unplanned* outages due to component failures. Storage system designers can employ various technologies, such as fault tolerance, to help a storage system remain online in spite of the failure of individual components. While the term *high availability* is widely cited in customer requirements and vendors' marketing materials, note that there are no industry standards quantifying "high" or classifying degrees of availability into low-medium-high types of classes.

Continuous operation refers to the ability of a storage system to remain available to users without requiring *planned* outages. Examples of activities that could potentially require planned outages in some storage system models include upgrading hardware (e.g., adding more drives), repairing hardware (e.g., replacing a failed component), upgrading software (e.g., replacing microcode with a new version), and making administrative changes to the logical configuration. Some storage systems are designed to perform some or all of these activities *nondisruptively*, meaning the system remains accessible to users. (That engineering achievement has been compared, albeit hyperbolically, to rebuilding an airplane in-flight.) Changes that are disruptive to system access can vary in the nature of the disruption. Perhaps maximum performance is reduced, or perhaps a redundant component must be taken offline so that a single point of failure temporarily exists, or perhaps some management functions are temporarily unavailable. Some system changes may not only be disruptive to operations, but may even be *destructive* to data, a situation the customer should carefully manage (e.g., by first copying data elsewhere, then restoring it).

Continuous availability refers to the ability of a storage system to support both continuous operation and high availability. That is, a system supporting continuous availability is designed to avoid both planned and unplanned outages. (The term "is designed to" is often used in the IT industry. It essentially means "is intended to." In this case, "is designed to" avoids implying outages cannot possibly occur – consider software bugs that are not part of the system design and remain unknown until they are discovered by the problems they cause.)

Business continuity is defined by SNIA as "Processes and/or procedures for ensuring continued business operations." So, business continuity in the context of storage refers to the ability of a storage system to support an organization's operations without disruption. An example is the ability of a storage system to make a copy of data for backup purposes while at the same time business applications continue to access the original data. Business continuity seems to be essentially synonymous with continuous availability.

Data integrity is related to availability but is a more specialized concept. It is defined by SNIA as "The property that data has not been altered or destroyed in an unauthorized manner." More broadly, the concept of data integrity often includes maintaining the accuracy and consistency of data, even if alterations are authorized, and that entails storage system and application responsibilities. Data that has lost integrity is said to be *corrupted*. For example, data loss due to the failure of a non-redundant drive inside a storage system is generally considered a loss of data integrity. Another example of losing data integrity is bits in a data record written by an application that have somehow "flipped" inside the storage system to their opposite values or have gotten permanently "stuck" as 0s or 1s, thus corrupting the record. Data corruption can lead to unpredictable consequences if it is not detected (and, ideally, repaired) before the data is used. (Some storage system design techniques to help protect data integrity are discussed later in this chapter.)

Tip: A vendor might assert their storage system has "high availability" as a marketing claim without necessarily defining what that claim means; no vendor is likely to ever say their system does not have high availability. So, customers may need to drill down to determine whether there is evidence that a storage system model they are considering for acquisition can likely meet their availability requirements.

Tip: Even if a vendor claims a storage system supports high availability, customers should ask what failures or activities could cause an entire system or significant portion of a system to become unavailable. Unknown system software defects are almost certainly such a potential cause in every storage system and vendors should acknowledge that. Human error by system administrators is an activity that could impair system availability. Some systems help reduce human error: for example, an administrator might accidentally command a system to delete a volume that is actually in use by applications – some storage systems detect that situation and deny the request. Other activities that could potentially impair system availability in some storage systems include certain repair actions, hardware upgrades, and software upgrades.

Tip: Some vendors publish a list of components in their storage system that are fault tolerant. The list may be long and seem impressive. What may be more important, though possibly difficult for customers to determine, is whether any components are not on the list. Similarly, if a system is claimed to have "extensive" hardware fault tolerance, keep in mind that "extensive" does not necessarily mean "comprehensive." For example, not all storage systems support redundant system consoles (aka service consoles, service processors, or management consoles) that may provide important functions such as "call home" in case of system problems and support the interfaces administrators use to make changes to a system's logical configuration. Those consoles are sometimes small computers (e.g., laptops). If a non-redundant console fails, some significant system capabilities may be unavailable even though data may remain available to applications.

Tip: Customers should consider both the probability of failure and the impact of failure of any non-redundant components. For example, some non-redundant hardware components may be essential to maintain system availability, but may be relatively unlikely to fail (such as a backplane connecting multiple components together); that situation may be considered high impact / low probability. Or, a subset of HDDs in a system may contain relatively unimportant data that is easily recreated or is expendable, so a decision is made to configure the drives without redundancy protection to save money; that situation may be considered low impact / high probability. (The meaning of "low" and "high" are relative and up to the customer.)

Tip: Storage system marketing collateral may use various terms to create an impression of high system uptime. Examples include claiming an entire system or system feature or system procedure is "highly available," or is "nondisruptive," or is "nonstop," or "supports mission-critical or business-critical operation." A situation that could compromise availability may be described as "in the (very) unlikely event that…"[47] These terms may convey an aura of high system uptime, but what specifically is being claimed may be less than clear. Customers can ask questions of vendors to provide more insight: What evidence (e.g., measurements based on customer experience) can the vendor cite to substantiate claims of high system availability? How improbable are "unlikely" situations that could compromise availability (e.g., have they ever happened to other customers)? What specifically is not disrupted by "nondisruptive" activities – availability or performance or function or all of those?

Tip: It is important to pay careful attention to a vendor's precise words. "Supports concurrent repairs" does not necessarily mean every component can be repaired concurrently. A vendor making such a statement without explicitly adding "for all components" should be asked whether there are any components that cannot be repaired while a system remains available to users.

- Measuring availability. Customers naturally would like a straightforward way to identify and compare the availability of storage system models they are evaluating for acquisition. There are a number of obstacles in the way of achieving this seemingly reasonable desire.

To begin, there is limited ability for customers to even roughly predict a storage system's availability based on published marketing and specification information. Such information is often written before a new system model initially ships to customers, in which case the information is not based on customer experience other than perhaps some beta test systems. Even a storage system with comprehensive and well-functioning hardware fault tolerance may have problematic internal software, something only time and customer experience may reveal.

Moreover, to this author's knowledge there are no public or for-sale statistics identifying or comparing the availability record (i.e., actual customer experiences) of different storage system models.[48] Vendors generally consider the availability statistics for their own systems to be confidential. Customer surveys on the matter typically capture only subjective opinions of the particular persons surveyed, not comprehensive quantified measurements.

---

[47] Statistically, an event could be called "unlikely" if it occurs anything less than 50% of the time. Hopefully, events characterized as "unlikely" occur with a much lower probability than that. Vendors can be forgiven for not publicly quantifying the probability of every failure event for a given population of storage systems.

[48] Decades ago, a company (not a storage system manufacturer) sold a report called Reliability Plus (aka R+). Customers who subscribed to the report sent mainframe-generated error logs for their storage systems to the company. The company returned a report comparing overall storage availability statistics for storage system models from different manufacturers. No comparable offering appears to exist today.

Instead of publishing statistics about the availability experiences of a storage system model in customer environments, vendors are more likely to publish claims of their design goals for the availability of the model. Vendors may publish statements in their marketing literature claiming a system is designed to support "high availability," but without more information such a claim has little value.

The industry has at least largely agreed on the types of measures that can quantify storage system availability. Below is a list of such measures. These would normally be averages that apply to a population of storage systems, not to any single unit in isolation. The definitions are presented as applying to systems, though they could also potentially apply to individual components. To keep the definitions relatively simple here, some details that can affect actual calculations are omitted.[49]

o **Mean Time Between Failures (MTBF)**: The average elapsed time a system will be operational before a failure occurs. The expectation is that there will be a pattern of uptime, then a failure, then more uptime, then another failure. (A related measure, Mean Time to Failure (MTTF), is appropriate for something that works until it fails one time and must be replaced, and so is (hopefully) not useful for measuring storage system availability.)

o **Mean Time to Repair (MTTR)**: The average elapsed time it takes to complete the repair of a failed system.

o **Annualized Failure Rate (AFR)**: The number of failures per year expressed as a percentage of a population. (AFR is often cited by drive manufacturers; an article by a drive manufacturer explaining why they switched from citing MTBF to citing AFR in drive specifications is at http://knowledge.seagate.com/articles/en_US/FAQ/174791en?language=en_US.)

o **Number of nines:** The average uptime of a system expressed using only the digit "9." This may now be the most commonly publicized measure or claim of overall system availability made by storage system vendors. For example, a storage system model might be described in marketing brochures as designed to support five nines availability, meaning it is designed to be available (at least) 99.999% of the time. Due to its widespread use, a discussion of this measure is warranted.

What does this kind of measure mean? A claim a system is designed to support 99.999% uptime translates to 5.26 minutes of downtime during a year.[50] An "is designed to" claim is an expected average that applies to a population of systems over some period of time, not to any one system unit. In the second decade of the 2000s, vendors' claims of storage

---

[49] Examples of such omitted details: Whether a failure impacts an entire system or only a portion of a system; the period of time to which the measures apply (e.g., all time since the first model was shipped or just for the last six months); whether mean time to repair (MTTR) includes the time from the discovery of a failed component or just the time beginning with the arrival of a service representative.

[50] There are 365 x 24 x 60 = 525,600 minutes per non-leap year. 99.999% uptime means .001% downtime. 525,600 minutes x .001% = 5.256 minutes. A table showing how various numbers of nines translate to average downtime per year, month, and week is at http://en.wikipedia.org/wiki/Nines_%28engineering%29#Percentage_calculation.

systems supporting five nines or "greater than five nines" availability are common. (A claim of the form "greater than x nines availability" does not indicate how much greater. It is likely the case that average availability is less than x+1 nines, else the more impressive claim would have been made.) Claims of six nines availability (31.5 seconds average downtime per year) – or even more nines – are rare and may apply only to multiple, coordinated storage systems (such as remotely mirrored storage systems with automatic failover, discussed in the *Inter-System Data Replication* chapter).

Tip: *Customers should ask vendors citing availability numbers whether those claims are based on the experience of a large population of systems or are estimates (predictions).*

Tip: *Availability (and other) measurements based on averages have benefits – and drawbacks.*

Benefits of averages include the simplicity of a single number, facilitating comparing availability claims or statistics for different system models. Averages provide a potentially meaningful indication of overall system model availability when they are based on experiences with a large enough number of systems over a long enough and recent enough period of time in enough different production environments to be meaningful. (A statistician might suggest what "large enough" and "long enough" should be, but it seems reasonable that five systems measured for one month is of little value, one hundred systems measured for six months is better, and one thousand systems measured for a year is even better.)

Averages also have a few drawbacks to keep in mind. Many result from the fact that averages are single numbers often not broken down to reveal important details. Consider:

o *An average over a population of systems provides limited if any insight into the (expected) availability of any individual system with its particular physical configuration (e.g., the number and type of drives), its particular logical configuration (e.g., the particular software functions used), its particular data center environment (e.g., the ambient temperature), and the particular pattern of I/O requests and function requests it receives from hosts.*

o *An average may not indicate whether events impairing availability impacted an entire system or only a portion of a system and, if only a portion, what portion.*

o *An average may not indicate the separate contributions of planned and unplanned outages.*

o *An average may not indicate whether availability varies for different models in the same system family, for different types of hosts, for different microcode versions, or for different hardware and software configurations.*

o *An average may not indicate the contribution of different causes of outages such as failures of particular hardware components, failures of particular software components, human errors, and environmental problems such as power outages.*

o *An average may not indicate how events impacting availability are distributed. For example, an average by itself does not indicate whether every system experienced availability near the average or whether some systems had no problems while others had major problems of long duration.*

o *An average that includes the earliest shipped systems of a new model or includes systems during their initial weeks after installation at customer sites may be lower, because of "early life problems," than averages that do not include those cases.*

o *An average is of little if any value for the earliest customers of a new storage system model or a new version of system software because it would be based on a low number of installed systems and a short duration of experience.*

o *An average of less than 100% availability does not indicate how many problems have been fixed (e.g., via improved component design or improved software) and so won't reoccur, and how many problems have been identified but are not fixed.*

At the end of the day, the most practical information for customers to draw on to evaluate and compare availability among storage system models they are considering acquiring can include: the customer's own experiences with the systems or prior generations of the systems, vendor reputation, analysts' perspectives, customer references, and selecting a few meaningful availability statistics provided by the vendors that can be compared among the systems.

Tip: *Vendors generally compile statistics that give insight into the nature of failures on their system models used by customers. Experience is more meaningful than estimates or unquantified marketing claims. Customers might consider asking their vendors questions such as the following: What availability measured as a number of nines have installed systems of this model achieved over the last year? How many availability-impact events have occurred per month over the last year, broken down by categories (such as hardware components and microcode versions)? What is the trend – is the number of availability-impact events decreasing, steady, or increasing? What has been the hardware Mean Time to Repair (MTTR)? In what percentage of component failures did the system's design permit it to continue to operate with no perceived impact to the customer (including no significant loss of performance)? In how many events was data temporarily unavailable? In how many events was data lost? What were the failure rates for software functions – were some functions more problematic than others?*

Vendors may consider answers to such questions to be confidential, but may be willing to share them via a non-disclosure agreement (NDA). (A customer should be concerned if a vendor says they do not have any of this information or are unwilling to share it.)

Good follow-up questions are: Are there actions customers could have taken to have avoided many or most of the problems that occurred? What actions is the manufacturer taking to reduce problem occurrence?

- <u>Multipath I/O drivers</u>. Storage system availability can depend not only directly on the storage system, but also on host-storage system connectivity. Hosts and storage systems are connected via paths (i.e., cables) either directly or through intermediate devices such as SAN switches, Ethernet switches, NAS gateways, and storage virtualization appliances.

Configuring multiple paths, and multiple intermediate devices (if any), between a host and a storage system helps protect against the failure of one path or device preventing access to the storage system.

Host software to manage multiple paths between a host and a storage system is called a *multipath I/O (MPIO) driver*. A multipath I/O driver can provide various functions. The two main availability-related functions are sending an I/O request down an alternate path when one path fails and reusing the failed path when it is again operational. In addition, multipath I/O drivers may help improve performance by distributing I/O requests across multiple paths, e.g., using an algorithm such as *round-robin* or *least-busy-path*. Some storage system vendors provide multipath I/O drivers for selected hosts; these may be provided at no extra charge or may be priced. Some host operating systems and some Independent Software Vendor (ISV) storage management software products include multipath I/O drivers.

Storage system attributes that significantly influence availability

Below is a list of storage system attributes that have a major influence on system availability. A given storage system model may support none, some, or all of these attributes. This list is not necessarily complete.

Because they know how important storage system availability is to customers, vendors often highlight facilities in the systems they are selling as evidence of how that system supports high levels of availability. In turn, that means customers are likely to hear about these technologies and terms that describe them. This discussion is more technical than most of this chapter, but customer personnel responsible for storage acquisitions will likely encounter the concepts and terms discussed below.

- Hardware reliability. For storage system hardware, high levels of availability can begin with a foundation of highly reliable hardware components, reducing the probability of a single component failure and the probability of multiple concurrent component failures.

  Consider one aspect of HDD reliability as an example. Disk media is formatted into fixed size chunks called *sectors*; a block of data read or written by a user may occupy one or more sectors, transparent to the user. HDDs in enterprise storage systems typically, perhaps universally, support error correction codes (ECC): extra bits derived from the data in a sector and stored with the sector as it is written to drive media. When a block of data is read by an I/O request, the drive retrieves the data and ECC from the associated sectors, recalculates the ECC, and compares the retrieved and recalculated ECC values to determine whether data integrity remains intact. If the ECC values differ, the drive, or the storage system, or the host may take actions to try to correct the problem.[51] (SSDs also use ECC internally.)

---

[51] A drive may be able to correct some bit errors (such as a "flipped bit" or a "stuck bit" in the sector; drives typically contain spare sectors to which data with erroneous but correctable bits can be relocated, transparent to users. A storage system may use RAID techniques (discussed later) to reconstruct corrupted data. A host may retry the I/O request.

- <u>Fault tolerance</u>. A design technique that builds on hardware component reliability to support high levels of availability even if a component fails is *fault tolerance* (aka *failure tolerance* or *self-healing*). A storage system supporting hardware fault tolerance means the system is designed so that the failure of a hardware component does not prevent access to data or function. A given storage system model may support hardware fault tolerance for all, some, or no components. A storage system can be designed to support fault tolerance in various ways such as the following:

  o *Pair redundancy*. A simple and common way to support fault tolerance is through configuring hardware components in redundant pairs.[52] Both components in a pair may normally be active at the same time and thus contributing to system performance, or one may be active and the other passive in a standby mode.

  o *N+m redundancy*. Another way to support fault tolerance could be called "N+m." The idea is that when *N* components are required to support a system capability, the system includes *m* additional components so that if one (or, in some cases, more) of the *N* components fails the remaining components are sufficient to maintain system availability. For example, a storage system might include N+1 or N+2 power supplies or fans where only N are needed for normal operation. Similarly, storage systems may include one or more spare drives so data on a failed drive can be regenerated onto a spare drive. (See the discussion of RAID later in this chapter.) N+m designs enable failed components to be quickly and automatically replaced by other components already installed in the system, promoting high levels of availability.

  o *Scrubbing*. Scrubbing is a technique to provide fault tolerance that makes use of ECC (discussed above). ECC can be supported for storage system DRAM cache as well as for drives. Bits stored on drives or in cache are each quite small and can be corrupted due to outside influences such as vibrations or cosmic rays.[53] Scrubbing is a storage system internal process that periodically scans media looking for bit errors indicated by ECC information and correcting them before they accumulate into uncorrectable bit errors. (ECC often provides information sufficient to correct only one or two bad bits in a group of bits.) A given storage system may support scrubbing for drives, for DRAM cache, for neither, or (preferably) for both.

  o *Metadata*. A technique similar to ECC that a storage system can use to help protect data integrity is adding *metadata* to each block of data received by the system from a host. That metadata stays with a block during its life in the system and is checked by the system whenever it accesses the block, helping to determine whether the block's data integrity has been compromised. Metadata might identify, for example, the location a block is supposed to be stored in, in case a system error causes it to be stored in the wrong location.

---

[52] Software generally does not benefit from redundancy the way that hardware components benefit. A logic bug in a program would exist in all identical copies.

[53] Reference: http://en.wikipedia.org/wiki/Data_corruption.

The idea of supporting metadata that helps protect data integrity by identifying certain types of data corruption within a storage system has been extended to a wider end-to-end level of protection that stretches from a host bus adapter (HBA) card in a host, through any network equipment, and into the storage system. This protection is defined as a formal standard by the T10 subcommittee of the International Committee for Information Technology Standards (http://www.t10.org). The standard defines a *data integrity field (DIF)* that an HBA can append to a block of data so it can be checked any time the block passes through devices supporting the standard, including when data written by a host to a storage system is later read by that host. A given storage system may support its own internal metadata protection, or the DIF standard for end-to-end protection, or both, or it may not provide metadata protection at all.

o *Component fencing.* If a component has failed or its failure is impacting other components, the system can potentially isolate (aka fence) the component so it cannot further impair system operation.

A useful storage system design attribute that complements fault tolerance is an ability to repair or replace (aka "hot plug" or "hot swap") a failed hardware component while the storage system remains online. That avoids the component being a *single point of repair (SPOR)*. Some storage systems require taking multiple components (e.g., drives or host attachment ports) offline to repair or replace one failed component; that can have negative implications for performance as well as for availability.

- Software reliability. Storage system software can help enable high levels of system availability. Software reliability results from good design, quality coding, and thorough testing. Software can be designed to keep a storage system available even if various hardware errors occur. In addition, storage software can contribute to system availability by being designed to allow itself to be replaced by a newer version, or be replaced by a previous version should problems occur in a newer version, all while the storage system remains online.

- Host-storage cooperation. Some techniques to support high levels of availability involve hosts and storage software working together. For example, some storage systems support high levels of availability through allowing customers to configure two storage systems as a primary-secondary pair that mirror their data. If the primary system fails, host-based software in cooperation with the storage system can quickly switch over to use the secondary system while applications continue undisrupted. (This ability is sometimes called *swapping,* discussed further in the *Inter-System Data Replication* chapter.)

Another technique to support high levels of storage system availability through actions by both a storage system and host is *dynamic volume expansion (DVE)*. DVE is the ability to increase the capacity of a volume while it is online.[54] DVE can be used to proactively avoid a volume running out of capacity, a condition that can cause applications to fail if they

---

[54] The opposite operation, nondisruptively contracting (reducing) the capacity of an existing logical volume, is typically not supported by storage systems. One reason is that storage systems have limited information about how a volume's capacity is being used by applications.

require additional capacity on the volume. For DVE to be nondisruptive to applications can require not only support in the storage system to increase a volume's capacity, but also that host software (typically a host's operating system) accessing the volume be informed of the increase in capacity. (Note that some implementations of DVE have the restriction that a volume being expanded cannot be part of an active copy process, e.g., the volume cannot be the source or target of an intra-system volume replication operation.)

- RAID. One of the best known techniques storage systems use to support high levels of availability is *RAID* which stands for Redundant Array of Independent Drives.[55] RAID is a way that a storage system can store data in a group of physical drives such that data remains accessible to applications even if one, or in some cases more than one, drive in the group fails. There are multiple RAID types (aka RAID levels) the most common of which are RAID-1, RAID-5, RAID-6, and RAID-10.[56] (Note: In addition to supporting high levels of data availability, RAID also has performance and cost considerations. Performance considerations are discussed in the *Performance* chapter and cost considerations are discussed in the *Prices and Costs* chapter.)

Many storage systems support multiple RAID types. A customer's decision of the type(s) of RAID to deploy is sometimes contentious: different individuals in an organization may have different preferences and different vendor representatives may have their own preferences. The decision has implications for availability, performance, and cost, so this topic deserves attention.

The most basic form of RAID is RAID-1. In a common implementation of RAID-1, pairs of physical drives are managed by the storage system to contain identical copies of data. To simplify this discussion, assume the pair of drives are seen by hosts as a single volume. Every write I/O to the volume received by the storage system results in two write I/Os inside the storage system, one to each drive in the pair. A read I/O to the volume is satisfied from the data stored in either drive (selected by an internal programmed algorithm). If one drive in the pair fails, the storage system directs all read and write I/Os for the volume to the functioning drive and can copy the data on the surviving drive onto another drive (e.g., a spare drive if available) to restore redundancy.

---

[55] "RAID" originally stood for Redundant Array of Inexpensive Disks. The idea came about in the late 1980s because at the time 5-inch diameter disk drives used in personal computers were much less expensive per unit of capacity than the larger drives (e.g., around 10-inch diameter) used in many enterprise storage systems. But "inexpensive" was perceived as meaning unreliable, and "disk" became inadequate once solid-state drives became prevalent. It just so happens that the English language has other appropriate words beginning with "i" and "d" that allow the original acronym to be preserved. Some storage systems use RAID-like designs, but do not use the term RAID.

[56] Another type of RAID, RAID-0, is defined as data striped across a group of drives for improved performance only. No redundancy is provided in case a drive fails. Since the "R" in RAID stands for *Redundant*, RAID-0 seems self-contradictory. (Data is striped across multiple drives in RAID-5, RAID-6, and RAID-10.)

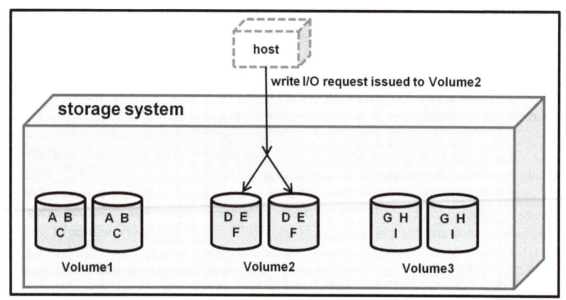

A storage system is shown with six drives configured as three RAID-1 pairs. Data is depicted as A, B,..,I. A write request from a host to a volume is automatically converted by the storage system internally to write operations directed to both drives in the pair.

To briefly summarize the most prominently used types of RAID:

RAID-1: Two copies of data are maintained. RAID-1 is sometimes called data *mirroring*.

RAID-10: Two copies of data are maintained but are *striped* (i.e., distributed) across multiple pairs of drives. This can improve I/O performance by increasing the number of I/O requests against the data (e.g., against a volume or file system) that can be processed in parallel. RAID-10 is sometimes called *striped mirroring*.

RAID-5: Instead of maintaining two copies of data, RAID-5 uses a simple calculation on the bits of the original data to create *parity* information that is stored in the RAID group; the benefit of parity is that less capacity is needed compared to RAID-1 and RAID-10 to preserve access to data in case a drive in the RAID group fails. (Data on a failed drive can be regenerated automatically by the storage system based on data on functioning drives plus parity information.) A RAID-5 group of drives requires only one extra drive's worth of capacity (distributed over the drives in the group) to preserve data in the group in case of a single drive failure; in contrast RAID-1 and RAID-10 require one extra drive for each drive's worth of data. An example of a typical RAID-5 group is one containing eight drives to support seven drives' worth of capacity plus parity.

RAID-6: This is similar to RAID-5, but maintains two types of parity information such that a RAID-6 group can preserve access to data even if up to two drives in the RAID group fail at the same time. RAID-6 is sometimes called *dual parity RAID*.

Tip: *The various types of RAID differ in the amount of additional physical capacity needed to protect data (resulting in different costs), in performance (where differences depend on the characteristics of an I/O request), and in the statistical probabilities of data loss. The way RAID support is designed in different storage systems can affect these differences. The point is, no one RAID type is necessarily better in all ways than other types.*

Tip: A given storage system model may not support the same RAID types for all supported drive types. Customers should ask vendors to identify the RAID types supported for the types of drives customers plan to install.

The sets of drives protected by RAID in different storage system models may be called different names. Common names are *RAID array*, *RAID group,* and *parity group.* Sometimes an entire storage system supporting RAID is called a *RAID array.* All but the smallest storage systems typically support multiple RAID arrays; such systems may allow an administrator to specify the RAID type separately for each RAID array. For example, in a single storage system supporting both RAID-5 and RAID-10, some drives could be configured as RAID-5 arrays and others could be configured as RAID-10 arrays.

The original RAID idea was to implement redundancy at a drive level so that all data on one drive is mirrored on one other drive. Some storage systems implement variations on that theme, mirroring data at the block or volume level and distributing the mirrored copies across different drives.

RAID techniques generally preserve data access (and protect against data loss) in case of drive failures inside a single storage system. However, some customers require protecting data access even if entire storage systems fail, or even if entire data centers in one or more locations suffer a disaster. Inter-system data replication techniques (aka remote mirroring) help with those situations; see the *Inter-System Data Replication* chapter.

A RAID-related issue of increasing concern among customers and in the industry is the time it takes for a storage system to rebuild data onto a spare drive from the drives that remain functional in a RAID group after a drive fails. As drives increase in capacity – and multi-terabyte drives are common today – it can take many hours, or even more than one day, to rebuild the data that was on a high capacity drive. The longer the time for rebuild to occur, the greater the statistical probability of other drive failures in the same RAID group that could prevent rebuild from succeeding. If rebuild of a failed drive does not succeed *all* data in the RAID group is lost (meaning special procedures need to be implemented by customers to recover the data such as restoring a backup copy then updating it to make it current).[57]

One way to address the time-to-rebuild issue is to use RAID-6. RAID-6 protects data with a dual parity scheme that allows up to two drives to fail concurrently in the same RAID group without loss of data. Some storage systems support parity schemes that can protect data against loss even if three drives fail.

Another way to address the time-to-rebuild issue recognizes that a major contributing factor to long rebuild times is that rebuilding data from functioning drives in the RAID group is normally done onto a single spare drive. That spare drive becomes a performance bottleneck. Some storage systems are designed to get around this bottleneck by

---

[57] While data on the functioning drives theoretically remains accessible, because logically consecutive data is usually striped (i.e., distributed) across the drives in the RAID group, the loss of a drive means there are "holes" of missing data. It is generally impractical to try to use the surviving data and somehow identify the holes and correct the situation. Instead, restoring all data in the RAID group from a backup copy is the practical approach.

maintaining mirrored copies of data blocks in the same system (just as RAID-1 and RAID-10 do), but distributing the copies among all drives in the system. If a drive fails, the data rebuild process accesses the distributed blocks that mirrored the data on the failed drive, creates new copies, and distributes them across multiple drives. That design allows the rebuild process to have a high degree of internal I/O parallelism, avoiding the performance bottleneck of rebuilding data onto a single spare. However, that design has the risk, albeit reduced by the fast rebuild process, that if a second drive failure occurs before rebuild is complete some data on every internal volume can be lost at the same time. And, as previously mentioned, mirroring all data internally adds to the cost of the system compared to parity-based RAID techniques.

As another way to address the risk of data loss due to multiple concurrent drive failures, and to give customers more choice over the degree of redundancy protection they want, some in the industry have turned to a form of drive availability protection called *erasure codes*. RAID designs are a special case of erasure codes. Erasure codes are techniques that can protect a set of n drives against m concurrent failures where n and m depend on system design and perhaps on customer-settable parameters. For example, an erasure code could be used to protect a group of 8 drives against 1 drive failure (comparable to RAID-5), or against 2 failures (comparable to RAID-6), or against 3 failures, etc. Similar to tradeoffs among RAID types, tradeoffs among erasure code implementations are in the amount of additional capacity needed, cost, performance implications, and the degree of protection against data loss.[58]

Protection of data by redundancy techniques such as RAID has been such a significant contributor to high levels of storage availability that it is nearly universally supported in storage systems. However, some storage systems, or portions of those systems, still do not have this protection. Those systems are often informally called *Just a Bunch of Disks* (*JBOD,* pronounced "jay'-bahd") or, for flash-based drives, *Just a Bunch of Flash* (*JBOF*).

Many hosts support some types of RAID, especially RAID-1 and RAID-10, through host software. Storage system support for RAID is generally preferred, however, because that frees host resources to be used by applications. Nevertheless, host-based RAID can be useful for supporting RAID in JBOD storage systems, for maintaining redundant data via RAID-1 or RAID-10 in two different storage systems thus protecting data access even if one of those systems is unavailable, and for migrating data between storage systems (by creating a mirror copy in a different system then deleting the original data).

Tip: Given the variety of RAID types and implementations in different storage system models, it is not surprising that storage system vendors often claim their system's implementation of RAID is better than competitors' implementations. Customers should evaluate a system's RAID capabilities against their storage requirements in terms of the impact on system availability, maximum system usable capacity, performance, and cost. If a customer's requirements are satisfied by a single type of RAID, then many questions can

---

[58] The term "erasure" refers to unavailable information such as due to the failure of a storage device. Erasure codes are a relatively complex technology. See http://web.eecs.utk.edu/~plank/plank/papers/FAST-2005.pdf.

be addressed at the system level; else they may need to be addressed at the array level for each RAID type.

Tip: *Customers can ask vendors how often, if ever, data has been lost in a given system model or family of models due to more concurrent drive failures in a RAID group (or entire system) than the system is designed to recover from. Comparing such experiences may be more meaningful than comparing calculations of theoretical failure rates.*

- Protecting the integrity of data written to cache. In addition to cache scrubbing, additional steps can be taken by storage systems to protect the integrity of data written to DRAM cache. Cache sizes are typically measured in gigabytes or terabytes; just one gigabyte of cache can potentially hold hundreds of thousands of 4KB blocks of data, a common size. Thus, protecting the integrity of data in cache is clearly an important aspect of overall system availability.

There are two situations that apply uniquely to data written to a storage system by hosts and stored by the system in cache but not yet destaged to drives. The situations do not apply to data read from drives into cache because that data is just a copy of data on drives and a well-designed storage system should be able to retrieve a good copy of that data from its drives if the cache copy is lost. The problem for writes is that, at least for some period of time, there may be only the one copy in cache and no other copy to resort to if that one copy is lost.[59] The following are facilities many (hopefully most if not all) storage systems use to protect write data in cache against loss:

1. Cache that can hold write data can potentially be designed to provide RAID-like protection for that data. During normal operations, contemporary storage systems often protect the integrity of write data in cache through maintaining two copies of each write block in separate caches. This is referred to as mirroring write data in cache and is similar in principle to RAID-1 protection for drives. It helps protect data integrity in case of failure of a cache memory component or in case there is a bit error beyond the ability of the system to correct (e.g., via ECC).

2. Storage systems typically include batteries to enable destaging write data from volatile DRAM cache to nonvolatile media (e.g., HDDs or SSDs) to preserve that data if the systems detect loss of external power, an emergency situation. These batteries should ideally be designed to last at least long enough to destage all write data from cache to nonvolatile media, perhaps even more than once before needing to be recharged (because recharging can take time). In some storage systems the write data in cache might be destaged directly to its intended media locations. In some storage systems write data might be destaged to internal drives reserved for that purpose. In some storage systems write data might be destaged to reserved locations on customer-

---

[59] The author once read an analyst paper that defended a storage system that supported only one copy of write data in its cache by claiming that if that copy was lost the storage system could simply ask the host to resend the data. As I pointed out to the analyst, hosts do not keep copies of data around in host memory just in case a storage system loses its copy some time after the system signaled the host that the write I/O operation successfully completed.

ordered drives. Wherever the data is destaged to should be protected against being a single point of failure.

Additional Tips

- *Some vendors offer "availability guarantees." See the* Marketing tactics *chapter.*

- *Storage system availability depends not only on the technologies built into the system, but also on how customers configure and manage the system. Here are examples of actions customers can take to promote storage system high availability:*

  o *A common type of availability issue in storage systems (and potentially in any product) is known as "early life problems." Storage systems sometimes have hardware quality problems and software defects not detected during manufacturers' testing. To help manage that fact of IT life, some customers prefer to acquire storage system models only after they have been in productive use by other customers for some period of time, e.g., at least six months, to help minimize the probability of encountering previously undiscovered problems. Similarly, some customers prefer to install new software versions only after they have been in productive use by other customers for some period of time, unless a particular release contains new function or fixes to problems that are critical to the customer's IT operations.[60]*

  o *Customers can test a newly installed storage system before deploying it in production. For example, customers can test actual applications using an expendable copy of a database. Customers can test system functions they plan to use such as making point-in-time copies. These kinds of tests can help uncover storage system software problems that would impact operations and can help uncover early life hardware problems that may be unique to the new system (e.g., due to a problematic batch of components used by the manufacturer). The testing period also gives administrators hands-on experience with the new system, helping to avoid human error when the system goes into production. Customers should install storage systems early enough to allow sufficient time for such testing.*

  o *Drives should be configured as RAID groups to support fault tolerance unless all data stored on those drives is trivial to reconstruct or is expendable. While different RAID types differ in their statistical levels of availability protection (and in associated performance and cost), any RAID type (other than RAID-0) provides far superior availability protection compared to no RAID at all.*

  Some storage systems always provide RAID protection for all drives, while other systems make that an administrator option. Not enabling RAID protection for some or all drives

---

[60] *Vendors know (or should know) which installed systems are running which releases of microcode. Customers can ask a vendor to share the number of installed storage systems running a given release to help indicate whether the software has been exercised by enough users to support confidence in the quality of that release.*

can reduce costs and increase usable capacity – both of which sound desirable unless some day data is lost due to the failure of a single drive and organization management is asking how that happened. Cost savings of not using RAID should be weighed against the consequences of losing data due to a drive failure.

○ *Customers may want to deploy data center facilities to help storage and other IT systems continue to operate through periods of loss of external power.*

Some storage systems provide the ability to ride through very short-term power losses (aka brownouts) that may last a few milliseconds to a few seconds. Such events are more common in some regions of the world than in others. Different storage systems support riding through different brownout durations, but that information is often not included in storage system specification sheets and so is something customers should ask their vendors about.

Some customers deploy uninterruptible power supplies (UPS, pronounced u-p-s) to provide data center power for some duration of time (perhaps up to a few hours) in case of loss of external power from utility companies. Some customers may deploy power generators for protection against even longer outages.

○ *Customers in earthquake-prone areas may want to ask storage system vendors about their systems' abilities to withstand earthquakes and any options or recommendations the vendors' have to help. For example, a vendor may support special hardware to help stabilize cabinets to protect components from damage during tremors.*

○ *A given failure could potentially impact a system for hours or longer. Customers should consider how they would manage such a situation, the potential business impact, and whether and how much they are willing to invest to reduce the probability of such a situation.*

For example, RAID-1, RAID-5, and RAID-10 are commonly used techniques to protect a group of drives against the loss of data in case of a single drive failure. Configuring RAID-6, however, can protect data against the concurrent failure of two drives in the same group of drives, but that can raise system costs due to the capacity overhead required by many RAID-6 implementations. As another example, configurations of two or more storage systems can work together to mirror data to help provide high levels of availability through automated or manually initiated failover – a generally effective approach, but more expensive than a single storage system. As an additional example, organizations with storage systems in locations lacking prompt response to hardware failures by vendor service representatives should consider configuring extra spare drives, using RAID-6 to help protect against data loss, and using storage system mirroring to help protect access to data in case of failure of an entire storage system.

• *Processes implemented in some storage systems to help maintain access to data, such as the ability to automatically rebuild data from a failed RAID-protected drive onto a spare drive and the ability to nondisruptively install a new version of internal software, can have side effects. Questions customers might ask vendors include:*

   ○ *How long does the process take?*

   ○ *Is system availability impacted during the process? (For example, Are any hardware components taken offline temporarily when system microcode is being upgraded, resulting in a temporary loss of redundancy? When one component fails, are any other components taken offline during the repair/replace process?)*

   ○ *Are there exception cases where the process cannot or should not be used? (For example, when nondisruptively installing a new version of internal software, a best practice is to do this during a period of relatively low storage system activity to minimize stress on the system that can cause problems.)*

   ○ *Is there a negative impact on performance? (A negative impact on system performance can occur when a failed component normally directly contributes to system performance in which case the component is sometimes said to be "in the data path" (in contrast to components such as power supplies). The negative impact on performance could be due to reasons such as the absence of the component's function or internal activities (e.g., data movement) initiated to manage the failure. Customers may want to ask their vendors what failures could result in degraded performance, what the degree of degradation might be, and what actions customers could take to minimize the impact.)*

- *Storage system availability can depend on how quickly a failed component can be repaired or replaced. The longer repair/replace can take, the greater the probability of another component failing in the same time period which can be a serious problem if both components in a redundant pair fail.*

   Some storage systems support customer-replaceable units (CRU, pronounced c-r-u) where the customer is responsible for replacing a failed component such as a failed disk drive. That enables quickly addressing component failures (and may also help reduce system and maintenance prices). When service representative assistance is needed, the time for the representative to respond to a problem can depend on warranty and maintenance agreement terms, e.g., is same-day response promised? Another consideration is where system parts are stocked. Customers may want to ask their vendors how close vendors' parts warehouses are to the customers' locations and how many service representatives are located in the customers' area. Some customers, usually larger customers using multiple storage systems from a given vendor, may be able to negotiate stocking some spare parts onsite.

- *Some storage system vendors have a policy to defer the maintenance (i.e., repair or replacement) of some failed (but redundant) components until multiple such components have failed. An example is a vendor that replaces failed RAID-protected drives in systems configured with multiple spare drives only when just a few spare drives (possibly just one) remain. This reduces the vendor's cost for maintenance because service representatives need to make fewer trips to customer locations. Customers concerned about the impact of this kind of maintenance policy on system availability should ask vendors whether they employ such policies and, if so, whether exceptions can be made, perhaps for a fee.*

- *The more thoroughly hardware and software are tested by the manufacturer prior to shipment, the fewer availability issues customers should see. Customers can ask vendors to describe their storage system testing procedures.*

- *Storage system manufacturers generally do not directly manufacture every component in a storage system; rather, they acquire some components from other manufacturers and integrate them into the system to be shipped.[61] The names of such original equipment manufacturers (OEMs) of components are often not divulged by storage system manufacturers. Drives, for example, may be sourced from multiple OEMs. That practice can benefit all parties because it eliminates dependencies on a single component supplier. However, the specifications of such components, while all presumably meet storage system manufacturers' requirements, may differ somewhat; customers generally do not have a choice about which OEM such multi-sourced components come from in a system they install.*

  In general, this is not a problem for customers. In some cases, however, customers may want to be aware of the suppliers of individual components in systems the customers have installed or in new systems or upgrades they are ordering. For example, sometimes an entire batch of drives (e.g., associated with a serial number range) from a particular drive manufacturer has problems and a storage system manufacturer will replace those drives in installed systems. While manufacturers may try to do this quietly to avoid bad publicity, many customers may become aware of this situation via press reports or blogs and wonder whether and how they are affected. Until they are replaced, there may be increased probability that the system will experience an issue with the problematic drives. Other risks include that the replacement process might be disruptive or lead to problems due to human error. Customers ordering a new system or new drives for an installed system may want to ask their vendor what manufacturer's drives are going to be installed so they can try to determine that those drives are not from a batch of drives known to be problematic.

---

[61] *That integration may (and arguably should) include testing the OEMed-in components in addition to the testing the OEM should have done. Storage system manufacturers who do such testing occasionally find problems in the OEM's components that the OEM manufacturer must then address. That indirectly benefits the OEM and any other manufacturers who buy the OEM's components. Unfortunately, storage system manufacturers who perform such thorough testing may not receive the credit they deserve.*

Performance

Storage system performance is about the speed at which storage systems can satisfy requests to read and write data and requests to perform data management functions. Performance objectives are among the most important requirements customers have for storage systems. While it is clearly essential that a storage system supports the hosts it will attach to, and that the system's data and function are available to applications and users on demand, it is nearly as essential to be able to access that data and function in a sufficiently timely manner to finish work on schedule and keep both internal and external users productive and satisfied.

Concepts and Facilities

- <u>Measuring performance</u>. Performance is not a single, indivisible storage system attribute. Different performance attributes apply to different types of I/O workloads; a system's performance might meet a customer's requirements for some types of work but not for other types of work. A vendor's simple, broad, but not uncommon, claim that their storage system provides higher performance than another storage system does not provide enough information to be of much value. The most important and measurable performance attributes include the following:

  o *Random I/O throughput.* This is a measure of the number of individual I/Os that are, or potentially could be, processed in a given amount of time. (Throughput essentially answers the question: "How many?".) Because storage systems are typically so busy and so fast, this measure is often expressed as *I/Os per second* (IOPS, sometimes pronounced "eye'-ahps"). The maximum IOPS a storage system can support varies based on factors such as: the speeds of hardware components, how a storage system's software manages those components, cache effectiveness, and characteristics of I/O requests, e.g., the amount of data read or written per I/O request and how I/Os are distributed across installed drives (which can promote, or hinder, processing multiple I/Os in parallel).

  o *Random I/O response time.* This is a measure of the time to process an individual I/O request. (Essentially, it answers the question: "How fast?".) Another term often used is *latency*. Response time can vary based on factors such as whether an I/O request is for reading data or writing data, the amount of data an I/O request is reading or writing, whether the request is satisfied quickly in storage system cache or less quickly in a backend drive, and the speeds of backend drives. It is interesting to note that I/O throughput is I/Os-per-time while I/O response time is time-per-I/O.[62] The following diagram illustrates the usual relationship between throughput and response time for random I/Os in a given storage system.

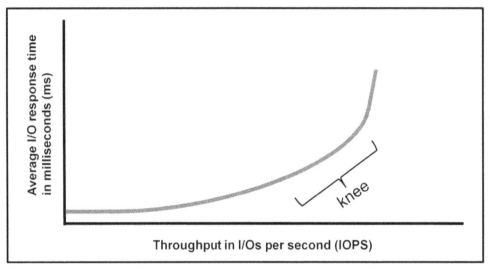

This graph illustrates the relationship between throughput and response time for random I/Os. The shape of the curve is typical of such curves.

The above diagram shows that as the number of I/Os per second increases average response time typically also increases because there is more work for a storage system to do, resulting in contention with other I/Os for system resources (i.e., some work has to wait in a queue for other work to finish using a resource). The increase in response time is initially zero or low until IOPS are high enough for requests to start significantly affecting each other's use of system resources.

Some curves rise faster and some rise more slowly compared to the diagram, depending on factors such as the storage system configuration, characteristics of the I/Os (e.g., the amount of data transferred per I/O), and the maximum I/Os per second shown at the far right of the graph. The general area where the curve starts to bend upwards more dramatically is called the *knee of the curve*. At and beyond the knee of the curve, the greater the impact a small change in the number of I/Os per second can have on response time. It is generally preferable for users to keep the maximum IOPS rate to the left of the knee of the curve to help ensure stable/predictable I/O response times.

---

[62] Technically, the time it takes to complete a single I/O request without any interference from other I/O requests is called *service time*. The time it takes to complete a single I/O request when multiple requests are contending for the same resources – a typical real-world environment – is called *response time*. These terms are used in *queuing theory* which is the mathematics used to model such things. In queuing theory, response time is calculated as service time plus delays due to queuing, e.g., a delay due to waiting to access a drive that can handle only one I/O at a time where other requests may already be in line.

Tip: *Curves showing response time as a function of IOPS can potentially be misleading depending on how they are drawn.[63]   For example, a curve could be truncated on the right side to avoid showing the knee of the curve or how steeply and quickly the curve rises at some IOPS point.*

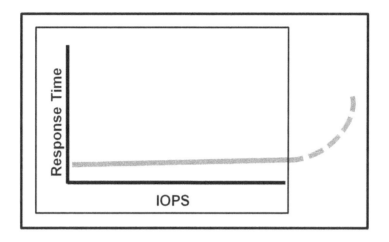

As another example, a vendor could draw a curve for a competitor's storage system showing each IOPS increment as very large (e.g., in incremental of 1 million IOPS) to make the curve for a storage system that supports up to 500K IOPS, say, with good response time rise quickly, implying response time is almost always high.

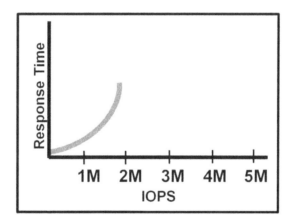

o *Sequential I/O throughput.*   (This term is sometimes called *bandwidth* or *sequential bandwidth*.) This is a measure of performance for sequential I/Os. The measure is often expressed quantitatively as megabytes per second (MB/s) or gigabytes per second (GB/s). (In networks or data paths where speeds are often expressed in *bits* per second, commonly used measures of sequential performance are megabits per second (Mb/s, Mbps) and gigabits per second (Gb/s, Gbps)).

Sequential I/Os typically differ from random I/Os in significant ways: They are usually for larger blocks of data than random I/Os. Sequential read I/O requests are predictable, enabling a storage system's cache algorithms to potentially be designed to *prefetch* data

---

[63] For a discussion of various ways graphs can be misleading see https://en.wikipedia.org/wiki/Misleading_graph.

into cache that is predicted to be accessed by future I/O requests, speeding performance. The basic principle is straightforward to illustrate: If a storage system detects successive I/O read requests to a given volume to be for block n, then for block n+1, and so on through block n+7, it can predict that block n+8 will soon be read and prefetch that block of data into cache before it is requested, thus improving the speed at which the data can be sent to the host when it *is* requested.[64]

o *Function performance.* This is an often overlooked area of storage system performance. There are two major considerations:

1) *How long the function takes to complete.* This can be thought of as the response time of a function. This time is important because some tasks cannot proceed until a storage system function they depend on first completes. Due to clever programming, some functions are designed to complete quickly in a logical sense (that is, they appear to have quickly completed and users can safely proceed as if that is the case), but they actually complete later. Many implementations of intra-system data replication work that way; see the *Intra-System Data Replication* chapter.

2) *The impact of a function on the performance of other work in the system.* Some storage system functions use system resources, reducing the ability of those resources to handle other work as fast as otherwise possible. An example is data movement due to I/O operations initiated inside a storage system. That internal data movement can degrade the performance of host-initiated production I/Os by adding activity to drives, internal paths, system cache, and internal processors. Vendors should be able to help customers estimate the performance impact of system functions. (As an example of internally initiated data movement, see the discussion of automated storage tiering later in this chapter.)

o *Overall system performance.* This indicates how a system performs when a combination of I/O workloads are running at the same time, e.g., random I/Os and sequential I/Os and function (internally initiated) I/Os. This can be difficult to model for a given environment and may require hands-on testing to be determined.

Tip: Storage system overall performance can far exceed the performance an individual application can attain. That makes it practical for multiple applications to share the same storage system at the same time and for each application to meet its performance goals. From one perspective, an application may issue I/Os at a rate less than the maximum rate the associated storage system can support. From another perspective, an application's

---

[64] Sequential prefetch algorithms in different storage systems may differ in ways such as: how many I/Os it takes before the system decides the pattern is sequential, how much data is prefetched into cache at one time, how many different sequential I/O streams can be supported by prefetching at the same time, and how quickly prefetched data is discarded from cache after it is read by a host.

Note that sequential data prefetching applies to read I/O requests. Even if a storage system detects that incoming write I/Os are being issued in a sequential pattern it must wait for a host to issue its next write I/O and cannot somehow prefetch it. However, sequential write I/Os can be optimized in another way: If a storage system detects a set of blocks written to cache will reside at consecutive locations on volumes, it can potentially write (destage) those blocks together to a drive or RAID group of drives with less overhead than writing each block individually.

I/O performance is limited by the particular set of storage system resources it can use or needs to use. For example, the application's data may reside on a subset of a system's drives, or its active data may fit in a subset of system cache, or its data transfer needs may be met using only a subset of the system's host ports.

Tip: *Watch for vendor claims describing storage system performance using qualifiers such as "up to" or "as high as." These qualifiers likely indicate a claimed performance benefit has dependencies in order to be achieved. The dependencies could be a specific hardware configuration, specific software features in use, specific software features not in use, specific I/O patterns, or some combination.*

For example, an "up to" claim might apply to only extreme (and rare in real-world applications) I/O patterns such as 100% reads from cache of very small blocks of data. The not uncommon use of such misleading claims illustrates the importance of "reading the small print" and questioning the usefulness of a claim when such detail is not provided.

As another example, a system model may be claimed to support sequential throughput to hosts of up to 6.4GB/s based on configuring the system's supported maximum of eight 8Gb/s (= .8GB/s) Fibre Channel connections. If a customer installs a system configured with only four 8Gb/s paths, sequential throughput cannot exceed 32Gb/s (= 3.2GB/s), half the potential throughput of the configuration with eight paths. (Note that this example assumes each path is 100% utilized, rarely practical, especially for random I/O workloads, for performance reasons.)

- Access density. This is an interesting measure of I/O performance that is less common than the measures cited above, but common enough to warrant mention. Access density is a measure of I/O throughput in the form of I/Os per second per gigabyte (IOPS/GB). Access density takes into account two aspects of storage: performance and capacity. Because IOPS is a factor, access density is relevant mainly for random I/Os, not sequential I/Os. Access density is sometimes thought of as a measure of I/O intensity.

Access density can apply to an application: what access density does its I/O activity generate? It can also apply to devices: What is the maximum random I/O request rate sustainable by a given device of a given capacity? (Here, "device" is used in a general sense and could be a single HDD or SSD, a group of such devices (such as a RAID array), or an entire storage system.)

Example 1: Assume an application uses 100GB of capacity and issues 100 I/O requests per second against that capacity. The I/O access density of the application is 100IOPS / 100GB = 1 IOPS/GB.

Example 2: Storage device *service time* is the time it takes to process a single I/O request that does not need to wait for previous requests to complete. (Service time is an intrinsic property of a storage device, ignores any time requests might spend in a queue, and so is less than or equal to response time.) Assume the average I/O service time for a random I/O to a 500GB HDD is 5 milliseconds (ms). The maximum access density the HDD can support is when it is 100% busy each second. The access density is derived in two steps:

1. Calculate maximum IOPS: (1000ms/second) / (5ms/IO) = 200 I/Os per second = 200 IOPS.

2. Calculate maximum access density: 200IOPS / 500GB = .4 IOPS/GB.

Tip: Access density can be useful for storage planning purposes. If a planned application is estimated to generate n IOPS/GB, then the storage system, or portion of a system, it will use should be configured to support at least n IOPS/GB. If the access density of a planned application isn't known, it might be estimated based on the IOPS/GB generated by a similar existing application.

Tip: Beyond its definition, there are a number of things to keep in mind about access density.

o *Access density calculations generally assume that I/Os are randomly (evenly) distributed across the capacity. If they aren't, it may be best to consider relevant subsets of capacity separately.*

o *I/O request characteristics that can affect the maximum access density of a device include the amount of data transferred per I/O request, the read/write ratio[65], and I/O patterns requiring longer or shorter HDD seek operations.*

o *Access density should be considered along with I/O response time. An application may have such a high access density that detailed planning is needed to create a storage environment that can support the desired response time. For example, while it might be interesting to determine the maximum IOPS/GB an HDD can sustain, i.e., the point at which it would be 100% busy, many applications have I/O response time goals which would require keeping drive performance utilization much lower. That, in turn, might require not using all of a drive's capacity.*

Applications with relatively high access densities and stringent I/O response time requirements generally require faster, more costly storage hardware than applications with relatively low access densities and loose I/O response time requirements. The first case may require high-speed SSDs and a large system cache, while the second case may be able to use slower, capacity-optimized nearline HDDs and a small system cache.

o *Access density is mainly applicable to usable capacity. For example, when considering the access density an entire storage system can support, the aggregate capacity of spare drives is irrelevant.*

o *The maximum access density of HDDs has generally declined over time because performance increases have been relatively minor while capacity increases have been*

---

[65] A *read/write ratio* is the percentage of I/Os that are reads vs. writes. It can be calculated for different application functions, for an entire application, for a host, or from the perspective of a storage system receiving I/O requests. If, for example, an application always issues three read I/O requests to read three blocks of data, then issues one write I/O request to store summary data based on its analysis of the three blocks of data read, the read/write ratio is 3:1, meaning 75% of I/Os are reads and 25% are writes. It is an important statistic because storage systems typically handle read and write I/O requests differently, with resulting differences in performance implications.

relatively major. SSDs provide much higher maximum access densities than HDDs for similar capacities.

o *An entire storage system may be capable of supporting an access density greater than the access densities of individual drives if a significant portion of I/O requests are satisfied by system cache.*

o *The number and speed of host-storage system paths can limit the achievable access density of a storage system.*

- Industry-standard performance benchmarks. Storage system benchmarks supported by storage industry standards organizations can help customers identify a system's potential performance capabilities. Prominent benchmarks for block-access storage systems include SPC-1 for random I/O workloads and SPC-2 for sequential I/O workloads from the Storage Performance Council (http://www.storageperformance.org). A prominent benchmark for file-access storage systems is SPEC SFS (e.g., https://www.spec.org/sfs2014/) from the Standard Performance Evaluation Corporation (http://www.spec.org).

Tip: There are important caveats to keep in mind about these standard performance benchmarks.

o *Benchmarks are generally run by storage vendors, not by the standards organizations that control benchmark specifications. Not all vendors publish results for all applicable benchmarks. A vendor may publish benchmark results for only some configurations of some of their storage system models. A benchmark result is published for a particular system configuration as of a certain date; vendors may not publish updated benchmark results, or not do so immediately, even if a system's performance capability improves later due to hardware or software enhancements.*

o *A given benchmark may support only certain types of servers.*

o *A benchmarked storage system hardware configuration may differ considerably from the hardware configuration a given customer would install.*

o *A benchmark's I/O characteristics may differ considerably from a customer's applications' I/O characteristics in terms of block size per I/O, the mix of random and sequential I/O, cache "friendliness," the read/write ratio, and more. The differences could potentially make the benchmarked system appear faster – or slower – than it would be if the benchmark was based on the customer's applications.*

o *A given standard benchmark may not work well with capacity optimization features (such as data compression) or the organization owning the benchmark code may not support storage systems that operate with such features enabled.[66]*

o *A vendor could potentially configure a system they benchmark with a large number of drives but only use a small amount of each drive's capacity. That can improve*

---

[66] *At least at one time this was an issue with the Storage Performance Council's SPC-1 benchmark. See http://www.purestorage.com/blog/why-doesnt-pure-storage-publish-a-spc-benchmark-result/.*

performance through supporting high levels of I/O parallelism, but not many customers may be willing to pay the cost of the unused capacity.

○ *A vendor could potentially configure a system with a large cache and a small amount of data so that most or all I/Os are satisfied at cache speed.*

That's a long list and is not necessarily complete. Nevertheless, the results of standard benchmarks can be useful as evidence of the potential performance capabilities of a storage system model when benchmark and system configuration details are published, when customers examine that documentation with a critical eye, and because vendors are usually, but not always, trying to demonstrate the maximum performance a system model is capable of.[67] Meaningful benchmark results can help customers determine which vendors' systems are worth further evaluation.

Tip: *Some benchmark results are published as an average of multiple "sub" benchmarks. For example, the SPC-2 sequential I/O throughput benchmark consists of three different sequential workload types. SPC-2 benchmark results are published showing the throughput of each individual workload as well as the combined average throughput. One storage system could have a higher overall SPC-2 average result than another storage system, yet not have a higher result for every individual workload type.*

Tip: *Vendor claims about maximum storage system performance should be viewed cautiously when they are not based on well-documented industry-standard benchmarks, particularly when the claims lack details about the system configuration or the characteristics of the I/O workload. Consider these examples:*

1. *Performance claims for random I/O workloads are often based on 100% read I/Os of small blocks of data where all the read I/Os are satisfied by data in cache. The claims do not always divulge those details. Such an I/O environment can provide very high IOPS throughout rates and low average I/O response times, but is unlikely to reveal performance real-world applications can achieve. (Unfortunately, because some vendors sometimes use this measure of maximum random I/O performance, other vendors may resort to it as well so their storage systems do not appear to be significantly slower.)*

2. *Currently, SSDs are generally based on flash memory technology. Because write I/O processing can slow down as flash memory fills up, writes to a new, empty SSD can be faster than writes to an SSD that has been accepting writes for a while. (The reason is that when a data record in a flash-based SSD is overwritten by an application, the new record is written to an empty location; making locations occupied by the original data usable to accept future writes adds internal overhead that degrades SSD performance.) Therefore, SSD benchmark results should either indicate the results apply to an empty SSD or should indicate that the SSD was first filled with data (i.e., has reached a steady-state) before the benchmark was run.*

---

[67] *It is not always the case that a vendor publishes benchmark results to demonstrate the maximum performance of which a storage system is capable. For example, a vendor might want to demonstrate the performance of a configuration that is lower cost than a maximal configuration, or a vendor might want to demonstrate the performance of a specific optional feature.*

3. *Techniques that optimize storage system capacity, such as data compression, can potentially reduce system performance. Some vendors may disable such facilities to maximize performance benchmark results, though many customers will want to operate the system they install with capacity optimization enabled.*

Tip: Tools customers can use to help run their own storage performance benchmarks exist in the industry. Two examples are Iometer *and* IOzone.[68] *Use of such tools does not guarantee meaningful results. For example, a tool might be used to run an artificial I/O workload that does not match the characteristics of the customer's applications.*

Storage system attributes that significantly influence performance

Below is a list of attributes that significantly influence storage system performance. The focus is on attributes a customer may have some control over via system configuration or administrative parameters. A given storage system may support only some of these attributes. This list is not necessarily complete.

Knowing how important storage system performance is to customers, vendors often highlight attributes of the systems they are selling as evidence of how those systems support high levels of performance. Customer personnel responsible for storage acquisitions will likely encounter the concepts and terms discussed below.

- Host ports. Host port speed and number have performance and cost implications. The IT industry has a history of increasing the speeds of major storage networks every few years, e.g., a record of increasing the Gb/s and IOPS capabilities for Fibre Channel and Ethernet ports. Higher speeds have three potential benefits:

  1) Data transfer time, a contributor to I/O response time, is reduced which is especially beneficial to large block I/Os, e.g., I/Os transferring 100s of kilobytes of data. However, the response time benefit is generally less significant for small block I/Os.[69]

  2) Path utilization is reduced which reduces I/O request queuing time which in turn reduces I/O response time.

  3) Due to lower path utilization, fewer total ports may be needed to support I/O response time and throughput goals; that may also reduce the number of ports in switches and hosts needed. (However, at least two paths between a storage system and each attached host is a best practice for availability reasons alone.)

Tip: Adapters supporting previous generation path speeds sometimes remain available at lower cost and may provide satisfactory performance for many customers. Some adapters

---

[68] References: https://en.wikipedia.org/wiki/Iometer and https://en.wikipedia.org/wiki/IOzone.

[69] Consider transferring a small 4KB block over an 8Gbit/s network. Networks generally encapsulate 8-bit data bytes into 10-bit transmission characters, so an 8Gb/s network speed supports 800MB/s of data. Transmission time is about 4000Bytes / 800MB/s = .000005 seconds = 5 microseconds = 5µs, almost negligible considering typical I/O requests take 100s of microseconds to a few milliseconds.

support auto-negotiation: the ability to support both current and previous generation speeds, allowing customers to migrate devices in a data path (e.g., host ports, network switch ports, and storage system ports) to a higher speed over time. Acquiring faster ports when new ports are needed, even if the higher speed cannot immediately be used end-to-end to advantage, helps position a customer for improved performance as other devices supporting faster port speeds are introduced into the data path over time.

Tip: The nominal speed of each port on a host adapter (e.g., 16Gb/s for a Fibre Channel port or 10Gb/s for an Ethernet port) does not necessarily mean all ports on the same adapter can run at that speed at the same time. That's because when adapters support multiple ports, the ports may share some resources on the adapter (such as processors) with the result that the maximum throughput and IOPS capabilities of the adapter may be less than the sum of the maximum performance capabilities of each port. Similarly, the maximum performance a storage system can support may be far less than the sum of the nominal maximum throughput and IOPS capabilities of all ports installed on the system. (The reasons some storage systems support more host ports than needed to support maximum system performance are (1) to allow direct connections to a large number of hosts and (2) to allow additional direct connections to hosts to enhance availability. Direct connections reduce or eliminate the need for network equipment such as switches, simplifying the overall configuration and potentially reducing cost.)

- Multipath I/O load balancing.[70] Many host-based multipath I/O drivers support algorithms to balance I/O activities across all the paths between a host and a storage system. Software designers have developed various algorithms to support this balancing. Alternating I/O requests among the paths in a round-robin manner is a common algorithm; assigning the next I/O request to the least busy path is another. Different drivers support different balancing algorithms.

Tip: The number and type of load balancing algorithms supported by a multipath I/O driver will vary. Some drivers support a relatively large number of path balancing algorithms to choose from; vendors selling such drivers may claim that means those drivers are superior to drivers with fewer algorithms. However, any differences in performance due to different algorithms may be small and it could take administrator time and effort to determine whether one algorithm is significantly better than others for a particular environment. Even the simplest algorithms (such as round-robin) generally provide good performance benefits in most environments.

- Active-active vs. active-passive controllers. When a storage system has one or more pairs of (redundant) controllers to enhance availability, the controllers may be designed to operate in an active-active or active-passive way. An active-active (aka active/active) design means both controllers in a pair are active, contributing to a system's performance capability; however, if one controller fails, system performance capability for the pair is cut in half. An active-passive (aka active/passive) design means only one controller in a pair actively contributes to supporting system performance while the other controller is inactive in a

---

[70] The general design principle of load balancing, which applies to multiple storage system resources, is discussed in *Appendix B. Load Balancing.*

standby mode unless and until the active controller goes offline; if the active controller fails, the standby controller takes over and system performance capability remains unchanged (and, therefore, remains stable under both normal and controller failure conditions).

The active-active and active-passive design alternatives can apply to any storage system with controllers in redundant pairs. However, the terms seem to most often be used to describe storage systems that have only one pair of controllers and hosts have one or more paths to each controller.

A variation of active-active and active-passive designs is a SCSI-based (block-access) industry standard called Asymmetric Logical Unit Access (ALUA, pronounced uh-loo'-uh").[71] While each controller is physically connected to all drives, each controller "owns" (i.e., is responsible for) I/O operations to only the volumes (i.e., SCSI LUNs) in a subset of those drives. If a controller receives an I/O request for a volume owned by the other controller it redirects the request to that controller, elongating I/O response time. Therefore, for best performance hosts should send I/O requests for a volume directly to the owning controller. The host-storage paths to the controller owning a particular volume are called *preferred* or *optimal* paths for that volume. For hosts and storage systems supporting industry-standard ALUA, hosts can query a storage system to determine which paths are preferred for which volumes.

An ALUA design is sometimes considered a variation of an active-active design because each controller can concurrently send I/Os to drives. ALUA is sometimes considered a variation of an active-passive design because each controller can actively access only the drives it owns and is effectively in standby mode to directly access the drives owned by the other controller if that other controller fails. The way ALUA works is standardized and it doesn't seem to matter which label one prefers to apply.

Tip: As is often true in IT, terminology is not always used consistently. The terms "active-active" and "active-passive" are generally defined as described above – but not always. Customers should ask vendors using those or similar terms (such as "dual active") to define what they mean by them. Also, if a vendor claims their storage system supports ALUA, a customer may want to determine whether that is industry-standard ALUA or just "ALUA-like." Many host I/O drivers support standard ALUA, but non-standard implementations may require customers install vendor-supplied drivers.

Tip: All else equal, an active-active design can potentially outperform an active-passive design. Unless maintaining a stable level of performance is a high priority requirement even if a controller fails, it is likely preferable to have the power of both controllers available to support work. Nevertheless, what matters more than which variation of a dual controller design a storage system implements is how well the system addresses a customer's overall storage requirements including requirements for availability and performance.

- Cache. Storage system cache to boost performance is commonly supported by today's enterprise storage systems. Storage system cache is typically solid-state DRAM memory

---

[71] The standard is owned by the T10 Technical Committee of the InterNational Committee on Information Technology Standards (INCITS, pronounced "insights"). See http://www.t10.org/index.html.

that is much faster than spinning drives (HDDs) and even faster than solid-state drives (SSDs) which typically use flash memory. In some storage systems that support HDDs for persistent storage, SSDs may be used as a cache, perhaps as a second-level cache "behind" DRAM cache.

The percentage of I/O requests satisfied directly via cache is called the *cache hit ratio*. A read hit ratio and write hit ratio are often measured separately. For example, a read hit ratio of 60% means that 60% of all read I/O requests are satisfied from data in cache. In contemporary storage systems, it is usually the case that 100% of write I/Os are satisfied by being "dropped off" in cache. A cache hit ratio can vary as I/O workload characteristics change and so can vary over time. The diagram below illustrates the typical shape of a cache hit ratio curve.

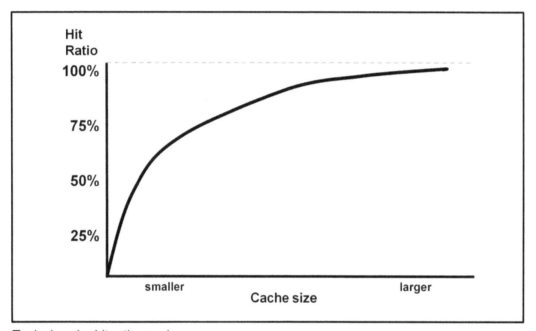

Typical cache hit ratio graph.

As the diagram shows, a cache hit ratio normally increases as cache size increases because the larger the cache, the more data it can hold. The curve asymptotically approaches a 100% hit ratio (shown by the dashed line). A consistent 100% hit ratio in an environment where all data is randomly accessed in short time intervals would require a cache size as large as the total data capacity of a storage system. That would be very expensive. It would also be unnecessary because high hit ratios can usually be achieved in practice using much smaller cache sizes.[72] Thus, cache sizes anywhere near maximum aggregate drive capacity for data are usually not supported even as a system option. Some storage systems come with a fixed cache size while others offer a range of sizes customers can choose from.

---

[72] The reason is the way storage is typically used by applications. In a given small interval of time, such as a few minutes, only a subset of all data in a storage system tends to be accessed and the same data is often accessed multiple times. The technical term for this observation is "locality of reference." Reference: https://en.wikipedia.org/wiki/Locality_of_reference. In many storage systems, maximum cache capacity is less than 1% of the maximum capacity for data stored on drives.

Tip: Customers sometimes define a requirement that a proposed storage system (from any vendor) must be configured with a certain minimum cache size. Or, customers may assume that systems configured with larger cache sizes must necessarily perform better. However, cache size alone is not a good indicator of either cache performance or overall storage system performance. A storage system with a more efficiently managed cache may meet a customer's performance requirements with a smaller cache (and a possible cost savings) compared to a system with a less efficiently managed cache.[73]

Customers, therefore, should generally not define a requirement for a specific cache size. Rather, customers should define requirements for overall system performance (e.g., average random I/O response time) and let the vendor determine the system model and configuration (including but not limited to cache size) that supports the requirement. (That said, if a customer has done their own analysis to determine a minimum cache hit ratio required to achieve their performance objectives, that hit ratio can be a reasonable requirement for vendors to address. A specific cache size requirement, if done properly, would need to be specified separately for each system model being considered for acquisition.)

Tip: Many storage systems support mirroring in cache of data received from write I/Os to help protect that data from loss. That mirroring is often a standard capability, but is sometimes an option that can be enabled or disabled. Some vendors have sometimes disabled mirroring of write data in cache when running performance benchmarks because doing so improves write I/O performance due to the system not needing to create the mirror copy. Because of this, customers should ensure that vendors' performance claims of interest to the customer apply when mirrored protection of writes in cache is enabled.

- <u>Drives - hardware</u>. Drive hardware significantly influenced system performance. The performance of read I/Os not satisfied by data in cache and the performance of write I/Os eventually destaged from cache are impacted by the performance of installed drives.

  One consideration is the speed of individual drives which affects I/O response time and throughput. Many of today's storage systems allow customers to configure a combination of different speed HDDs, or (much faster) SSDs, or a hybrid combination of both HDDs and SSDs.

  Another consideration is the number of drives. Multiple drives of any type support I/O parallelism: the ability for each drive to potentially be handling an I/O request at the same time (assuming requests are fairly evenly distributed across drives and internal data paths can handle the resulting data movement). Some customers with relatively stringent performance requirements have sometimes added drives to a storage system just to

---

[73] Cache is managed by internally programmed algorithms and the efficiency of those algorithms can vary by system. For example, one system model's cache may be managed as relatively small fixed-size units of cache capacity (e.g., a few kilobytes each that can be dynamically grouped together to accommodate large blocks of data), a design well-suited to support both random I/O requests that are typically for small data blocks as well as sequential I/O requests that are typically for large data blocks. In contrast, another model's cache may be managed as only relatively large fixed-size units of capacity (e.g., dozens of kilobytes) that result in unused cache capacity when I/O requests are for smaller blocks of data.

support increased I/O parallelism, not for additional capacity. That has usually been done only for HDDs since the innate high speed of SSDs generally obviates the need to increase performance even further; an SSD can generally handle multiple I/O requests in the time it takes an HDD to handle one request. (In the industry, the term *short-stroking* refers to using only a portion of an HDD's capacity in order to improve performance by minimizing mechanical arm movement.)

Tip: Determining an efficient mix of cache and drive types to meet the goals of capacity, cost, and performance is not trivial. Customers should ask vendors for their recommendations because vendors often have tools to model the performance of configurations with different combinations of cache and drive types.

Considering just drive types, a mix of types, such as high-speed SSDs along with slower high-capacity HDDs, can often meet performance needs at lower cost than an all-SSD configuration. A feature of some storage systems called automated storage tiering, *discussed later in this chapter, can help manage data placement across different types of drives in the same storage system.*

- Drives - RAID. A group of drives can be managed as a RAID array. Different types of RAID arrays have different performance characteristics. However, no one RAID type necessarily always outperforms all others, all else equal (such as drive speeds and the effectiveness of system cache).

Performance differences among RAID types are more common for write I/Os than for read I/Os. For read requests for data in RAID-5 and RAID-6 arrays there is a single copy of data to access. For read requests for data in RAID-1 and RAID-10 arrays there are two copies so that a storage system could, if designed to do so, distribute read I/O requests among the copies which could have a performance benefit when drives are very busy. Keep in mind, however, that many storage systems keep the most frequently read data in high-speed cache, supporting faster read I/O performance than any type of RAID and reducing the read I/Os that go directly to drives.

Writes are the more interesting, and more complex, case. It turns out that to handle a write I/O request to locations in a RAID array, additional I/O operations are internally generated; that is commonly called the *RAID write penalty*. (A) For writing a single random block of data, RAID-1 and RAID-10 write the block and also generate one internal I/O operation to write a copy. So, in that case, there is one internally generated write operation in addition to the original write I/O request. (B) For RAID-5, in addition to writing the block in the original write I/O request, it turns out that three extra internal I/Os are needed to update the associated parity data: read the old block before it is replaced, read the old parity data, then write the updated parity data after the contribution of the old block to the parity data is computationally backed out and the contribution of the new block is included. (C) RAID-6 adds even more internally generated I/Os due to supporting two levels of parity for each block of user data.

Knowing only that much makes it sounds like RAID-1 and RAID-10 significantly outperform RAID-5 and RAID-6 for write I/Os, case closed. However, it's not that simple. Here are three reasons; others may apply depending on system and application design.

1. Read/write ratios, the relative number of read I/O requests and write I/O requests, vary by application. For many applications, there are far more reads than writes, though in some cases just the opposite. When the percentage of writes is low, that indicates the RAID write penalty is experienced by only a minority of I/O requests, reducing the impact of the RAID write penalty on overall I/O performance.

2. Storage system cache accepts write I/O requests at cache speed so "write I/O complete" indications are quickly returned to hosts. Thus, applications may not be delayed waiting for the additional internally-generated I/Os of RAID-5 and RAID-6 that adjust parity data. (However, those additional internal I/Os may degrade the performance of other host I/Os, depending on timing and which system resources (e.g., drives) are involved.)

3. For sequential write processing, RAID-5 and RAID-6 (where redundancy is based on parity data) may outperform RAID-1 and RAID-10 (where redundancy is based on a copy of data). An example of sequential processing is writing data to logically consecutive storage locations in a new, initially empty, file.

   The potential parity-based RAID performance advantage for sequential processing is due to some storage systems being designed to detect when successive write I/Os are sequential. To illustrate the principle, assume seven sequential write I/Os are sent to such a system containing an eight-drive RAID-5 array. The system temporarily holds the blocks in cache, detects the seven blocks are logically consecutive, internally generates a block containing the associated parity data for the seven blocks, then writes the seven blocks and associated parity block to drives in the array for a total of writing eight blocks. In contrast, if the same seven sequential write I/Os are sent to a storage system with a RAID-1 array, the system writes those blocks and also internally generates seven more write I/Os to make the copies, for a total of writing fourteen blocks.

Tip: *The point is, no RAID array type necessarily has superior performance to other RAID types based on type alone. It's one of those "it depends" situations where system attributes besides RAID type influence the performance of RAID arrays. What matters in the end is that the RAID type(s) configured in a given storage system contribute to a customer's requirements for maximum usable capacity, availability, performance, and cost. Those system attributes depend on many aspects of system configuration and design, not on RAID type in isolation.*

- Drives - data striping. Not all data is equally busy. At any given time, more I/O requests are almost always directed to some data than to other data. This can result in some drives being busier than others, known as *I/O skew*. Drives that are so busy they significantly slow down I/O performance are called *hot spots*.[74]

---

[74] Drive utilization is the percentage of time during which a drive is busy servicing I/O requests. The impact of drive utilization on response time increases nonlinearly. Assume a drive has an average service time of 1ms (1 millisecond) when a new I/O request arrives and the drive is not already busy. For that I/O request, the response time is the same as the service time, 1 ms. In comparison, based on a simple queuing theory model (M/M/1), a drive that is 25% busy increases average response time to 1.3ms. A drive that is 50% busy increases average response time to 2ms. A drive that is 90% busy

Data striping (aka wide striping) is a technique for distributing where data is stored that can help reduce or even eliminate drive hot spots. Assume a storage system has multiple drives. It could conceivably be that as data is written to the system the first drive is filled with data, then the next drive, and so on. Data striping, instead, manages drive capacity so that consecutive storage locations are assigned to a set of drives in a round-robin manner. This results in storing logically consecutive data (e.g., block-1, block-2, block-3, and so on) on different drives. If I/O access patterns are random enough (meaning roughly equally distributed across the locations where data is stored) then the utilization of the drives should be nearly balanced, eliminating or at least significantly reducing I/O skew and drive hot spots. A common implementation for block-access storage stripes each volume across a set of drives as illustrated in the diagram below.

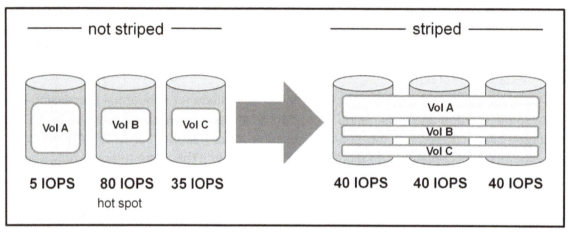

At the left are three drives each containing one volume. The average I/O rate to each drive is shown below it for a total of 120 I/Os per second for the three drives. Some volumes, and thus the drives they reside on, are busier than others. Here, the drive containing Vol B is a "hot spot" (relative to Vol A and Vol C) because it receives the most I/Os per second and likely has the highest utilization and slowest average response time per I/O. At the right are the same three volumes each striped across all three drives. In this case each drive handles a portion of the I/Os to each volume and the I/O rate tends to be about the same on each drive.

Many storage systems support data striping. Host software sometimes supports data striping which can be useful if a storage system lacks that support. In any case, whether data is or is not striped across drives is normally transparent to users other than for its performance impact.

Tip: In some cases, customers may have control over the number of drives that volumes are striped across. That control can influence data availability. Assume a group of volumes is striped across multiple RAID arrays. If any one of those arrays fails (e.g., two drives fail at the same time in a RAID-5 array, however unlikely that may be), then at least some data on every volume in the group is lost. That likely means all volumes in the group need to be recovered, perhaps from a backup copy. The point is: customers may want to avoid striping volumes over too many drives in order to limit the amount of data lost in case of a failure of a RAID array.

---

increases average response time to 10ms. From another perspective, reducing drive utilization from 90% to 50% results in an 80% reduction in response time ((10ms-2ms)/10ms=80%), a big benefit.

- Drives - I/O load balancing. Data striping, discussed above, helps balance I/O activity through distributing groups of consecutive storage locations across multiple drives. However, data striping determines initial data placement only; sometimes I/O activity is skewed across drives due to data access patterns even if data is striped. In that case, performance can be improved if a storage system is designed to detect skewed I/O activity and automatically shift some data around to better balance that activity. Some storage systems are designed to hat way.

  In addition to ongoing performance optimization, a scenario where this kind of load balancing is very useful is when new empty drives are added to a storage system; if a system automatically rebalances I/O activity, that avoids the need for an administrator to manually relocate some data to make use of the new drives.

  Tip: Implementations of I/O load (re)balancing vary among storage system models. Some implementations automatically rebalance I/O activity across drives periodically without manual intervention; some implementations do this rebalancing only on administrator command. Some implementations rebalance only thin provisioned volumes. Some implementations balance only drive capacity utilization, not drive performance utilization; balancing drive capacity utilization may not help balance drive performance utilization or may not do so as effectively as an implementation designed specifically to balance performance utilization.

- Drives - automated storage tiering. Automated storage tiering (aka auto-tiering) is a capability supported by some storage systems. Drives of different speeds (e.g., 10K RPM HDDs, 15K RPM HDDs, and SSDs) are considered to be separate *tiers*.   Tiers are sometimes numbered (e.g., tier 0, tier 1, and so on) where the lowest numbered tier supports the highest speed; SSDs are typically considered to be tier 0.

  A system configured with multiple tiers of drives, especially if both SSDs and HDDs are installed, is sometimes called a *hybrid* configuration. Potential benefits of hybrid configurations include cost savings (compared to a configuration of only the fastest drives) and energy savings (compared to a configuration using drive types requiring more energy than other drive types). Auto-tiering helps manage hybrid configurations by automatically and nondisruptively relocating data to the drive tier that optimizes price-performance. In this way, auto-tiering optimizes data striping in hybrid configurations.[75]

  Price-performance optimization is possible because faster drives generally cost more per unit of capacity than slower drives and which data can benefit from higher speeds varies over time.

---

[75] The drives that can be in a given tier may vary by storage system model. For example, some models may give the user the flexibility to determine which speed drives can be in separate tiers while other models may group drives with similar performance (such as 10K and 15K RPM drives) into the same tier.   Some storage system models may support configuring multiple, different sets of tiers. For example, one set could be SSDs + nearline HDDs while another set could be 15K RPM HDDs and nearline HDDs; a given volume is striped only across drives in the set of tiers to which the volume is assigned. Hybrid systems configured with two or three tiers (in a given set of tiers) may be the most common implementations.

When different drive speeds were first able to be intermixed in the same storage system, administrators manually moved data among them to manage price-performance by putting data needing the highest performance on the fastest drives and data needing less performance on slower drives. This approach is still used in storage systems lacking auto-tiering, mainly when large groups of data, such as entire volumes, are known to be constantly busy or are known to be much less busy over long periods of time (e.g., weeks or months or longer). Manually managing a hybrid configuration has drawbacks including: possibly needing to make the data being moved temporarily unavailable to applications, moving only relatively large amounts of data at one time such as entire volumes even though some data in a volume may be much busier than other data, and the practical limitation of being able to relocate data only occasionally.

Automated storage tiering, supported by many storage system models, addresses the drawbacks of manual management of hybrid configurations. Auto-tiering can relocate data nondisruptively. The amount of data relocated to a different speed drive can usually be relatively small, e.g., one gigabyte or less, often called a *subvolume* amount of data. Relocation can occur frequently based on a storage system's analysis of I/O activity over short periods of time by human standards (typically a few minutes or hours). The most active data (i.e., the *hottest* data) that a storage system determines is not being read from cache (perhaps because cache is full of even busier data) will be moved from slower to faster drives. Similarly, the least active data (i.e., the *coldest* data) will be moved from faster to slower drives.

This scheme, originally implemented only for the drives inside a storage system, has been extended as follows. Flash memory, usually in the form of solid-state drives (SSDs), can be installed in hosts to serve as a *host-side* cache for the most active data. This is usually a read cache, meaning write I/Os are sent to a storage system for persistency and to enable using storage system-based functions such as backups, data sharing, and remote mirroring. Some storage system models communicate with host software managing the host-side cache for additional efficiencies such as avoiding caching the same data in both the host-side cache and the storage system's cache.

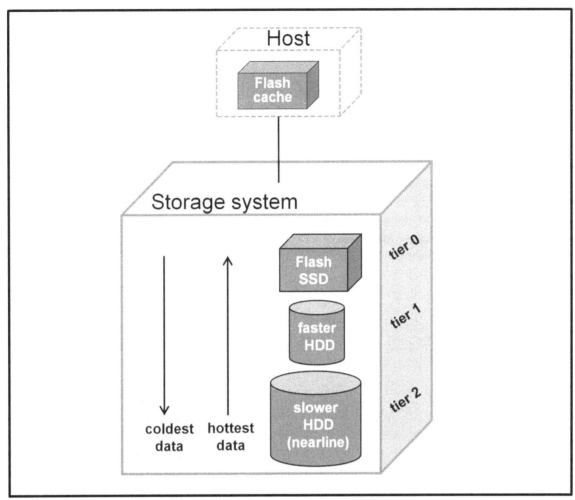

Inside a storage system there can be a set of tiered drives, e.g., tier 0 is flash SSDs, tier 1 is the fastest HDDs, and tier 2 is the slowest HDDs often called nearline drives. The number of supported tiers can vary by storage system; two and three tiers are common. The storage system automatically migrates the most active data to the fastest tiers and the least active data to the slowest tiers. Some hosts may have host-side flash memory-based cache which contains a copy of selected data that resides in the storage system; write I/Os are sent by the host to the storage system.

Tip: When auto-tiering is implemented it is common that less than 10% of total drive capacity needs to be solid-state technology to significantly boost I/O performance compared to disk technology, especially for cache read miss I/Os. The appropriate percentage can vary by storage system model and configuration, application data access patterns, and customers' performance requirements.

Tip: Some vendors selling storage systems that support auto-tiering have tools that can analyze a customer's I/O activity to help assess an appropriate mix of drive speeds and capacities, and the performance changes that should occur if auto-tiering is implemented. The tools may be limited to analyzing data generated only by selected storage system models.

- Processor pooling. Enterprise storage systems often contain multiple processors, sometimes dozens or more in the largest systems (not counting the processors inside drives). Some storage system models organize at least some internal processors into pools that can be shared across multiple types of work. In contrast, other storage system models dedicate each processor to a specific type of work (e.g., supporting only I/Os to a subset of internal drives). The result is that processors dedicated to handling one type of work, even if completely idle, cannot be dynamically assigned to help busy processors dedicated to handling other types of work.

Without system-managed processor sharing, administrators may have to manually tune a system to optimize performance by attempting to better balance the workload across processors. That could entail activities such as moving data around inside the system or moving cables from hosts to different ports on the system. Moreover, those kinds of actions can only be done after the administrator determines that the processors in question are causing a performance problem.

- Quality of service. Some storage systems support quality of service (QoS) facilities. The intent of these facilities is to help customers ensure that system users are able to meet specified performance objectives regardless of activity by other users using the same system at the same time. Storage system models differ in the kinds of QoS facilities they support, and in the effectiveness and efficiency of that support.

  In this context, *quality* refers to consistent, predictable performance. Users are often referred to as *tenants*, and storage systems supporting multiple users are said to support a *multitenant* (or *multi-tenant*) environment. While there is no generally accepted industry-standard definition of *tenant*, for the purposes of this discussion a tenant (of a storage system) could be an application or a host. (Of course, hosts and applications don't reside in a storage system, but are users of a storage system.) While the prevalence of the terms *tenant* and *multitenant* in a storage context is relatively new, many enterprise storage systems have been able for decades to support multiple hosts and/or multiple concurrently running applications in a host.

  It may be possible to configure a storage system to meet the performance objectives of all tenants at the same time even if every tenant's peak I/O activity occurs at the same time. However, such a configuration, even if possible, may be relatively expensive. In lieu of such a configuration – and that probably includes most installed storage system configurations during at least some time in their useful lives – the performance of some or all tenants can suffer as they contend for shared resources such as host ports, cache, and drives. This situation is sometimes called the *noisy neighbor* problem. Storage system QoS facilities help administrators manage this situation when it is acceptable to preserve the performance of more important applications at the expense of reducing the performance of less important applications, if necessary. Below are examples of types of QoS facilities. Different storage systems may support none, one, or more such facilities.

  o *Volume priorities* allow administrators to assign performance priorities to individual volumes. If a volume is assigned to one application or a set of related applications, the volume can be viewed as a proxy for the application(s). When there is contention for system resources shared by multiple volumes, I/Os to higher priority volumes can be given preferential access to those resources. How this is done can vary by storage system.

For example, if a storage system detects that the response time of random I/Os to higher priority volumes is being degraded due to contention for system resources by I/Os to lower priority volumes, the system might artificially slow down processing the lower priority I/Os to reduce that contention.

o *Host data rate controls* allow administrators to limit (or cap) the maximum data rate (in terms of I/Os per second or megabytes per second) accepted from a given host. This can prevent a host from using so much storage system performance capability that the performance of I/Os from other hosts degrades unacceptably. This QoS control can help enforce contracted limits on storage system use or can help prevent overly high resource contention (perhaps due to a runaway application in a program loop issuing I/Os).

Tip: One drawback of QoS controls over a host's data rate is that the limit applies to an entire host without an ability to assign separate limits to different applications. Another drawback is that even if there are sufficient storage system resources available to let a host exceed its data rate limit without degrading the performance of other work, or if other work is not even running, the maximum data rate may be enforced regardless.

o *Cache partitioning* is a QoS control allowing administrators to divide storage system cache into subsets called *partitions* and assign each partition to a different group of volumes. In this way a subset of cache can be indirectly assigned to one or more specific applications. Partitions assigned sufficient cache to achieve higher cache hit ratios can generally support better I/O performance than partitions achieving lower cache hit ratios (all else equal). A given implementation of cache partitioning may or may not be able to automatically reassign cache among partitions based on current I/O workload patterns. A related control in some storage systems is a capability to bind (meaning permanently keep) administrator-selected data in cache, ensuring it always receives cache-based performance.

Tip: Cache partitioning can have drawbacks. For example, if a partition does not need all the cache assigned to it there may be no automatic or speedy way to reassign that cache to another partition that could benefit from improved performance. As another example, there may be more tenants running concurrently than the maximum number of cache partitions supported; some cache partitioning implementations may allow assigning some applications to dedicated cache partitions and all remaining applications to a shared cache partition.

Binding selected data to cache – more precisely, binding selected locations of data into cache – also has drawbacks: The data uses cache capacity whether or not it is frequently accessed. If binding is done by parameters set by administrators that identify specific locations in volumes and the data (on drives) is later moved or deleted, it can take extra administrative steps to update those parameters (assuming administrators remember to do so). Binding selected data in cache was of most value in the early days of storage system cache when cache was even more expensive than it is today, cache capacity was relatively small, storage systems did not support SSDs, host-side flash-based cache was not supported, and storage system built-in cache management algorithms were less sophisticated than they are today.

o *Pacing* is the ability to control the speed of moving data around inside a storage system to support certain internal processes. The functions whose I/Os can be paced can be thought of as specialized applications that happen to run inside the storage system. Examples include: rebuilding data onto spare drives, intra-system data replication, automated storage tiering, and administrators manually moving files to different drives. These activities move data using the same internal resources (such as cache, drives, and internal paths) also used by host-initiated I/Os. Contention for the same resources as host I/Os can potentially degrade host I/O performance. Some storage systems automatically give host-initiated I/Os priority over at least some internally initiated I/Os. Some storage systems let administrators control the pacing of selected types of internal I/Os.

A potential drawback is that pacing controls may apply to specific types of data movement independently of the priority of an application needing the movement. For example, the pacing of the I/Os to make a copy of a volume may be a constant set by an administrator that does not vary based on the importance of a user requesting the copy.

Tip: QoS facilities can only *help customers ensure that system users are able to meet specified performance objectives regardless of activity by other users using the same system at the same time. QoS facilities supported by a given storage system may not address every potential point of resource contention. And, customers must configure their storage systems with sufficient resources to support the performance goals of concurrent users; QoS cannot make up for insufficient resources such as a too small cache.*

Tip: It is important that a storage system provide reports on QoS attainment. Administrators and tenants may require such reports. Are the performance goals of tenants being met? If not, does the system provide enough information to help administrators determine why not? Perhaps a tenant is using more resources than planned for in which case a performance cap may need to be set or more system resources may need to be installed. Perhaps a QoS parameter was not set properly.

Tip: Regardless of whether QoS facilities are supported by a given storage system, many systems support the ability to assign as least some hardware resources to specific tenants, eliminating contention for those particular resources by other tenants. Examples include dedicating host ports or even entire host port adapters to specific hosts and dedicating a set of drives to a specific tenant. Such configuration options can be used in conjunction with QoS facilities; in some cases they may reduce or eliminate the need to employ QoS facilities. However, dedicating certain resources to specific tenants means those resources will not be available to be used by other tenants even if the assigned tenants are not busy; manually reassigning resources to different tenants to address changing demands is usually not practical over short periods of time (e.g., measured in hours or even a few days if cables must be moved or data must be relocated).

Additional Tips

- *This chapter frequently refers to "average(s)." A Tip discussing benefits and drawbacks of averages is in the* Availability *chapter.*

- *Some vendors offer "performance guarantees." See the* Marketing Tactics *chapter.*

- *Performance from the user point-of-view often warrants a "big picture" perspective. While "faster" I/O is generally better than "slower" I/O, whether measured in throughput or response time, it may not always make a significant difference in terms of quicker application response times or earlier completion of long-running applications. Once interactive users perceive an application's response to pressing the Enter key as virtually instantaneous, they likely won't be more productive or more satisfied if that response is made another millisecond faster. Although I/O time in commercial applications is generally the largest contributor to application response time, sometimes that contribution is small compared to network time or host time; in that case, improving the performance of those latter resources may provide more leverage than improving I/O performance.*

- *Some forms of vendor evidence to support claims of high performance can sound impressive, but really say little if anything about system performance users and applications can see. In some cases, such claims might be a form of distraction intended to avoid disclosing more relevant, though less impressive, details of system performance. Here are some examples:*

  1. *Some vendors claim their storage system supports a high "internal bandwidth," sometimes called "data bandwidth" or a similar name. There is no industry-standard definition for what this value applies to, but it is usually a claim about sequential data throughput (e.g., in GB/s) supported by only selected internal system components. For example, it might be a claim about the maximum data flow possible through cache or the maximum data flow across internal connections between certain components. Internal bandwidth does not indicate performance applications can attain. In particular, it provides no information about the response time of random I/Os which are typically the most common type of I/Os in commercial applications.*

  2. *Some vendors draw attention to the number of processors or speed of processors inside their storage system as evidence of high system performance. However, the number and speed of processors omit several important points about processors that can influence performance. Processor number and speed do not indicate whether processors are 32-bit or 64-bit architecture. They do not indicate how efficiently or inefficiently the processors are programmed. They do not indicate how processors are managed: Are processors in a shared pool so they can be dynamically assigned to meet workload needs[76], or are they dedicated to managing specific system resources so that if one processor is very busy, other less busy or idle processors cannot help?*

---

[76] *A host with multiple processors that can be dynamically assigned to processes (aka jobs or tasks or threads) by the host's operating system is said to have a* symmetrical multiprocessor (SMP) *design.*

3. *A vendor might claim that their storage system model has no I/O bottlenecks or that I/O bottlenecks have somehow been eliminated in their new system. Such a claim doesn't indicate performance applications can see. If such a claim is taken literally (which is likely not the intention) and a storage bottleneck is the slowest component in the path between a host and data inside a storage system, then having no bottlenecks could mean all those components are no faster than the speed of the slowest component, often a mechanical disk drive.*

- *A general vendor claim that a given storage system model supports resource load (re)balancing is ambiguous until the details are known. Load balancing, if implemented at all, can be implemented by different storage system models in different ways and for different types of resources. One system may balance drive I/O load, another may balance processor use, while another may balance how multiple types of resources are used. One system may balance (some) resource use dynamically (i.e., while the resource is in use), while another system may require the resource to be offline. One system may do balancing on a particular schedule (e.g., at certain time intervals or based on certain events), while another system may use a different schedule, while still another system may only balance certain resources based on manual commands.*

- *Some storage systems support performance-related controls in the form of parameters for system administrator use. A vendor may highlight support for such parameters and emphasize they aren't supported by competing systems, but the reason competing systems don't support them may be due to their limited value.*

  The limited value of an ability to bind selected data locations in cache was mentioned previously. Consider another example. Some storage system models give an administrator the ability to control what data resides on the outermost tracks of a disk drive. These areas hold more bits than inner tracks because the outer tracks are longer (i.e., the track circumference is larger). That means more data can be stored on fewer outer tracks than on the same number of inner tracks, potentially reducing the time for the disk arm to seek among the outer tracks. One reason this provides limited benefit is that it requires manual time and effort to control the placement of data on disk drives. Another reason is that modern storage systems automatically keep the most active data in cache, providing higher performance than the fastest disk drives. Yet another reason is that storage systems are increasingly configured with tiered drives of different speeds where the system automatically relocates the busiest data to the fastest tier which typically consists of solid-state drives that do not incur seek time.

- *Storage system performance depends not only on the maximum performance a given system configuration is capable of, but also on the ease of achieving that performance. Some storage systems may require more ongoing manual performance tuning to achieve and maintain desired levels of performance than other systems supporting more self-optimizing performance. Thus, the ease of managing system performance can be as important as the potential performance capability of a system. If a storage system needs a lot of manual "care and attention" (i.e., micro-management) to provide satisfactory performance, that can require significant time and skills from storage administrators yet still result in inconsistent delivery of I/O performance to users and applications. This is further discussed in the* Logical (Software) Configuration Management *chapter.*

- *Customers should not assume that storage systems supporting larger maximum data capacities necessarily have superior performance compared to storage systems supporting smaller maximum data capacities. There are many more factors that influence storage system performance than the maximum data capacity supported or the maximum number of drives supported. For example, too many drives sharing the same internal data paths may make it impractical for all those drives to run at satisfactory performance concurrently. Or, an inefficiently managed cache may not adequately support the performance needs of a large number of busy drives.*

- *When considering performance requirements and vendors' storage system performance claims for random I/Os, it is important to consider I/O response times, not only maximum I/Os per second (IOPS).*

  A vendor's claim about I/O response time may be about an average *response time, in which case the distribution of individual response times that yield the claimed average can be important to know. Are they all close to the average or do they vary significantly and possibly unacceptably? How do they vary as IOPS varies? A claim of an impressive maximum IOPS capability may not reveal that the average I/O response time at that IOPS level is so high as to be unacceptable to most customers.*

  Consider how *Storage Performance Council SPC-1 benchmark results (http://www.storageperformance.org/results/benchmark_results_spc1_active) address this. SPC-1 is designed to represent an online transaction processing (OLTP) workload, common in commercial environments. SPC-1 benchmark results have been published by many vendors. Both IOPS and average response time at various IOPS points are published in graphical form for easy interpretation (and also published in tabular form). Looking at the published SPC-1 results for multiple storage systems shows that average I/O response times can vary considerably, typically increasing in each system as IOPS increases. For some storage systems, response time increases so much as IOPS increases that at some point a high IOPS value is impractical in real-world applications. (Some vendors and industry watchers focus on only the maximum IOPS values measured; a vendor may cite the maximum measured IOPS for their storage system as a "bragging right," but without citing the corresponding response time at that IOPS point it has little usefulness.) The point is: customers should consider and compare average I/O response times at relevant IOPS points when comparing different SPC-1 benchmark results, not only maximum IOPS in isolation.*

- *The need for improved performance is one of the most common reasons for acquiring a new storage system, whether a customer has quantified performance objectives not being met or just wants "to make the system run faster" to address complaints.*

  There are actions a customer can take to improve the performance of an installed system, potentially delaying the acquisition of a new system. It is useful to compare alternative actions to take to achieve desired performance rather than just "throw" changes and money at the problem. Ideally, the best actions have the least cost, require the least effort, take the least time to implement, and are the most effective and efficient. It's not always possible to attain all these goals at the same time.

Here is a list of potential actions to enhance storage system performance. The list is ordered so that generally preferred actions are listed first.

o *Use automated tuning facilities. The degree to which optimizing performance is managed automatically by an installed storage system can help reduce administrator workload and help keep the system performing well at all times, rather than only after manual tuning activities. Some facilities may work "out of the box" while others may require initial setup and occasional updating of parameter settings. Some may be standard while others are optional at extra charge. Examples of automated performance tuning facilities include cache management algorithms, wide striping, automated storage tiering, automated rebalancing of drive activity, and quality of service (QoS) facilities.*

o *Manually tune the system. This addresses tunable areas not supported by automated tuning facilities. Manual tuning can be an ongoing process as the system configuration and the I/O workload change over time. It can require significant technical skill. It can be done by an organization's storage administrator or perhaps by hiring a consultant from the vendor or an independent contractor. Manual tuning includes activities such as: Monitoring performance reports to determine when manual tuning is needed, relocating data among drives to address drive hot spots, and relocating data to drives attached to different internal controllers to keep controller utilization at levels that support performance objectives. In data centers with multiple storage systems, manual tuning can include redistributing data among those systems to control how their resources are utilized.*

o *Upgrade system hardware. Unlike manual tuning or using existing automated running facilities, hardware upgrades cost money. What hardware to upgrade depends on determining where hardware performance bottlenecks exist. For example, increasing cache size may help increase cache hit ratios to reduce random I/O response time; adding more drives and redistributing data may enable more I/Os to be handled in parallel.*

o *Install host-side flash memory read cache. A host-side read cache can accelerate read I/O performance even more than storage system-based cache. Host-side read cache not only reduces the response time of I/Os satisfied from that cache, but can also reduce host-to-storage network traffic and the number of I/O requests the storage system must directly handle. That in turn potentially boosts the performance of the I/O activity the storage system does handle and potentially enables growth in that I/O activity while still meeting performance objectives. (Keep in mind that this activity requires modifying host hardware; that can be limited to the hosts most in need of faster I/O.)*

o *Redesign applications. This is late in the list because it is usually not under direct control of a storage administrator or even a data center. Application redesign can include activities such as: (1) adjusting data transfer sizes (aka block sizes), because smaller sizes can reduce the response time of each I/O while larger sizes can reduce the total number of I/Os; (2) establishing or tuning application facilities (such as database and filesystem buffer pools) that keep frequently read data in host memory, because accessing data from host memory is even faster than accessing it from storage system cache; and (3) modifying programs to allow or increase the parallelism of I/O processing and other processing.*

- o *Add another system.* *This is usually not desirable due to the complexity of managing an additional system. However, it may be a feasible alternative if workload growth projections or internal organization politics warrant the need for an additional system, or if the first system cannot be upgraded or replaced on a timely basis. Perhaps the current model is top-of-the-line, larger next-generation systems are not going to be available anytime soon, and the customer requires system compatibility.*

Replacing an installed storage system with a faster system may be necessary if other alternatives are not feasible. For example, it may be determined that no amount of tuning can address the problem; or, perhaps hardware upgrades are not practical because a system is already maximally configured or end-of-lease dates are near.

- *Vendors often support tools they can use to model storage system performance based on a proposed system configuration and I/O workload profile. Vendors can be asked to do that modeling and review the input, assumptions used by the model, and results with customers.*

- *This chapter discussed performance goals in terms of the application or user experience (e.g., random I/O response time). This can conflict with another possible organization goal of maximizing the use of storage (or other IT) hardware assets to maximize the return on hardware investment. The intent of such a goal may be to get all possible value out of an asset before incurring the expense of replacing it or upgrading it. After all, from an economic perspective a simple, high-level question may be asked: Why replace an asset that is not 100% utilized? The financial goal may sound reasonable on the surface. However, it is unlikely to be a practical goal for storage systems.*

One reason is that storage systems contain multiple hardware components of various numbers and speeds and the way a system is used is unlikely to result in every component being 100% busy at the same time. In other words, some components may reach performance saturation before other components.

Another reason involves the nature of the HDD and SSD drives in a storage system. Each drive provides both capacity for data and speed to access that data. It is usually difficult to simultaneously use all capacity while also meeting performance objectives, especially for HDDs because they are inherently slower than SSDs yet often contain more capacity. For example, trying to fill 100% of usable drive capacity with data can result in such a high I/O rate as that data is accessed that application I/O performance (and, in turn, application overall performance) becomes unacceptable. It is best to view a drive as a resource designed to support a certain amount of data capacity and speed, but not designed for users to necessarily be able to both maximize capacity and achieve desired performance at the same time.

Intra-System Data Replication

Storage system intra-system data replication creates copies of data in the same storage system as the original data.[77] Intra-system data replication may be the most popular storage system software-based function after basic system management. Data movement required for replication is handled by a storage system without using host resources. A copy can usually be made while applications continue to access the original data.

Internal replication has many use cases such as: (1) making a copy of data to be backed up to tape while applications continue operating, (2) making a copy of (production) data for use in testing new or changed applications, (3) making a copy of data for use by reporting or data mining applications, and (4) making a copy of data for use as a version (aka checkpoint) of data an application can fall back to if the current copy becomes corrupted or lost.

While the idea of making a copy of data may seem straightforward – read data to be copied and write it somewhere else – this chapter reveals many factors that affect the capabilities available to users.

Concepts and Facilities

- Purpose. The main function of intra-system data replication is to create a *point-in-time (PiT)* copy of data. That means the data in the copy initially matches that of the original data at a specific point-in-time, usually when a command to create the copy is received by the storage system. Over time, the contents of the original data and a copy may increasingly differ; for example, production applications continue to read and write the original data while a new version of an application being tested reads and writes the copy.

---

[77] In the case of multiple storage systems managed by a storage virtualization facility, the copies may reside in physically different storage systems, but that can be considered to be a single system when viewing the virtualization facility and the systems it manages together as defining "a storage system."

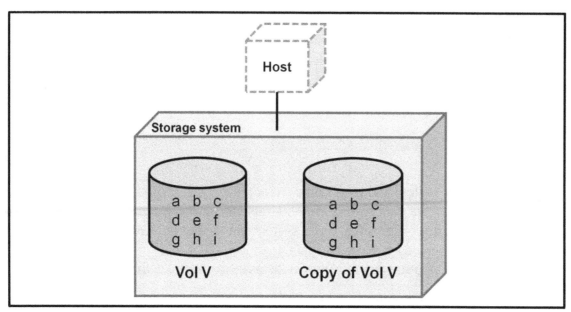

Initially, there is a single copy of Volume V. When the storage system receives a command to create a replica of Volume V, it creates a copy as a separate volume.

Tip: Intra-system PiT data replication is more complicated than a simple "does or does not support it" attribute of a storage system, as this chapter explains. The capabilities of PiT replication features may vary considerably between different storage system models. Some storage system models support multiple different PiT replication features, each of which supports an optimization or use case other PiT replication features in the same system do not support (or do not support as well).

What matters most is that the features of a storage system model support a customer's requirements, not that one storage system has more internal replication features or capabilities than another system. One customer may find that one such feature satisfies all their intra-system replication needs while another customer may want to use multiple different features in the same storage system for different purposes.

Therefore, customers should determine their intra-system replication requirements at a deeper level than simply "The storage system must support making point-in-time copies of data." And, customers should ask vendors to explain the tradeoffs between intra-system replication features if multiple features are supported by a proposed system.

- Supported data types. PiT copies can potentially be made for various types of data items; in practice these are mainly files, objects, volumes, and groups of those items. The types of data items that can be replicated vary by storage system model. For example, block-access storage systems usually support volume replication, but not file replication, because block-access storage systems are "aware" of volumes (created by storage administrators using a storage system management interface), but are not aware of individual files (created by hosts to reside inside volumes).[78] For simplicity, the remainder of this chapter refers to

---

[78] Block-access storage systems supporting IBM z Systems z/OS (mainframe) hosts typically support the ability to replicate individual files (called *data sets*), but only by the host sending the storage system detailed information about the location of the files inside a volume.

volumes as the type of data being replicated, but keep in mind that some storage systems support replicating other types of data.

- Terminology. Vendors often give the storage system features that support intra-system replication distinct names. However, several terms are commonly used in the industry when discussing intra-system replication:

The basic function is often described by terms such as *snapshot, cloning,* and *mirroring.* (The term "mirroring" in this context should not be confused with RAID-1 or RAID-10, also sometimes called "mirroring." RAID presents a volume as a single entity even if there are actually two mirrored volumes "under the covers" to help protect against data loss in case one volume becomes inaccessible due to a hardware failure. Mirroring as a replication function presents each copy of a volume as a separately accessible volume.)

A copy of *primary* or *production* or *source* data may be called a *copy* or *replica* or *secondary* or *snapshot* or *target.* While, as a result of a copy operation, there are initially two (or more) copies of the same data – source and target(s) – generally only a copy made from source data is called a *copy*; that includes the case of a copy of a copy. *Copy* and *snapshot* are sometimes used as verbs as in "We need to make a copy of Volume V" or "We need to take a snapshot of volume V."

A copy of data is sometimes made by creating an extra continuous RAID mirror of data, then *splitting off* the mirror as a separately accessible entity.

The process of using a target's data to replace the source data (e.g., in case the source data was lost or corrupted) is called *restore.*

A copy may be a bit-for-bit *physical copy* (aka *clone* or *full copy*). Or, a copy may be a *logical copy* (aka *space-efficient copy* or *virtual copy*) based on clever programming that can reduce the physical capacity needed to hold the copy compared to the capacity used to hold the source data. Applications cannot normally tell the difference between a physical copy and a logical copy.

Storage system attributes that significantly influence intra-system replication

Below is a list of attributes that influence the capabilities of intra-system replication. A given storage system may support only some of these attributes. This list is not necessarily complete.

- Data type support. This identifies the kinds of data that can be replicated. For example: volumes or files.

- Host support. Some storage systems support different PiT replication capabilities for different types of hosts. Therefore, simply querying a vendor to determine whether a given copy capability is supported by a particular storage system may elicit a "yes" response, but a better query would ask whether the capability is supported for all hosts or specific hosts to be attached to the storage system.

- Target read/write capability. Some replication features may create read-only copies. Some features may create writable (i.e., updateable read-write) copies. Some features may create up to a certain number of copies all of which can be read-only or a subset of which can be writable. (Making a read-only PiT copy for backup purposes is likely acceptable; making a copy of a database to test a new application may require that the copy can be updated.)

- Degree of application disruption. Ideally, an active application should be able to continue to run while a PiT copy of data it is using is being made. (Some users may prefer to temporarily pause an application in order to make the copy while the application and its data are in a particular state.)

- Time until a copy is usable. Ideally, from a user's point of view the time to effectively make a usable copy should be negligible (sometimes described as "near-instant") and any internal data movement from a source to a target occurs asynchronously in the background. In the particular case of planning to concurrently make a large number of copies, customers should ask their vendors how long it takes before the entire set of copies is usable.

- Maximum copies per volume. Some use cases require maintaining multiple copies of a volume, whether identical copies (perhaps for testing purposes) or different versions created over time (perhaps serving as fallback copies as a long-running application progresses). The maximum number of copies a replication feature can support for a given volume may vary based on the type of host.

In some cases it is necessary to distinguish the number of copies that can be made which can remain in a relationship with their source volume from the number of copies which can become completely independent of their source volume. The reason is that some replication functions may require maintaining the relationship. For example, an ongoing source-target relationship between two volumes may be required to support the ability to update the target data with only the changes made to the source data since the time the copy was made or since the time the last changes-only update was made.

- Maximum number of copies supported for an entire storage system. In some storage systems, that number may be fewer than the maximum number of copies per volume times the maximum number of volumes. For example, assume a particular storage system supports up to 100 copies of a volume and supports up to 100 volumes. If a maximum of only 1,000 copies are supported in that system, that is far fewer than (100 volumes) x (100 copies/volume) = 10,000 copies.

- Physical capacity required to hold copies. This is the amount of physical storage capacity needed to support all the target copies that can exist at the same time. This can be less than the sum of the nominal capacities of all targets if capacity optimization technologies such as thin provisioning or data compression can apply to targets.

Taking advantage of properties of copies of data, technologies to reduce capacity requirements for copies are supported by some storage system models. In that case the copies are described as *logical copies* (as opposed to physical copies) or as *space-efficient copies*. A related consideration is whether physical capacity used to hold target copies must be pre-allocated (i.e., dedicated) to copy use, or whether system capacity is dynamically assigned to copy use as needed. The following diagram illustrates how a space-efficient copy may be implemented.

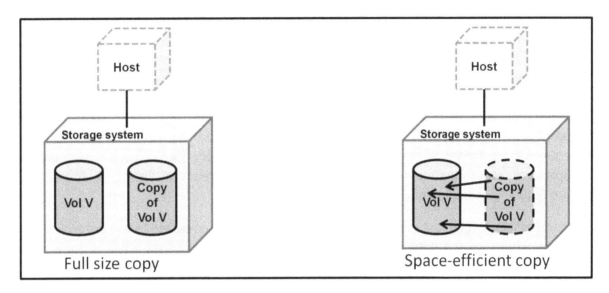

At the left, a physical (full size) copy of a volume uses the same physical capacity as its source volume. At the right, a space-efficient copy appears to have the same capacity as its source volume, as indicated by its dashed outline, but may occupy much less physical capacity. This is possible because, instead of holding an actual byte-for-byte copy of the original source data, the target volume contains pointers (i.e., the addresses of locations) to data on the source volume that existed when the PiT copy was created. Pointers are typically just a few bytes each and thus require much less space than the relatively large blocks of data they point to. The use of pointers is managed internally by the storage system so that applications can typically access physical copies and space-efficient copies the same way. (If an I/O request changes a block of data on the source volume, the pre-change block is preserved by the system by being moved to the target volume or some other location.)

Some storage systems may support intra-system replication features that create full size copies (aka clones) and also support other features that create space-efficient copies. (The term "snapshot" is ambiguous and could refer to full size or space-efficient copies, depending on the context.)

Whether full size copies or space-efficient copies or a mix of both types of copies are best for a given customer depends on the cost, the relative benefits and drawbacks, and (of course) the copy features a particular storage system supports. While it may seem that space-efficient copies should always be preferred because they save money by reducing the amount of physical capacity needed to hold copies, full size copies have their own advantages. Consider these points:

o Some space-efficient replication features reduce the physical storage capacity needed by a target copy through maintaining only one copy of data blocks common to the source data and a target. (At the time a copy is made, that means all blocks.) In that case, if a common block is lost or corrupted due to a system error, both the source and target are affected. Therefore, that kind of copy is of limited use as a fallback version. An independent full size copy can avoid this exposure.

o A customer may have performance-sensitive applications and a storage system may provide better performance for full size copies than for space-efficient copies. As noted above, many space-efficient replication features maintain only one copy of data blocks common to a target and its source. I/Os to the target that access those common blocks can impact the performance of I/Os to the source that access the same blocks or even other blocks on shared drives. Creating copies that are physically separate from the source can reduce or avoid contention for shared drives and other shared system resources. In addition, for HDDs in particular, full size copies may provide better sequential performance than space-efficient copies. That's because on space-efficient copies the target data may be stored physically in a different order than the source data, thus requiring more mechanical arm movement.

o Space-efficient copy features based on pointers may be best-suited to the case of making copies where source data undergoes relatively few if any changes while a copy exists. That's because the longer a target exists, the more capacity it can consume since the storage system must preserve for target use the original contents of any source data blocks that change. Given enough time, a space-efficient target could physically grow to match the size of its source volume (or even exceed it due to internal control information needed to manage the copy), negating its space-efficiency. That is likely not an issue for copies with a short lifespan, such as copies created as input to backup processes and then immediately deleted, which is why that is a good use case for space-efficient copies.

Tip: A customer should ask a system's vendor to help estimate the physical capacity needed to support the way the customer plans to use the system's intra-system replication features.

- Performance impact on other work. Intra-system data replication has a potential negative impact on the performance of other work in the storage system because replication involves the overhead of system software managing the copy process and the overhead of data moving through internal hardware resources. This can potentially degrade the performance of host-initiated I/Os received while copy operations are active. (The situation is not unique to PiT data replication. Any internal system activity not performed to directly process a host's I/O request for data could potentially impact host I/O performance; multiple internal activities could impact each other's performance as well.)

Many customers appear to not consider this aspect of intra-system replication, essentially take their chances in the matter, and not have resulting performance problems. For example, some customers make few copies and may do so mainly for backup purposes during periods of relatively low storage system activity. However, customers with stringent performance requirements should consider whether intra-system replication activity will allow application I/O performance objectives (if formulated without considering the impact of replication) to be met by a given storage system configuration. The performance impact of copy operations will vary based on multiple factors including at least those in the following list.

o The number of copies of the same data made at the same time

o The number of copies of different data made at the same time

o The algorithms used to make and update copies[79]

o Whether a copy is a physical copy or a logical copy

o Whether any system hardware resources used by source and target data are shared

o Whether the system supports facilities to help manage the performance impact of copy activity.   An example is parameters that let users control the pace of internal data movement.   Slower data movement to make a physical copy means less short-term interference with other work, but also means it will take longer for an internal physical copy process to complete.

o Whether hosts' write I/Os to change source data the target copy depends on are handled synchronously or asynchronously.   Assume a space-efficient target volume contains pointers to data in the associated source volume for data that is unchanged since the point-in-time the copy was made. If a host's write I/O arrives that would change pointed-to data in the source volume, the storage system must preserve that data for target use by moving it to another location (e.g., in the target volume).   The issue is whether the host's I/O write request has to wait for that movement to occur before the host is signaled that the I/O request is complete.   If the system makes the write I/O request wait (synchronously), the I/O's response time would be elongated.[80]   Some PiT copy features are designed to avoid the I/O response time elongation by quickly signaling the host that the write I/O request is complete and handling the internal data preservation movement later (i.e., asynchronously).[81]

---

[79] The names of two prominent PiT algorithms may be mentioned by vendors or storage administrators in replication discussions.   Copy-on-write (COW, aka copy-on-first-write): source data is updated in place, requiring the original data to be preserved for target use by being moved to another location. Redirect-on-write (ROW): updates to source data are written to a new location so the original source data is preserved as the PiT copy.   Different algorithms have different implications for performance.   As this bullet item's Tip notes, the performance impact of a copy operation depends on many factors of which the copy algorithm is only one.

[80] Some applications issue write I/Os asynchronously, meaning a portion of application processing may not wait for write I/Os to complete before continuing.   The performance of such applications may not be impacted by synchronous copy-on-write I/O processing.

[81] An asynchronous design may work something like this: The storage system accepts the write I/O request into cache (as it may do for all write I/O requests).   The system detects the I/O request wants to change data that happens to be the original source data in a PiT copy relationship, meaning the system needs to preserve that original source data before it is overlaid.   The system schedules (but does not yet execute) an internal process to do the data movement later and before the newly written data is

Tip: Because of the number of factors that can impact the performance of other work in the system when copy processes are active, customers are advised to ask vendors for help in determining whether and how much host I/O performance would be degraded in a particular environment.

- Incremental update/refresh. Once a target copy is made, some replication feature designs allow that target to be *updated incrementally* (aka *refreshed*) from the source volume by copying only changes made to the source volume since the target was initially made or since the previous incremental update was made. Copying only changed data should have a lower impact on storage system performance than a refresh performed by copying all source data again.

  Support for an incremental refresh optimization can be useful for targets that are physical copies of source data (i.e., clones). However, this optimization may not be applicable to space-efficient replication designs that can quickly create a new, current PiT target by using pointers without needing to copy any source data.

- Consistency groups. A consistency group is a user-specified group of two or more volumes such that a copy of the group includes a copy of all the individual volumes in the group at the same point-in-time. This is important when a group of related items – such as a database management system's (DBMS's) tables, logs, and control files residing on different volumes – must all be copied at the same point-in-time.

  Consistency group support ensures the data in the group of copies is *time-consistent*, similar to the state the data would be in if a server suddenly stops working (aka "crashes") and cannot write more data until it is rebooted. (For that reason, *time-consistent* is sometimes called *crash-consistent*.) DBMS's in particular are generally designed to be able to successfully restart from time-consistent data; a DBMS uses its log to identify any partially completed transactions and backs out (undoes) any changes those transactions made to the database.

  The value of consistency group support is seen by considering a scenario describing what can happen in its absence. A single database transaction often needs to issue multiple I/Os to change multiple records in the database. Without consistency group support, only some of the changes made by a completed transaction against a large multi-volume database may be captured in a point-in-time copy, yet the database log captured in the copy can indicate the transaction completed successfully. A financial transaction to transfer funds between two accounts could result in the database copy showing a withdrawal from one account (with data on one volume), but not the corresponding deposit to another account (with data on another volume), even though the log copy (on yet another volume) indicates the transaction completed normally. In that case, the copy of the database has lost integrity. A more detailed discussion appears in *Appendix C. Intra-System Replication Consistency Groups.*

---

destaged from cache. The system now signals the host that its write I/O request is complete. This design avoids delaying the write I/O request until the internal data movement to preserve the original source data completes.

Tip: Customers requiring support for consistency groups should determine the consistency group scalability they need and include that in their storage system requirements: What is the maximum number of volumes that can reside in one consistency group? How many consistency groups need to coexist at the same time? Can a consistency group include multiple volumes residing in multiple storage systems (which can occur for very large applications) and, if so, how many volumes in how many systems? (Note that to support consistency groups that span multiple storage systems an external facility to coordinate the copy creation process, such as host-based software or a storage virtualization-based facility, may be required.)

- Copy creation concurrency. Some PiT replication facilities support the ability to make multiple copies of the same source data at the same point-in-time via a single command. (An alternative can be to create one copy, then later create other copies of that copy.)

- Cascading. Some PiT copy features allow copies to be made from other copies, sometimes called *cascading*. Example: source → target → copy_of_target. (In storage systems that do not directly support cascading, an alternative may be to separate the target from any further relationship to its source, then make a copy of the target.)

- Feature interoperability. In some storage systems making PiT copies is not supported under certain conditions. For example, the ability to make a PiT copy of a volume may be limited or not supported if the volume is also in an inter-system (remote mirroring) replication relationship.

- Management. There is more to supporting copies than just the ability of a storage system to make them. Management facilities can add important ease-of-use functions. Examples include scheduling when copies are to be made, coordinating copy creation with host-based applications, helping with data restoration activities, and automatically deleting older copies when new copies would exceed the maximum supported number of copies. These kinds of management facilities may be provided by an intra-system copy feature or by separate host-based software. Some host-based replication management offerings support heterogeneous storage systems.

Additional Tips

- *In some cases, host-based replication can be an acceptable solution to address data replication requirements. Unlike storage system-based replication, host-based replication may operate at an application level, e.g., making a copy of specific files rather than making a copy of all data on a volume or set of volumes. Host-based replication can place a copy of data in a different storage system than the source data. Host-based replication provides a facility that can support heterogeneous storage systems attached to the same host. On the downside, host-based replication uses host resources that can impact application performance; while storage system-based replication uses storage system resources, many of those resources (such as the drives containing source and target volumes) are used by either storage-based or host-based replication. Host-based replication may not support as many functions as storage-based replication because the latter has received a lot of attention by storage companies.*

Storage system vendors may not suggest using host-based replication if their company does not sell it or it does not count towards their sales quota.

Inter-System Data Replication

Storage system inter-system data replication (aka *remote mirroring* or *remote copy*) creates and maintains copies of data located in one storage system in one or more separate storage systems. Data movement required for remote replication is generally handled by the storage systems without using host resources. The remote copies can be made and updated while applications continue to access the original data.

Inter-system replication has several use cases such as: (1) Supporting disaster recovery (DR) in case of events such as natural or man-made disasters that prevent use of a local storage system (or even an entire local data center) for an unacceptable period of time; operations can be resumed using current (or near-current) data preserved in remote storage systems. (2) Supporting data migration between storage systems. (3) Supporting backing up or archiving data to a remote storage system. (4) Supporting copying or relocating data from one storage system to another for any reason.

While the idea of making a remote copy of local data may seem straightforward, this chapter reveals many factors that affect the capabilities available to users, as was true for intra-system copy discussed in the previous chapter.

Concepts and Facilities

- <u>Purpose</u>. The main function of inter-system data replication is to create and actively maintain a current or near-current copy of data in one storage system in another storage system. In contrast to intra-system point-in-time copies where a copy in the same system reflects data at the time the copy command was issued, inter-system copy propagates updates to the source data to another storage system (or systems) as the updates are made, or (as we'll see) soon after. (For simplicity, the remainder of this chapter refers to *volumes* as the type of data being remotely replicated, but keep in mind that some storage systems support replicating other types of data such as a NAS system that can replicate files.)

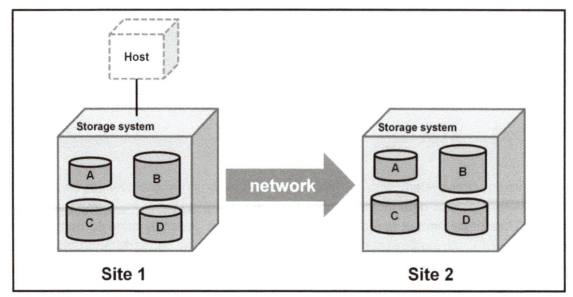

Data written to the storage system at Site 1 is replicated over a network to the remote storage system at Site 2. It is not necessary to have hosts connected to the storage system at Site 2 until that system needs to be accessed by hosts.

Tip: Remote mirroring is more complicated than a simple "does or does not support it" attribute of a storage system. The capabilities of remote mirroring features may vary considerably between different storage system models. What matters most is that the features on a storage system a customer considers for acquisition support the customer's requirements.

Therefore, customers should determine their remote replication requirements at a deeper level than simply "The storage system must support remote replication of data." The most fundamental requirements should specify at least these items:

1) The distance to be supported between storage systems

2) The currency of data in the remote system relative to the local system

3) The maximum acceptable performance impact of remote replication on production applications

4) Whether 2-site or 3-site or other configurations are needed.

Additional remote mirroring capabilities that may be required by some customers are discussed later in this chapter.

- Terminology. Vendors typically give unique names to their storage system that support inter-system replication. However, several terms are commonly used in the industry when discussing inter-system replication:

The basic function is often described by terms such as *remote replication*, *remote copy*, and *remote mirroring*. (The term "mirroring" in this context should not be confused with RAID-1 or RAID-10, also sometimes called "mirroring." RAID is generally a way to manage multiple drives within a single system to help protect against data loss in case of certain hardware failures. Also, unlike RAID mirroring, in some types of remote mirroring (discussed later in this chapter) the remote system's data is not as current as the local system's data.)

A minimum remote mirroring configuration is a *2-system* (aka *2-site*) configuration.[82] (Remote mirroring configurations with more than two systems are discussed later.) The *local* site or system (where production work runs) is also called the *primary* or *source* or *production* site or system. The *remote* site or system is also called the *secondary* or *target* or *recovery* site or system.

Sometimes the terms "storage system" and "site" (where a site might be a data center or building or campus or other geographical location) are informally used interchangeably. For example "If local storage system A fails, operations can be resumed using remote storage system B" and "If local site A fails, operations can be resumed at remote site B" may sometimes be stated interchangeably. However, their precise meanings differ; consider that a storage system can fail yet other equipment at the same site can remain operational.

Managing the local-remote storage replication process so that the remote storage system becomes the production storage system is called *failover*. Failover may be planned (e.g., scheduled in advance for DR testing purposes) or unplanned (e.g., initiated due to a disaster). Following a failover, the original local hosts (if operational) may be redirected to use the recovery storage system (if connected), or hosts at the recovery site may be used instead such as in the case of a total local data center disaster. After a failover, the reverse process of again making the original local storage system the production storage system is called *failback*.

The desired maximum time following a failover operation until the recovery storage system is ready for use by applications is called the *Recovery Time Objective (RTO)*. Note that RTO could be defined from a storage system's point-of-view (meaning the storage system is ready to accept application I/Os) or could be defined from an end-user's point-of-view (meaning the application is ready for productive use, perhaps following its own recovery actions).

The degree of data currency in a recovery storage system (compared to the production system) is called the *Recovery Point Objective (RPO)*. RPO is a goal, not a certainty, because unforeseen circumstances (such as a temporary outage of communication links between storage systems) can cause a remote system's copy of data to fall further behind the production copy than desired by a customer. RPO is an important consideration because in some remote replication features the remote system normally lags the production system in data currency, and for good reason (discussed later). In practice, RPO is commonly measured in time, not as a number of transactions or I/O requests or bytes of data. Customers' RPOs commonly vary from zero (aka zero data loss) to a few seconds to multiple hours. An RPO greater than zero may be necessary in some circumstances, but can mean lost business transactions following an unplanned failover.

---

[82] There is an exception. Some storage systems can act as both a local and remote system for the same volumes. That is, one system would contain production volumes and also contain their "remote" copies. That capability can be used, for example, to help train administrators on use of a remote mirroring feature before a planned 2-system configuration is installed.

Tradeoffs between shorter and longer RPOs are considered in the discussion of protocols later in this chapter.[83]

Tip: *The terms* local *and* remote *are sometimes used ambiguously when considering a post-failover condition because the system or site that was local before a failover may be viewed as remote from the point-of-view of the recovery site. It is important to clarify the meaning of these terms in discussions and documents. Naming the sites or systems, such as Site-My_city and System-Remote_city, can help.*

- <u>Interoperability</u>. Remote mirroring is generally supported only between models of storage systems in the same system family. Further, interoperability between selected older and newer models or between selected older and newer microcode versions may not be supported. This is generally because the systems have to cooperate with each other to send and receive data, but there are no industry standards for that and different storage system models may use incompatible protocols.

Remote mirroring between heterogeneous storage systems is supported in some cases. Some storage virtualization facilities and specialized appliances support remote mirroring between selected heterogeneous storage systems. In addition to local I/Os being handled by a local storage system, the facility (or appliance) also propagates write I/O requests to a remote facility (or appliance) that writes the data to a remote storage system. In this way, the local and remote systems do not have to communicate directly with each other and may not need to directly support remote mirroring at all.

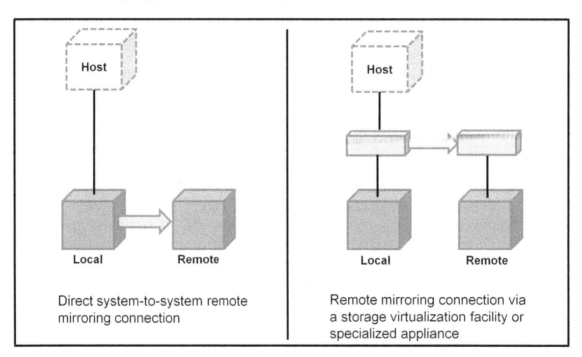

| Direct system-to-system remote mirroring connection | Remote mirroring connection via a storage virtualization facility or specialized appliance |

---

[83] Customers not using storage system-based remote mirroring sometimes make a daily backup onto tape cartridges and ship those cartridges to another location. In that case, the RPO is about 24 hours. Compared to that, a remote mirroring RPO of a few minutes or a few hours may be a significant improvement that many customers consider acceptable.

Tip: *Interoperability restrictions limit which storage systems can participate together in a remote mirroring configuration. Such restrictions could require that a customer wanting to replace either a local or remote system finds they have to replace both at the same time. Customers should consider a vendor's history of supporting remote mirroring interoperability between different model generations and different microcode versions. Storage virtualization facilities and specialized appliances can provide more flexibility to combine heterogeneous storage systems ("behind" the facilities) for remote mirroring, though these facilities and appliances have their own interoperability requirements.*

Storage system attributes that significantly influence inter-system replication

Below is a list of attributes that influence the capabilities of inter-system replication. A given storage system may support only some of these attributes. This list is not necessarily complete.

- <u>Data type support</u>. This identifies the kinds of data that can be remotely replicated. For example: volumes or files. The types of data that can be remotely replicated by a storage system vary by the type of storage system and the capabilities of a system's replication feature(s). In particular, remote mirroring for block-access storage systems commonly works at a volume level of granularity because storage systems are "aware" of internal volumes created by system administrators, but are not aware of host-created files that reside in volumes.

- <u>Host support</u>. Some storage system models support different remote mirroring capabilities for different types of hosts.

  Tip: Simply querying a vendor to determine whether a particular remote mirroring capability is supported by a particular storage system model may elicit a "yes" response, but a better query would ask whether the capability is supported for the specific hosts the customer plans to attach to the storage system.

- <u>Inter-system communication ports</u>. When s local storage system receives a write I/O it propagates the data to a remote system. This is done over a network. The kind of networks supported can vary by storage system model. A Fibre Channel storage area network (SAN) is commonly supported; if necessary, it can work with other network equipment to change the network protocol to something else such as IP over Ethernet. Some storage systems support integrated Ethernet ports that can avoid needing protocol conversion equipment.

  The number of ports needed can vary based on the amount of data to be transmitted, port speed, whether data compression is used in the storage system or in network devices, and the efficiency of the remote mirroring software in the storage system.

  Tip: A minimum of two ports, each on a separate host port adapter, is a best practice to preserve disaster recovery protection in case one port or adapter fails. However, unavailability of one out of two ports would double the utilization of the functioning port. If that would lead to performance issues, more than two ports may be preferred even if not strictly needed for performance reasons when all ports are operating normally.

- <u>Synchronous and asynchronous protocols</u>. Local and remote storage systems interact by exchanging information over communication links. These exchanges influence attributes such as the maximum practical distance between systems, local application performance, and data currency in the remote system.

  These exchanges are called *protocols*, but are distinct from (and at a higher level than) the underlying inter-system network protocols such as IP. The two most prominent protocols are technically described as *synchronous* and *asynchronous*. (Vendors generally have unique names for their remote mirroring features which may not clearly indicate which protocol a feature supports.) Which of these protocols (or combination of protocols) is best for a given environment depends on a customer's remote mirroring requirements (e.g., for RPO).

  o *Synchronous protocols* are designed to keep data on a remote storage system synchronized (i.e., current) with a local system so there is no loss of data if operations are failed over to the remote storage system. In other words, a synchronous protocol supports an RPO of zero seconds.

  However, achieving this data currency objective can degrade application performance because an application is not notified its write I/O request has completed successfully until both storage systems are updated.[84] Thus, the response time applications see for write I/Os elongates as the distance between storage systems increases because of the time it takes a message to travel over distance. Further, at least one round trip, from source to target and back, is required for a storage system to propagate a write I/O and receive a "propagation successful" acknowledgment from the remote system[85]; some designs have required more than one round trip for each propagated write I/O, further elongating write I/O response time.

---

[84] Many applications issue a write I/O request then wait for an indication it completed before continuing. Some applications issue write I/Os asynchronously, allowing the applications to continue immediately. Some applications divide their work into processes (aka threads or tasks) that can execute in parallel; one process may be waiting for a write request to complete while other processes continue running in parallel.

[85] For example, the speed of a signal in a fiber optic cable is about 2/3 the speed of light (i.e., 2/3 × 300,000km/s). It takes about .5 milliseconds for that signal to travel 100km. (100km / (2/3 × 300,000km/s) = .0005s.) So, one round-trip for a message between two storage systems 100km apart takes about .001s = 1ms. This compares to the typical speed of accessing a local HDD of perhaps 3-5 ms and the speed of accessing a local SSD of under 1 ms. The round-trip time is affected by several factors including the communications media, intermediate communications equipment, the size of a block of data being transferred, actual distance traveled (vs. straight line map distance), and the number of round trips required by the protocol implementation.

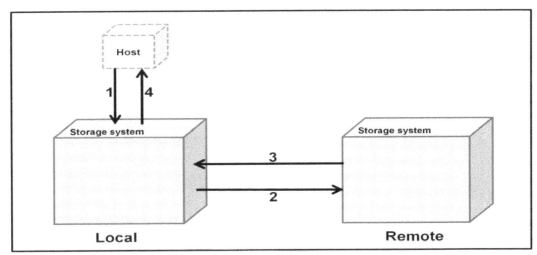

The figure shows the steps of how a host's write I/O request is processed when a synchronous protocol is used: (1) The write request is issued by the host to the local storage system. (2) The local storage system stores the data and propagates the request to the remote system. (3) The remote system sends a message to the local system indicating it successfully received the request. (4) The local storage system notifies the host that the I/O request is complete.

Different storage systems support different maximum distances for synchronous protocols. Some vendors allow those distances to be extended in some cases, e.g., after reviewing the performance implications with the customer.

Synchronous protocols are best-suited for storage systems located relatively close together, e.g., in the same data center or on the same campus or in the same metropolitan area, all of which are sometimes said to be in the same *region*. Unfortunately, that proximity of systems means they are potentially susceptible to a regional disaster such as a power outage, flood, or earthquake; the solution to that problem is asynchronous protocols, discussed next.

o *Asynchronous protocols* are designed to support arbitrarily long distances between local and remote storage systems, and to maintain application write I/O performance at a level similar to what it would be without remote mirroring. Asynchronous protocols achieve this by eliminating the need for applications to wait for write I/Os to be propagated to a remote storage system. Instead, an application is informed a write I/O is complete almost immediately after a local storage system receives the write I/O request, similar to how read I/Os are handled (because read requests are normally not propagated to a remote system). The local system then asynchronously (i.e., at a later time) propagates the write request to a remote storage system.

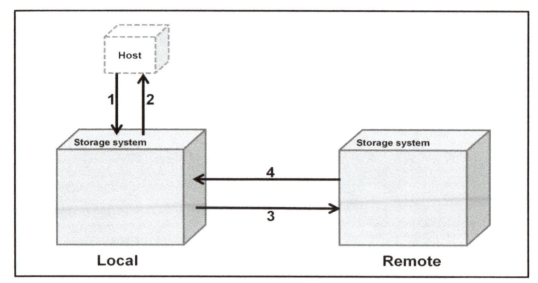

The figure shows the steps of how a host's write I/O request is processed when an asynchronous protocol is used: (1) The write request is issued by the host to the local storage system. (2) The local storage system stores the data and notifies the host that the I/O request is complete. (3) The local storage system propagates the I/O request to the remote system. (4) The remote system sends a message to the local system indicating it successfully received the request.

Achieving these performance and distance benefits means there may be loss of the most current data if operations are failed over to the remote storage system. (There should be no loss if all write I/Os previously received by the local storage system have been successfully propagated to the remote system. This is generally not the case in environments with high write I/O rates.)

An asynchronous protocol is best-suited for environments where the RPO is greater than zero and/or the distance between storage systems is so long that the performance elongation of a synchronous protocol on writes is not acceptable. The amount of remote system data loss can typically vary from a few seconds to many minutes or even hours, depending on the remote mirroring feature design and any customer-settable parameters. For example, some asynchronous remote mirroring features are designed to transmit local writes to the remote system as soon as possible. Alternatively, some features are designed to periodically (e.g., once every hour) take point-in-time snapshots of local volumes and transmit the snapshot data to the remote system. In that case, an optimization is for the local system to compare each new snapshot to the previous snapshot and transmit only the changed data, saving transmission time and network bandwidth.

A variation of asynchronous protocols is an optimization for copying an entire volume to a remote storage system on command (rather than copying individual data blocks as write I/Os are issued to a volume). The elapsed time for copying an entire volume is usually reduced by copying the data blocks in the order in which they are physically stored on drives because that minimizes seek time (i.e., arm movement) for HDDs. One use case for this optimization is initializing the contents of a remote system. Another use case is moving volumes for migration purposes.

- <u>Recovery Point Objective (RPO)</u>. Some remote replication features allow a customer to specify the Recovery Point Objective time the customer wants to achieve. (This applies to asynchronous protocols; synchronous protocols have an RPO of zero by definition.)

  Tip: Regardless of the range of RPO parameter values a system allows an administrator to set, a customer should ask vendors to identify RPO times other customers have successfully achieved in practice for the feature the customer would use. This applies to minimum RPO values in particular.

- <u>Multi-site configurations</u>. While the minimal remote mirroring configuration has two systems (aka a 2-site configuration) and is widely implemented, 2-site configurations have limitations of concern to some customers: They cannot support zero-data-loss (RPO of zero) at long distances due to performance degradation. And, if one system is unavailable, the operating system does not have DR protection. (A system may be unavailable for reasons such as a site disaster, system maintenance, in-place upgrades, or migration to another system.)

  Some storage system models can help customers overcome these limitations by supporting remote mirroring configurations consisting of three or more storage systems connected by combinations of synchronous and asynchronous protocols. A common 3-site configuration has one remote system located near (e.g., on the same campus as) the local system using a synchronous protocol to minimize the performance impact and preserve data currency; the other remote system is located farther away via an asynchronous protocol to support long distance between systems. The configuration can be implemented in one of two ways:

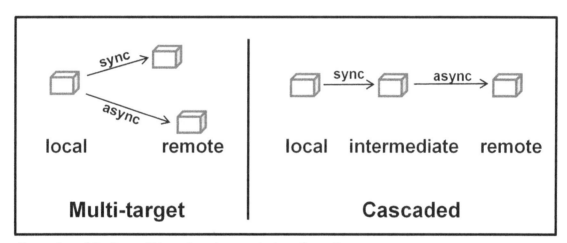

Examples of 3-site multi-target and cascaded configurations.

  1) In *multi-target* configurations, a local storage system is directly connected to two (or more) remote storage systems. In the example shown, one remote system is connected synchronously and the other asynchronously; other combinations may be supported by some storage system models. A facility may be supported to synchronize data in the two remote systems if the local system is unavailable. If so, the remote systems can be synchronized to contain current data and either could be used to resume operations while the other then provides DR protection.

  2) In *cascaded* configurations, a local storage system is connected to one remote system which in turn is connected to another remote system. In the example shown, the first

connection is synchronous and the second connection is asynchronous; other combinations may be supported by some storage system models. The intermediate system propagates write I/Os it receives from the local system to the farthest remote system, so the farthest system may normally lag in data currency, but would become current if only the local system stops operating. In some implementations, if the intermediate site becomes unavailable the local site can communicate directly with the farthest remote site. Because the local system propagates write I/Os to only one other system, there is less overhead in the local system than in multi-target configurations where the local system must propagate each write I/O it receives to two other systems.

Some storage system remote replication features support four or more sites. One possible configuration is illustrated below.

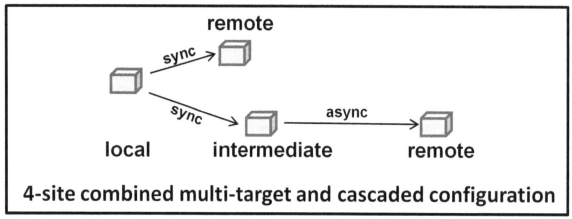

4-site combined multi-target and cascaded configuration

Example of a 4-site configuration.

In this example, a multi-target configuration and a cascaded configuration are combined. A local storage system connects directly to two systems via synchronous protocols where the synchronous target systems are located near the local system to minimize elongation of write I/O response time. One of those synchronously connected systems in turn connects to a remote system via an asynchronous protocol to provide DR protection at long distance.

A use case for a 4-site configuration such as the one illustrated above is when an especially high degree of data availability and data currency is required (hence the two synchronously connected storage systems) along with long distance DR protection in case of a regional disaster.

• Swapping. Some storage systems support a capability, sometimes called *swapping*, that can help support high levels of storage availability in non-disaster scenarios. Two storage systems are connected to the same host(s). The two storage systems are in a synchronous remote mirroring configuration so they both have the same current data. Normally, host I/Os are directed to the system the customer designates as the *primary* system; that system propagates write I/Os to the other storage system called the *secondary* system. If the primary storage system fails (while the host remains operational), the swapping capability automatically redirects host I/Os to the secondary system, allowing applications to continue to operate without disruption despite the failed storage system. (The capability may also be invoked by manual command in case the primary system has a planned outage.) Support for swapping may require special host software to detect a failure of the primary storage system and manage redirection of host I/Os; thus, a given storage system's swapping capability may be supported only for selected hosts.

- Volume pair scalability. This is the maximum number of local-remote volume pairs that are supported by an entire storage system.

  Tip: In some storage systems, this number may be less than the maximum number of volumes a system supports, limiting system capacity scalability in remote mirroring configurations in a way customers may not anticipate.

- Target read/write capability. Some remote mirroring features limit target data to read-only access by hosts until a failover occurs, helping to ensure the local and remote copies are consistent. Some remote mirroring features may permit write access by hosts to a remote system. If so, that must be carefully managed by customers because the data in a remote system could be changed (1) by hosts attached to the local storage system (via the change being transmitted to the remote system) and (2) by hosts attached to the remote system. Those changes would be uncoordinated which could corrupt remote system data integrity.

- Active-active configurations. Recent years have seen increased interest in *active-active* (aka *active/active*) configurations where storage systems in different locations are essentially peers (in contrast to primary-secondary pairs) all of which can accept writes to the same logical volume from different hosts and propagate those writes to other peers. An active-active volume is sometimes called a *stretched volume* or *distributed volume*.

  Depending on implementation, an active-active volume may be backed by a physical copy in each storage system or in only one storage system. If backed by a copy in each storage system, access to data can continue without needing a customer-initiated failover process if one system fails (assuming users are connected to hosts that are connected to surviving storage systems).

  Maintaining data integrity requires that the application owning the volume support multiple hosts updating the same volume at the same time.[86] An active-active configuration may be supported by capabilities of a storage system or by virtualization facilities that sit between hosts and storage systems.

- Bi-directional support. Some remote replication features allow two storage systems to be both local and remote relative to each other. A given storage system can contain both primary volumes (with remote secondary volumes) and secondary volumes (with remote

---

[86] A single instance of an application on a single host can preserve data integrity by controlling the order of changes to data it manages because it is aware of *all* changes. In contrast, when an application runs on multiple hosts where those application instances can all access the same data, some form of communication between the instances is needed so all those hosts don't try to change the same data (such as a set of related records in a database) at the same time in a way that could compromise data integrity. That kind of data sharing capability is supported, for example, by some database management systems communicating over a network or via a shared storage system.

primary volumes). This capability supports two data centers serving as the recovery site for each other.

- Consistency groups. (Consistency groups were previously discussed in the *Intra-System Data Replication* chapter. While both inter-system and intra-system data replication consistency groups are designed to preserve the time-consistency of a copy of data, they do so in different ways.)

  In inter-system data replication, a consistency group is a user-specified set of volumes managed by a storage system such that if a write I/O request cannot be successfully propagated to any remotely mirrored volume in the set, all remote volumes associated with the consistency group are "frozen" to maintain their contents at that point in time. This ensures data on the group of remote volumes remains *time-consistent*: all write I/Os up to a point-in-time are captured and no I/Os beyond that time are captured. That is similar to the state of stored data if a server crashes (which is why the term *crash-consistent* is sometimes used).

  Some applications, such as database management systems in particular, are designed to maintain and recover successfully from time-consistent data. For example, if, when restarted, a database manager determines from its log that a transaction had updated the database but had not completely finished, the database manager would undo any updates made by the uncompleted transaction.

  The value of remote mirroring consistency group support can be seen by considering what can happen in its absence. Assume a database is being remotely mirrored from a local storage system to another storage system and consistency groups are *not* supported (or are supported but not enabled). The two storage systems are connected over two (or more) communications links, a best practice for availability. The local storage system propagates write I/Os it receives from hosts using both communication paths. As a result, due to timing issues (such as recovering from temporary errors on one of the links), write I/Os could be sent by the local system, and thus received by the remote system, out of order. Assume a "transaction complete" log entry arrives at the remote system before the transaction's update to a database table entry was able to be successfully sent, then a disaster occurs at the local site and operations are failed over to the remote site. When the database manager is restarted against the remote copy of the database, the database log indicates the transaction completed normally, but in fact the update to the database table entry is missing. The database has lost integrity. If the database had been in a consistency group, that would have ensured all write I/Os received by the local storage system for the consistency group up to a point-in-time were captured by the remote system and no I/Os beyond that time were captured. (The program logic to make that happen can vary by storage system.)[87]

---

[87] Real disasters are sometimes called "rolling disasters" because IT systems and components do not all fail at the same instant, but rather fail over a period of time in a somewhat random manner as the effects of a disaster "roll through" a data center. Storage systems are not able to distinguish whether failure events signal a small temporary problem or are part of a rolling disaster. Consistency groups help protect remote site data integrity regardless. If the situation is a real disaster, remote system data

An additional potential benefit of consistency groups is the ability to manually failover/failback individual consistency groups. That is useful for DR testing purposes because it is less disruptive and less complex than failover/failback of all data in a storage system.

Tip: Customers requiring support for consistency groups should determine the consistency group scalability they need and include that in their storage system requirements: What is the maximum number of volumes (or other data types) that can reside in one consistency group? How many consistency groups can coexist in one storage system? Can a consistency group include multiple volumes residing in multiple storage systems (which can occur for very large applications) and, if so, how many volumes in how many storage systems?

- Data resynchronization. Local and remote storage systems sometimes need to *resynchronize* their copies of data, i.e., take action to make the remote system's data match the local system's data after some event has prevented normal local-to-remote propagation of data. Such events include failed communication links or a remote system being offline. Sending previously unpropagated data is called *resynchronization*.

A significant optimization in terms of time and link utilization is for the local storage system to transmit only the updates that could not be transmitted rather than reinitialize the remote system with all local data. When normal propagation of write I/Os from a local to a remote system cannot occur, applications normally continue to access the local storage system for both read and write I/Os. (Customers usually don't want to stop or applications or have them fail just because, say, a gopher ate through underground communication cables and there is no disaster.) During this time, a local system can keep track of the data that can't be propagated to the remote system. Later, when the problem preventing propagation is fixed, the local system needs to send only the previously unsent data to the remote system to bring the remote system to data currency.

Similarly, a significant resynchronization optimization is that during failback the (original) remote system transmits to the local system only data from write I/Os it received after the failover. This can be useful, for example, after a failover/failback test where production was temporarily moved to the remote storage system.

Tip: Customers may find it useful to ask vendors what conditions (other than first time initialization of the data in a remote storage system) require transmitting all data between remotely mirrored storage systems (in either direction) rather than transmitting updates only. Retransmitting all data can take significant time and inhibit using the remote system for DR recovery until data transmission is complete and the data integrity of the remote copy is ensured.

- Data resynchronization and data integrity. It is important that storage systems and administrative procedures protect against an exposure to losing data integrity than can

---

integrity is protected. If the situation is not a disaster, perhaps just a temporary failure of communications links, when the links are again operational any data previously unable to be sent from the local to the remote system can be sent to resynchronize the systems.

potentially occur during local-remote storage system data resynchronization due to the nature of the resynchronization process.

Here is the crux of the matter: The data being resynchronized may not always be transmitted in the original write order in which case the remote system's copy of data lacks integrity until all those writes are received.[88] If a disaster occurs during resynchronization but before it completes, the remote system may have lost integrity and a customer may not even be able to determine whether and to what extent that is the case. (The customer may notice indirect evidence over time such as a client complaining that a funds transfer they requested resulted in a withdrawal from one account but no corresponding deposit to another account.)

The usual way of protecting remote site data integrity is to make a point-in-time intra-system copy of the remote data (sometimes called a *safety copy* or a *gold copy*) prior to resynchronization for fallback use in case resynchronization cannot complete successfully. If fallback is required there can be loss of the latest data, but data integrity (time consistency) is preserved. Some storage system remote mirroring features protect data integrity by automatically making a safety copy prior to resynchronization, some systems support a facility to make a safety copy but do not require customers use the facility, and some storage systems may not even support such a facility. A scenario using a safety copy, here called the gold copy, is illustrated in the following diagram.

---

[88] A method of identifying unsent writes employed by many storage systems is using a set of bits (called a *bitmap*) where each bit indicates a range of storage locations such as HDD track1, HDD track2, and so on. A bit set to 1, say, indicates data on the associated track has been updated but not yet sent to the remote system. A bitmap does not indicate the order in which tracks were updated and different blocks on the same track may have been updated at different times. The unsent writes are generally not simply put in a time-ordered (first-in first-out, (FIFO)) queue for use by the resynchronization process because the problem preventing propagation might persist for an unpredictable amount of time that could require an unpredictable amount of capacity for the queue. Some storage systems do use such a queue to handle propagation problems of relatively short duration, but when the queue fills up these systems generally resort to using bitmaps.

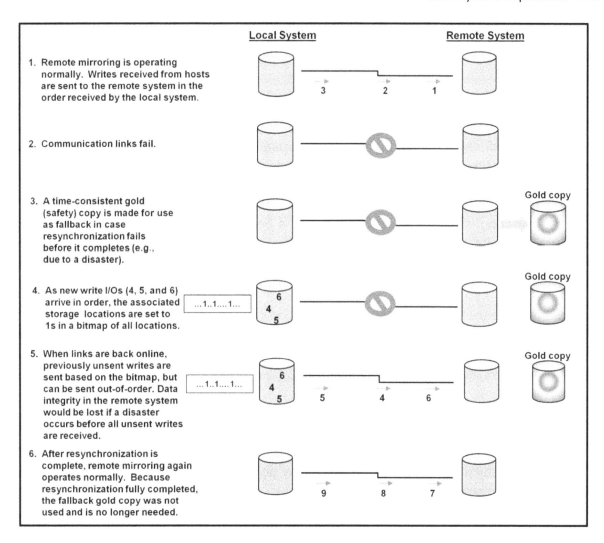

Local System   **Remote System**

1. Remote mirroring is operating normally. Writes received from hosts are sent to the remote system in the order received by the local system.

3   2   1

2. Communication links fail.

3. A time-consistent gold (safety) copy is made for use as fallback in case resynchronization fails before it completes (e.g., due to a disaster).

Gold copy

4. As new write I/Os (4, 5, and 6) arrive in order, the associated storage locations are set to 1s in a bitmap of all locations.

...1..1....1...   6 4 5

Gold copy

5. When links are back online, previously unsent writes are sent based on the bitmap, but can be sent out-of-order. Data integrity in the remote system would be lost if a disaster occurs before all unsent writes are received.

...1..1....1...   6 4 5

5   4   6

Gold copy

6. After resynchronization is complete, remote mirroring again operates normally. Because resynchronization fully completed, the fallback gold copy was not used and is no longer needed.

9   8   7

Tip: Customers should understand this issue and the risks they would be taking by not protecting remote site data from scenarios that can compromise data integrity. It would be unfortunate, to say the least, if a customer invests in implementing remote mirroring only to learn after a disaster occurs that the remote copy of data is not useful or is causing problems due to lost integrity and that restoring a backup copy may be needed to continue the business.

Tip: A vendor selling a remote mirroring feature that either makes using a gold copy optional or that does not even support making a gold copy may try to sell that feature without discussing the data integrity issue with a customer. The vendor may perhaps be hoping that the cost savings of not requiring a gold copy will make their proposal look favorable compared to competing storage systems designed to always implement that protection. The vendor may be hoping a customer does not even understand the issue. (A vendor's product manuals may discuss the issue and recommend customers implement the data integrity protection if it is optional, but that does not ensure vendors' representatives point that out to customers or that customers read the technical product manuals before acquiring a system.)

Tip: *Implementing a safety copy requires additional remote system capacity to hold it, raising system cost. Some storage systems can make a space-efficient copy, reducing that cost.*

- <u>Suspend/resume</u>. It is useful if a remote mirroring feature supports the ability for administrators to suspend remote mirroring data propagation on command and later resume it on command. An example of where this is useful is suspending communications while data is in a desired state so a copy can be made in the remote system of the data in that state, after which data propagation is resumed. Another example is if there is a problem with a remote system or communication links, and the problem is best addressed while remote mirroring is not transmitting data. (As a best practice, it is generally preferable to command remote mirroring to suspend rather than "surprise" the feature by an unexpected situation such as turning off network equipment. The feature is hopefully designed to handle such a situation well, but it is likely better to avoid finding out.)

A suspend capability can preferably specify a particular local-remote system relationship or even a particular volume-pair to be suspended, host applications can continue to write to the local storage system, and the remote system can later be resynchronized with local write data received while data propagation was suspended.

- <u>Fan-in and fan-out</u>. *Fan-in* and *fan-out* specify the number of storage systems that can communicate in a remote mirroring configuration where there is a 1-to-1 relationship between source and target volumes. (Fan-in and fan-out are not to be confused with multi-target or cascading configurations though it may be possible to configure fan-in and fan-out layouts in those configurations.)

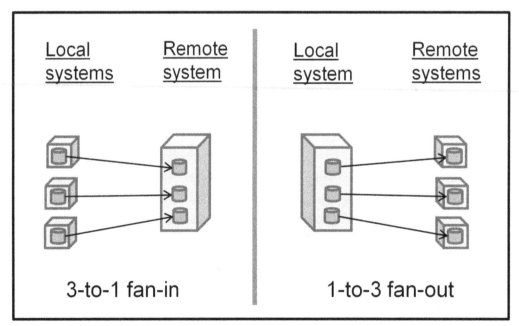

Examples of fan-in and fan-out.

Fan-in: Some storage systems support the ability for different secondary volumes in one remote storage system to each be paired with a primary volume where the primary volumes are located in up to n local systems. That is an n-to-1 fan-in capability from the remote system's point of view. A use case of fan-in is the ability to have a single (larger) storage system at a remote site serve as the recovery system for several (smaller) local storage systems located at different sites.

Fan-out: Some storage systems support the ability for different primary volumes in one local storage system to each be paired with a secondary volume where the secondary volumes are located in up to n remote systems. That is a 1-to-n fan-out capability from the local system's point of view. A use case of fan-out is when multiple local and remote systems are initially configured in 1-to-1 pairs and later the local systems are consolidated into fewer systems while the number of remote systems remains unchanged.

Tip: *Customers interested in fan-in and fan-out capability should ask vendors about the maximum number (n) of storage systems supported in each case. The number may vary based on whether a synchronous or asynchronous protocol is used. It may also vary depending on whether the configuration has only two sites or more sites.*

- Optimization for intra-system copy. In many storage systems, intra-system (point-in-time) copy and remote mirroring can be active at the same time for the same volume. Often, the two copy processes run independently which can lead to some operational issues. Consider the following scenario. A local storage system receives a command to make a point-in-time clone of a volume in that system and the target volume is remotely mirrored. Almost immediately after it receives the copy command, the local system responds that the copy operation is (logically) complete. However, the internal write I/O operations to actually populate the target occur after that and could take minutes to hours. Each of those internal write I/Os is propagated to the remote system as it occurs.

As a consequence, while applications can be using the local target, the remote system is unaware that a copy process is even occurring and just populates its copy over time from the individual writes it receives from the local system. This can complicate recovery operations in case of a failover because the local and remote systems are in different states. It may be difficult or time consuming for administrators to determine that let alone what to do about it. Also, the utilization of the local-remote communication link is increased due to propagating to the remote system each local system internal write I/O to the copy target.

Some storage system models are able to avoid the problem through an optimization that notifies the remote storage system of a copy command as soon as it is received by the local system. That is, the local system propagates the copy *command* similar to how it propagates write I/Os; of course, the remote system must recognize the command as such and handle it appropriately. This optimization results in the copy being logically complete on both systems at the same time, so both the local and remote copies are in the same state after a failover. (There is no need to coordinate the timing of how the physical copy processes separately proceed inside the two systems.) Moreover, the individual copy I/Os inside the local system no longer need to be propagated to the remote system because the remote system internally makes its own copy, thus reducing link utilization.

Tip: *Customers who want to run intra-system copy and remote mirroring against the same volumes should ask vendors how their storage system handles the situation. Whether the combination of features is supported at all for a given volume, as well as the way it is* *supported, may vary for different types of intra-system replication and different types of remote mirroring configurations.*

- <u>Optimization for storage tiering</u>. Automated storage tiering, discussed in the *Performance* chapter, relocates data across different drive tiers (i.e., groups of drives of similar speed) based on I/O activity to help optimize price-performance. In a remote mirroring configuration, the optimization may not occur in a coordinated way on local and remote systems. To see why, assume a 2-system remote mirroring configuration where the local and remote systems are configured identically. The remote system is normally unaware of local system read I/O activity and, therefore, normally would not make the same data relocation decisions as the local system. Thus, if there is a failover and the remote system must handle the I/O workload formerly handled by the local system, remote system performance may not be as good as it was in the local system for some time until the remote system relocates data based on I/O activity it monitors.

Some storage systems support the ability for local and remote systems in a remote mirroring configuration to communicate so changes to data locations in the local system made by an automated storage tiering function are made known to the remote system, avoiding the time and overhead it would otherwise take the remote system to optimize price-performance by relocating data after a failover. This proactive communications capability is most effective if the local and remote system drive configurations are the same.

- <u>RAID-like availability protection</u>. Some storage system remote mirroring features allow a remote system to cooperate with a local system to enhance data availability by a capability analogous to RAID protection. If a local drive becomes unusable, data can instead be read and written to a corresponding drive in the remote system, transparently to applications.

Tip: This capability was of most value in the days when RAID was not common in enterprise storage systems, while today RAID is nearly universally deployed in these systems. The value of this capability in contemporary RAID-protected storage systems may be small. In addition, if all I/Os to an unusable local drive must be forwarded to a remote drive, both read and write I/O performance from an application's point-of-view can degrade substantially. Moreover, the data on the remote drive must eventually be transmitted back to the local system once the failed local drive has been replaced.

- <u>Command forwarding over local-remote links</u>. Some remote mirroring features support the ability for users of a local storage system to submit commands to be sent to remote storage systems. The commands are issued to the local system which forwards them to the appropriate remote system over the same communication links the two systems use for remote mirroring. Without this capability, it might be necessary to have a local host connected to the remote storage system in a way required to issue commands (e.g., a channel path connection or Ethernet connection), or it might be necessary for someone at the remote site to issue commands to the remote system. The ability to issue commands to the remote system in this way may be limited to certain remote mirroring configurations and certain commands.

- <u>Management</u>. Inter-system replication may be managed by storage system facilities; those management facilities may be augmented by host-based software offerings. Examples of management functions are: reporting on remote mirroring activity, helping to preserve remote system data integrity during activities such as data resynchronization, helping with testing disaster recovery procedures, automating failover when certain conditions are detected, and coordinating host and storage failover. This kind of management assistance can help administrators be more productive and can help reduce human error. System-based management can be especially beneficial in the unlikely case an actual disaster occurs because storage administrators might not be available in a timely manner or might not be well-practiced in the procedures to follow.

Additional Tips

- *Remote mirroring is one of the most complex, costly, and important storage system capabilities. Therefore, it is prudent for a prospective customer to ask vendors to identify other customers using remote mirroring configurations in production in ways comparable to what the prospective customer plans to implement.*

- *Customers should determine whether any remote mirroring capabilities are required or recommended by relevant government and industry organizations.*

- *Some storage systems' remote mirroring features use considerable amounts of system cache. Customers should ask vendors about how their system's feature uses cache because significant use can negatively impact the performance of production work or can raise the cost of the system if additional cache needs to be configured to avoid performance problems.*

- *The price of a remote mirroring feature can vary among storage systems in various ways. Some storage systems include remote mirroring features as standard at no extra charge. Some storage systems support separate pricing for features based on synchronous protocols vs. features based on asynchronous protocols. Some storage systems require separate features for different types of hosts. Because of these pricing variations, it is generally best to consider a storage system's total acquisition and total ownership costs rather than making acquisition decisions based on comparing the prices of different storage systems' similar features in isolation. (Acquisition and ownership costs are discussed in the* Prices and Costs *chapter.)*

- *The cost of implementing and supporting remote mirroring can potentially be reduced in several ways. This list may not be complete.*

  o *The local and remote systems may not have to be identically configured. Some customers may find it acceptable for performance capabilities on the remote system to be less than on the production system if it is likely the remote system will be used only in a disaster situation and some performance reduction is deemed acceptable in such a (hopefully rare, if ever) situation. However, if DR testing is done by actually failing over to the remote site on occasion, it may be required that both sites support the same levels of performance.*

Remote system configurations that can potentially reduce costs compared to the local system include: a smaller cache, fewer but larger capacity drives, and RAID types that have lower capacity overhead than the RAID types configured on a local system.

Another possibility is not installing software features that would not be needed until some time after a failover, if they can be installed soon enough after that event. Or, a customer might negotiate with a vendor to let the customer install those features now, but delay charges until/unless they are used.

Another possibility is installing older storage systems at the remote site, perhaps by redeploying systems from production use to recovery use as they age and are replaced. Customers will want to be sure that any functional capabilities used on the local system are either supported by the (older) remote system or are expendable in case of a failover. It is also important to ensure that the vendor supports interoperation of the different generation systems; that includes both hardware and microcode considerations.

o *Space-efficiency techniques (such as compression or thin provisioning) that may not have been acceptable on the production system for performance reasons might be acceptable on the remote system. (Note: Unlike space-efficient techniques for making logical intra-system point-in-time copies that rely on storing only one copy of unchanged data blocks that reside on both the source and target volumes, in remote mirroring a single copy of duplicate data cannot be shared between local and remote storage systems because the copies reside on separate systems and a disaster may make the local storage system inaccessible.)*

o *Communication link costs can potentially be reduced by compressing data being transmitted. That may be supported by the storage systems or by communications equipment. (In some storage systems, data may be stored on media in a compressed form, but that does not necessarily mean that data is transmitted to a remotely mirrored system in compressed form.)*

o *Not all data may need to be remotely replicated. Being selective about which data is remotely replicated can reduce costs in these ways: (1) Communication costs may be reduced by needing fewer or slower links. (2) Some storage systems charge for replication feature licenses based on only the portion of storage system capacity that is being replicated. (3) Rather than continually transmitting all contents of a database, it may be acceptable to transmit only the transaction logs and apply them at the remote site to update database contents; this is sometimes called* log shipping.

o *Some storage systems use link bandwidth more efficiently than others. That efficiency can reduce the number or speed of needed communication links. For example, in their implementations of asynchronous protocols, some storage systems propagate write I/Os as soon as possible after they arrive at the local system if link bandwidth is available. However, other storage systems implement asynchronous protocols by collecting write I/O data temporarily in local cache or drives and transmitting that data only after fixed intervals of time. That can result in some available-but-unused link bandwidth so that users need faster or additional links to support a required level of data throughput. (Related issues are that delaying data propagation in this way can add to a system's cache or drive requirement and can also elongate best-case achievable RPO.)*

o *Some storage systems support native Ethernet connections for remote mirroring, potentially reducing communication costs compared to native Fibre Channel connections that may require additional communication equipment to convert the connections to Ethernet.*

o *Some customers create point-in-time copies of remote system data for use in testing DR procedures.[89] These copies require extra capacity in the remote system. One potential savings is to use a space-efficient copy technique to create the copy to be tested. Another potential savings is to test only subsets of the remote data at any one time. In addition, in some storage systems it may be possible to use the same capacity for both the test copy and the previously discussed "safety copy" (aka gold copy) needed to help protect remote site data integrity when local-remote data must be resynchronized.*

- *While it might seem efficient to use a remotely mirrored system to concurrently support both backup and DR, achieving this efficiency has challenges. DR favors maintaining current data while backup favors maintaining older data that predates problems such as accidental deletions of files or application bugs causing data corruption. One technology approach to addressing the issue is called* continuous data protection (CDP). *CDP maintains a history of all changes to data (back to some point-in-time, comparable in principle to database transaction logs) and thus supports a copy of current or near-current data as well as past point-in-time copies of data. To-date, however, CDP appears to have limited acceptance in the IT marketplace, especially as an alternative to facilities optimized for DR. In particular, CDP offerings may not support all the DR-related capabilities supported by storage system inter-system replication features. Other issues are the amount of capacity needed to hold changes and challenges in determining the appropriate point-in-time to restore data to.*

- *In some cases host-based replication can be more efficient than storage system-based replication. Unlike storage system-based replication, host-based replication may operate at an application level, e.g., maintain a remote copy of a specific file rather than all data on a volume or set of volumes. Host-based replication operates independently of a storage system and thus can provide a common approach that supports heterogeneous storage systems. On the downside, host-based replication uses host resources that can impact application performance. Storage system vendors may not suggest using host-based replication if their company does not sell it or it does not count towards their sales quota.*

---

[89] *One reason to test with a copy of data rather than testing using the remote data directly is to maintain active DR protection during the test. That avoids first suspending remote copy activity, performing a test, then resuming remote copy activity when testing is complete, a process that results in the remote data falling behind in currency. Another reason to do the testing on a copy is to allow write I/Os to the copy; if writes were issued directly to the remote data used for recovery that could cause it to lose synchronization with production data in a way that could not readily be undone.*

Security

An organization's ability to protect its assets against unauthorized access helps create a reputation that can attract and reassure customers, while helping to prevent situations that can damage that reputation and the assets themselves. No organization wants to be the subject of a news story that begins "Today, the 'WeTryToProtectAllYourStuff Company' acknowledged a major security breach…"

A significant aspect of the security of any organization is the security of its data and the storage that holds that data. Although there are multiple enterprise storage system capabilities that can help limit access to storage data and functions to authorized users only, those capabilities are often overlooked in the requirements organizations place on their storage systems. (Many data breaches occur through accessing servers via the Internet and through accessing point-of-sale devices. It might seem that enterprise storage systems are protected by being almost invisibly "behind" that equipment. However, there are many ways the contents of storage systems can potentially be exposed to unauthorized access – and many ways to protect against that.)

Concepts and Facilities

- <u>Physical security</u>. A starting point for storage system security is protecting access to associated physical equipment. An enterprise storage system, like physical IT assets in general, should be in a secure location and the doors to its cabinets should be locked with the key available to only appropriate personnel. Many enterprise storage systems are heavy refrigerator-size cabinets, but smaller systems might warrant protection against being carted away.

- <u>Security of data-at-rest</u>. Securing *data-at-rest* on drives is an important capability. The term *data-at-rest* is commonly used in the industry to distinguish data residing on storage media from data-in-use (such as data in host memory) or data-in-motion (such as data being transmitted over a network). Securing data-at-rest helps prevent unauthorized access to data in case drives are removed from a storage system (e.g., stolen or replaced after failing) or after an entire system is repurposed within an organization, transferred to another organization, decommissioned, or stolen.

An effective method to protect data-at-rest is to use *encryption*: encoding (i.e., translating) data in a controlled way to make it difficult – ideally, nearly impossible – to interpret (given current technologies). Encryption can use sophisticated algorithms to alter data based on a sequence of bits called a *key* so the true data (aka "data in the clear") cannot be identified unless the encrypted data is decrypted (i.e., decoded) using the same key or an algorithmically related key.[90] It is possession of the key(s), the length of the key(s), and the sophistication of the encryption algorithm that provides the security.

It is important to understand that data-at-rest encryption often applies to all data on a drive and so does not help control authorization to access individual data items such as named files when drives are used as intended. Applications normally view data in the clear because encryption/decryption is performed somewhere between the application and storage media unless an application specifically implements its own form of encryption, not usually the case. (Generally, authorizing users or applications to access specific data items – such as authority to read only selected files on a drive containing multiple files – is managed by means such as Unix-based filesystem permissions in a host or NAS storage system.)

There are two basic approaches to supporting data-at-rest encryption. A diagram follows the descriptions.

1) <u>Internal encryption</u>. Encryption is performed inside a storage system. This can be done in either of two ways. A storage system may use drives supporting full drive encryption (FDE, aka full disk encryption), also known as self-encrypting drives, produced by drive manufacturers. Or, a storage system may use its own encryption software running on processors on internal system controllers (such as a processor on a system's front-end host adapter).

2) <u>External encryption</u>. Encryption is performed by facilities outside the storage system. One approach is to use host-based software supporting encryption. Another approach is to use network equipment such as Ethernet or Fibre Channel switches supporting encryption.

---

[90] When speaking of encryption in this chapter, the ability of a facility to both encrypt and decrypt data is implied.

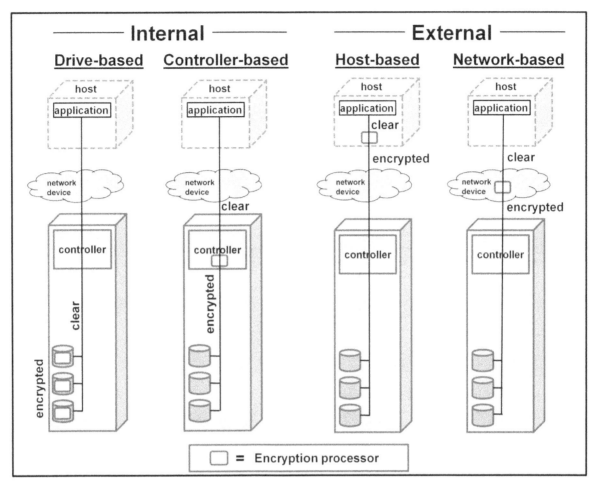

Two major approaches to encrypting data-at-rest, Internal and External, each with two variations, are shown. These approaches to encryption are compared by showing the different locations of the processors that perform the encryption/decryption function. The processors may be specialized for encryption or may also be used for other functions. In the diagram, data is in the clear only "above" the processors.

Tip: An advantage of the internal approach encryption is that it is an integrated part of the storage system. No host or network support for encryption may be required.

An advantage of the external approach to encryption is that the encryption facility may support different storage systems in a consistent way, including storage systems that do not have their own internal encryption capability. Another advantage is that data is encrypted not only on a storage system's drives, but everywhere inside the storage system (including in any nonvolatile memories such as cache), on the paths (cables) between the encryption device and the storage system, and over any remote mirroring communication paths. However, when enterprise storage systems reside in the same data center as the attached hosts, there is little benefit to encrypting data over host-to-storage paths; networking equipment supporting encryption can be used for remote mirroring environments.

Storage system encryption keys are managed by a facility called a *key manager* to help manage key creation, distribution, deletion, and recovery. A key manager may be internal software in the storage system or may be software that runs in an external host (or two external hosts for redundancy). An internal key manager may have the advantages of being simpler to use and possibly lower cost than an external key manager. An external key manager may have the advantages of an ability to centrally manage encryption keys for multiple, different IT devices (e.g., disk-based storage and tape storage) and the ability to house keys in different storage than in the storage system being encrypted.

Tip: Encryption can be a relatively complex capability to understand and implement. (For example, for security reasons implementations can involve encrypting the keys that are used to encrypt data-at-rest if those keys are transmitted over a network.) Customers may want to ask vendors what assistance or education they can provide beyond just selling the capability.

Tip: Customers interested in data-at-rest encryption should ask vendors questions such as the following:

Does the storage system support encryption of data-at-rest?

How strong is the encryption key? (As a point of reference, consider the U.S. government's National Institute of Standards and Technology NIST Special Publication 800-131A standard. Compliance with this NIST standard includes supporting a minimum specified key length for encrypted data, and more. Reference: http://csrc.nist.gov/publications/nistpubs/800-131A/sp800-131A.pdf.)

What is the granularity of capacity covered by a unique key? Does each drive have a unique key assigned to it, or are unique keys assigned to only groups of multiple drives? (If a group of drives are encrypted using the same key, then if one drive in the group is somehow decrypted, the entire group is exposed.)

Does the storage system support data-at-rest using internal system facilities or using external facilities in hosts or networks?

What is the performance impact of data-at-rest encryption during normal operations? Does performance vary based on the number of drives or the amount of I/O traffic?

If a storage system implements encryption using specialized (dedicated) processors, what is the performance impact if an encryption processor fails, even assuming data availability is protected by redundant processors?

What is the cost of the encryption capability for initial implementation and for storage system upgrades compared to the same system without encryption? Does that include the cost of an external key manager if needed or preferred?

What drive types are supported by self-encrypting drives in storage systems that use that approach to encryption?

Do configuration options allow for encrypting no drives, or all drives, or only a user-specified subset of drives?

If both compression and encryption are supported, in what order are they applied to data? (It is best to apply compression first because encrypted data generally appears as random bit patterns that may not be able to be compressed well.)

Must encryption be enabled when the storage system is first installed or can it be enabled later? If it can be enabled later, is that disruptive? (For example, encrypting data that is already stored but is not encrypted may not be directly supported if encryption capability is added to a system; instead, that data might need to be re-stored. Or, if a system supports encryption only through self-encrypting drives and such drives are not currently installed, non-self-encrypting drives would need to be replaced by self-encrypting drives.)

What key managers are supported? Does the key manager support the Key Management Interoperability Protocol (KMIP) standard for how encryption facilities and key management facilities can communicate? (Reference: http://en.wikipedia.org/wiki/Key_Management_Interoperability_Protocol)?

- <u>Secure data erasure</u>. The ability to intentionally erase data in a storage system, sometimes called *data sanitizing*, is an important security protection.[91] For business or legal or national security reasons, it can be necessary to ensure that all or selected data in a storage system has been securely erased. There are multiple methods that can help accomplish data erasure; combinations of methods may be used as an extra precaution.

  o *Erasing encrypted data (aka crypto(graphic) erase).* If data is encrypted, simply erasing the encryption key (e.g., deleting it from the key manager) is a fast way to effectively erase the data without having to take time and resources to physically erase the data. After data is cryptographically erased, anyone accessing the data would see only the encrypted data and would not have the key to decrypt it.

  o *Overwriting data.* Overwriting data erases it by replacing it with other data. This is sometimes called *data wiping* or *data shredding*. Overwriting typically replaces data with a meaningless bit pattern (such as all zero bits); overwriting data multiple times, possibly with different patterns, is called performing multiple *passes*. There is some controversy in the industry over the effectiveness of overwriting and the optimum number of passes.[92]

  If a drive has failed in a way that prohibits processing I/O commands, normal overwrite procedures do not work and other approaches to erasure, such as physical destruction of drives, would be necessary. Such procedures are still necessary due to the possibly of being able to access data stored in a "failed" drive. Searching the Web for *recover data*

---

[91] The U.S. National Institute of Standards and Technology (NIST) has published *Guidelines for Media Sanitation*, December 2014, available at http://nvlpubs.nist.gov/nistpubs/SpecialPublications/NIST.SP.800-88r1.pdf. The publication states: "Media sanitization refers to a process that renders access to target data on the media infeasible for a given level of effort. This guide will assist organizations and system owners in making practical sanitization decisions based on the categorization of confidentiality of their information."

[92] For example, see http://www.infosecisland.com/blogview/16130-The-Urban-Legend-of-Multipass-Hard-Disk-Overwrite.html and https://www.cs.auckland.ac.nz/~pgut001/pubs/secure_del.html. Some erasure programs support U.S. Department of Defense (DoD) standard 5220.22-M which recommends 3 passes of different bit patterns. However, the December 2014 U.S. National Institute of Standards and Technology (NIST) *Guidelines for Media Sanitation* (http://nvlpubs.nist.gov/nistpubs/SpecialPublications/NIST.SP.800-88r1.pdf) states "For storage devices containing magnetic media, a single overwrite pass with a fixed pattern such as binary zeros typically hinders recovery of data even if state of the art laboratory techniques are applied to attempt to retrieve the data."

from a failed HDD or *recover data from a failed SSD* finds articles on the subject and companies in business to help do that kind of data recovery.

Tip: *When using overwriting, it can be important to ensure* all *media locations are handled. That's because, although applications using standard read I/O requests would return only the data used to overwrite previously written data, specialized equipment might be able to access data in all locations, some of which are not visible to host software and would not have been overwritten. (The time and expense of using such equipment might be worthwhile to the "bad guys" if retrievable information is considered sufficiently valuable.)*

What media locations might be missed by a data overwrite procedure? An example is data in bad HDD sectors; bad sectors once contained good data, but applications see only the spare sectors that replaced them. Another example is storage where updated data is always written to a new location, rather than directly overlaying the data being updated, and the contents of the original location are not instantly erased. That could occur in storage systems using a log-structured file *design to manage how updates to data are handled; see* https://en.wikipedia.org/wiki/Log-structured_file_system.

o *Erasing residual data.* The way a host or storage system or storage device manages capacity for data can result in a user's request to delete data leaving it potentially accessible to other users. (This isn't a bug, but a consequence of the way capacity management is often designed, as will be explained.) The data remaining potentially accessible after the deletion operation is called *residual data.*

For example, consider block-access storage systems where host software assigns capacity within volumes to files created by users. The storage system itself is unaware of these files. When an authorized user issues a command to host software to delete a file, the host merely changes information it keeps in a table (e.g., a directory) in storage that identifies the names and locations of files that exist and the locations of unused capacity. The capacity the file occupied is made available to hold other files (perhaps after the "deleted" file is temporarily placed in a computer's "trash" or "recycle" bin for potential retrieval in case the user changes their mind). For all these actions, a storage system sees I/O requests but has no awareness of what the requests mean.

Here's the security problem: While a deleted file may no longer be accessible to users by name, the host may not erase the data in a deleted file in any way; that would take time and potentially degrade the performance of other work. If any portion of a deleted file's capacity is later assigned to a new file, the residual data in that capacity could potentially be accessed by users via standard read I/O commands, even if new users of the capacity were not authorized to access the deleted file. While this example is based on files in block-access storage, the principle could apply to entire volumes as well as to other data access types.

Various methods can help prevent unauthorized access to residual data. Which methods, if any, are supported varies by host software and storage system. A host or storage system may automatically overwrite a deleted file as part of the deletion process. Or, a storage system might overwrite (e.g., initialize with binary zeros) the contents of media locations assigned to a new file when it is created. Or, a storage system may not allow users to read data from unwritten locations in newly created data structures it is aware of; for example, if a new volume is created, attempts to read data at a location in the volume would not be allowed unless data had been written to that location since the time the volume was created.

Some host software and storage systems cooperate through interfaces allowing the host software to inform those storage systems of the storage locations of a deleted file the storage system would otherwise be unaware of. A storage system supporting such an interface could be designed to overwrite the data in the deleted file. (An additional benefit of that cooperation is supporting thin provisioning efficiency by making the storage system aware of now unused capacity so it can be reassigned to other uses.)

Tip: When a customer plans to repurpose or dispose of a storage system, including reselling it to another organization, the customer should ask the vendor whether any residual application data could exist in areas of the storage system reserved for system use and, if so, how that situation should be handled to protect data security. For example, some storage systems use dedicated internal drives or regions of capacity on customer-ordered drives to save data written to cache when there is a loss of external power to the system. Procedures to erase data by overwriting only storage locations accessible to users may not be able to overwrite data in areas reserved for system use.

Tip: For a broader discussion about residual data, see https://en.wikipedia.org/wiki/Data_remanence.

o *Physical destruction.* Techniques that physically destroy media or its contents can prevent unauthorized access to data in the media. (But note that, given the high bit densities of many storage devices, even a seemingly small piece of media could contain meaningful data.) One technique is to physically destroy individual (removed) drives or an entire storage system by crushing or incineration.[93] A technique that can physically erase magnetically stored data is *degaussing* (i.e., *demagnetizing*). Degaussing can be applied to HDDs because data in HDDs is stored as magnetic states. Degaussing cannot be applied to SSDs when data is not stored magnetically, such as in flash-based SSDs.

Tip: Some vendors offer tools and services to assist customers in securely erasing data. Vendors offering data erasure services may be able to provide customers with a certificate indicating the erasure procedure was successfully run. That may be useful for legal or regulatory purposes.

Tip: Because HDDs and SSDs are based on very different technologies, different technical considerations apply to ensuring all data is completely erased. Customers should consult their vendors for more information.[94]

---

[93] A video illustrating this technique is at https://www.youtube.com/watch?v=DUnSp87gSsM.

[94] *For an academic perspective see* http://cseweb.ucsd.edu/~swanson/papers/Fast2011SecErase.pdf.

- <u>Administrator security</u>. Administrators have significant control over a storage system. As an extreme example, an administrator might be able to erase all data from a storage system. Thus, system security warrants that, at a minimum, administrator access should require a userid and password.

Many storage systems support pre-defined administrator *roles* each of which identifies the specific tasks an administrator assigned that role is allowed to perform. For example, one administrator may be allowed to modify a storage system's logical configuration (e.g., create or delete volumes) while another administrator may be able to only view system status. Going beyond a few pre-defined roles created by the system manufacturer, some storage system models provide the flexibility for customers to define the specific actions a given administrator or host are allowed to take against a storage system, e.g., which commands can be entered against which volumes.

Some enterprise storage system models maintain administrator information in a directory inside the storage system; in that case the information may need to be manually entered into the internal directory of each storage system. To reduce that complexity, some storage systems support an external directory accessed through the industry-standard Lightweight Directory Access Protocol (LDAP, pronounced "l-dap," rhyming with "map").[95] A directory supporting the LDAP protocol can be shared among storage systems, servers, and applications supporting that protocol and communicating over a network with the LDAP server managing that directory. Of course, if a shared external directory is used, customers should take actions to protect *its* security.

Tip: After a storage system is installed, administrators' userids and passwords should be changed from any default values that ship with new storage systems. Those defaults may be public knowledge (among the technical community). Administrator userids and passwords should be managed with the same precautions commonly recommended for Internet users such as long passwords that are changed periodically and not easily guessed.

- <u>Vendor security</u>. Vendor representatives may need to access a storage system for tasks such as hardware upgrades, microcode upgrades, and problem management. (In some cases, upgrades are performed by the customer and in some cases upgrades are performed by the vendor.) In some cases, vendor access to a storage system is on-site and in other cases over a network.

Here are examples of relevant security controls that could be implemented: Customers can ensure on-site system access is limited to authorized vendor representatives who show credentials demonstrating who they are. On-site vendors could be accompanied by customer personnel (e.g., a storage administrator). Access to vendor-oriented (console) system interfaces should require an authentication method, e.g., entering a password, perhaps limited in time and known only to the vendor. Customers may want to ensure that vendors cannot access sensitive customer-generated data, e.g., that such data is not transmitted to the vendor over a network without explicit customer permission.

---

[95] Reference: https://en.wikipedia.org/wiki/Lightweight_Directory_Access_Protocol.

- Network security. Storage systems may connect to multiple networks. That raises the risk of network traffic possibly being intercepted (or inserted) by unauthorized parties, e.g., a man-in-the-middle attack[96]. Host-storage connections over cables in the same data center, such as a block-access storage system connecting to hosts via a Fibre Channel SAN entirely in the same building, generally have low risk of being compromised. Other networks may be more vulnerable. For example, enterprise storage systems may communicate over WAN networks with administrators (e.g., for system management via a browser-based interface), with host-resident management software (e.g., device managers and encryption key servers), and with vendors (e.g., to "call home" in case of system problems or to download new microcode). If these networks could potentially be accessed by unauthorized parties, data should be secured during transmission, e.g., by using encryption.

- Host authorization to access storage. Controlling which hosts can access which storage systems is another important security consideration. This discussion focuses on facilities that apply to SAN-attached block-access storage to illustrate issues involved.

  One simple (and perhaps obvious) form of security is to not configure physical paths between hosts and storage systems for hosts that should not access that storage. However, it is common that multiple hosts can access and share (parts of) multiple storage systems and security in such cases needs further consideration.

  Many Storage Area Network (SAN) devices for block-access storage support *zoning*, the ability for a SAN switch to be configured by an administrator to specify which hosts and which storage systems connected to that switch can communicate with each other by being defined to reside in the same zone. Sharing fewer switches may cost less than installing a higher number of switches. (If a host and storage system are connected by direct paths without an intermediate SAN switch, the situation is similar to the host and storage being defined to be in the same SAN zone.)

  To provide more granular security protection than zoning by controlling which volumes in a shared block-access storage system can be accessed by which hosts, many block-access storage systems support *LUN masking*.[97] LUN masking is important when multiple hosts can access the same storage system, but should not be accessing each others' volumes. (Note that some host operating systems support the ability for a host administrator to identify which storage systems the host is allowed to access, a facility comparable to storage system-based LUN masking, but possibly not under the control of a storage administrator.) Zoning and LUN masking are illustrated below.

---

[96] Reference: https://en.wikipedia.org/wiki/Man-in-the-middle_attack.

[97] "LUN" stands for Logical Unit Number. A LUN is how (logical) volumes are identified in I/O requests in the SCSI I/O protocol for block-access storage. The SCSI protocol is supported by Fibre Channel Protocol (FCP), by Fibre Channel over Ethernet (FCoE), and by iSCSI.

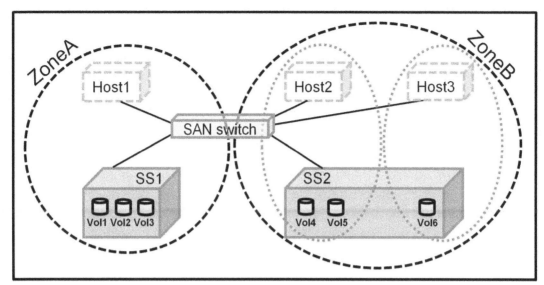

Host1, Host2, Host3, and storage systems SS1 and SS2, are all connected via the same SAN switch. An administrator has configured the switch to support two zones, ZoneA and ZoneB, so that SS1 can be accessed by only Host1 while SS2 can be accessed by only Host2 and Host3. Through LUN masking configured by an administrator for SS2 (and shown as two vertical ellipses in ZoneB), only Host2 can access volumes Vol4 and Vol5; only Host3 can access Vol6.

Tip: *Host-based facilities to help protect storage system security can be an important extension to storage system-based security facilities. For example, a block-access storage system may support LUN masking to identify which hosts connected to the system can access which logical volumes in the system. However, a block-access storage system does not provide a way to manage the security aspects of how different applications on the same host access the volumes the host is allowed to access. Not every application may warrant being allowed to read or write to every file on every accessible volume. This more granular security can be provided by facilities such as host-based software designed for that purpose, e.g., the "permission" facility in Unix-based file systems. These facilities may go further than a simple "yes" or "no" level of access control; for example, a given application may be allowed to only read certain files, only update certain files, and not access other files at all.*

- Protection against malware. Some storage systems internally use commercially available operating systems (such as Linux and Windows) that may be the targets of computer malware including viruses; those operating systems might be used in the main storage system or in integrated management consoles (aka service processors). Administrators can sometimes access storage system management facilities through personal computers or mobile devices via the Internet. Therefore, it is important that these storage systems and devices for accessing management facilities be protected against malware (such as key loggers that could transmit userids and passwords to unintended parties).

Tip: *Customers should ask their vendors whether proposed storage systems include commercial software known to be a target for malware. If so, the vendor should be asked: What steps are taken to ensure that software and fixes are shipped to customers free of*

*malware? What steps does the storage system take to prevent penetration by malware?
What steps should customers take to prevent storage system penetration by malware?*

- <u>Read-only data</u>. Some storage system models support the ability to designate all data or selected data (e.g., a given volume) as read-only. (The phrase *write-once, read-many (WORM)* is often used to describe such storage.) Some host-based facilities also support this kind of control.   Designating data as read-only can be important for archiving or regulatory purposes.

- <u>System change auditability</u>. Even a small change to a system's logical or physical configuration can have a significant impact on system operation, including changing its security characteristics (e.g., by changing an administrator's authority) or even causing loss of data (e.g., deleting a volume). Therefore, it is important that a storage system support an auditing facility that identifies the history of administrator and vendor activities on a system including for each activity: what action was performed, who did it, and when the action occurred. The system's log of activities should be protected against modification.

Additional Tips

- *If a (failed) drive is removed from a storage system by the vendor (or other service provider), the vendor may normally keep the drive. Some customers want to retain any drives removed from a storage system so they can track the location of those drives and destroy them if desired, for security and audit purposes. Interested customers should ask their vendor whether that can be arranged.*

- *Some types of applications have associated industry organizations that publish recommended or required standards for protecting application security including the security of stored data. An example is the Payment Card Industry (PCI) PCI Security Standards Council (https://www.pcisecuritystandards.org/). Customers should ask vendors whether their storage systems support, or enable the customer to comply with, the standards of relevant organizations.*

- *Some customers may want to restrict how a vendor can access a storage system over a network, e.g., for uploading diagnostic information or for downloading microcode fixes into the storage system. That can be discussed with the vendor, including how support the vendor normally provides over a network might be handled in alternative ways.*

- *Customers may want their vendors to ensure that any data transmitted by the storage system to the vendor cannot include customer-created data. For example, if a system error occurs and data is transmitted to the vendor for analysis, customers may want to ensure the storage system is designed so the transmitted data does not include customer-created data.*

- *Customers should consider asking storage vendors whether they are aware of any security breaches other customers have experienced for proposed storage systems. Similarly, customers should consider asking whether storage systems being proposed have any known security issues or exposures the customer should be aware of.*

Physical (Hardware) Configuration Management

The saying "one size fits all" definitely does not apply to enterprise storage systems. There are many storage system models with significantly different capabilities available for customers to choose from.

While a storage system's capabilities depend on both its hardware and software, hardware is often the most visible, and certainly the most tangible, aspect of a system. Many system models can be customized to support different *physical configurations* (aka *hardware configurations*) of components to meet different customer needs.

Concepts and Facilities

- Flexibility. Customers sometimes state they want a storage system to be "flexible" without clarifying what they mean. In this Guide, a storage system is flexible to the extent it supports the ability of customers to define and modify its configuration to meet their needs.[98]

  Physical configuration flexibility includes a customer's ability to select hardware component attributes such as: the number of components of a particular type, component speed, and component capacity. Flexibility can include the ability to modify (i.e., add or change or replace) components over time. Flexibility is not unlimited, but applies within the constraints of the hardware and software supported by a given system model.

- Customer vs. vendor installation. Some storage systems are installed or upgraded with new features by vendor personnel. Some systems are installed or upgraded by the customer (aka customer set-up); in that case, vendors may offer to optionally perform the installation or upgrade for a fee.

  Customer set-up can potentially reduce vendor's internal costs and, in turn, system prices, if it allows vendors to hire fewer personnel. However, unless the process is relatively quick and infrequent, customer set-up can take time from other work customer personnel might do. Unless the process is very simple there is a risk of human error, especially if the process is rarely performed by the customer.

- Upgrades and replacements. Some storage system models support hardware upgrades, meaning selected components in the system can be added or enhanced.

---

[98] Sometimes the terms *agile and agility* are used instead of *flexible* and *flexibility.*

An important consideration is whether an upgrade can be done completely *nondisruptively,* meaning all system capabilities remain intact during the upgrade procedure, or whether, instead, the procedure temporarily degrades some or all of a system's capabilities. A related consideration is whether an upgrade can be done with data remaining in place or whether, instead, some of all data must be relocated (at least temporarily) either to different drives in the same system or even to another storage system.

When an entire storage system is replaced by a new system and data from the old system is migrated to the new system, that is sometimes called a *forklift upgrade.*

Tip: Customers should ask vendors to clarify what they mean by "upgrade." A vendor might claim a system can be upgraded, but that might mean only that the system could be replaced by a more capable compatible system in the same family. In particular, if a proposed or installed system is configured with its maximum supported components, the only upgrade path is to add another system or replace it with a more capable system, if available.

Tip: Customers should ask vendors to clarify what they mean by claiming an upgrade procedure is "nondisruptive." Even if access to data remains undisrupted during an upgrade procedure, sometimes a system capability may be temporarily degraded during the procedure, a situation many customers would consider to be a form of disruption. Examples include a degraded ability to access function, protect system availability, or meet performance goals. Any such issues could affect the time the customer prefers to schedule the upgrade. Customers should also ask how long the upgrade is expected to take and consider what actions they can take if an upgrade takes longer than planned. As a best practice and to minimize any impact on the organization should problems arise, upgrades should preferably be scheduled for periods of low or no storage system activity.

- Scalability. A key attribute of physical configuration flexibility is how storage system hardware components can *scale:* how the system can be modified by adding components or increasing component capability. Examples include adding more drives and increasing cache size by replacing parts. Various terms are used by vendors to discuss types of hardware scaling such as *scale-up, scale-out, scale-deep, elastic scaling, horizontal scaling,* and *vertical scaling.* These terms may not always be used consistently in the industry. There are two forms of scaling frequently cited by vendors and users.

  - Scale-up (aka vertical scaling): This is the ability to add more components or increase component capability in one storage system. Which components can be scaled-up can vary by system model. The components may be added into existing cabinets if empty space is available, or may be added into additional cabinets connected (wired) to existing cabinets.

○ <u>Scale-out (aka horizontal scaling)</u>: This is the ability to connect multiple storage systems together to form a larger system (sometimes called a *grid* or *cluster*).[99]   The multiple storage systems communicate/cooperate with each other.

The following diagram illustrates and contrasts scale-up and scale-out:

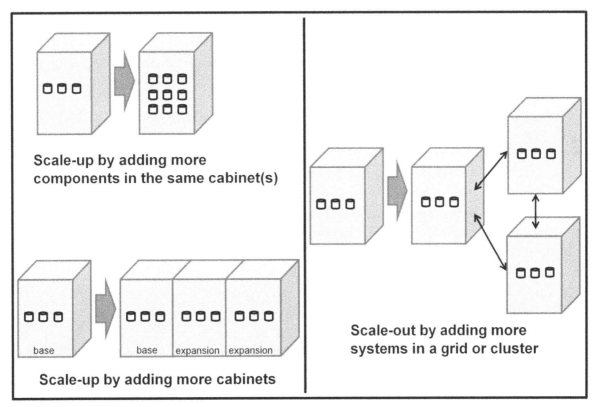

Examples of scale-up and scale-out configurations to add more drives to a storage system. In each case the system starts with three drives and grows to nine drives. Only internal drive components are shown.

Both scale-up and scale-out preserve the property that the storage system remains a single system from a management and data access point of view. For example, physical capacity remains a single pool potentially shareable among hosts; a file-access (NAS) system retains a single namespace.

A given storage system model may support scale-out, or scale-up, or both, or neither capability. Some storage systems have been described as scale-out when major internal components that work together are comparable to individual storage systems even though the components could not be acquired as independent systems, may reside inside a shared cabinet, and the system is upgradable by adding those components over time in a scale-up fashion.

---

[99] There does not appear to be widespread agreement on the definition of these terms, or how they are distinguished. They are often used when separate storage systems (or hosts) communicate/cooperate with each other. However, sometimes the terms may be applied even to a storage system in a single cabinet if it consists of multiple controllers of different types that work together. It's also possible these terms might be used for marketing purposes to add cachet to a system's description.

Neither type of scaling is necessarily better than the other. What matters most is whether a system's overall attributes meet a customer's requirements, including that the system can scale to meet initial and projected needs. Another important consideration is whether upgrading a particular system to increase its scale is nondisruptive or temporarily disruptive; if disruptive, for how long and in what way (such as temporarily degraded performance).

While at first glance they may not seem to be examples of scaling, the technologies of *virtual storage* and *federated storage* can provide some interoperability among separate systems so they act like single systems in some ways. (See the *Architecture* chapter and *Logical (Software) Configuration Management* chapter.)

For completeness, it should be mentioned that unless floor space or power is at a maximum limit, customers usually have the option to scale their storage environment by adding additional, independent storage systems. There may be no practical limit to this form of scaling other than physical space and energy to support the systems.

- Granularity. A storage system attribute related to scalability is component *granularity*. The granularity of a component is the increments in number or capacity in which that component can be ordered or upgraded. Granularity is important because it can impact initial system and future upgrade costs. Granularity often applies to front-end ports, cache, back-end ports, and drives. For example, a given storage system model may support adding drives of a given type in only increments of eight to match a built-in RAID group size.

- Component types and combinations. Another form of physical configuration flexibility is the ability to support – and, sometimes, to mix – different types of similar components in the same storage system. Examples include:

  1. Configuring a block-access system with a combination of Fibre Channel and Ethernet ports to connect to hosts

  2. Configuring a system with HDDs of different speeds and capacities

  3. Configuring a system with both HDDs and SSDs, sometimes called a *hybrid* configuration

Tip: *Some storage system designs limit the combinations of components that can be installed. That reduces configuration flexibility for both the initial configuration and future upgrades. To illustrate:*

o *Assume a storage system supports up to eight host ports. Host ports must be ordered at a granularity of four ports of the same type and three types of host ports are supported (say, Fibre Channel, Ethernet, and InfiniBand). In this case, a given system can have no fewer than four ports of one type, no more than eight ports of one type, and at most only two types of ports with four ports of each type.*

o *Assume a storage system is designed with a fixed number of internal slots where each slot can hold one of two types of adapter cards. One type of adapter card supports front-end ports to hosts and the other type supports back-end ports to drives. System specifications might cite a maximum value for each type of adapter card (say, up to 16 each), yet the system has fewer total slots (say, 24) than needed to support the maximum number of both types of adapter cards at the same time.*

- <u>Floor and rack space flexibility</u>. An important physical configuration consideration is the amount of space a storage system requires on a floor or in a rack. There are multiple attributes customers and vendors should consider.

  Some storage systems are housed in vendor-supplied or customer-supplied industry-standard 19-inch racks while other systems require vendor-supplied floor-standing cabinets of other sizes.[100] Some storage systems consist of small drawer-size enclosures that can be housed in customer-supplied 19-inch racks along with other equipment in the same rack, promoting efficient use of rack space.

  The capacity per unit of floor space, e.g., terabytes per square foot or per square meter, is important to help customers support their capacity requirements in environments with floor space constraints. Some storage systems support a variety of capacities for a given drive module form factor. Higher capacity per module can increase capacity supported per unit of floor space, while generally reducing the cost per unit of capacity. However, higher capacities per module may increase the I/Os per second a module must support, potentially stressing its performance capabilities. (A system supporting automated storage tiering can help in that situation by allowing customers to configure a mix of drives of different speeds and capacities where the system automatically relocates data to appropriate drives based on data activity.)

  A related consideration is incremental floor or rack space requirements: minimum space, maximum space, and the increment of space required for each additional cabinet. A physical configuration flexibility supported by some storage systems and useful in environments with limited physically contiguous floor space is the ability to place different cabinets of the same storage system physically dispersed from each other (up to a supported maximum distance apart) rather than only physically adjacent to each other.

  Another related floor and rack space consideration is the maximum distance supported between the storage system, hosts, and network equipment. For cabling under the floor or through the ceiling, segments of vertical distance contribute to the overall distance.

  It is important to distinguish the physical space occupied by enclosures during normal system operation with enclosure doors closed, and the area needed when doors must be opened during installation and maintenance. That latter area is called "service clearance." The clearance areas needed by adjacent systems can potentially overlap.

  The weight of cabinets and racks also needs to be considered. The floor that cabinets and racks will sit on must be designed to be able to support their weight as it will be distributed on the floor. The weight of individual large storage system cabinets can be as high as a few thousand pounds (over 1,000 kilograms).

---

[100] Information about the history of 19-inch racks and the specifications of such racks is at https://en.wikipedia.org/wiki/19-inch_rack.

Tip: Storage systems requiring cabinet sizes other than industry-standard 19-inch racks may not fit, efficiently or at all, in floor space areas previously occupied by other systems.

Tip: Several strategies can potentially reduce floor space needed by reducing the number of HDD or SSD modules needed. (1) Using higher capacity drives to support the usable capacity requirement. The feasibility of this strategy can be increased by reducing I/O traffic to back-end drives by using a larger storage system cache, a larger host-side cache, or larger host-side filesystem and database buffer pools. (2) Using RAID-5 or RAID-6, rather than RAID-1 or RAID-10. (3) Using capacity optimization techniques such as compression and deduplication. (4) Replacing multiple, short-stroked HDDs by fewer SSDs. (5) Deleting obsolete data. (6) Archiving data that needs to be saved to tape.

Tip: It is important for site structural engineers and vendor installation planning personnel to work together to ensure heavy equipment can be safely delivered from a loading dock all the way to its final location on a data center floor. Some storage system vendors support options to reduce the weight of shipped cabinets, allowing the assembly of heavy cabinets to be completed at their final location.

- <u>Energy use</u>. Efficient use of energy has become increasingly important around the world. The ability of a storage system to help minimize energy use (for power and cooling) can be of immense value.

  Some governments support programs to promote or verify energy efficiency. An example is the U.S. government's ENERGY STAR program; see https://www.energystar.gov/. ENERGY STAR international partners are identified at
  http://www.energystar.gov/index.cfm?c=partners.intl_implementation.

  The Storage Networking Industry Association (SNIA) runs the SNIA Emerald Program (http://www.snia.org/emerald) that publishes the results of a test of a storage system's energy use. Emerald is part of SNIA's Green Storage Initiative (http://www.snia.org/forums/green).

  Tip: System attributes and customer strategies that promote efficient use of energy include the following. (This list may not be complete):

  o *Support for* hot aisle / cold aisle *data center layouts. These layouts help support efficient airflow.*[101]

  o *Support for 3-phase power. This is more energy-efficient than single-phase power, but can be costly to install. It is often used by larger data centers. Some storage systems support both power options.*[102]

---

[101] Reference:
https://www.energystar.gov/index.cfm?c=power_mgt.datacenter_efficiency_hotcold_aisles.

[102] Reference: https://en.wikipedia.org/wiki/Three-phase_electric_power.

o *Support for strategies mentioned above that can help save floor/rack space by reducing the number of drives, especially HDDs. These strategies can also save energy. Repeating them here and adding to the list: (1) Using higher capacity drives to support the usable capacity requirement. Capacity-optimized drives generally use less energy than performance-optimized drives. The feasibility of this strategy can be increased by reducing I/O traffic to back-end drives by using a larger storage system cache, a larger host-side cache, or larger host-side filesystem and database buffer pools. (2) Using RAID-5 or RAID-6, rather than RAID-1 or RAID-10. (3) Using capacity optimization techniques such as compression and deduplication. (4) Replacing multiple, short-stroked HDDs by fewer SSDs. (5) Deleting obsolete data. (6) Archiving data that needs to be saved to tape. (7) Using SSDs (to at least some extent) rather than HDDs. (8) Using a storage system that supports spin-down of idle HDDs if there is an extensive amount of low-use data that must be online in HDDs; this capability is sometimes called a* Massive Array of Idle Disks *(MAID).*[103]

- Host port type flexibility. Some storage systems support the ability to change one host port type to another type without a change in hardware. This is a rarely supported capability. One requirement is that the physical port connections (e.g., the size and shape of the plug) are the same for the different types of ports – the difference is in the microcode that supports the protocol used by the ports. An example of this flexibility is a storage system that allows a host port to be reconfigured in-place between Fibre Channel and FICON (which use the same cables and connectors but different software-driven protocols). This is useful if a customer plans to migrate hosts or applications between IBM z Systems mainframes and other types of hosts while attaching all those hosts to the same storage system.

- Support for restrictions on hazardous substances. Multiple jurisdictions have implemented or are evaluating policies restricting the sale of electronics equipment, including computer storage systems, containing various hazardous substances. For example, the Restriction of Hazardous Substances Directive (RoHS, pronounced "row'-hahs") is a policy adopted by the European Union (EU) that restricts the use of lead, mercury, and several other substances in electronics equipment. Storage system manufacturers are motivated to comply with such policies to help maximize their market. Customers should ask their vendors whether systems of interest comply with pertinent policies.[104]

- Software licenses. The last aspect of physical configuration flexibility discussed here is licensed software features. In the context of physical configuration, this discussion is about how licensed software features are configured *as* system features, not about the functional capabilities of the software features.

---

[103] "Online storage systems are designed to be on all the time and use approximately 80% of their peak energy capacity while simply idling their spinning drives." Source:
https://www.energystar.gov/about/content/data-center-storage-products-earn-energy-star-certification.

[104] For more information see
https://en.wikipedia.org/wiki/Restriction_of_Hazardous_Substances_Directive.

Licensed software features are configured in ways that vary by storage system model. Some licensed software features may be required for system operation while others are optional. Some licensed software features may be included in a system as standard at no extra charge, while others may be priced. Some licensed software features may be installed in the initial system shipped from the factory or later installed as a system upgrade at a customer's site. Some licensed software features may be pre-installed in a storage system and enabled after system installation by a vendor-provided key if and when they are licensed by a customer. Some licensed software features may require that other software or hardware features also be installed; the other required features are sometimes called *prerequisites*.

Additional Tips

- *Some storage systems bundle multiple components together so that a set of components (such as host ports, processors, cache, and back-end ports) always come together with limited, if any, flexibility for customers to more precisely select the combination of components they need. The problem is that not all storage environments need the same combination of hardware components. Examples: (1) Applications needing more capacity for data do not necessarily also need more internal storage system processing power. (2) When a customer needs to install another host port or two to connect a storage system to another host, they do not necessarily also need more system cache.*

  The number of such bundles that can be installed in a given system may vary. Adding more bundles supports physical scaling, but does not eliminate the inflexibility of component bundling.

- *While a given storage system may support a high degree of hardware configuration flexibility at the time it is being evaluated, customers should ask vendors about their policies for making customers aware of plans to discontinue selling hardware upgrades for the system such as additional drives. Vendors may make such plans as older systems age significantly and there is no business case to continue to manufacture new or replacement parts.[105] Or, perhaps the manufacturer wants to motivate customers of the older systems to migrate to newer system models. Regardless of the reason, how much notice will the vendor give before upgrades to a storage system model are no longer available?*

---

[105] *The decision to discontinue support for various upgrades is not always under direct control of a storage system manufacturer. Sometimes, the supplier of an internal system component decides to no longer make that component. For example, that often occurs as drives of a given capacity and speed are made obsolete by faster or higher capacity drives and demand for the older drives decreases too much to warrant continued manufacture.*

Logical (Software) Configuration Management

As soon as a customer installs a storage system, the quality of its operation, especially from the point-of-view of system users, depends greatly on how well the customer's IT organization manages the system. That includes planning, implementing, monitoring, and adjusting the system over time.

A significant aspect of storage system management applies to a system's *logical configuration*. The logical configuration can be thought of as a layer of software-based function that conceptually "sits above" the system's hardware components and provides management interfaces for administrator use. Managing the logical configuration involves managing system parameter settings that affect how the system is accessed from the perspective of applications, hosts, and administrators. Examples of logical configuration items include the number and capacity of individual logical volumes, the authorities different administrators have over system operation, and how system software functions should behave under various conditions.

Storage systems with a logical configuration that is easier to manage can mean smoother operation as well as reduced administrator time and effort. A logical configuration that is more difficult to manage can mean uneven operation, more user complaints, and, as a result, increased scrutiny of the IT organization by upper management. This chapter focuses mainly on the area of *ease-of-management* (aka *ease-of-use*) of logical storage system configurations, a significant subset of storage system management.[106]

Concepts and Facilities

- Flexibility. Customers sometimes state they want their storage systems to be "flexible" without clarifying what they mean. As previously mentioned, a storage system is flexible (or agile) to the extent it supports the ability of customers to define and modify its configuration to meet their needs. That flexibility is not unlimited; storage system flexibility applies within the constraints of the hardware and software that compose a system model. Logical configuration flexibility, in particular, refers to a customer's ability to initially determine and later adjust a system's logical configuration.

---

[106] This focus omits a number of other storage management topics that, while certainly important, are beyond the scope of this Guide. One example is managing backups. Another example is reporting on how various storage system resources are used, an area addressed by storage resource management (SRM) software products.

- <u>Ease-of-management is relative</u>. Storage system management is rarely, if ever, *easy*. All storage systems require some manual time, effort, and skills to manage. Ease-of-management is a relative consideration – some systems are easier to manage than others.

A sometimes heard administrative complaint is that a given storage system model is difficult to manage. Management complexity generally correlates to the amount of installed capacity, the number and complexity of system functions that are not self-managing, the number of systems to manage, and the number of servers, users, and applications to support. All those factors can grow over time as organizations grow.

It is important that ease-of-management items be included in a customer's storage system requirements rather than being left to chance or to taking broad marketing claims about ease-of-use at face value (considering it's unlikely any vendor has ever claimed their system is not easy to manage). Evaluating storage system ease-of-management can be challenging, however, because ease-of-management is not a single, easily identifiable storage system attribute. (No storage system appears to have an orderable feature such as #Sys123456_Ease_ of_Management.) In practice, it is a system attribute that usually must be considered case-by-case for the deployment and ongoing use of different storage system features. There are no industry standards for measuring ease-of-use, at least not in a quantified way, though some ways to compare relative ease-of-use are discussed below.

Tip: Once a vendor mentions a system function a customer is interested in, the customer should consider asking: How easy is it to implement and manage? What management challenges do existing users of the function have to deal with? In addition to a vendor's answers, insights may be provided by the customer's own administrators' experiences as well as by the experiences of other customers.

Tip: Ease-of-use increases when a function is designed in ways that reduce management complexity. The following list identifies a few general ways function design can increase ease-of-use. (Additional ways are identified later in this chapter.) Note that these points are indicative of relative ease-of-use.

- *Ease-of-use increases as the number of steps (e.g., the number of mouse clicks) required for a given procedure decreases. For example, some implementations of dynamic volume expansion, a nondisruptive way to increase a volume's capacity, automatically add a requested increment of capacity to a volume in a single step, while other implementations require that an administrator first create a new volume of the incremental size then concatenate that new volume to the original volume.*

- *Ease-of-use increases as the time a step or procedure takes decreases. One reason is that a step that completes quickly keeps administrator attention, enabling rapid transition to the next step in a sequence.*

- *Ease-of-use increases as storage system documentation (such as user guides and white papers) increases in comprehensibility. As part of storage system evaluation, administrators might be asked to rate a few segments of storage system documentation in terms of readability.*

o *Ease-of-use increases as the degree of automation increases. Avoiding manual time-and-effort to manage a storage system or particular function may be the ultimate way to support ease-of-use (assuming a customer is satisfied with the way automation is implemented). A deeper discussion of automation is the next topic.*

- Automation. The more automated function a storage system supports, the less manual time-and-effort administrators need for activities such as provisioning capacity to users, tuning performance, maximizing availability, and handling problems. Automation can also reduce the chance for human error.

  A system or feature with automated operation is sometimes said to be *autonomic*. Another often-used term is *self-managing*. Specific areas where self-management may apply include *self-healing* (to help support high levels of availability), *self-tuning* (to help support high levels of performance), and *self-optimizing* (to help support efficient use of system resources).

  Automation in enterprise storage systems is rarely if ever comprehensive. To-date, these systems may all require some amount of human management, meaning time and effort and skill are needed.

  Tip: *The extent to which a given storage system function is automated can vary. Consider the following functions in order of decreasing ease-of-use.*

  o *A function that is fully automated and never needs administrator time and effort. This applies to many cache management algorithms and to handling many types of system failures.*

  o *A function that can be set up once and is automated thereafter, where the function is simple to set up. For example, a single system parameter may merely need to be set to "on."*

  o *A function that can be set up once and is automated thereafter, where the function is complex to set up. The function might require complex administrator-written scripts or might have numerous system parameters to manage. Administrators may need good technical skills, possibly a good understanding of the application environment, and be diligent in documenting scripts and rationales for parameter choices.*

  o *A function that must be manually invoked, but is easy to use and used infrequently.*

  o *A function that must be manually invoked, but is difficult to use and used frequently.*

  Tip: *Customers should not assume that just because a function is automated it works efficiently.*

  For example, many storage system cache management algorithms are automated, but the algorithms in different systems can vary significantly in efficiency. In particular, the effectiveness of prefetching data for sequential read I/Os can vary by system. The ability to efficiently use cache capacity (and thus help support high hit ratios) can vary by system.

As another example, some storage systems support drive rebalancing, a technique to potentially improve I/O performance by relocating data on (a subset of) drives to improve the use of system resources. Some systems invoke rebalancing automatically while others invoke rebalancing only by administrator command. Some storage systems rebalance the I/O load (i.e., drive performance utilization) across a set of drives to optimize performance, while other systems rebalance only the amount of data stored on each drive (i.e., drive capacity utilization) which can leave some drives very busy while other drives are less busy. Some storage systems can rebalance more types of data than other systems (e.g., not all block-access storage systems may support rebalancing for both thick and thin volumes). The point is, while automation can be an important ease-of-management attribute, the quality and capabilities of a function being automated must be considered as well.

Tip: *When determining requirements and comparing systems, customers should consider which is more important to them: A higher degree of built-in automation or a higher degree of customer-managed customization.*

Vendors offering storage systems supporting a higher degree of automation may highlight that attribute as supporting more ease-of-management, while vendors offering storage systems with less automation may highlight the ability of administrators to manually customize the system to their specific environment. How effective an automated function is at supporting different environments, so that customization is either not needed or can be kept to a minimum, depends on the implementation.

Some administrators may prefer manual management (aka do it yourself, DIY) over automation. They may prefer to manually control at least some storage system functions rather than let the system automate them "under the covers" even for functions that could be automated. While some administrators may have the technical skills to do a good job at what may be micro-management, customers should determine whether that applies to their IT staff, whether micro-management is a good use of their staff's time and effort, and whether there is worthwhile if any benefit to the organization of that approach to storage management, especially considering that automated management capabilities supported by many contemporary storage systems have been increasingly optimized over time.

Consider an example. When different speeds of drives were first able to be intermixed in the same storage system, administrators manually moved data (such as volumes) among them to try to optimize price/performance by putting the most active data on the fastest drives. Many modern storage systems go further by supporting automated storage tiering (aka auto-tiering) that automatically relocates data at a granular (e.g., subvolume) level across different speed drives based on I/O activity over short periods of time (typically a few minutes or hours). This can provide superior system price/performance compared to the capabilities and reaction times of a human administrator. Some storage systems support auto-tiering with a high degree of automation and minimal customization needed. Other implementations of auto-tiering support a significant degree of customization that can require a good deal of administrator time and effort. Another alternative is to not use auto-tiering features but, instead, manually place data on desired drives. Which approach or combination of approaches is preferred is a customer decision, but it should be made for good reasons, not for a preconception such as "I don't trust the storage system to do as good a job as I can do."

- Performance management. Logical configuration performance management is the process of controlling how system resources are used to help achieve the performance objectives of applications.   A system obviously cannot perform better than the capabilities of its hardware.   But how hardware resources are used is often controllable by logical configuration options.   Such options (such as Quality of Service) are discussed in the *Performance* chapter.

Automation is also important.   In particular, the better the job a storage system does of automatically sharing internal hardware resources, the less administrators need to try to manually compensate.   Automation of resource sharing can help avoid some resources becoming so busy that I/O performance objectives are not achieved, while other resources have the capacity to handle more work but go underutilized.   For example, if a system has multiple internal controllers each of which is dedicated to supporting a subset of drives, some controllers can be very busy while others go underutilized.   In that case, administrators may spend time using logical configuration management tools to manually move data around, trying to more efficiently distribute the workload among controllers.   It's arguably better to not need to do that work at all than to have a requirement that a storage system support logical configuration management tools to help administrators relocate data.

- Provisioning management.   Storage *provisioning* is the process of making storage resources (such as capacity, performance, and function) available to a user.   Provisioning can involve numerous steps such as identifying the details of what the user needs, determining which installed or new storage system(s) should be used to satisfy the user's request, providing physical connectivity between hosts and storage, defining data structures (such as logical volumes or file system directories) of the appropriate sizes and RAID types, controlling which hosts are allowed to access the user's data, establishing remote mirroring disaster recovery protection if needed, and invoking host-based procedures to recognize the assigned storage.   Different storage system models vary in their ability to automate parts of the provisioning process.[107]

Recent developments by some in the industry make it easier for users to request storage resources.   The idea is for users to access an online interface to specify "what I want to achieve," minimizing the need to specify details such as "what needs to be done to make that happen."   Users can select from a menu of pre-defined provisioning options (aka policies), categorized in ways such as "platinum, gold, silver, and bronze," each representing a particular combination of data management attributes such as capacity, availability, performance, and function.   This kind of self-service provisioning is sometimes called *storage-as-a-service (SaaS, rhymes with "mass")*, especially if provided by an outside organization.

---

[107] Comprehensive automation of provisioning does not currently appear to be supported in the market. In particular, the market is still waiting for an offering where robots handle the task of physically cabling hosts to storage systems.

- <u>Management interfaces</u>.   A storage system may support multiple interfaces for administrators to use to control the logical configuration. Contemporary enterprise storage systems generally support one or more of the following management interfaces: graphical user interfaces (GUIs), command line interfaces (CLIs), and application programming interfaces (APIs). A GUI provides an interactive interface with ease-of-use facilities such as help information, wizards, diagrams, icons, drag-and-drop, graphical reports on system status (such as capacity and performance), and so on. A CLI provides text-based commands, especially useful for combining into *scripts*: files of multiple commands that support procedures that can be invoked at any time by simply entering the name of a script. An API provides programmable commands that allow computer programs to invoke other programs to carry out specific tasks, simplifying and standardizing software development.

A related interface consideration is location: where can administrators perform their management tasks? This may be limited to locations at or near the storage system. Some systems support management interfaces over Web browsers or mobile devices such as cell phones that could potentially be anywhere worldwide. This kind of flexibility can be important; consider a problem that an administrator can address from home or while on "vacation" rather than having to travel to where the storage is. Keep in mind, however, that security, always an important concern, is even more so once storage system administrative access can be off-site.

Tip: *Often, a storage system function can be invoked using any of multiple interfaces. In that case, the choice of which interface(s) to use is up to the customer. For example, the choice might be based on an administrator's personal preference, or based on consistency with interfaces the customer already uses, or based on a capability supported by only one interface.*[108]

Tip: *CLIs and GUIs are generally proprietary, i.e., unique to a given storage system model or family. An API may also be proprietary. However, some APIs are based on industry-standards such as SNIA's SMI-S (discussed later), enabling storage systems to be managed by third-party (ISV) products. Some APIs conform to a style of interfaces called REST (which stands for the nearly indecipherable "Representational State Transfer"); RESTful APIs are sometimes provided by cloud storage providers. RESTful APIs can be invoked by a program or by being entered into a Web browser.*

Tip: *GUIs have significantly increased the ease-of-management of storage systems compared to text-based CLIs (though CLIs often have advantages over GUIs such as programmed logic and scripting for reuse). However, the ease-of-management of GUIs of different storage system models can vary considerably. Customers evaluating the usability of a system's GUI interface may want to consider the following attributes: Support for all the functions supported by the CLI, consistent terminology with the CLI, a "dashboard" summary of system status, fast response time, easy navigation among tasks, small number of pages*

---

[108] *It's interesting to note that, over time, many API, CLI, and GUI interfaces have added capabilities that reduce some of the differences between them and allow them to interoperate. Some CLI script languages support program-like functions (such as "IF x is true THEN do y") and the ability to invoke other scripts and even APIs. Some programming languages support the ability to invoke scripts just as if a script was another program. Some GUIs support the ability to enter a CLI command interactively.*

(screens) needed to accomplish a given task, wizards that help a user through multistep tasks, use of color to indicate system and component status (e.g., green is good and red is bad), appropriate national language support or icons providing language-independence and intuitive use, commonly desired information displayed without requiring manual calculations (e.g., unused capacity displayed as both gigabytes and percentages), extensive help information, use of photographic images when depicting the location of system hardware components an administrator may need to access (e.g., the location of a failed drive), charts to supplement or summarize text and tables, an ability to filter information to be displayed (e.g., show only volumes with names beginning "DEPT1"), similar GUI look-and-feel among a vendor's different storage systems (if planned to be used), and more.

- Customer notification of abnormal system events. It is important that storage administrators and perhaps other customer personnel be quickly made aware of significant system events such as hardware and software failures and almost-out-of-capacity alerts. Ease-of-use supports choices in how this information is communicated such as by one or more of the following methods: a message to a system management console, a phone message, a text message, an email message, and/or a Simple Network Management Protocol (SMNP, pronounced letter by letter) message that can be received and acted on by a computer program. Ideally a storage system can send these notifications to multiple recipients designated by the customer.

- Virtualization. This topic was introduced in the *Architecture* chapter. The focus here, however, is mainly on management considerations.

In the context of IT, *virtualization* can be broadly defined as the principle of presenting capabilities to users that may differ from the supported capabilities of computer resources (such as servers and storage systems). In other words, the presented capabilities are *virtually* there. Typically, virtual capabilities are provided by software that resides between a user and computer resources that may not inherently support the capabilities.

The concept of virtualization is sometimes described in ways that align with its management benefits. Virtualization supports the computer science principle of separating policy from mechanism. A (management) policy is about *what* is to be done. A mechanism is about *how* it is done. A related view separates the *control plane* from the *data plane*, terms originating in the networking world. The control plane consists of software-based policies for managing storage (e.g., allowing users to specify their requirements for storage in terms such as capacity, availability, and performance) while the data plane consists of hardware where data is stored; portions of the data plane are provisioned to users by the control plane based on the users' requirements. Regardless of the conceptual framework, the key principle is separation of the software that manages storage from the hardware being managed.

Virtualization can promote ease-of-management in various ways.

- o Virtualization can preserve interfaces originally designed to support a specific technology so that different (perhaps newer) technology can be used "behind" the interfaces without requiring users to change interfaces they already use. For example,

SSD modules were able to replace HDD modules in storage systems without applications or other host software needing to change.

o Virtualization can support an appearance of relative simplicity to users while underlying complexity is handled "under the covers." For example, provisioning of capacity and function can be handled through an interface that allows a user to specify their requirements; software supporting virtualization then determines which storage system best satisfies those requirements and assigns capacity from that system to the user.

o Virtualization can add capabilities not inherently supported by the resources being virtualized. For example, data compression might be supported by virtualization software for storage systems that lack that inherent capability.

In some cases, virtualization is entirely internal to a storage system. A widely known example is letting administrators create *logical volumes* (aka *virtual volumes* or *LUNs*) that can be different capacities than the physical drives installed in a block-access storage system.

In practice, however, the term "storage virtualization" (or "virtualized storage") most often refers to external facilities to control storage systems by treating individual systems as components of a virtual system. In recent years, a form of storage virtualization that has increasingly gained in popularity provides a facility to manage storage systems that are connected to and accessed through the facility; the storage systems conceptually sit "behind" the facility. The virtualization facility may reside inside a conventional storage system or may be a stand-alone appliance that has no internal storage of its own. This facility is sometimes called a *storage hypervisor* (analogous in some ways to host-based hypervisors). *Software-defined storage (SDS)* is a relatively new term to describe storage virtualization facilities, especially those in a host or a stand-alone appliance.[109]

---

[109] As mentioned previously, this Guide uses the terms "storage virtualization facility," "virtualized storage," "storage hypervisor," and "software-defined storage" interchangeably unless otherwise noted. Some in the storage industry use the terms differently. For example, SDS may sometimes be defined as using commodity servers to run the software, but this Guide does not treat that as a defining characteristic.

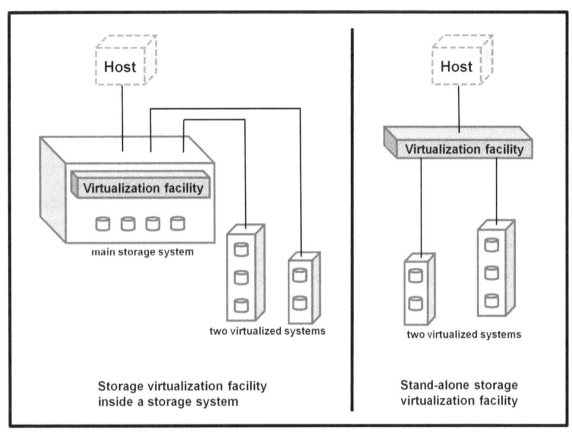

The left side of the diagram illustrates a virtualization facility within a storage system; the storage system has its own drives and also emulates a host to attach two storage systems it virtualizes. The right side illustrates a stand-alone virtualization facility that is not a storage system in its own right, but exists only to manage other storage systems. In both cases, an I/O request proceeds from a host through the virtualization facility to a virtualized storage system. Hosts cannot distinguish the type of virtualization facility or what storage system a logical (virtual) volume managed by the facility resides in.

Tip: The above diagram shows in-band designs: the virtualization facility is in the data path, meaning I/O requests (commands and data) pass through the facility. Out-of-band designs have also been available in the marketplace. While there have been debates over which design is best, in-band appears to be the simplest and most common approach. Caching in the virtualization facility can potentially address any concern that placing the facility in the data path degrades performance. As this Guide often states, what matters most is how well a given product addresses a customer's requirements; engineering debates over the nuances of alternative designs are less relevant.

Different storage virtualization facilities provide different ease-of-management benefits. Management benefits that can be provided by these facilities include:

o Supporting centralized storage management interfaces that provide administrators with a common look-and-feel or common command syntax, even if the storage systems being virtualized support different management interfaces.

o Supporting capacity pooling; capacity in the virtualized systems is managed as a single pool. This could be capacity for volumes in block-access storage or a common namespace for file-access storage.

o Supporting many data management functions even if the externally attached storage systems do not directly support the functions on their own. In particular, first-generation storage systems sometimes support limited data management functions; putting such systems behind a virtualization facility can add that function. Data management functions supported by many virtualization facilities include: nondisruptively relocating volumes, intra-system and inter-system data replication, thin provisioning, data compression, and automatic storage tiering. In the case of data movement functions (e.g., relocation and replication), the source and target storage systems can be separate, even heterogeneous systems.

o Supporting nondisruptive data migration between storage systems

o Extending the useful life of older storage systems that may lack functions supported by the virtualization facility

o Emulating different types of storage. For example, a virtualization facility might allow a file-access storage system to be accessed by object-access protocols.

Tip: In addition to easier storage management, a significant benefit of storage virtualization is the flexibility for customers to choose a combination of storage hardware and SDS software they prefer. A customer may choose the storage hypervisor or SDS software product they like and separately select the storage systems they want it to manage. Reasons for preferring particular storage systems to be managed by an SDS facility can include cost, capability, vendor preference, or that the systems are already installed.[110]

On the other hand, potential benefits of the traditional storage system approach of bundling hardware and software together include pre-integrated/pre-tested configurations, a single-vendor point-of-contact for any problems or questions, and potential technical benefits such as levels of capacity scalability, performance, and function not (currently) supported in virtualized environments. (That latter point applies to relatively large, high-performance high-function storage systems in particular.)

Either or both manufacturer-integrated storage systems and customer-integrated storage systems can work in most customer environments. What matters most is whether the system meets a customer's requirements, and whether a customer prefers the benefits of a pre-integrated storage system or prefers the flexibility of combining major hardware and software components to, in effect, build their own storage system.

---

[110] *In some cases, an SDS facility may support only selected storage systems, limiting customer choices to some extent. Some vendors sell only the virtualization software and customers have some flexibility to select the servers to run it on. Other vendors pre-package the SDS software in a particular server model; that can help ensure server quality, adequate performance, and that the vendor supports the server/software combination. In any case, it is usually the flexibility to choose the combination of SDS software and the particular storage system models it will manage that is of most interest to customers.*

Tip: A facility that virtualizes other storage systems does not make those other systems entirely invisible to administrators. For example, those systems still typically need to be manufactured, upgraded, and maintained by their respective vendors. They need to have their own "call home" facilities. They need to be logically configured by the customer's storage administrator (requiring time, effort, and system knowledge). For example, the administrator needs to define the logical volumes that the external system presents to the virtualization facility. Administrators still need to occasionally work with the management interfaces (e.g., GUIs and CLIs) supported by the external storage systems.

It's also possible that an SDS server and the managed storage systems may support some comparable functions in which case a customer may be able to choose which to use. SDS-based function has the advantage of being applicable to all managed storage systems in a consistent way.[111]

Therefore, it is important to understand that what storage virtualization facilities offer is generally a form of data management, not comprehensive system management or virtualization of every external storage system capability. The external storage systems generally cannot be treated by a customer as simply a set of drives (aka JBODs: just a bunch of disks) with no other system support functions that need customer involvement. A strategy of buying the lowest-cost storage system anytime more capacity is needed and placing it behind a virtualization facility to provide management and function could lead to a proliferation of incompatible storage systems from multiple vendors, resulting in the indirect costs of dealing with complexities in both system management and vendor management.

Tip: Stand-alone storage virtualization facilities may support the ability for the storage systems they manage to be accessed by two facilities to protect availability; if one facility is offline access to data continues through the other facility. In contrast, a virtualization facility inside a conventional storage system may not be designed to preserve access to the external storage systems it manages if the managing system is offline (e.g., due to an internal software-based failure in the conventional system). Also, if the managing storage system is being replaced by another system, access to the external storage systems being managed may be disrupted. Customers should consider such scenarios, not only the benefits of virtualization when systems are operating normally.

Tip: Some vendors market storage virtualization facilities as providing vendor independence. There's some truth to that because the facilities often support selected storage system models from different vendors. However, the customer will be adding a dependency on the virtualization facility itself and different virtualization facilities from different vendors are not interchangeable. Examples of differences between virtualization facilities include management interfaces, function, performance, which hosts and storage systems are supported by the virtualization facility, and the ability to interoperate with peer facilities for high levels of availability such as remote mirroring.

---

[111] Support by both an SDS server and an external storage system of a given function does not necessarily always give a user the choice of which function to use. For example, logical volumes presented to hosts by an SDS server may differ from the logical volumes created in an external system. In that case, even if both the SDS server and external system support making copies of logical volumes, only the SDS server would be aware of volumes visible to hosts.

Tip: As is true for storage systems generally, newer SDS offerings created "from scratch" may have limited capabilities compared to SDS offerings available for a longer time. However, that is not necessarily the case. Some vendors have created new SDS offerings from existing, time-tested software+hardware storage systems by offering the internal software as a stand-alone product, allowing customers to select the hardware to run it on. (That's most practical when the original system used commodity hardware such as x86-based servers.)

Tip: A customer should ask vendors whether they can provide references of other customers who use the combination of SDS software and storage system models the asking customer plans to use.

- Federation. Customers often install multiple storage systems of the same data access type (e.g., block-access storage) in the same data center. Reasons can include requiring more data capacity than one system supports, or more performance than one system supports, or different users/departments having the authority to choose their storage systems. A data center may have multiple system models from the same system family or may have a mix of different system models from one or more vendors.

With a few exceptions such as inter-system replication (i.e., remote mirroring) between compatible storage system models, these systems have operated independently for most of the history of storage systems. This is changing.

Some storage systems now support the ability for multiple systems to communicate with each other directly over a network (e.g., a Fibre Channel SAN) as a set of *peer* systems to provide various ease-of-management functions. This is sometimes called *storage federation*[112], though vendors assign various names to features supporting this kind of capability. While federated storage systems are usually from the same system family or at least the same manufacturer, in a few cases even heterogeneous storage systems communicate with each other.

Federated storage offerings provide the following ease-of-management capabilities. This list may not be complete and new capabilities may be added by vendors over time. Supported capabilities can vary by system model.

1. *Centralized management.* A single console may be used by an administrator to manage systems in the federation. That can include configuring and monitoring those systems. Applications may be able to access information about the systems in the federation via a single application programming interface (API).

2. *Data mobility.* Data (e.g., volumes) can be moved between storage systems for purposes such as balancing workloads, data migration, and maintaining access to data initially residing in a system scheduled to be temporarily taken offline. This federation function is illustrated in the following diagram.

---

[112] SNIA defines storage federation as "making multiple storage systems appear to a user as a single system." (See http://www.snia.org/education/dictionary/s.) While that definition would also encompass many storage virtualization offerings, it is largely consistent with how the term is used here. Actual federation offerings differ by degree of federation; it's not all or nothing.

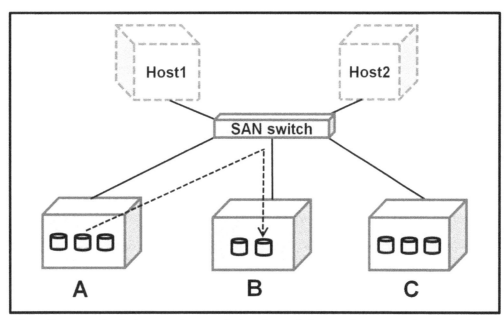

The diagram illustrates a storage federation of three storage systems that can communicate through a SAN switch. The dashed line shows a volume in system A being copied to system B.

This kind of data movement may be manually initiated, allowing customers to specify the "from" and "to" systems. The "to" system emulates a host by sending read I/O requests to the "from" system; the "from" system does not need any special support for this function. In contrast to traditional methods of moving data where a host reads data from the "from" system and writes it to the "to" system, host utilization is reduced.

3. *Cross-system consistency groups.* Some large applications have data residing in multiple storage systems. In such environments, making a snapshot copy of all that data at the same point-in-time or preserving point-in-time consistency of remotely mirrored data can be required.

- Interoperation. Ease-of-management through *interoperation* among different kinds of storage systems is emerging in the industry; this might be viewed as a step beyond a federation of similar systems as described above. Here are two examples: (1) An HDD/SSD-based storage system may be able to communicate directly with a conventional tape system or virtual tape (i.e., HDD/SSD-based) system to back up data. (2) A local storage system may communicate directly with public cloud-based storage to archive data.

  System interoperation provides several benefits for storage management. It can simplify workflow. It can improve performance by transmitting data directly between storage systems without having to pass it through an intermediate host. Accordingly, host utilization is reduced. To-date, storage system support for interoperation as described here is limited, but is likely to increase over time.

- Hardware consolidation. Storage system ease-of-management can depend on factors other than just a system's innate capabilities. In particular, ease-of-management can be facilitated by a customer choosing to consolidate storage systems. Two basic forms of consolidation can be distinguished:

1. The most common form of storage consolidation is replacing multiple storage systems – whether like or unlike models – by a single storage system. That single system would require sufficient capacity, performance, availability, and function to accommodate the systems it is replacing.

   Potential benefits include fewer systems to manage, possibly fewer vendors to manage, and a single pool of hardware resources that the system can draw on (in contrast to separate systems where one system with little work to do cannot assist another system that is overloaded, or one system with extra capacity cannot give it to another system that needs it).

   A potential drawback is putting "all storage eggs in one storage basket" such that a system problem or human error could potentially impact the larger (and possibly the one-and-only) system rather than being confined to one of multiple systems.[113]

2. Another form of storage consolidation may be less common. Some data centers install multiple, separate "boxes" (i.e., physically separate devices or appliances) to support specialized storage functions such as remote mirroring or file-access to block-access storage systems. The resulting collection of storage systems and other devices can be difficult to manage due to different management interfaces and possibly different vendors to deal with. In addition, support by such specialized devices for the storage systems and hosts the customer installs may not be available in the time-frame a customer needs it.

   The need for specialized devices can be reduced or eliminated if storage systems supporting the desired functions in an integrated/consolidated way can be installed. One benefit of this form of consolidation is reducing the number of different devices, and perhaps the number of vendors, a customer needs to manage. Another potential benefit is a performance gain if I/O requests pass through fewer devices. Another potential benefit is easier problem solving due to fewer devices and fewer vendors to deal with.

   A potential drawback of eliminating specialized devices is a potential cost savings they may provide. A specialized device may be able to support multiple generations of storage systems or multiple, heterogeneous storage systems, avoiding any cost to provide comparable capability directly in each storage system. Another potential drawback is giving up any desired capabilities unique to the specialized devices.

   Here are examples of this form of consolidation:

   o Installing a storage system with a large number of host ports can reduce or eliminate the number of SAN switches needed.

---

[113] From one perspective, storage consolidation has gone on implicitly for years. When users outgrow the maximum capacity or performance of an installed system, the preferred solution is often to upgrade the system to support higher capacity or performance, or to replace it by a larger/faster system, rather than install another system next to the first.

o Installing a storage system supporting an integrated storage virtualization facility (i.e., the ability to attach and manage other storage systems) can reduce or eliminate the need for separate storage virtualization appliances. It can also facilitate system migration by avoiding host-based data migration software.

o Installing a storage system with both built-in block-access and file-access support (aka unified storage) can eliminate the need for separate block-access and file-access storage systems or for configuring file-access gateways in front of a block-access system.

o Installing a storage system that supports remote data mirroring as an integrated function can eliminate the need for specialized appliances at the local and remote sites to implement that function.

- Management consolidation. Some storage management software offerings provide ease-of-use through supporting a single management interface (e.g., a single GUI console) for managing aspects of multiple, possibly incompatible, storage system models from one or more vendors. These management offerings typically reside in a host outside the storage systems. Unlike storage virtualization, there need not be a facility that adds functions to or somehow consolidates the storage systems. Unlike storage federation, there need not be direct storage system-to-storage system communication.

Some such management offerings, especially for heterogeneous storage systems, support the Storage Networking Industry Association (SNIA) storage management application programming interface (API) standard called the Storage Management Initiative Specification (SMI-S); see http://www.snia.org/forums/smi. A storage management software offering supporting SMI-S can help manage storage systems that also support the SMI-S standard.

SMI-S supports (meaning it can be used to invoke) some functions in storage systems such as defining volumes and making point-in-time copies of volumes. However, many storage systems support functions not supported by SMI-S. For example, a storage system may support variations of intra-system data replication that cannot be specifically invoked via SMI-S. For that reason, a storage system manufacturer's system-specific management interfaces are often preferred over management based on (and limited to) the SMI-S standard.

Tip: Some vendors' storage management offerings are claimed to support storage systems from that vendor and other vendors. That support may be limited to specific system models and not all functions of the offering may be supported for all models. Customers interested in such offerings may want to determine how quickly a vendor's storage management offering adds support for new storage system models (from any vendor).

Tip: A storage management offering may be described by a marketing claim that it provides a "single pane of glass" (i.e., a common GUI) for storage management of heterogeneous storage systems. That can be misleading because the offering may support only selected storage system models and because customers often use multiple storage management products from multiple vendors (e.g., for managing logical volumes, managing backups, managing archiving, and providing various reports) where the products do not work together and each has its own GUI with its own look-and-feel.

- Scalability. Many aspects of a logical configuration are scalable up to system-supported maximums. This is analogous to hardware scalability for system attributes such as data capacity and the maximum number of host ports. Here are some examples: The maximum capacity of logical volumes an administrator can create usually has an explicit software-defined limit (and is also indirectly limited by the aggregate capacity of installed drives). There can be a limit to the number of point-in-time intra-system copies of data that can be made. A file-access (NAS) storage system may place a software-defined limit on the maximum size of a file.

Tip: While customers often place specific requirements on physical configuration scalability, e.g., the minimum usable capacity supported, logical configuration scalability is sometimes neglected. Such an oversight can result in system migration problems. For example, migrating from one storage system to another is more difficult if the customer configured some logical volumes each with, say, 16TB of capacity on the "from" system, but the "to" system supports a maximum logical volume size of only 4TB. Migration can also be more difficult if a customer has procedures to create and maintain 24 copies (versions each created hourly) of an important file on the "from" system, but the "to" system supports only up to 10 copies of a file.

Tip: Ease-of-management can be reduced if the scalabilities of related logical configuration items are inconsistent. Some storage systems, for example, support the ability to create more logical volumes than the maximum number of local-remote volume pairs allowed in a remote mirroring configuration. Adding remote mirroring to such a system after it has been logically configured with a large number of volumes could require extra work to reduce the number of volumes to within limits imposed by the system's remote mirroring implementation. Because vendor representatives may not point out such issues or the information may be buried in user guides, it is up to customers to ask appropriate questions.

Tip: Host-based software, such as an operating system, can place its own limits on aspects of storage system scalability, outside the control of a storage system. Examples: A host's operating system or logical volume manager (LVM) may limit the maximum number of logical volumes it can support to fewer than the number supported by attached storage systems. A database management system (DBMS) may limit the maximum size of a database it can support to less than a storage system's maximum usable capacity. A given host's multipath I/O driver may support fewer channel paths between a host and storage system than the number of paths that could be physically installed. The point is, when determining their storage system requirements, customers should consider both host and storage system limits on storage system scalability.

- System parameters. Storage systems often include functions with administrator-settable parameters analogous to mechanical knobs, levers, dials, and switches. A system or function supporting a relatively large number of parameters may allow a customer to highly customize the capability for their environment. On the other hand, the more parameters there are, the more time and technical skill it can take to understand each one and determine the value to set it to.[114]

Here are two ease-of-use attributes customers can look for that can help them deal with a large number of parameters:

Helpful documentation.   Documentation should ideally go beyond merely listing parameters and their values. It is helpful if parameters are organized within functional areas and if their descriptions indicate the problems or goals they address. Documentation could indicate the relative importance of different parameters, such as which parameters are likely to have the largest impact for most customers.

Default values. Ease-of-use is promoted when parameters have default values: values that take effect unless a specific (overriding) value is specified by a user. This reduces the number of parameters that must be manually set.

Tip: *More important than whether default values exist for a given function is whether they are relevant to the customer. Customers can ask their vendors about whether they had an intended environment in mind when they created their default values. Customers can also ask referenced customers about their experiences using a system's default values.*

Tip: *Default values sometimes change in new releases of microcode. Customers should ask their vendors how customers are notified of such changes so they can consider the impact on their environment.*

Tip: *Just because a parameter supports multiple values does not indicate every value is necessarily useful. (Some values may be supported for architectural or marketing reasons.) For example, suppose a storage system supports a function to transmit some data to another storage system over a communications link. Only one instance of the function can run at a time. The function supports a parameter allowing it to automatically run at fixed intervals, from 1 to 1,000 seconds. If the function always takes, say, 30 seconds to complete, setting the parameter to a value under 30 seconds does not make sense.*

- <u>User-assigned names</u>. The ability for administrators to assign meaningful names to storage resources (e.g., logical volumes) promotes ease-of-use. That stands in contrast to resources that have only system-assigned names. User-assigned names help reduce the chance for human error when referencing resources. User-assigned names can also help new administrators understand how a system's logical configuration relates to hosts and applications.

---

[114] One can imagine various reasons why a function might have been designed with a large number of user-settable parameters. Such a design could allow supporting one function customizable via parameters rather than multiple functions each based on fixed values. Perhaps the designer wanted to impress customers with the degree of customization supported, for competitive purposes. Perhaps an important customer asked the manufacturer to support specific controls over the function. Perhaps the function's design resulted in high use of system resources so that it was necessary to allow customers to optionally limit the conditions under which the function operates. More generally, perhaps the designer couldn't figure out how to make the function work satisfactorily in all environments without many user-settable options.

- <u>Named groups</u>. An ease-of-management principle that applies to many aspects of storage management is the ability to assign a name to a group of related items. Named groups make it easier to manage and manipulate multiple items compared to handling them individually. In general, support for named groups can enable administrators to create and delete groups, add and remove items from groups, invoke functions to be applied to all items in a group, and request information about groups (such as listing all members of a group).

Here is an example of how groups can promote ease-of-management. Assigning subsets of volumes to named groups can make it easier to manage capacity provisioning. To illustrate, the IDs of one hundred volumes to be shared among four hosts could be typed in once and assigned a group name by an administrator. Then, to allow access to the group of volumes, just the group name is assigned to each host rather than typing one hundred volume names four times. And, any change made to the group (such as adding or removing a volume) could immediately apply to every host the group is assigned to.

Whether and how named groups are supported varies by storage system model. In general, user-assigned names are more meaningful than system-assigned names.

Additional Tips

- *Customers can ask their storage administrators to estimate the time they spend on various tasks. Customers can then ask vendors to describe whether and how their particular storage systems help minimize the time and effort required for the most frequent and most time-consuming tasks.*

- *Some storage system models require vendor assistance for at least some changes to the logical configuration. In some systems, the procedures for making logical configuration changes may be so complex that customers prefer to rely on their vendors to assist in the process. Vendor assistance may involve charges and scheduling delays before desired changes can be implemented.*

  Customers should ask vendors whether any logical configuration changes require vendor assistance, whether there are logical configuration changes for which other customers frequently ask for vendor assistance even if it is not strictly required, whether vendor assistance in making logical configuration changes is a free or fee service, and how long it can take a vendor to make a change to a system's logical configuration once it is requested by the customer.

- *Using common tools for some storage management tasks can minimize the complexity of managing multiple, different storage system models from the same vendor or sometimes even from multiple vendors. While storage system configuration is generally best managed by a tool designed for a particular system model, some aspects of storage management such as reporting on how storage system capacity is used may be able to be handled using common tools.   These tools often fall under the generic term* storage resource management (SRM).

Storage Technology Trends

This chapter overviews some of the major technology trends in the storage industry that should be of interest to organizations that want to consider such trends in their acquisition decisions. While such speculation is always intriguing, keep in mind that organizations can acquire only offerings available in the marketplace. The trends below are not in any particular order.

- <u>SSD vs. HDD</u>. Decreasing prices and increasing capacities for solid-state drives (SSDs) promote a trend towards increasing use of SSDs and decreasing use of hard disk drives (HDDs). While early hybrid enterprise storage system configurations often had three tiers of drives in a system – SSDs plus fast lower-capacity HDDs plus slower higher-capacity HDDs – this may move towards a two-tier approach of SSDs and slower high-capacity HDDs. The use of host-side SSD-based cache is expected to continue as a means to accelerate read I/O performance. When solid-state storage will completely replace mechanical drives remains to be seen, but seems inevitable.

- <u>Beyond flash for SSDs</u>. The industry is researching various solid-state technologies to replace the flash solid-state memory technology that has been the primary form of storage in SSDs. While flash has offered significant benefits over HDD technology, especially for improved read I/O performance and reduced energy requirements, other solid-state memory technologies are being investigated that provide benefits over flash. Examples of these technologies are resistive RAM (RRAM) and phase-change memory (PCM). In 2015, Intel and Micron jointly announced 3D XPoint, a solid-state technology that is nonvolatile and much faster than flash memory; see http://newsroom.intel.com/community/intel_newsroom/blog/2015/07/28/intel-and-micron-produce-breakthrough-memory-technology?wapkw=xpoint.

Keep in mind that the IT industry has proven to be good at incrementally improving existing technologies, and the development of new technologies sometimes takes longer than expected. Thus, it can take time for a new technology to broadly replace technologies already proven and widely accepted.

- <u>Public cloud storage</u>. Public cloud storage (i.e., Internet-based storage) is already widely used by consumers for sharing data and holding backups. Many smaller enterprises, and some departments in larger enterprises, do not need to have their own on-premises data centers and storage; cloud storage can satisfy their requirements. Cloud storage also offers a significant benefit to start-up companies because they can focus on their core competencies and avoid the "distraction" of also running a data center.

- ODM storage. Original Design Manufacturers (ODMs) produce specialized storage systems based on designs requested by other parties, typically organizations with unusually large requirements for storage. This is sometimes called "white box storage." Large Internet companies, especially those offering cloud storage, are typical users of white box storage where the main goals are low-cost and high-speed.

- System classifications. As different block-access storage systems evolve to have more hardware components (e.g., types of drives) and more software-based functions (e.g., replication, encryption, and compression) in common, traditional distinctions between entry, midrange, and high-end storage systems will continue to blur. At least one industry analyst has already dropped the distinction in favor of including all block-access oriented systems in a "general purpose storage system" category. Further, as unified systems supporting multiple data access protocols become more common, and as software-defined storage facilities that translate one protocol to another become more common, the distinction between block-access, file-access, and object-access storage systems may also lessen. To be clear, the different access protocols will likely continue, but it may be increasingly common that any given storage system model can be configured to support one or more access protocols.

- Number of manufacturers. As storage capabilities percolate down from the highest-end storage systems to smaller systems, differences between systems decrease. Price becomes a more significant decision criterion when other system capabilities approach commodity status. Vendor profits will decrease. The result could be some manufacturers dropping out of the industry, or being acquired by or merging with other manufacturers.

- Host connectivity. Having one way to do something that is good enough or better than good enough is preferable to having multiple ways of doing the same thing that require specialized skills and devices, raising costs and complexity. Thus, the use of high-speed Ethernet for all access protocols will likely increase, just as the TCP/IP communications protocol triumphed over competing protocols. In particular, whether the SCSI protocol over Fibre Channel connection is supplanted by iSCSI (which runs over Ethernet) or by Fibre Channel over Ethernet (FCoE) still remains to be seen, but decreasing use of specialized Fibre Channel devices seems likely.

- Capacity optimization. Data compression, deduplication, and thin provisioning will increasingly be employed in storage systems as ways to reduce the amount of physical capacity needed to support a much larger amount of usable capacity.

- Data redundancy. Protection against data loss remains one of the most prominent storage requirements. Since the 1990s, RAID (redundant array of independent drives) has provided dramatically increased protection against data loss compared to previous decades of non-redundant drives. However, ever larger drive capacities without commensurate increases in drive performance have resulted in longer rebuild times for failed drives – often running into many hours, increasing the possibility of additional failures in the same RAID array resulting in data loss. Solutions include RAID-6 which can tolerate two drive failures in one array, though that is still subject to long rebuild times and reduced performance compared to other RAID techniques. Other redundancy schemes that provide faster rebuild times will be increasingly deployed.

- Host-storage synergy. Cooperation between hosts and enterprise storage systems is likely to continue. The goal is to increase the efficiency of storage operations by a host and storage system sharing information or taking actions not supported by basic read and write I/O commands. This cooperation can be driven by operating system vendors and by vertically integrated vendors selling both hosts and storage systems.

  There are multiple current instances of such cooperation. One example is storage functions supported by the VMware host hypervisor (e.g., VAAI, vStorage APIs for Array Integration). Another example is a capacity reclamation function supported by ISV Symantec in its Storage Foundation (formerly Veritas Storage Foundation) product to optimize capacity use in storage systems supporting thin provisioning. Yet another example is the use of host-based caches and how the software managing those caches cooperates with storage systems attached to the host (e.g., to avoid double-caching the same data in both the host cache and the storage system cache). A final example is storage functions supported by IBM's z Systems z/OS mainframe operating system such as the ability to inform a storage system of the priority of the application submitting an I/O request.

- Software-defined storage. Software-defined storage (SDS), also known as *storage hypervisors* and *virtualized storage*, implements data management functions (such as provisioning, compression, data replication, and a system management interface) in a facility separate from the storage media. The goal is to provide extensive data management capabilities in a common, centralized way that is independent of, and conceptually sits on top of, the facilities or systems providing data capacity. Accordingly, SDS offerings are sometimes said to be "hardware-agnostic"

  Multiple SDS offerings are already available in the marketplace. Implementations differ significantly. Some SDS offerings are proprietary products and some are open source software.[115] Some SDS offerings manage conventional storage systems on a SAN. Some manage multiple hosts each of which is directly connected to storage in an arrangement sometimes called a *Server SAN*. The particular hosts and storage systems supported can vary by SDS offering.

  Regardless of implementation[116], SDS threatens conventional storage system architectures by potentially providing storage function at relatively low cost in a storage system-independent way. SDS also increases customers' flexibility in selecting hardware+software configurations, in contrast to conventional storage systems that bundle hardware and software together in one proprietary facility.

---

[115] Open source software can take some time to gain acceptance in production environments. But this can happen – consider the Linux operating system. Vendors can make a profit offering open source software through services and pre-integrated hardware+software systems.

[116] In IT, it sometimes seems that if someone can think of a way to do something not previously done, it will likely be turned into a product. That is not a predictor of success.

One way SDS use may evolve could result in conventional storage systems increasingly being replaced by boxes of capacity that contain drives and only minimal function because other functions are provided by a central SDS facility.

- Converged and hyperconverged systems. In brief, this is about simplifying data centers by replacing separate server, storage, and network systems integrated by customers with systems pre-integrated by vendors.

  A *converged system* is an integrated bundle of server, storage, network products, and software; these components may also be sold separately. A converged system is a sort of miniature data center implemented as pre-integrated products that may even come from different manufacturers. A converged system may be pre-racked, pre-cabled, and pre-tested by a vendor to support a particular level of performance, perhaps for a specific type of workload.

  Converged systems offer benefits such as reduced complexity, workload optimization, potential cost savings, single vendor support, and fast deployment. A downside is reduced customer flexibility to mix-and-match different hardware and software products. To the degree storage systems become increasingly less differentiated, which storage system hardware is included in a converged system may be less important to many customers than the overall system capability (e.g., host operating system, overall system performance, storage capacity, workload optimization, and ease-of-management).

  A *hyperconverged system* further reduces the variety of components in converged systems via a server-centric approach. Basically, processing power and storage devices are installed together in a server; a hyperconverged system can scale-out by adding more servers. From a storage perspective, the configuration is like a Server SAN where the servers can also run applications. Storage is accessed through SDS (virtualization) software running in the servers and is sharable among the servers in a hyperconverged system. The resulting hyperconverged system has benefits and drawbacks similar to those of a converged system. It may also have lower cost and better scalability. In addition, the management interfaces of a hyperconverged system may provide a consolidated server/storage view that is easier to work with than separate management interfaces for independent hardware and software components.

  The descriptions here of converged and hyperconverged systems are very general. The capabilities of particular offerings – such as availability, performance, capacity, and data management function – can vary significantly. In some cases, server administrators may view hyperconverged systems as a way to retain or regain control over storage in contrast to separate storage systems managed by a group of storage administrators.

- Unanticipated, disruptive industry changes. This final topic is pure speculation, inserted merely for completeness. Any of the following developments could have significant impacts on the enterprise storage system industry: Ultra-small and/or ultra-fast and/or ultra high-capacity and/or ultra-cheap storage media. Ultra-fast, ultra-cheap processors. Significantly reduced demand for block-access storage in favor of file-access and object-access storage. Severe economic conditions forcing major reductions in budgets for storage, thus limiting the amount of capacity available to an organization to hold data. Major industry changes that result in storage system models used by many customers no longer being offered. New, unanticipated storage system architectures with extremely compelling benefits.

From a different angle, consider the increasing commoditization of storage systems, and competition from public cloud storage, leading to enterprise storage system differentiation increasingly based on price, in turn leading to vendor sales and support models that are mainly Web-based and call center-based to reduce the cost of geographically dispersed, face-to-face sales and support personnel. That could be augmented by increases in customer-managed system setup, upgrades, and repairs.

Part III.

Insights into
Storage System Vendors

While a customer's main focus during storage system evaluation is on how well a system addresses their product requirements, customers should keep in mind they are acquiring both a storage system and a relationship with a vendor.

Armed with knowledge about the kinds of values vendors can offer, and with knowledge about how vendors go about marketing and selling to customers, organizations can separate pertinent vendor claims from irrelevant claims, determine their vendor requirements, and determine the vendor best able to meet those requirements.

Vendor Capabilities

Customers have a variety of storage system vendors to choose from. The industry is flourishing with dozens of vendors, many with international presence.

Just as different storage system models can differ dramatically in their attributes, so can vendors. Just as customers can develop requirements for storage systems by knowing the values those systems can potentially offer, customers can develop requirements to help identify the vendors they want to do business with by knowing what values vendors can potentially bring to the table.

Landscape

- <u>Types of vendors</u>. The storage industry includes several types of vendors selling storage systems. Sometimes multiple vendors even compete with each other to sell the same storage system models.

A vendor selling a storage system model may be the *original equipment manufacturer* (*OEM*) of that model. Some vendors are *business partners* of one or more manufacturers: independent companies that sell manufacturers' products to customers. Some vendors are *value added resellers* (*VARs*), independent companies that add value to a product, generally additional features or services, and sell the package as an integrated solution.

Manufacturers often refer to their vehicles for selling systems as (*sales*) *channels*. Sometimes "channels" refers only to business partners and VARs, not to a sales force employed directly by a manufacturer.

Tip: Manufacturers sometimes have formal programs to help support business partners. Such programs may include logos a partner can use indicating it has demonstrated a level of proficiency certified by the manufacturer. When such certification programs are in place, some customers may prefer doing business with certified partners rather than with uncertified partners. More generally, some customers may prefer working with business partners with significant experience with a storage system model being considered, rather than working with business partners with less experience with that model.

Tip: Don't assume that a vendor who is not the manufacturer would have to charge a higher price for a storage system because they buy the systems they sell from the manufacturer. Because a storage system manufacturer typically sells a relatively large number of systems to other vendors (or to distributors who stock systems and ship them as requested to vendors), those vendors receive a higher discount than customers normally receive. That allows those vendors to charge a higher price than they pay for the system, thus making a profit, but not necessarily charging a customer a much different price per system than the manufacturer would charge. The manufacturer can afford to do this because, for one, business partners and VARs reduce or eliminate the need for the manufacturer to hire (as many) direct sales personnel.

Tip: *A customer spending a relatively large amount of money with a vendor may be able to use that to motivate the vendor to offer a higher discount.*

Tip: *There can be advantages to customers who buy directly from the manufacturer. If the vendor is also the manufacturer, the customer may be able to forge a useful relationship with the manufacturer's system experts and management. Customers spending a relatively large sum of money or indicating a potential for substantial future business may have leverage to motivate the manufacturer to prioritize supporting future storage system capabilities the customer wants.*

- Product portfolios. Some vendors have storage product portfolios consisting of a single storage system or system family intended (or optimized) to address specific use cases. Some vendors have more comprehensive storage portfolios consisting of multiple storage system families intended (or optimized) to address different use cases. Some vendors have IT product portfolios extending beyond storage alone, including other offerings such as servers, host-based software, and network equipment. And some storage vendors are part of conglomerates that also sell products outside of IT offerings.

Tip: *Being able to acquire multiple types of IT products from one vendor – sometimes called "one stop shopping" – can help customers reduce the number of vendors they deal with. (A vendor focusing on only storage may claim that focus in itself is an advantage over vendors who support a variety of products. However, having such a focus does not necessarily indicate an advantage in either product capability or vendor capability compared to vendors with broader portfolios.)*

Tip: *Some storage system vendors sell different system families with significant overlap in supported capacities, supported levels of performance, and supported function. (There can be various reasons for such overlap. For example, a storage manufacturer may have acquired an additional storage family from another manufacturer and plan to eventually merge the families.)*

A vendor might claim, at least for marketing purposes, that this overlap increases customer choice. However, supporting two (or more) overlapped storage families can require more development, manufacturing, marketing, sales, and services resources than supporting one family. Vendors may deal with this inefficiency by eventually reducing investment in one of the system families or by attempting to merge multiple families into a single family (e.g., attempting to evolve one family to provide a superset of the functions of the overlapped families, a strategy that may not be easy to implement).

Customers may want to ask vendors selling overlapped storage system families about the vendors' commitment and direction for the families: Will one family generally support new features first? Does each family have a multi-year development plan? Are there plans to discontinue one of the families or to attempt to merge families and, if so, what will be the migration path for current users at that time? If a family will be discontinued, how much notice will the vendor provide to customers?

Tip: Some vendors who are business partners sell systems from multiple manufacturers. This can widen a customer's choice of systems while dealing with a single vendor. Because such vendors are one step removed from the manufacturers, customers will want to determine whether the vendors they deal with have expertise the customer can depend on; merely selling a system does not necessarily indicate in-depth expertise is there. Further, if a customer relies on such a vendor to recommend the best system for the customer's needs, the customer will want to know the vendor is acting in the customer's best interest, unswayed by a manufacturer's incentives such as high rebates for selling that manufacturer's systems.

Tip: A vendor may buy storage systems from an original equipment manufacturer (OEM) and rebrand them. (That may be in addition to storage systems the vendor itself manufactures.) The original manufacturer is sometimes said to OEM-out a product and the rebranding company is said to OEM-in that product. The rebranding company may make system modifications, may support more or fewer system configuration options than the OEM-out vendor supports, and may have different sales terms and conditions (such as different feature prices and warranty duration). The OEM-in vendor may have limited influence over product plans depending on the terms of the deal. The OEM-in vendor may have limited expertise, at least initially, in the acquired offerings. If an OEM relationship ends, customers who acquired OEM-in systems may have to deal with uncertainties: Will customers be able to upgrade installed systems? If a customer chooses to migrate to systems from the original OEM-out manufacturer, will that customer have to deal with incompatibilities between the installed system model and the corresponding system model from the original manufacturer?[117]

Tip: A vendor may grow their storage portfolio by merging with or acquiring another vendor. (These actions are sometimes referred to together as M&A). That can be an implicit endorsement of each others' company and offerings. When an acquired or merged company is a manufacturer, customers may want to determine whether the technical leaders behind products the customer is interested in continue to work on those products (rather than having left for other ventures or having been assigned to other projects). Customers may also want to understand the (possibly revised) product plans (which vendors may share under a non-disclosure agreement). An inability to retain technical leaders, or post-M&A reduced investment in a product, could lead to less frequent product

---

[117] *An OEM relationship can end for various reasons. It may end after a contracted period at the discretion of either party; to alleviate customer concern about that possibility vendors may announce a renewed contract before the previous contract expires. The relationship may end in a de facto way before a contract expires if a vendor selling an OEM-in product starts to offer a competing product developed in-house and the vendor's sales force no longer actively sells the OEM-in product.*

enhancements and to falling behind competitors. (Of course, such situations could potentially happen even to in-house (aka organically) developed storage systems.)

- <u>Services portfolios</u>. Vendors differ in the portfolio of IT services they offer. Examples of such services include: technical education (where variations can include classroom, Web-based, and customer-site training), assistance in implementing system features, and outsourcing of storage or storage management.

    Tip: *Even if a vendor who is a business partner offers few if any such services, it may be that desired services are offered by the system manufacturer.*

- <u>Financing offerings</u>. Vendors differ in the financing offerings they may support for system acquisition. In addition to purchase, financing offerings could include options such as month-to-month rent, fixed-duration lease after which the system is returned to the vendor, full payout over *n* months where the customer then assumes ownership, delayed initial monthly payments, *volume discounts* if at least certain numbers of systems are acquired, and trade-ins of older systems or competitors' systems to reduce the price of a new system. A related financial consideration is possible vendor support for capacity-on-demand, discussed in the *Marketing Tactics* chapter. Additional financial considerations are discussed in the *Prices and Costs* chapter.

- <u>Vendor viability</u>. Vendor viability – the ability to survive and profit over a long term – can vary. Consider the contrast between a Fortune 500 company in the storage business for decades with a large base of loyal customers compared to a startup without a customer base trying to break into the market.

    Viability can be measured in various ways such as reputation, financial health, geographic presence, market share, a diversified set of offerings addressing different markets (vs. a single one-size-fits-all storage portfolio), an ability to support popular new technologies in a timely fashion or even drive industry developments, and a history of delivering on planned future offerings. Another measure is whether a vendor has a significant focus on (investment in) storage or, instead, has an extensive product portfolio where storage may be treated as a potentially expendable "sideline." Yet another measure is whether a company is currently defending itself against patent infringement lawsuits; that may be an issue for startup companies in particular.

    Tip: *Market share is usually measured in terms of quarterly or yearly revenue, but sometimes in terms of the amount of data capacity shipped or in the number of individual storage systems shipped. A vendor's revenue accrues not only for each storage system sold, but also for subsequent upgrades of installed systems. Market share applies not only to vendors, but to individual products in a market of comparable products.*

    Market share, by itself, is only a limited way to determine a vendor's (or product's) viability. Consider that whenever a new vendor or storage system model enters the market its market share is initially zero and its viability is unproven by time. Clearly, that has not prevented many vendors and storage systems from becoming successful due to the value they offer. While there may be more customer risk when acquiring a new, unproven system from a new, unproven vendor, market share should be only one consideration when evaluating vendor (or system) viability as part of an acquisition decision.

Tip: Professional appearing websites and brochures are not a good indicator of vendor viability. Many tools and firms-for-hire exist to help create such polished documents. While a poor-quality document should raise questions about the associated vendor's quality, high-quality documents are not difficult to put together. In any case, what matters most is substance and facts, not appearance.

Tip: Some IT industry and investment analysts publish assessments of the viability of selected vendors, usually for a fee.

- <u>Local vendor personnel</u>. Different storage vendors may have different numbers of personnel in a given locality. Vendors usually cultivate different skills in different personnel who provide direct customer support: sales representatives, customer-facing technical support (aka system engineers), and product service engineers who perform system maintenance or help diagnose and fix system problems. Customers may want a vendor's assurance that there are sufficient local personnel to support them and other nearby customers, including at any time of the day or week and when some vendor personnel are on vacation, ill, or otherwise not available.

Tip: Some vendors have a presence in many countries worldwide. Other vendors may have more limited presence. A wider international presence can be important to customers with global locations or global aspirations.

- <u>Maintenance service representatives</u>. Some vendors (often the manufacturers) provide their own service representatives to support system installation and maintenance. Some vendors may hire other firms to provide that support; that is most likely for smaller vendors with a limited workforce or a presence in limited locations.

Tip: If system maintenance is provided by a third party, customers should determine the viability of that party. Also, it might be the case that unusually difficult problems require the maintainer to have to contact the manufacturer, possibly elongating the repair process especially if the manufacturer is located in a distant time zone.

Tip: Some manufacturers can maintain not only their own products but also selected products from other manufacturers. That can reduce the number of different maintenance representatives a customer needs to deal with. Interested customers should determine a vendor's qualifications for servicing the different systems and what the cost implications are.

- <u>Help desk support</u>. (Similar terms are *service center*, *call center*, and *contact center*.) Some vendors and manufacturers support the ability for customers to contact product experts by phone or email to get answers to product questions. Examples of such questions are: "How do I make the system do x?" or "I can't figure out what this system message means; can you help?". A vendor's help desk can be of particular value for customers dealing with recently installed storage systems or relatively complex storage systems and functions. It's also of value to less experienced administrators.

Help desk support may be provided free or as a priced service. A help desk may be organized by levels such as "level 1" handling initial contact and relatively simple questions and "level 2" handling more complex questions.

Tip: *Customers should ask vendors about help desk staffing and the impact of time zone differences on staff availability if the help desk is in a different time zone than the customer.*

- Location of parts inventory. Customers will want to ensure their vendor can deliver replacements for failed system hardware components in a timely manner. That can necessitate the vendor maintaining a local area parts inventory. Some customers, likely those who do significant business with the vendor, may be able to motivate the vendor to keep spare parts at the customer's site.

- Terms and conditions. Vendors may differ in their terms and conditions (aka T & C, or T and C) for contracts and warranties. Examples of T & C items include warranty duration and limitations if a customer wants to resell a purchased storage system to another customer.

- User community. Some vendors facilitate communication with and between users through means such as user groups, newsletters, online forums, occasional roadshows in different locations, and annual conferences. These vehicles can provide ways customers can share views and experiences with other customers, enhance their skills, keep up with industry developments, and perhaps meet a vendor's business and technical leaders. Additionally, some vendors support programs allowing customers to submit requirements for currently unsupported, but desired, storage system capabilities. (Engineers can't be expected to think of everything by themselves.) Some vendors may invite selected customers to a special briefing to solicit their feedback about possible future storage offerings.

Tip: *Customers sometimes view events such as roadshows and conferences as ways to reward employees as well as increase their skills. Customers should send personnel to such events based on their ability to benefit from the topics. For example, if topics being presented are technically oriented, customers may benefit more by sending storage administrators than by sending CIOs; if presenters are vendor executives, the opposite may apply. Note that if sending customer personnel to attend a conference is not possible, some vendors post videos of the sessions on the Web.*

- Coopetition. When competing companies cooperate in an endeavor they consider to be to their mutual advantage, the situation is often called *coopetition*.

Some storage system vendors may have formal relationships with other storage or IT vendors. One or both parties may call the relationship by names such as *partnership* or *alliance* or *coalition*.

These kinds of relationships can be about almost anything. For example, a relationship may be one manufacturer acquiring the specifications from another manufacturer of interfaces to a software function.[118] Or, a relationship may be only a declaration of a plan to work together on a project at some time in the future.

Tip: There are no industry standards for the terms used to describe these relationships, so what a given relationship entails depends on the specific agreement between the vendors, not on the term a vendor calls it. Only one vendor in a relationship might use a term such as "alliance" to describe an agreement. A vendor may highlight its relationships with other vendors; the purpose may be to imply some sort of endorsement by the other vendors, though a business relationship, especially for a limited purpose or with a competitor, may not in fact be an endorsement.

- Industry contribution. Some storage manufacturers invest to help drive product and industry advances. Examples include technology research, patent portfolios licensed to others, active participation (not merely membership) in industry-standards organizations, and contributions to open source software used in many manufacturers' storage systems. Doing business with such a manufacturer, whether directly or through a business partner, recognizes their industry contribution and helps sustain it, potentially benefiting everyone. Customers of such a manufacturer may also benefit by being able to consult its research organization.

Additional Tips

- *Some vendors have received awards for diverse reasons such as business ethics, community service, and product design. In particular, customers may want to ascertain whether a vendor can cite evidence they conduct business in an ethical manner.[119] Some vendors create business conduct guidelines that employees are required to follow for legal and ethical reasons. (Of course, there is no guarantee an individual employee will follow these guidelines; ethical business practices can depend on a company's culture and individuals' conduct, not only on a document.)*

- *Customers may want to ask vendors about their visions for their storage business. That includes both technology and customer support considerations. Of course, a vendor's public vision is likely crafted to sound appealing to customers and commentators, so the actual value of a particular vision may be limited. Nevertheless, knowing the vision may foster a discussion that yields useful insights into the vendor and its plans.*

- *Customers may want to determine whether a vendor, especially a manufacturer, complies*

---

[118] Interface specifications may be exchanged for money or for technology. Paying a competitor for interface specifications may be viewed by the purchasing manufacturer as lower cost than losing sales revenue due to lack of or incompatible support of a function, and lower cost in the long run compared to attempting to reverse engineer such interfaces and any future enhancements.

[119] *For example, the* Better Business Bureau *has a* Torch Awards for Ethics *program. See* http://www.bbb.org/council/international-torch-awards/about. Corporate Responsibility Magazine *publishes a* 100 Best Corporate Citizens *list each year; see* http://www.thecro.com.

with International Standard Organization (ISO) 9000 quality management standards.   See
http://www.iso.org/iso/home/standards/management-standards/iso_9000.htm.

- It can be useful for a customer to reflect on qualities they want in their storage system vendor representatives. Here are suggestions:

An ideal storage system vendor will have an understanding of the customer's business and IT applications.

An ideal vendor will listen to what the customer says are their objectives and requirements for storage; their wants and needs. The vendor will strive to understand a customer's problems: their constraints and challenges (sometimes called "pain points"). The vendor will explain how their offerings support the customer by addressing those wants, needs, and problems, and not merely cite product specifications.

An ideal vendor will communicate at a level appropriate to the customer audience. IT administrators generally prefer technical information which is sometimes relatively detailed. Executives generally prefer business perspectives and want information to be summarized.

An ideal vendor should share experiences or offer references of other customers using the vendor's storage system model to support environments relevant to the current customer.

An ideal vendor will get back to the customer in a timely manner with answers to questions that cannot be answered immediately.

The vendor will propose a fair price.

An ideal vendor who has won an opportunity will monitor project status before, during, and after installation, soliciting frequent customer feedback on how the project is going. They will not sell-and-run.

An ideal vendor will identify backup personnel supporting the storage systems the customer has in case someone assigned to a customer is unavailable (e.g., on vacation, taken ill, etc.).

An ideal vendor may suggest how they can help the customer improve their storage operations in ways the customer may not have considered. (The customer is always free to ignore such suggestions or to ask the vendor to stop sharing them.)

An ideal vendor may recognize when the customer is struggling in an area that the vendor is quite good at and arrange for the relevant executives in each organization to talk. (This is an "extra credit" item not limited to only IT issues. For example, supply chain management is employed by many companies.)

An ideal vendor will proactively remind the customer of any current equipment with lease dates nearing expiration, providing ample time for customer action.

An ideal vendor will keep the customer informed of product enhancements and new offerings that may bring value to the customer's organization.

Perhaps the ideal vendor can be summarized with the expression "easy and a pleasure to do business with." The ideal customer-vendor relationship should be win-win.

Product Announcements

Product announcements by enterprise storage system vendors are a way to inform existing customers, potential customers, industry watchers, investors, and other interested parties about new storage systems or enhancements to existing systems. These announcements are usually designed to draw attention to new products or new product capabilities with the intention of motivating those parties, especially customers, to learn more. Thus, they can be viewed as an aspect of product marketing, discussed later.

Vendors sometimes refer to product announcements as *launches* or *rollouts*. In the industry, announcements of enhancements to existing system generations (such as new releases of microcode designed to improve performance) are sometimes informally called "the next turn of the crank" or "midlife kickers."

Landscape

• <u>Formal announcements</u>. Formal storage system announcements are often made via press releases that follow a pattern something like this:

"My company, a [or the] leader in [an area of storage or IT], today announced..."

A high-level description of what was announced...

Comments from company officials, industry analysts, and customers...

Disclaimers and footnotes

Beyond press releases, announcements may be published or summarized via social media such as a vendor's Facebook page, a LinkedIn discussion group, Twitter, and YouTube. For major announcements, vendors may run roadshows in multiple cities, possibly featuring vendor executives and product architects as speakers.

Tip: In an offering's announcement information, it is important to distinguish any remarks made by vendor executives and industry analysts from remarks made by customers. Scanning the remarks too quickly can potentially overlook who made them. In any case, because the vendor controls the text of an announcement, expect to read only positive remarks in announcement materials.

Tip: Because many storage system announcements include comments from early users –

and because vendors generally like to cite such comments to add credibility – announcements lacking any customer comments can raise questions about product readiness and customer experience to-date.

Tip: *In an offering's announcement information, any customers' and analysts' comments should be read carefully to determine whether they are based on hands-on experience or on only vendor-provided information.*

Tip: *Storage system or feature names are sometimes changed when a new version of a storage system is announced, or perhaps when models in a storage system portfolio are rebranded with new names. The purpose may be to draw attention to significant changes in the new version compared to previous versions. Or, the purpose may be to make the changes sound more significant than they are. Or, the purpose may be to assign a more contemporary name aligned with industry trends. Or, the purpose may be to imply the new system version is very different from previous versions that may not have a good reputation.*

- Informal announcements. Storage vendors sometimes make less than official product announcements. Here are ways this is commonly done:

  1. Some announcements are not made public until weeks after they have been communicated to some or all of a vendor's existing customers and the new products or product enhancements are in use by some customers, e.g., in a "beta test" or "early ship program." One reason may be to enable a vendor to announce that the enhancements are already in use by multiple customers, adding credibility to the official announcement. Another reason may be for a vendor to gather enough customer experience with the new offerings that the vendor has confidence in their quality, helping to avoid bad post-announcement publicity that could result from early-life problems. Yet another reason may be to enable the official announcement to include testimonials from customers who have successfully used the offering.

  2. Some official announcements may include high-level *previews* or *statements of intent* or *statements of direction* about future product offerings.

  3. Some vendor personnel may provide informal, high-level insights into planned future announcements through social media including blogs and videos. Such insights are likely provided with the knowledge and permission of vendor executives; such insights are sometimes provided *by* those executives.

Tip: *The use of informal announcement vehicles allows a lot of freedom in what is said and how it is said compared to a formal announcement. Because this type of information is disclosed prior to a formal announcement, details can both emerge and change over time. Informally announced offerings sometimes never become real offerings.*

- Hyperbole. Storage system announcements often include attention-grabbing terms such as "breakthrough," "game changing," "raises the bar," "redefines," "unprecedented," "unparalleled," "unmatched," "revolutionary," "disruptive," and "next generation." An adjective that should be viewed with particular caution is "unlimited"; even "infinite" has been used.

Tip: Impressive terms may be warranted when what is being announced is truly significant and worthy of attention. However, such terms are often used for effect, unaccompanied by substantiation or quantification. They may be relative to a vendor's previously announced products, but not relative to (all) competitors' products.

Such impressive terms sometimes apply to only a storage system's architecture. To illustrate, a given storage system's architecture might support up to one yottabyte (one trillion terabytes) of capacity while the models a customer can order are limited to a maximum of one petabyte (one thousand terabytes) of capacity due to the maximum number of drives supported and the maximum capacity of each of those drives.

- <u>First-to-announce</u>. A storage system vendor may strive to be the first vendor to announce a particular system capability not currently supported by competing products, even if that capability won't be available for some time. Whoever announces first has advantages: They may get the most media and analyst headlines; customers wanting the new capability initially have only one place to go. However, whoever announces later (informally called "me too") has different advantages; they can evaluate what other vendors have announced, their marketing approaches, and customer and analyst feedback, enabling those later announcers to potentially offer (or claim to be working on) something as good or even better.

Tip: While being first-to-announce has its advantages, being the vendor first able to deliver a capability may provide more tangible value. Also, being first-to-announce does not necessarily equate to delivering the best.

Tip: Manufacturers have various motivations to be first-to-announce. It can help win business from customers buying "today" who choose the manufacturer's system over competing systems if those customers believe they can later upgrade the system to obtain the new capability. Another manufacturers' motivation is promoting an image of technology leadership or thought leadership.

However, not every new technology quickly (or ever) receives widespread customer demand or delivers on initial expectations. Some manufacturers may choose to focus on delivering and enhancing technologies proven to provide the most value to the most customers, rather than trying to be the first to deliver something new as early and often as possible in an attempt to grab media, analyst, and customer attention.

- <u>General availability</u>. Announcements often include a *general availability (GA)* date: the date when the product is planned to be able to be shipped to customers after formal announcement. The GA date may be the same or later than the announcement date. Lack of citing a specific GA date (e.g., year-month-day), or at least a time frame (such as "fourth quarter"), may indicate the product is still in development/test. In fact, development/test may continue for any new offering up to the date it can ship from the factory to customers (and perhaps beyond that date, allowing vendors to claim they delivered on schedule even if the offering was not completely ready yet). Lack of citing a specific availability date may indicate an attempt to stall the market, meaning an attempt to discourage customers from acquiring anything from competitors at least until more information about the new offering is available.

Availability of new systems and new capabilities is sometimes constrained in various ways. Announcements sometimes indicate *limited availability*, meaning that for some period of time the new system or capability is going to be shipped to only selected customers. Announcements sometimes state a next-generation storage system will be available as of a given date, but some capabilities (possibly including some capabilities already available on the current generation system) are delayed until a later date.

Tip: If an announcement indicates a new product is available "immediately," customers wanting that product as soon as possible should investigate its quality to a greater extent than for a product that has been available for some time. New products may have few if any references of customers using it in production, or few if any references of customers with configurations similar to what a new buyer wants, increasing the risks of being a "pioneer." New products are more susceptible to early-life problems than more established "customer-proven" or "field-proven" products. An especially thorough testing process by customers may be warranted.

Tip: Motivations behind statements in announcements about delayed or planned (but not yet available) system capabilities may not be stated. A motivation may be to ship a storage system to start earning revenue since not all customers may require any delayed or planned capabilities. A motivation may be to support an announcement date and associated events planned long in advance that could not easily be changed. A motivation could be to make a "me too" claim for competitive reasons.

- <u>Superseded systems</u>. Storage system vendors may continue to sell the current version of a product as well as the new version being announced.

Reasons for continuing to market and sell an apparently superseded storage system may include: clearing inventory, having something to sell to customers before the new system is generally available, attracting new customers by offering the current system at a reduced price, attempting to minimize dissatisfaction among customers who recently bought the current version (because no customer wants to think they may have been the last buyer of a superseded storage system), continuing to provide a product supporting capabilities not (yet) available on the new version, and being able to provide products to customers who only install products that have passed an organization's internal certification process or that have been on the market for some period of time.

Tip: Before making a product decision, customers should inquire about manufacturer plans, including timing of general availability, of next-generation systems. That may require that the customer sign a non-disclosure agreement because manufacturers and vendor representatives generally do not want such plans to be widely known since that could impact current business if customers decide to wait for the new system. (On the other hand, if a current generation storage system is not selling well, vendors may want some information about the next-generation system to "leak out" to help stall the market.)

Tip: *The announcement of a new version of a storage system model or level of microcode may provide insights into problems and weaknesses in the version being superseded that were not previously well-known. The vendor likely positions newly introduced capabilities as highly valuable, while the absence of those capabilities in the previous system may have been a subject the vendor avoided when selling that system.*

Additional Tips

- *Storage product announcements often identify multiple new or enhanced capabilities. Customers should focus most on items that address their particular environment. Not all customers assign the same importance to each announced item. A particular customer may even assign different levels of importance to the same item if they consider installing multiple systems for different applications.*

- *Customers do not buy new enterprise storage systems or new features on existing systems based on announcements alone. They will (or should) have many questions for the vendor. Unless the new product is needed right away, it can be prudent to wait a while – perhaps a few months – before asking a vendor to do an on-site presentation of the new offering. Presenters are often local sales and field support representatives (in contrast to product architects and developers) who will need some time to really understand the product and be best able to address questions on the spot.*

- *Searching the Web in the days and weeks following an announcement can reveal commentary from storage industry analysts and others in media articles and storage blogs. This commentary can help clarify what was – and was not – announced. (For example, commentary about what was not announced could include information about current product issues that remain unaddressed or could indicate rumored enhancements that were not announced.) Analyst commentary may mention initial reactions from interviewed competitors; competitors may publish views on their own blogs. Search criteria should include the vendor and product name, and perhaps a date or date range to narrow the search results if supported by the browser.*

- *Sometimes it is said (perhaps by a vendor, an industry watcher or just in casual conversation) that a new version of a product makes previous versions "obsolete." That is likely hyperbole and is rarely the case.*

  The previous version was presumably "current" even the day prior to the new announcement. Vendors generally, if not always, continue supporting previous-generation systems with upgrades, maintenance, and sometimes enhancements for years after a next-generation system is announced.

  Announcements of new enterprise storage systems (or enhancements to existing systems) often introduce technical capabilities months to years ahead of the requirements of many customers. Many customers successfully operate storage systems that are five or more years old, even though newer generations are available, because the installed systems continue to meet the customer's requirements. Some customers may even have a policy of only buying used storage systems because they are good enough for the customers' purposes and typically have a lower cost than new systems.

For customers deciding whether to acquire the latest generation of a system model or a previous generation, useful questions include: Is there significant financial savings in buying the previous generation system rather than the new one? Can the previous generation system be (nondisruptively) upgraded in-place to a newer generation system? Will the previous generation system be enhanced with any of the capabilities of newer systems or with new technologies such as now drive models, or are its capabilities/specifications effectively "frozen"? How long will the vendor support maintenance on the previous generation system? How long will the vendor continue to offer previously announced hardware upgrades, software upgrades, and fixes to software problems for the previous generation system?

To summarize, previous generation systems may be "good enough" for many customers until there is a compelling reason to replace them. Such reasons could include a high cost of maintenance, or an increasing frequency of system problems, or a requirement for hardware or software capabilities not supported by the installed system.

- *A pattern often seen in customer and analyst reaction to new products beginning at announcement time (or earlier if information is publicly disclosed or leaked) goes something like this: At the start there is high excitement and high expectations based on initially provided information. That is later followed by diminished excitement and expectations, perhaps even disappointment, as more information (such as hands-on experience) becomes available. Eventually there is a levelheaded assessment of what the product really can do as well as knowledge of how the relevant industry as a whole has responded (e.g., with different approaches to provide comparable or better value).[120]*

---

[120] A discussion of this pattern is at http://en.wikipedia.org/wiki/Hype_cycle.

Marketing Tactics

Enterprise storage system vendors use marketing as a tool to help them achieve their sales objectives.[121]

Marketing can motivate prospective customers to consider acquiring a vendor's offerings. Marketing can appeal to customers through generating emotions ranging from curiosity to excitement to the fear of being left out. Marketing can help shape a product's image and help generate customer interest, even customer demand.

What ultimately should matter to customers, however, is the value of the storage systems they would acquire and the vendors they would work with, not the style with which storage systems and vendors are marketed.

Landscape

- Delivering marketing messages. Enterprise storage system marketing messages are delivered via media known as collateral or deliverables. Examples are press releases, websites, specification sheets, data sheets, brochures, white papers, vendor Webcasts, product manuals (such as user guides), customer testimonials, social media (such as blogs, YouTube videos, LinkedIn discussions, and Twitter), fly-in briefings, presentations, conventions, roadshows, and advertisements. Even reports and opinions from analysts and commentators sometimes repeat vendors' marketing messages.

  Tip: Marketing collateral generally focuses on the positive aspects of a storage system: "the good news" story. This collateral generally avoids any mention of weaknesses, drawbacks, restrictions, limitations, or negative customer experiences (except, perhaps, when those negative experiences apply to competitors).

  Therefore, it is up to customers to identify any product issues that may impair their IT environment if they were to acquire a particular storage system. Issues can include product limitations and restrictions as well as other customers' problems with product quality.

  Information to help identify issues can often be gleaned by searching vendor publications –

---

[121] The American Marketing Association defines marketing as "the activity, set of institutions, and processes for creating, communicating, delivering, and exchanging offerings that have value for customers, clients, partners, and society at large." (Source: https://www.ama.org/AboutAMA/Pages/Definition-of-Marketing.aspx)

especially product manuals (such as user guides) and technical papers – for terms such as: unsupported, *not supported, can not, cannot, can't, must not, mustn't, should not, shouldn't, is not, isn't, are not, aren't, not allowed, limitation(s), restriction(s), restricted, caution(s), and* warning(s).

Other useful information is published documents from manufacturers and possibly other vendors identifying recently fixed problems and known-but-unfixed problems. These documents go by names such as release notes *or* microcode release information *or* customer advisory *– there is no standard name for such information. These documents may be on the vendor's website and available to everyone, or may require a userid/password. When this information is not on the public Web, customers should ask vendors to make that information available to them, e.g., a history of reported problems and fixes for, say, the previous twelve months. (The kinds of problems of interest may vary by customer; however, most customers will want to at least get a feel for the frequency and number of problems that have resulted in loss of access to data or even loss of data itself.)*

Other sources of potentially useful information are claims about a vendor or product made by competitors; those claims generally focus on "the bad news." This is discussed in the Competitive Tactics *chapter.*

- Puffery. Enterprise storage system marketing messages communicate the main points a vendor wants customers to pay attention to. These messages often make broad, high-level claims using vague, even flowery, language that can make it difficult to determine what a product can really do. Nevertheless, marketing messages can at least help customers identify products that are worthy (or not) of further consideration.

  The concept of *puffery* may not be well known beyond the legal and advertising industry. "Puffery is commonly defined as 'publicity or acclaim that is full of undue or exaggerated praise'. Commercial entities use puffery as a key marketing strategy allowing them to advertise their product as 'the best,' 'the better choice' or even 'the world's most effective.'…The Third and Ninth Circuits [U.S. courts] define puffery as 'exaggerated advertising, blustering and boasting upon which no reasonable buyer would rely.' "[122] In the U.S., at least, puffery is not illegal; it is up to the audience to determine which vendor claims can be glossed over as mere puffery and which claims warrant substantiation.

- Leadership claims. Vendor claims of leadership are common. Some enterprise storage system vendors may claim to be *a* leader in the industry or even *the* leader in the industry or some aspect of the industry. Such claims could be about technology, or revenue, or market share, or first-to-announce a capability, or first-to-deliver a capability, or something else.

  Tip: *To-date, no vendor is the leader in* all *aspects of enterprise storage systems. Considering just technology, given so many storage system attributes to compare (such as maximum capacity, performance benchmark results, functions, floor space, etc.), virtually*

---

[122] A. Gurnani and A. Talati, *"The World's Most Trusted Article on Puffery": Non-Actionable Puffery or Misleading?,"* Update magazine, The Food and Drug Law Institute (FDLI), November/December 2008. http://www.americanbar.org/content/dam/aba/administrative/litigation/materials/2012_food_supplements_2nd_annual_cle_wrkshp/2012_aba_panel3_the_worlds_most_trusted.authcheckdam.pdf.

any vendor can find something about their storage system that is better than at least one competitor's system. Strictly, all it takes to legitimately claim to be "a leader" is to be ahead of at least one other system or vendor in at least one area.

Tip: Marketing claims that a system or system feature is "best" are common. Consider claims that a storage system model or feature is "best of breed" or is "best in class." That prompts the questions: What other systems are considered to be in the same breed or class? Who decided that and what were the criteria? Consider claims that a storage system model is "the system of choice" or is "the gold standard." (That latter claim might even be misinterpreted as indicating the system (or feature) is an officially designated industry standard or is viewed as a standard by other vendors or customers.) Such claims are likely puffery and customers should request substantiation if such claims are important to them.

Tip: A vendor being the first to announce or deliver a storage system capability may claim to be the leader. Such leadership is often short-lived. All storage vendors don't announce their new offerings on the same day. A vendor announcing industry-leading performance today may be matched or leapfrogged by another vendor tomorrow.

Tip: Claims of market share leadership in particular should be considered carefully. The purpose of making such a claim may be to create an impression that acquiring a certain storage system model or acquiring storage from a certain vendor is safe because that is what many other customers are doing. The claim may be about majority share leadership, or perhaps just plurality share leadership since in many market segments no vendor has a majority share. (Citing market share as an answer to the question "Why should I buy from you?" brings to mind an old business saying of the form "No one ever got fired buying from vendor wxyz." All vendors would presumably like to be in that position.)

When evaluating claims of market share leadership it is important to determine what market segment is being referred to. There are technology questions to consider: Is the claim being made about all types of enterprise storage in all environments?   Is the claim about only internal storage installed inside server cabinets (and perhaps sold only by the server vendor), or about only external storage, or about both types of storage together? Is the claim about only storage supporting a specific capability, e.g., about only file-access storage or about only storage attaching to a certain type of server?

There are also more general questions to consider: How is market share being measured: by total revenue generated, or by total physical capacity shipped, or by total units shipped (a measure that can place systems supporting larger capacities at a disadvantage), or by something else? What vendors and products are included (and not included) in the market share comparison? What countries does the claim apply to? Is the claim substantiated by a credible third party?

The time frame being considered also matters. Market share is usually measured by calendar quarter or year. It can take multiple quarters or years to detect trends in market share that are due to more than short-term fluctuations. It is important to use the same time frames for all vendors or products being compared because of seasonal variations that are often repeatable year after year. In particular, the fourth quarter of the calendar year usually sees a higher amount of storage buying than other quarters. One reason may be customers determining there are budget funds left to spend and not spending those funds risks a budget reduction for the next year. Another reason is vendors working extra hard to close deals to make their year-long sales quotas. For vendors whose fiscal year does not coincide with the calendar year, their revenues may be higher towards their last fiscal quarter. To help compensate for these variations, market share percentages are sometimes calculated as a rolling average (aka moving average): the value at each quarter shows the market share calculated as the average share for the most recent four quarters combined.

The following diagram illustrates a typical market share graph showing the percentage shares of three (fictional) vendors at each of four quarters. If all vendors in the market segment were shown the percentages at each quarter would add to 100%.

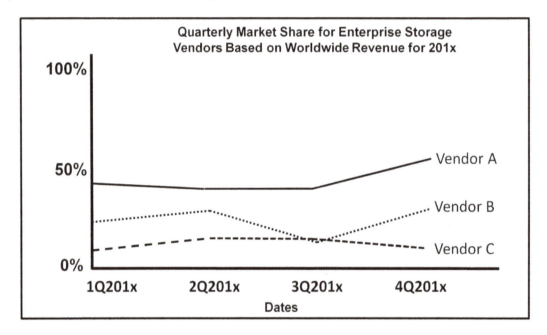

Market share by itself may have limited value as an indicator of a vendor's or product's leadership. Consider that whenever a new vendor or storage system enters the market its market share is initially zero. Clearly, that has not prevented many new vendors and products from becoming successful due to the value they offer. Market share should be only one consideration in an acquisition decision.

- Entry / midrange / high-end classifications. Placing storage systems into broad *low-medium-high* classes remains a challenge in the industry given the variety of systems and possible system configurations in the market. While classification terms such as *low-end (or entry), midrange (or mid-market or mid-tier), and high-end (or enterprise or tier-1)* are common, there are no industry standards for classifying a particular storage system or system configuration using those terms.[123]

Attempts at such classifications of storage systems have usually been based on relative capability (e.g., *high-end* applies to storage system models with the highest maximums in capacity, performance, and function), but other criteria – such as ranges in average selling price, or support for certain types of servers, or the impact on performance of a hardware component failure – have also been used. To add to the classification challenge, storage systems that today might be considered midrange, just a few years ago might have been considered high-end.

Tip: Many different storage system models often do not fall into perfect superset/subset relationships. That is true regardless of whether systems are compared across different system families or more narrowly compared across the models in one system family.

There are additional classification obstacles. Some capabilities in what are often considered midrange storage systems are not supported by some storage systems often considered high-end. Examples include higher maximum capacities for data, higher maximum performance (especially in all-flash storage systems that may otherwise have limited function), and support for both block-access and file-access protocols.

A vendor's marketing messages may take advantage of the lack of classification precision by using classification terms intended to evoke positive impressions for marketing purposes, but without clear justification. To illustrate, consider a marketing claim such as "My storage system provides high-end capabilities at midrange prices."

Clearly, low/medium/high classification schemes are rough at best. They may be more meaningful within a given vendor's storage system portfolio rather than industry-wide. And, even then, a vendor may position a storage system model into a higher "class" than it would seem to warrant, simply for marketing purposes.

The moral of the story: broad low-medium-high classification schemes for storage systems may have little if any value to customers making a storage system acquisition decision. A customer should not define a requirement requesting vendors to bid only "high-end storage systems." What is important is for customers to identify their specific storage system requirements and determine the system(s) best able to meet them.

- Guarantees. Some vendors offer guarantees that selected attributes of a storage system will work in a certain way. A vendor agrees to provide a remedy to a customer if the guarantee fails to be met.

---

[123] In the author's view, the term *enterprise* is best used to mean a unit of economic organization, e.g., a business or government. "Enterprise storage", then, is storage designed for use by enterprises and is thus distinguished from "consumer storage" such as a hard disk drive inside a personal computer.

On a related note, it is important to not confuse the size of a customer organization with the classification of a storage system. For example, an organization may be classified (by some criteria) as mid-market or small-medium business (SMB) or small-medium enterprise (SME), but that by itself does not indicate the class of storage system they do or should use. In particular, a very large organization may employ multiple classes of storage systems in different departments.

Vendors may have various motivations for offering such guarantees. They may be offered as evidence of a vendor's high confidence in their system's capabilities. They may be a marketing tactic to help attract customers' interest and win business (and the vendor is willing to risk reduced revenue in cases where a guarantee isn't met and a remedy must be incurred). They may be offered as a way to stand out from competitors or to match competitors who provide similar guarantees. They may be offered because the vendor wants to deflect attention away from system weaknesses or bad press.

Tip: Customers should understand the specific terms and conditions of a storage system guarantee. The following are questions customers can ask: What evidence is there that the system will support what is being guaranteed? How long does the guarantee last? What is the vendor's remedy for the customer if the guarantee is not met? How soon must any deserved remedy be provided? How are customer-vendor disagreements about whether a situation violates a guarantee handled? A particularly interesting question to ask a vendor is: How many times has the vendor had to provide the guarantee's remedy for the storage system model in question during the past year?

The most common types of guarantees are described below (along with a tip identifying a type of guarantee that may be of interest to customers, but which may not be offered by vendors):

o <u>Capacity guarantees</u>. Some vendors offer customers a *capacity guarantee.* This may take the form of claiming a storage system model can reduce the amount of physical capacity needed by at least x% to provide a given amount of usable capacity, compared to the system being replaced. That can represent a potential cost savings to a customer since the cost of capacity, future capacity upgrades, and post-warranty maintenance for drives are often a major portion of overall system cost.

Tip: Customers should ask vendors offering capacity guarantees for evidence that claimed savings will be attained in the customer's environment. Such evidence could be the output of a vendor-provided tool run against an installed storage system and designed to estimate potential capacity savings of the proposed storage system.

Tip: In case achieved capacity savings on the new system turn out to be less than guaranteed savings, customers should ensure ahead of time that an acceptable remedy will be offered. An example of such a remedy is the vendor taking the following actions: adding physical capacity to the new system to address the capacity gap at no extra charge, not charging for any additional components required to support that added capacity (e.g., enclosures for drives or additional system controllers), not charging for associated post-warranty maintenance, and not imposing charges that would otherwise apply due to software features priced based on physical capacity.

One reason actual capacity savings may be less than the guaranteed savings is that some customers are already using techniques to optimize physical capacity. In that case, another storage system may not be able to significantly further reduce physical capacity requirements. A vendor will presumably want to determine whether that is the case before offering a specific guarantee.

o Availability guarantees. Some storage system vendors offer customers an *availability guarantee*. An availability guarantee is generally about providing a remedy to a customer if storage system availability is impaired. It is not a kind of metaphysical assurance that a storage system's data and functions will be available to users 100% of the time without exception.

Tip: Customers should understand what storage system attributes an availability guarantee applies to. Does it apply to maintaining access to all data at all times? Does it apply to maintaining access to all function at all times? Does the guarantee apply to hardware problems or software problems or both? Does it apply to performance remaining acceptable even if a system component fails and, if so, how is "acceptable" defined? (If a component failure results in unacceptable performance, it may be reasonable to judge availability to be (indirectly) impaired.)

Tip: Customers should understand what an availability guarantee's remedy is. For example: Is it money to compensate the customer for the impact to the customer's business? (That is unlikely because it is not under a vendor's control.) Is it a fixed sum of money or is it based on the amount of time availability was compromised? Is it an extension to the system's warranty? Is it pre-paid maintenance? Is it a discount on future upgrades or products or maintenance from the same vendor?

o Performance guarantees. Some vendors offer a *performance guarantee* to help assure a customer that a storage system configuration to be installed meets the customer's performance requirements.

Tip: Customers generally are not storage system engineers. They rarely have the skill or time prior to operating a storage system to determine whether it will meet their performance requirements. Unless, before making an acquisition decision, a customer can evaluate a system's performance by running their own performance benchmark that effectively represents the planned application environment, they will (or should) want evidence the proposed system will meet their performance needs.

Evidence could include: a customer's prior experience with the model or previous generation models, performance modeling results performed by the vendor based on customer input, a vendor's internal performance benchmark results if the I/O workload and system configuration are applicable to the customer's environment, industry-standard benchmark results if the I/O workload and system configuration are applicable to the customer's environment, and testimonials from other customers who are running the proposed model with a similar I/O workload and system configuration.

Tip: Performance guarantees should be carefully reviewed by customers because (understandably) vendors may write them mainly to protect themselves. A guarantee should be clear about what constitutes acceptable performance; that may apply to all I/O workloads or to only specific I/O workloads. A guarantee might state that any I/O workload not performing satisfactorily must be the same as the I/O workload measured on the replaced system (and it may be the customer's responsibility to prove it).

Tip: Customers should understand what a performance guarantee's remedy is. The remedy could initially involve a vendor's experts helping the customer tune the system. If that does not eliminate the problem, the remedy could then involve the vendor adding hardware or software features or even replacing the system by a faster model (or even a competitor's storage system), all at no additional cost to the customer.

Tip: There are various reasons why a newly installed storage system may not deliver promised performance. It may be because of planning errors by either the vendor or customer. More unfortunately, it may be because of an unscrupulous vendor under-configuring a system's performance capability to win business based on price. That's easy to do because performance is not a tangible component like capacity, but more of an experience when using a storage system. An unscrupulous vendor may hope that, once the underperforming storage system is installed, the customer will decide it is better (e.g., less risky and less time consuming) to pay for additional hardware (such as more cache or more drives) than to go through another migration to another storage system. Or, the vendor may pay for those upgrades as a penalty but still expect to make a profit on other upgrades, future maintenance, and follow-on systems. Customers can help protect themselves against these kinds of situations by insisting vendors provide performance guarantees.

Tip: If a vendor does not formally offer a guarantee a customer wants or that a competitor offers, the vendor may be willing to create one if that is what it takes to win or at least compete for the business.

Tip: It may be that no storage system vendor offers anything like a general "security guarantee" for their storage systems. The Security chapter discusses system attributes such a guarantee might cover such as absence of malware in a system's software.

- Capacity-on-demand. Some vendors offer *capacity-on-demand (CoD)* marketing programs for selected storage systems. These programs provide pre-installed capacity that can be quickly put into productive use (and paid for) at a time determined by the customer. This is sometimes described as "pay as you grow." Potential benefits include: delayed costs (compared to paying for the capacity ahead of time) and assurance the capacity is available for use immediately rather than having to order it, then wait for it to be delivered and installed.

Tip: The details of a capacity-on-demand program can vary by vendor and by storage system model. There are multiple questions customers can ask vendors about the program. Customers should keep in mind that, while CoD programs provide flexibility to customers, they also have work and cost implications for vendors; it's reasonable for CoD programs to have limits and restrictions. Questions to ask vendors include:

   o *Basics:* What is the approximate time it currently takes if additional capacity is ordered as a normal upgrade rather than through the CoD program? (Of course, that can change if circumstances, such as unanticipated supply problems or spikes in demand, occur in the future.) What are the complete terms and conditions of the program? What customers can participate in the program? Can the vendor provide references of other customers using the program?

o *Prices: How would using the program compare financially to using the normal upgrade process? Is there any charge to participate in the program (before CoD capacity is used)? What charges occur when CoD capacity is used? Can any or all unused capacity in the pool be returned to the vendor at no charge or for at least partial reimbursement of paid charges? If configuring CoD capacity requires additional enclosures or cabinets or other system components, how and when are they charged for? Can capacity withdrawn from the CoD pool be used temporarily (e.g., for only end-of-quarter use) and then returned to the pool with charges only for the time the capacity was used?*

o *Management: What types of drives can be pre-installed? What are the minimum, maximum, and incremental amounts of capacity that can be pre-installed? Can more drives be added later to an installed CoD pool? Can a CoD pool of capacity be added to an installed storage system that does not already have a CoD pool? Can capacity be withdrawn from the CoD pool and put into productive use at any time without disrupting system operation? What increments of capacity can be withdrawn from the CoD pool at one time? Is there a time limit on how long CoD capacity can be installed without being paid for?*

- Limited time offers. Some vendors may offer special incentives to customers for a limited period of time only. Examples of such incentives include reduced or no charges for selected system features normally charged for, or delayed payments, or free trials (aka "try and buy") of a system or feature, or free vendor services (e.g., assistance with data migration), or an option to exchange a storage system purchased now for a newer model (perhaps not yet formally announced, but expected to be announced) within some time frame.

Tip: These kinds of offers can provide value to customers. However, customers should give some thought as to why the incentives are offered. They may be offered simply to help boost near-term sales or to gain publicity without permanently reducing prices. Or, perhaps the offers are made to match similar offers from competitors. On the other hand, such offers may be attempts to increase sales of a system model or feature that is not selling well; if so, that prompts questioning why sales have been low. Or, perhaps the offers are made to help clear inventory of a system model soon to be replaced by a next-generation model.

Customers should consider possible undesirable consequences of accepting such offers. There may be unanticipated costs of "free" features such as post-warranty maintenance charges. Any additional data capacity acquired might result in increased charges for software features priced by capacity. Customers installing a system or feature for a free trial should consider what would be entailed to uninstall it if they decide not to keep it.

Tip: Customers may want to determine whether a limited time offer is an official vendor program, or is merely a sales tactic by a particular vendor representative to motivate a customer to act quickly and perhaps not fully evaluate competing systems.

Tip: Customers may want to proactively ask their vendors whether such programs are currently offered. A vendor may mention a limited time offer only if they think they need it to win a particular opportunity. (From the vendor's perspective, the offer decreases revenue and profit.) Even if an offer a customer would like (perhaps one available from another vendor) is not available from a given vendor, or if a limited-time offer has expired, the customer may be able to negotiate comparable deals with the vendor who may agree rather than lose business. In any case, as the saying goes, "It doesn't hurt to ask."

- <u>Relocating drives between systems</u>. Some vendors support the ability to relocate drives from one installed storage system to another, compatible system. This can be useful if a customer wants to shift workloads among storage systems. Whether this flexibility is supported by a vendor may be a marketing decision rather than a technical decision.

- <u>Replacing drives in a system</u>. Some vendors support the ability to replace at least some drives in a system by other drives. For example, a customer might have the option to replace previously installed drives with faster or higher capacity drives at a discount if the replaced drives are returned to the manufacturer. This process can require the customer to first move their data off the drives being replaced. Some storage systems support commands to "depopulate" user-selected drives, making replacement easier. Whether a replacement option is supported by a vendor may be a marketing decision rather than a technical decision.

Additional Tips

- *Marketing collateral often highlights "bragging rights": storage system attributes that are particularly impressive, especially compared to competitors' offerings. For example: Marketing messages might emphasize that a particular storage system model has achieved the highest result to-date in an industry-standard performance benchmark, or that a particular storage system model supports a higher maximum capacity than competitors' systems.*

  Repeating a major point in this Guide: What matters most is how well a product and vendor can support a customer's requirements. Capabilities (and weaknesses) that do not relate to requirements should have low priority in the decision process, no matter how impressive bragging rights claims may be. In any case, bragging rights are often short-lived, leapfrogged by other vendors' achievements.

- *It is useful to identify the date a marketing document was published. For text documents, this is usually near the front or near the end of the document. A relatively old date may indicate the product is not receiving frequent or notable enhancements.*

  Further, claims in marketing deliverables may not be updated in a timely way to reflect industry developments that occur after the deliverables were published. Consider a vendor marketing claim of the form "only my system can do such-and-such." Has the vendor actually compared the claim against every other storage system? Is the claim true given current competitors' offerings? (A published claim could potentially be invalidated by a competitor the day it is made. It is reasonable to give a vendor a little time to correct or update such a claim, but the process should certainly not take years.)

- *Claims comparing a storage system in vague relative terms provide little information. Consider these terms: "reduces," "increases," "simplifies," "is faster than," "is more efficient than," and "provides the highest levels of." They all prompt the question: Compared to what? Can the claim be quantified? (A claim that system A is faster than system B does not indicate whether it is 100% faster or only 1% faster.) If the claim is about multi-faceted storage attributes such as availability or performance, what particular aspect of those attributes does the claim apply to? Whatever the answers, customers should consider whether the claimed improvement would be relevant and significant in their environment.*

- *Verbs often misused in marketing messages include "maximizes" (ask: Is it really as large as theoretically possible?) and "minimizes" (ask: Is it really as small as theoretically possible?). "Optimizes" is ambiguous (ask: In what way or to what extent? Is the claim that the function is as efficient or effective as theoretically possible, or, perhaps, that it is just improved and, if so, relative to what?). Another verb to be wary of is "ensure" such as a vendor's claim that a system ensures access to data never fails. A customer should ask: How can the vendor or storage system ensure that some condition will not happen – perhaps a latent software bug or a failure (however unlikely) of redundant hardware – that can result in a problem, perhaps as serious as loss of data access or even loss of data?*

- *Various adjectives vendors use to describe their storage systems may sound impressive, but by themselves do not provide quantified value. Consider: "advanced," "agile," "easy," "effective," "efficient," "extreme," "flexible," "high [good attribute like availability]," "intelligent," "low [bad attribute like overhead]," "powerful," "smart," "sophisticated," and "trusted." Adjectives sometimes used to describe system or feature performance include "blazing," "fast," "lightning," and "rapid."*

  Qualifying adjectives with adverbs such as "dramatically," "most," "significantly," "substantially," "ultra," and "very," may be done to try to impress the audience, but really does not add useful information.

  It's not that using such terms is wrong. Rather, customers should withhold making judgments based on such terms until more information is provided.

- *A vendor may describe a function as completing "instantly." Any computer or storage function takes some amount of time to complete. The time may be short from a human perspective, but a term such as "near-instantly" would be more accurate. Also, while a simple invocation of a function may complete near-instantly, the time may take longer in certain cases such as if the command invoking the function has a long list of items the function is to be applied against. For example, making a logical copy of one volume may complete near-instantly, but making a copy of 1000 volumes all at the same time may take perceptively longer.*

- *Marketing claims such as "our new system's performance is 2x better" or "our market share doubled" may sound impressive, but without knowing the base reference point the claim has little meaning. Consider that a startup storage system company may announce their market* share increased by 100%. The claim may be accurate, but its significance will be interpreted one way if the increase was from 1% to 2% of a market, but in quite another way if the increase was from 25% to 50%. (Other questions, such as how the market segment is defined, are also warranted.)

- Clever marketing can sometimes divert attention from product weaknesses. Emphasizing benefits without mentioning drawbacks is a straightforward approach; consider a marketing focus on high performance without mentioning lack of useful data management functions found in competing products. A marketing message to make the best of a system with an active-passive controller design may highlight that system performance remains consistent even if a controller fails.

- Vendors sometimes introduce new marketing campaigns (e.g., using new themes or new messages) to reposition the market's perception of a given storage system model. For example, if a model isn't selling well when the emphasis is on its support for high capacity, the marketing focus might change to reposition the system as an ideal platform for consolidating multiple smaller storage systems into a single system. Or, a vendor losing sales due to customers choosing competing systems with more data capacity might shift its marketing focus to another system attribute such as performance or function. The system model hasn't changed, but the vendor is hoping customers' perceptions of the system will change.

- Claims of a storage system's superiority compared to unspecified "other systems" can be ambiguous. Is the comparison to a previous generation of the same storage system, or to another storage system family from the same vendor, or to a specific competitor's current system, or to a competitor's older generation system, or to all other storage systems in the market, or to something else?

- A claim to be wary of is that a storage system has "no compromises." What does such a claim mean? Unless the system has attributes such as infinite capacity scalability, every component supporting the fastest speed available in the industry, any degree of hardware redundancy a customer might desire, and support for every publicly known storage function and optimization, it appears design compromises were made.

- A claim that a storage system provides "extensive" support for some capability is not the same as saying it provides "comprehensive" support. "Extensive" implies something could be missing.

- A claim such as "my storage system supports function F" warrants asking: Does the support apply to my environment? It should not be assumed that a system's function does what a customer wants it to do simply because marketing deliverables say the function is "supported" without further information about what that means. Drilling down, perhaps using more technical documents, can reveal any "small print" details such as: exceptions, limitations, implementation complexity, incompatibilities with other features, and less than clear product manuals administrators have to rely on.

- *A claim such as "my system's function F is compatible with industry standard S or with function G as implemented in another storage system" warrants questioning. In particular, "compatible" could mean "is 100% identical to in all ways," or "is a subset of," or "is similar to with exceptions," or something else.*

- *A storage system feature may sound like it inherently provides a function, but watch for qualifiers indicating otherwise such as "helps to" or "enables" or "provides the foundation for." (A claim such as "my storage system enables improved xyz" implies that something in addition to what is being described may be needed to achieve the improvement – what is it?) Another qualification to be aware of is "designed to."*

  These kinds of qualifiers may be included at the request of vendors' lawyers to protect against potential legal actions by customers in case their expectations are not met. (Customer: The system did not make the copy of data I requested; I'm going to sue. Vendor: We clearly said that the system was designed to make the copy, not that it actually would without fail.)

- *Products are sometimes marketed as "new" for quite some time after they have been available.[124] Customers may need to research the dates of initial announcement and general availability to help them judge whether a product warrants being called "new", or how new it really is. In addition, a vendor may re-announce (aka re-launch) a product or feature long after it was originally announced, as a way to re-advertise it; that may be because the original announcement did not receive the publicity or customer interest the vendor hoped for.*

- *Sometimes an analyst's paper about a generic technical storage capability includes statements like "This important capability is supported by products such as vendor X's storage system." That may indicate the vendor hired the analyst to write the paper, especially if competing products are not mentioned by name. (Sometimes an analyst's document will state it was written at the request of a vendor or that a mentioned vendor is a client, but not always.)*

- *An important marketing skill is creative writing. Almost anything in the marketplace can be described in ways that make it seem good (if it's your offering) – or bad (if it's a competitor's offering). One storage vendor once characterized virtualized storage as "Frankenstorage" because customers integrate multiple, potentially incompatible storage systems together (via a virtualization facility), in contrast to conventional storage systems integrated in the factory. When that same vendor later introduced a storage virtualization offering, it was described in rather glowing terms. The point is, customers need to look beyond simple, often clever, characterizations of storage products and determine for themselves whether or not there is real value to be had.*

---

[124] *The U.S. Federal Trade Commission (FTC) has advised adhering to a six month time limit. See http://www.consumeradvertisinglawblog.com/2010/02/how-long-can-your-product-be-new-and-improved.html.*

Sales Tactics

Vendors focus on selling products and services. That begins with an announcement, continues with marketing, and completes with a sales process and closing (followed by installation and upgrades).

A vendor may use a variety of tactics during the selling process to persuade a customer to acquire their storage system.[125] Many tactics are perfectly legitimate and certainly not limited to only the storage industry. However, some tactics that may be employed some times by some vendors are at least questionable if not potentially unethical.[126] By being aware of these potential vendor tactics customers can avoid being caught off-guard and can better evaluate the quality of their relationship with a vendor.

The question for customers is: Vendors will try to manage your decision process – don't you want to manage your vendors?

Note: Because there are so many sales tactics not directly related to costs and so many sales tactics that are directly related to costs, cost-related topics are covered in the *Prices and Costs* chapter.

Landscape

- Attention to the customer. A vendor may pay a lot of attention to a prospective buyer during the sales process. Vendor representatives may call on multiple relevant parties in the customer's organization. That can include vendor executives calling on customer C-level executives such as the CIO and CFO, and other vendor representatives calling on lower level decision makers and decision-influencers.

  Tip: Vendor representatives may carefully choose which customer parties they call on and which messages they communicate to each party. That's reasonable considering the CFO

---

[125] The term *tactics* is not intended to be disparaging. Other terms that could be used are *methods* and *actions*. The interaction between buyer and seller in many transactions is sometimes contentious with each party trying to achieve their own, sometimes inconsistent, goals. A seller generally wants a customer to pay the highest possible price and wants to complete a transaction in the shortest possible time. A buyer generally wants to pay the lowest possible price and wants sufficient time to make a well-thought-out product and vendor decision.

[126] Many vendor companies have formal policies for appropriate business conduct, but individual representatives may not always act accordingly. Unethical sales behavior is hopefully a rarity.

likely doesn't want to hear about technology and the IT staff may have limited interest in finance. However, there are possible negative consequences to this selectivity. A vendor may focus on only those parties they think will support their proposal, avoiding parties who might find weaknesses in the proposal or even disapprove of it. It's possible that, in the end, no party has a complete picture of the proposal. Customers should manage the evaluation and decision process to avoid these pitfalls.

Tip: *Vendor representatives may have a healthy expense account allowing them to treat decision makers and influencers to meals and events, perhaps even gifts, hoping to increase "face time," strengthen the relationship, create loyalty, and instill in customers a feeling that "I owe the vendor something." A customer may appreciate all the special attention they receive during the sales process, but should question whether it will be ongoing after the sale and, more importantly, to what extent it is relevant to the product decision.*

Customers who accept vendor offers to pay for meals, events, and gifts should consider how that might influence the decision process. Upper management might choose to allow at least some such activities as a way to foster a customer-vendor relationship, but should proactively warn the organization's participants against letting such activities unduly influence a decision or recommendation. Some customers have policies that constrain or prohibit such vendor activities.

- <u>Good news focus</u>. Sales representatives' messages, such as in face-to-face discussions and product presentations, generally focus on presenting a high-level "good news" story. That includes highlighting product and vendor capabilities, and highlighting customer goals, opportunities, and concerns the product and vendor can help address, while avoiding any topics that could be possible objections to a sale such as product weaknesses. For example, when all-flash storage systems were designed specifically for only flash technology (not HDDs), vendors emphasized the systems' high performance while deemphasizing the absence of data management functions common in more established systems. (A way to compensate for this weakness was installing the flash system behind a storage virtualization facility, though that raised costs and complexity.)

Tip: *Sales representatives may try to delay discussing cost considerations, especially if that is not a competitive advantage, until after the representatives have created a favorable customer impression of product and vendor capabilities.*

- <u>Customer and analyst views</u>. Aware that customers like to know reputable third parties have had positive experiences with the vendor and positive assessments of its offerings, vendor sales representatives may actively distribute customer testimonials and positive analyst reports.

Tip: *The sales representatives may not expect a customer to read that material to assess its applicability to the customer's environment, but at least hope to create the impression that other customers and industry experts have favorable assessments of the vendor and its products.*

- <u>Focus on maximum capabilities</u>. Sales representatives may emphasize maximum storage system family capabilities (such as the maximum capacity or maximum performance of a model in a family of compatible models).

  Tip: This can occur even when those maximum capabilities exceed those of the system configuration proposed as sufficient to meet a customer's requirements, or even when the proposed family model is not upgradable in-place to the high-end family model.   Such emphasis is particularly likely if those maximum capabilities exceed the corresponding maximum capabilities of competitors' systems.   (A high-speed sports car in the showroom window may draw customers into a car dealership that mainly sells family sedans.)

- <u>Non-incumbent vendors</u>. A sales representative from a vendor a customer currently does not do business with may (and probably should) work especially hard to persuade a customer to switch vendors. Vendors know that customers prefer to stay with what works or is at least "good enough" unless there is a compelling reason to change. Non-incumbent vendors may identify such reasons; it is up to a customer, of course, to decide whether those reasons are truly compelling.

  Tip: A vendor, especially a non-incumbent vendor, may assign a technical resource (sometimes called a systems engineer*) to work with the customer's technical staff during the sales process, to help build a relationship and build confidence in the vendor. Will that resource still be around if the vendor wins the business? Will it be the same person(s) or someone with comparable or better skills? How often will that resource be at the customer's site or otherwise easy to contact? Another issue for customers to consider is that, if the resource provides significant help to manage the new storage system, the customer organization might view them as additional no-cost staff; changing vendors could add the cost of hiring personnel to replace the vendor-provided resource.*

- <u>ISV assistance</u>. A vendor sales representative may bring in a representative from an ISV (Independent Software Vendor) for a host-based software product (such as a database management system) the customer uses or is evaluating, to talk about how well that software and the vendor's storage system work together.

  Tip: While that can certainly be useful information, customers should question whether any benefits are unique to that vendor's storage system and whether the benefits apply to the customer's environment.

- <u>Turning a unique feature into a requirement</u>. A vendor may focus on any capability of their storage system that is unique relative to competing systems and try to persuade a customer to make that capability a requirement or at least a preferred system capability.

  Tip: Certainly, a customer may determine adding such a requirement is justified in some cases. However, making a feature that is unique to one particular system model or family a requirement could inhibit a customer's flexibility to choose among alternate storage systems or could discourage other vendors from even bidding.

- <u>Briefings</u>. Vendors often invite customers to briefings at an off-site vendor-run or manufacturer-run briefing center. The customer will likely meet experienced product experts and vendor management, perhaps get a tour of a manufacturing plant, and gain insights into the storage system and plans for future enhancements generally beyond insights a sales representative can provide. The vendor hopes to have the customer's full attention for a day or two to help strengthen the customer-vendor relationship.

Tip: These briefing centers are sometimes called "Executive Briefing Centers" to add an aura of importance, though in practice many attendees are a customer's technical staff and many presenters are not executives.

Tip: Briefing center personnel, no matter how knowledgeable (they give presentations and answer customer's questions for a living) and personable (a critical quality for a briefing center presenter), are likely not the vendor representatives who will be directly supporting the customer after the sale.

Tip: Customers may not realize that vendors often agonize over whether to schedule a vendor-site briefing (or even a customer-site presentation) before or after the customer attends a competitor's briefing (or presentation). Will the customer best remember only the most recent messages they heard? Or, can the vendor going first tell the customer what they can expect to later hear from the competitor and suggest tough questions to ask, all in the hope of undercutting the competitor's messages?

- <u>Future product enhancements</u>. A vendor may focus on discussing planned future product enhancements. Motivations could include highlighting a future competitive advantage or indicating "me too" when the vendor is currently at a competitive disadvantage.

Tip: A vendor's claims of future storage system capabilities (aka directions, intents, plans, or roadmaps) sometimes become reality, but sometimes do not. Vendors may (or may not) clearly indicate whether the status of a future capability is a concept merely being considered or is a commitment funded by the manufacturer (e.g., development costs are in the budget with a planned product availability date). A future capability may or may not be planned to be supported on a storage system sold "today."[127] Regardless, the vendor's plan could potentially change at any time – another point for customers to consider.

Unless there is an acceptable penalty in case a compelling potential future enhancement ends up not being offered on the storage system model a customer is considering or ends up not being offered in a time frame desired by a customer, it can be risky to base an acquisition decision on it.

---

[127] *Storage system manufacturers often struggle with which approach to take. Supporting a new hardware or software capability on only a next-generation storage system can help increase sales of that system. However, also adding that capability to previous generation systems can bring in revenue by selling it as a priced upgrade and can foster customer satisfaction by protecting/enhancing the value of installed systems. A downside of supporting an upgrade to installed systems is additional manufacturer expense for development and testing as well as possible delayed revenue if some customers use the upgrade as a reason to delay migrating to the next-generation system.*

Because of the uncertainty involved, some customers may choose to limit storage system evaluations and comparisons to offerings that are currently announced and available. Some customers may give lower value in an evaluation process to future capabilities the farther out in time they are estimated to be available. (An announcement a vendor states is planned for a month from now is more likely to happen on schedule than one planned for a year from now.)

- <u>Dual vendor strategy</u>. Some customers employ a "dual vendor strategy" as a way to help manage vendor relationships and storage system decisions. The idea is that a customer buys all their storage systems from (at least) two vendors.

***Tip:** There are several benefits to this strategy. For one, it limits the number of different vendors and systems a customer needs to evaluate, simplifying the decision process and the data center environment. The customer hopes that each vendor is motivated to provide good prices and good service because each vendor knows there is always an incumbent competitor the customer seriously considers for their business. The strategy also allows the customer to compare the quality and capabilities of the vendors' systems and support based on direct experience. The customer may decide to replace one of the vendors in the small group of vendors they work with if that vendor's offerings deteriorate.*

There are also several drawbacks to a dual vendor strategy. Working with a single vendor provides a single point of contact, sometimes described as "one back to pat and one throat to choke."[128] Migration between incompatible storage systems can add administrative time and effort and increased business risk. A related drawback is that a customer may decide that, to facilitate migrations and make it easy to shift data between storage systems, they should avoid using any capabilities on one vendor's system that are not supported on the other vendor's system, a "lowest common denominator" approach. Another drawback is that a customer may miss out on alternatives in the market that would better support their environment.[129]

Note that a customer can potentially subvert their own dual vendor strategy by strictly alternating which vendor they buy their next storage system from, a pattern the vendors can likely figure out. If a vendor believes "it's my turn this time" they may not make the best possible offer. If a vendor believes "it's not my turn to win the business this time," they may exert minimum time-and-effort trying to do so.

---

[128] *Problem solving is especially complex when hardware and software from multiple vendors reside between a user and their data. Consider a server from Vendor A running software from Vendor B where the server is connected to a SAN switch from Vendor C that in turn connects to a storage virtualization facility from Vendor D that manages storage systems from Vendors E and F. If, say, data returned to the user is corrupted, who is at fault? Problems without an easily identifiable culprit can, unfortunately, result in finger-pointing ("I didn't do it; you must have done it.") between a customer and multiple vendors, delaying a solution.*

[129] *Given the large number of storage system vendors and products currently in the market and the frequency at which storage innovations are being introduced, the chance of missing out on storage vendor offerings that could be valuable to the customer is higher than ever. An exception is when a customer's requirements are so specialized that only a small number of vendors can possibly meet them; an example is storage system support for IBM z/OS mainframe environments.*

- Keeping the old system's serial number. A vendor may propose replacing an installed system they previously sold a customer with a newer model with the same serial number. The customer can then potentially position the change as a system upgrade to avoid a formal bidding process or having to deal with replacing equipment not yet fully depreciated. (Maintaining a system's serial number after an upgrade is sometimes referred to as having a *Velcro serial number*.)

Tip: There may be government rules or accounting practices that regulate how to deal with true in-place upgrades vs. system replacements.

- Early system replacement. Sometimes a customer may complain about the quality of an installed storage system if it has a serious problem (e.g., suffers a long outage that hurts the business) or has a history of frequent (even if minor) problems. The system's vendor may address the situation by recommending the customer replace the problematic system with another system. The recommended system may be a different, but compatible, model in the same family, or may be a system the vendor sells that is incompatible with the installed system. Unless the problems are believed to be inherent to the system family or to the way the customer operates, moving to another compatible system may be a reasonable plan because it helps reduce migration complexity and may provide other benefits such as additional capabilities if the recommended model is a next-generation system.

Of course, there are other considerations to keep in mind. The vendor may be motivated to push a replacement solution rather than other solutions due to the revenue it would bring in, perhaps much earlier than had been forecast. Unless the problems were so severe that the vendor offers the new system at no charge, it will cost the customer money, perhaps long before that money was planned to be included in the budget. There may be accounting issues such as the current book value of the problematic system. The customer should negotiate with the vendor for help with these issues, such as a significant discount or delayed payment for the replacement system, along with vendor assistance with the migration. The vendor will hopefully be eager to please since the problem was in their product and they don't want to risk losing the customer to a competitor.

- Closing. Closing a sale is a climactic moment that marks achieving a major milestone in both sales and acquisition processes. However, getting to closing can sometimes be a stressful process for both the customer and vendor.

Tip: Some sales representatives are sometimes reluctant to ask a customer for the business because they are afraid of hearing "No." In contrast, some sales representatives are relatively aggressive in pursuing closing business. They may ask something like "What can I do to get your business today?" or "If I can fulfill the request you just made, do we have a deal?"

Tip: A vendor, if not awarded the sale, may go over the head of the decision maker to higher management to try to have the decision overturned. The vendor may think they have nothing to lose. Perhaps the current sales representative expects to not remain assigned to the account long enough to have to deal with any ill will this tactic may create.

Tip: *Following a successful close, a vendor might arrange for a lavish celebration, hoping to cement the relationship in a memorable way to influence future business.*

Additional Tips

- *Ideally, vendor sales representatives are motivated to propose offerings in the best interest of the customer. But customers should not assume that is necessarily the case because conflicting motivations can come into play. Consider a sales representative's possible motives: make money (and keep one's job) by achieving quota (and separate quotas may apply to profit and revenue for the overall deal, for hardware, and for licensed software features), earn a raise, earn a promotion, qualify for a bonus, pursue other sales opportunities as quickly as possible, and sell what they are told to sell by their management (who may have their own motivations).[130]*

- *There is an old saying that customers buy from sales representatives they like. Certainly, customers do not want to do business with someone they do not trust, or who they feel lacks expertise, or is overly pushy, or who they are just uncomfortable with.*

  Before making an acquisition decision, a customer should consider meeting with the vendor's representatives (e.g., sales, technical, and product service (maintenance) personnel), and perhaps their direct managers, who would be officially assigned to support the customer. If there are any personnel issues the customer is concerned about, it's best to find that out before an acquisition decision is made. (Customers sometimes ask a vendor to replace a particular representative the customer does not want to work with.)

  Vendors often have their best customer-facing personnel (i.e., most knowledgeable, most charismatic) assist with selling, but they may not be the personnel who directly support the customer after a sale. For example, many vendors have representatives skilled in giving product presentations and providing comparisons against competitors, but those representatives often travel widely and are unlikely to be permanently assigned to any one customer.

- *Vendors sometimes strive for* account control, *a situation where a vendor has sold most or all of a customer's storage (or even most or all of the customer's IT equipment). A vendor with account control has significant advantages over competitors in future selling opportunities. An incumbent vendor usually has an existing, even long-term, relationship with the customer that is comfortable for both parties. An incumbent vendor may be willing to renegotiate existing contracts if that helps keep out competitors. An incumbent vendor can propose proactively upgrading installed storage systems to help keep out competitors*

---

[130] *Sales representatives typically earn a substantial portion of their income in the form of commissions paid based on business they close. Accordingly, sales representatives are sometimes said to be "coin operated." This isn't to say technically-oriented vendor representatives aren't motivated by money, but they are often also motivated by the pleasures and challenges of working with computer technology.*

proposing new systems; upgrades are usually lower cost and less business risk than new, unfamiliar systems.

It is widely recognized by vendors that winning additional business from a customer is easier – usually significantly easier – than winning initial business. On the other hand, competitors also know this and therefore are motivated to offer especially attractive proposals to make their (initial) sale, which can be to a customer's advantage at least in the short term.[131]

- *When selling to a customer who already has storage systems installed from multiple vendors and who wants to add one new system or replace only one installed system, a vendor may make a proposal supporting system coexistence which is what the customer requested. However, the vendor may decide their best strategy or opportunity is instead to propose replacing all storage (aka sweeping the floor). Or, the vendor may decide their best strategy is to make two proposals, coexistence and sweeping the floor, so that the customer is choosing among the two proposals from that one vendor (and hopefully paying less attention to other vendors).*

- *Be aware of the possibility of a bait-and-switch tactic. For example, this might take the form of a vendor shipping a different system configuration than the customer expected. The vendor might claim it was a mistake that cannot be corrected in an acceptable amount of time so the customer is advised to accept the system as is. The shipped system may include extra capacity or performance capability which the vendor hopes may delay a future acquisition process that would open the door to other vendors. The vendor may offer concessions such as not charging the customer for the extra capabilities until they are used or perhaps offering the extra capabilities immediately at an attractive discount (rather than having to uninstall the system or return unneeded components to the manufacturer).*

- *An incumbent vendor may have little incentive to help a customer use their current storage capacity more efficiently because the customer would then need less additional capacity in the future which could reduce or delay sales revenue.*

  A capacity analysis *can help identify how storage capacity is currently used, often focusing on inefficiently used or excess capacity. The analysis could be done in-house or by a storage vendor or a hired consultant. Recommendations resulting from a capacity analysis may include deploying various data management procedures and technologies to use storage capacity more efficiently. (See the* Capacity *chapter.)*

  For vendor-performed capacity analyses, a non-incumbent vendor may have more incentive than an incumbent vendor to help the customer use current capacity more efficiently because that can help win future business by generating good will and sending the message that the incumbent vendor has been taking the customer for granted. The non-

---

[131] *Reasons a customer may choose to stay with a particular vendor or particular storage system family can vary. The incumbent system and vendor may be "good enough," satisfying needs and causing no serious problems to-date. Or, a customer may not want to undergo the risks of change or may not want to take the time and effort to identify and analyze other offerings in the marketplace, even if there might be benefits to be had.*

incumbent vendor may even offer to provide a capacity analysis at no charge. (However, customers should not ask a vendor to invest the time and effort to perform a no-charge analysis if the customer has no intention of doing further business with that vendor.) Keep in mind that vendors whose products do not support a particular capacity-optimization technology may be reluctant to recommend a customer use that technology.

Beyond technology recommendations, a business-oriented recommendation could identify an organization's users who would benefit from using currently unused (excess) storage capacity.

- *When a storage system and host are installed from the same vendor and the customer wants to replace that storage with storage from another vendor, the incumbent vendor's representative may claim the storage will not work with their host or may claim that the vendor will no longer provide host maintenance if the customer connects the other vendor's storage to it. Unless there is official documentation from the incumbent vendor to substantiate such a claim (e.g., a document on host-storage interoperability), the claim may be just a scare tactic by the incumbent (and worried) sales representative. A customer should talk to the representative's management to clarify the issue. A customer statement that the vendor will not receive future business if they take an uncooperative stance may help resolve the issue.*

Competitive Tactics

With a worldwide market measured in tens of billions of U.S. dollars annually and many vendors vying for that revenue, it is not surprising that the enterprise storage market is intensively competitive. The good news is that this competition gives customers choices of products and vendors, helps drive technology advances, and helps keep prices lower than they otherwise might be. But this same competition often results in intense battles fought among storage system competitors with claims and counterclaims for customers to sort out.

Landscape

- <u>Getting beyond good news</u>. Storage system vendors, like most vendors in most industries, tend to focus on communicating the benefits and competitive advantages of their offerings – the "good news" story – while hoping to avoid or at least minimize customers' awareness of weaknesses. Therefore, caveat emptor (Latin for "let the buyer beware"); it is up to customers to probe to identify any product and vendor weaknesses.

  High-level examples of storage system weaknesses include unsupported capabilities, limitations and restrictions on supported capabilities, complicated data management procedures, and hardware or software quality problems. Examples of vendor weaknesses include objectionable items in a contract's "small print," high customer support personnel turnover, and business viability issues. No storage system or storage vendor appears to have a reputation of being weakness-free.

  Tip: *Customers are users of storage; comprehensively evaluating a storage system's technology and quality is not their core competency. Identifying weaknesses in storage systems considered for acquisition can be challenging, especially given customers' constraints such as limited time and, often, lack of relevant hands-on experience. That leaves avenues such as reading specification sheets, reading marketing literature, attending vendors' presentations, reading product manuals (e.g., user guides that together can run into thousands of pages for a single storage system), reading industry watchers' views, and talking to other customers who have used the systems being considered.*

  There is another resource customers can access that is potentially extremely helpful. To help make their case versus competitors, vendors are motivated to take the time and effort to study competitors' offerings looking for weaknesses. And vendors are understandably eager to share their findings with customers.

Unfortunately, customers cannot assume that all information a vendor provides about a competitor is accurate or at least not misleading. A vendor, whether intentionally or accidentally, may make inaccurate or misleading or outdated claims about a competitor. By focusing on only a competitor's weaknesses, a vendor may present an overly negative picture that ignores the competitor's strengths. Customers should listen to what a vendor has to say about its competitors, but should also be on the watch for these pitfalls.

- FUD. "FUD" (rhymes with "mud") stands for *fear, uncertainty, and doubt*. This term has been used for years in the marketing and sales world to characterize many claims vendors make about competing vendors and products, especially inaccurate claims or innuendos of weaknesses. All, some, or none of the claims or innuendos may be true in a given case.

Tip: A vendor may believe spreading FUD has multiple benefits for their sales strategy. It is a way to keep a competitor defensively occupied with supplying responses to the customer for questions prompted by the vendor. It is a way to keep a customer focused on possible weaknesses of a competitor's system, avoiding focus on strengths of the competitor's system and weaknesses of the vendor's system. A vendor using this strategy may hope that even if every FUD claim has a satisfactory response the customer will hear so many negative claims they may think something must be wrong with the competitor's system. (However, a vendor constantly making false or misleading claims about a competitor may find the strategy backfires if the customer sees the competitor is able to provide acceptable responses every time.)

Tip: Here are examples of FUD:

- o *A common FUD claim from a storage system vendor may quickly follow a competitor's announcement of a new system or enhancement: "It is new and therefore unproven; it sounds good on paper, but does it work?" (That may be followed by "Anyway, we're working on something even better.") Such points can be valid to consider, perhaps prompting a customer to gather additional information. Not surprisingly, however, vendors who raise questions about competitors' new announcements typically do not raise them about their own announcements.*

- o *A vendor, faced with a customer interested in a competing storage system, may say "We've never seen any of those systems installed anywhere. They must not be selling well." Even if the representative making the claim is being honest about their particular observation, they likely directly deal with only a few customers out of thousands on the planet. Even a vendor as a company doesn't know what storage systems every customer has installed. (The vendor selling or manufacturing the system being questioned is likely the best reference to ask for statistics about their system's "install base.")*

- o *After a vendor discontinues one storage product in a large portfolio and based on no other evidence, a competitor may say something like "That could indicate they are going out of the storage business, so buying from them could be a big mistake."*

- o *A vendor may make a claim such as: "A customer replaced a different vendor's storage system with my storage system and achieved significant benefits" (such as reduced application elapsed time or reduced floor space or some other benefit). That can sound bad for the replaced system, but often the details of the replaced system are not identified. Why did the customer replace the system? How old was the replaced system? Was the new system doing the same work? How do the configurations compare? Was the new system equal or better in every way?*

○ *A vendor may make a claim of the form "Only my storage system can…" Taken literally, that means the vendor has compared their storage system against every other storage system – is that really the case? A twist on that claim takes the form of "Unlike other storage systems, my system can…" That prompts the question: Which other systems? A vendor may make these kinds of statements hoping to discourage customers from looking at competitors' offerings in the market; after all, if "only my system" can do something a customer wants, why would a customer waste time looking elsewhere?*

○ *A vendor may make a claim of the form "The competitor's system (or a feature of that system) doesn't work." The term "doesn't work" is too broad to be meaningful. It could mean anything from a total continuous malfunction impacting all customers to a minor occasional annoyance experienced by only a small number of customers. It might not be accurate at all. Customers should ask the vendor making the claim for more specific information and evidence.*

○ *A vendor might claim their system was designed from the beginning to support a certain capability that competitors supported only later as an "add-on." The implication is that there is something superior about the former approach and problematic about the latter approach. What matters most, however, is the quality of the capabilities and how well the overall system addresses requirements. Was the new capability added cleanly into the system or does it seem to not fit well? The history of how a system evolved over time to support its current capabilities may be interesting, but is generally less important.*

Tip: By being aware of the FUD strategy, customers can manage their vendors, and their system and vendor evaluation process, to get a fairer view of all candidates. Some customers invite vendors to comment on their competitors. In contrast, some customers ask vendors to discuss only their own offerings. That latter approach may help to at least reduce FUD, but runs the risk of the customer remaining unaware of legitimate points vendors might raise about their competitors.

- <u>Downplay</u>. When a vendor or vendor's storage system lacks a capability supported by a competitor, the vendor may claim that the capability offers little if any value and that customers don't need it. (The author once heard this point cleverly summarized in the competitive server environment as a vendor theoretically telling a customer: "If we don't have it, you don't need it. When we have it, then you'll need it.") Of course, the value, or lack of value, of any particular system capability is up to the customer.

- <u>Compatibility</u>. When one storage system's feature has proven to be popular with customers, other vendors may want to create an impression of "me, too." Some vendors offer unique implementations of comparable hardware or software capabilities. Some vendors offer features they claim are "compatible" with features of another vendor's storage system, e.g., the features support the same user interfaces. Compatibility is sometimes claimed for software-based features in particular and can include support for the same command syntax; that support can potentially allow CLI scripts to run (with fewer or no changes) on all the "compatible" systems, simplifying the coexistence of heterogeneous systems and simplifying system-to-system migration.

Tip: The term "compatible" is ambiguous. "Compatible" likely does not mean "identical." "Compatible" could mean "similar to" or "a subset of." There may be restrictions and limitations relative to the feature being compared to; or, there might even be advantages. (Some vendors have even included the term "compatible" in the name of a feature marketed as compatible with a competitor's feature.) Customers considering a system's "compatible" feature should consult the system's technical documentation, such as user guides, to help identify exceptions and limitations.

Tip: The vendor offering the original feature may plan future enhancements to it. It is unlikely a vendor claiming to support a compatible feature would be able to guarantee, without advanced knowledge of what those enhancements are, to ever implement them in the future, let alone within a specified period of time.

- Visible vs. invisible system attributes. Storage systems have attributes that are visible to customers (such as I/O performance, availability, and floor space) and attributes that are essentially invisible to customers (such as the speeds of connections between internal system components). Customers find the most tangible value in what is visible to them; attributes that make a difference they can experience. But vendors sometimes criticize attributes of competitors' systems that are invisible to customers. Customers should ask themselves: Do invisible attributes make a difference when evaluating and comparing different storage systems?

Tip: What are here being called "invisible attributes" are important in the sense that they make a system's visible attributes possible; knowing about them may provide evidence to support claims about external system behavior and capabilities. But external system behavior and capabilities are generally more important to customers day-to-day operations than the internal system design behind them. Nevertheless, a vendor may try to impress customers with claims their storage system has some superior internal attributes compared to competitors' systems, even though customers cannot readily tell those attributes are there.

For example, a vendor may claim their storage system has a superior hardware architecture compared to competitors' storage systems. While vendors usually share some high-level aspects of a system's architecture with customers, architectural details are usually locked in a proprietary (confidential) document identifying the design guidelines for a storage system model, including (if the document is comprehensive) known design weaknesses. Different hardware architectures have different tradeoffs – to-date there is no proven best storage hardware architecture. (Strong evidence for that is the different architectures of different storage systems sold by the same vendor, and how many different storage system architectures are used successfully by customers.)

As another example, rather than compare system performance measured by fair benchmarks, a vendor may claim their storage system has more or faster internal components of some type than a competitor's system, hoping the audience thinks that indicates the vendor's system must be faster. Such claims may be about the number of internal processors, or about cache size, or about other components. Without a lot more detail such claims really do not provide useful information about performance users see, regardless of how impressive a vendor may make their claims sound. Consider that vendors are likely to highlight any components in their system that are faster than those in a competitor's system, but not mention any components that are slower. Consider that having more components of a given type at first glance implies higher aggregate performance for that set of components; however, it may be that the competitor's system needs fewer such components of that type because it uses faster components or because the competitor's software manages component performance more efficiently. In the end, the performance that matters to customers is the performance applications and users can obtain from a storage system – *not the speed or number of particular components "under the covers."*

- Negative references. A vendor may use a "negative reference" tactic: identifying customers who will talk about problems they have had with competing storage systems or vendors.

  Tip: There may not be a storage system model that works flawlessly everywhere it is installed and there may not be a vendor who has never had a customer unhappy with at least some aspects of the customer-vendor relationship.

  Tip: Information customers receive from negative references won't provide a balanced picture. The vendor offering the negative references will neither be citing customers with positive experiences about the competition nor citing customers with negative experiences about the vendor itself. A vendor might highlight a customer who is particularly vocal about a bad experience, but that does not indicate the experience is widespread. On the other hand, lack of a vendor citing negative references does not mean unhappy customers do not exist. Some customers have a policy of not being a reference and so are not willing to talk negatively (or positively) about a vendor or product. Some vendors may have policies discouraging the use of negative references.

  Tip: Just because a customer is named on a list as an unhappy user of a particular storage system does not guarantee the inclusion is valid or that the facts are as the vendor – or customer – describes them. A referenced customer may be critical of a vendor or product for reasons that may be relevant to the current customer, or for reasons that may have low or no relevance to the current customer. Examples of the latter are issues with a particular vendor representative, or problems with a different system model or system generation than the one being evaluated.

  Tip: Vendors may take actions to avoid their own customers becoming negative references who would willingly share information about problems with the vendor or the vendor's storage system. For example, after a serious problem (such as data loss) caused by their storage system, a vendor may provide a system upgrade or even an additional storage system at no charge to the customer. A vendor executive may call on the customer to try to save the system and relationship. This responsiveness and "customer care" may even leave a customer more satisfied with a vendor than before the problem occurred.

Tip: Storage vendors sometimes point customers to media reports about failures of competitors' offerings in production settings, e.g., if a problem in a customer's IT infrastructure led to a loss of data or a temporary loss of consumer Web access. While customers may peruse such reports hoping to glean useful information about a storage system model, the reports may provide limited useful information in that regard. Media reports often lack significant details such as whether a problem was caused by a storage system and, if so, what model storage system, or was caused by the vendor during a service call, or was caused by customer personnel (i.e., a "user error"). Many customers do their best to avoid such information ever getting to the press due to the resulting negative publicity for the organization. Or, a customer (perhaps encouraged by their storage vendor) may simply describe a problem as a "computer glitch."

- Vendor-based performance comparisons.   A vendor may claim their storage system outperforms a competitor's system based on the vendor's own testing, and show graphs to "prove" it.

Tip: Customers should be very skeptical about taking such claims at face value. It can be easy for a vendor to run a test biased in their favor, but not necessarily easy for customers to determine the test was not fair. For example, it is often possible to configure a competitor's system to reduce its maximum performance, though the competitor would never configure, and never recommend a customer configure, their system that way. In one case this author is personally familiar with, a vendor measured their storage system against a competitive system where the competitive system was configured so that only half its performance capability could be used.

Because vendors running their own performance benchmarks often publish limited, if any, details about system configuration and benchmark characteristics, and because customers unfamiliar with a given system won't have the expertise to know how it should be properly configured, it can be difficult for customers to determine that a test was inherently unfair.

See the Performance chapter for additional information on measuring the performance of a storage system and comparing the performance of different storage systems.

- Open vs. closed capabilities.   A vendor might criticize a competitor by claiming the competitor takes a closed approach to (some of) their offerings, in contrast to the vendor's open approach. What does that mean?

Many storage capabilities conform to industry standards.   Such standards are often described as *open*.[132] Support for industry standards provides benefits such as promoting interoperability between devices from different manufacturers, reducing manufacturer's costs, and preserving administrator's skills when using different products supporting the same standards. Some standards, such as SCSI I/O commands, Ethernet networks, and open-source software projects are controlled by widely recognized standards bodies. Some less formal standards include interfaces (e.g., APIs) developed and controlled by

---

[132] The terms *open* and *standard* are not always used consistently. See: https://en.wikipedia.org/wiki/Open_standard.

manufacturers, and licensed to other manufacturers. (It is the licensing to other vendors that makes the interfaces "open.")

Many storage capabilities are owned and used by a single manufacturer and do not conform to industry standards. That may be because an appropriate standard does not exist or the manufacturer believes they have developed a superior approach over existing standards. Such capabilities are generally considered to be *closed* or proprietary. Sometimes, closed interfaces to capabilities later become industry standards.

Tip: *"Open" does not necessarily mean "better"; "closed" does not necessarily mean "worse." The quality of the (hardware or software) technology behind either an open or closed interface can vary based on its implementation.*

Customers weighing acquiring open vs. closed approaches to a capability should consider questions such as the following: What are the near-term and long-term consequences to my organization of choosing an open vs. a closed capability? Would acquiring products complying with open standards present more choices for other products it can interoperate with? Would products complying with open standards make it easier to find relevant skills in the job market? Would complying with open standards make migration among systems easier? Would a closed offering provide compelling benefits that make it worthwhile to give up the benefits of an open offering? How important is the open-vs.-closed consideration in the context of an entire storage system decision?

- Vendor lock-in. This topic is closely related to the previous discussion of open and closed capabilities.

Storage system vendors strive to provide advantages that attract customer interest. That often means supporting system and feature capabilities no one else in the industry is providing. Vendors offering such capabilities will naturally emphasize the benefits those capabilities can bring to their customers.

A vendor lacking comparable capabilities might try to evoke a fear in a customer's mind of *vendor lock-in* (aka *customer lock-in* or *proprietary lock-in)*, meaning the customer would be so dependent on the competitor's offering they would find it difficult (e.g., unduly expensive) to migrate to a different offering. What if the competitor decides to impose exorbitant maintenance charges in the future, or fails to enhance their offering to keep up with industry developments or customers' requirements, or decides to discontinue the offering?

Tip: *The "proprietary" label does not always warrant significant customer concern. All storage system models are proprietary to at least some extent in that each is manufactured by only one company (even if some models are OEMed-out to other companies). Different storage system families even from the same vendor typically have proprietary API, CLI, and GUI management interfaces so that invoking even similar functions in different families can involve different syntax and different parameter options. In practice, customers often migrate from one storage system family to another and manage these kinds of proprietary incompatibilities without too much trouble.*

There may not be such a thing as an absolute form of storage vendor lock-in from which there is no escape. There seem to always be alternative ways to address a storage requirement. Customers should weigh the benefits of using proprietary capabilities and the cost (including finances, time, and effort) to potentially switch to an acceptable alternative. Here are examples of how that cost might vary, where a customer might view higher costs as indicating higher degrees of lock-in: (1) A relatively low cost is replacing an installed storage system with a different model whose integration into a data center requires mainly education of administrators and perhaps modifying existing administrator-written scripts. (2) The cost would be higher if there was also a need to change existing host-storage cabling. (3) The cost would be higher still if there was also a need to modify applications that use the storage.

As is true for business in general, the case for switching from a proprietary offering to an alternative can warrant a cost-benefit analysis. That's very different from claiming such a switch is not even possible.

- <u>Influencing requirements placed on competitors</u>. A vendor may try to persuade a customer that competitors must configure certain models or features in order to meet the customer's needs. The vendor is hoping to gain a price advantage. Here are two examples:

1) Suppose vendors A and B are vying for the opportunity to sell a storage system to a customer. Vendor A might tell the customer they have determined that at least 200GB of storage system cache is needed to meet the customer's performance requirements, so the customer should also require at least that size from vendor B. Vendor A may do this because they know that their system supports a 200GB cache size while vendor B would need to configure 256GB of cache due to the particular cache sizes B's system supports. But, as discussed in the *Performance* chapter, cache size alone is a limited indicator of cache performance as well as a limited indicator of overall system performance. It is more important that a vendor assures a customer that the total storage system configuration they are proposing (i.e., the combination of model, cache size, drives, software features, etc.) meets the customer's performance requirements.

2) A vendor might claim that the (midrange) storage system they are proposing is so much faster than the competitor's proposed (midrange) system that the competitor should be required to propose their high-end system. Alternatively, a vendor may change their proposal from their high-end system to their midrange system after learning a competitor is proposing their high-end system, claiming that the vendor's midrange system meets the customer's needs at a lower price. In such cases, customers should be especially diligent in seeking evidence of storage system performance and other capabilities.

- <u>How competitive information is delivered</u>. Vendors may communicate criticisms of competitors in various ways. Communications may be written or spoken. They may be papers, presentations, or informal conversations. They may be comparisons (highlighting advantages) of the vendor's offerings to a competitor's offerings, or they may be entirely dedicated to criticizing a competitor. They may be simple "Yes / No" checklists or may include discussions and evidence of claims.

Tip: Some vendors freely share with customers the vendor's documents containing claims about issues with competitors' storage systems, even knowing the documents may be turned over to competitors. That may indicate a high degree of confidence in the claims, though it is still not a guarantee of accuracy. In contrast, customers should be wary if a vendor states that its claims about a competitor are "confidential." That may be an attempt to prevent the customer from consulting the competitor to determine whether the claims are accurate. A vendor unsure of its claims or knowingly making less than accurate claims has obvious reasons to want to discourage customers from checking out those claims with the competitor.

Tip: It is a good idea to check any written claims a vendor makes about a competitor for the date the document was published. Be sure the date of publication is the date the document content was initially published and not merely the date the document was printed or emailed. Be wary of undated material. Older documents may be less accurate because vendors announce new products and new product capabilities (e.g., new versions of internal software or support for new types of drives) from time to time. Vendors publish new or updated product documentation such as user guides from time to time, sometimes multiple times per year.

Tip: Customers should be wary of documents about competitors distributed by a vendor where the documents do not identify the vendor or author. They may be documents by vendor representatives acting on their own that do not represent the vendor's official position. Such documents may be more likely to contain misleading or inaccurate information than documents a vendor stands behind.

Additional Tips

- As mentioned, it can be very helpful to ask a vendor for their views of their competitors – at least the competitors a customer is considering. Vendors often have expertise and significant motivation to identify weaknesses in their competitors' offerings.

  However, customers cannot be certain that a vendor's claims about a competitor are necessarily accurate or current. Therefore, it is equally important – and in the best interests of both the customer and the accused competitor – to give the competitor a chance to respond to any criticisms.

  Customers should ask a vendor to provide evidence to support any claims it makes about a competitor. For example, evidence could be statements from a competitor's public website or from product manuals. Even if evidence is provided the competitor should still be contacted for their side of the story: is the evidence cited current and accurate? Was a statement taken out of context? Does the competitor have a way to address the issue?[133]

---

[133] A vendor may validly claim that a competitor's storage system does not support a certain capability. However, the competitor may have alternate ways to provide the desired result. For example, the competitor may support or recommend a host-based function rather than the function implemented

In lieu of any evidence, a customer could reasonably take the stance of saying they are not giving the claim any credence or are not going to bother competitors by asking them to respond to claims made without evidence. (Unfortunately, once a claim is made with or without evidence, it may stick in a customer's memory, which may be something the accusing vendor hopes for.)

Some claims are easy to state and may be backed by just enough evidence to seem credible on the surface, yet still be inaccurate or misleading in fact. For example, a vendor may claim their storage system has internal paths to drives that are two times faster than the internal paths in a competitor's system and therefore the vendor's system has superior performance. The claim may be backed up by specification sheets showing the path speeds. That may sound like an open and shut case. However, it may be that the slower path speed is more than sufficient to support higher levels of system performance than the customer requires. Or, it may be that the supported drives in each system can transfer data from media only at a much slower speed than either system's internal path speed. Or, it may be that the system with the slower path speed has other performance attributes (such as a more efficient cache) that more than compensate.

The point is, a vendor may make claims about competitors that seem credible on the surface and take only seconds to make, yet may still not be relevant. Unfortunately, the defense against or refutation of a claim can reasonably take more time and detail than it took to make the claim. A vendor may take advantage of that by making simple claims, hoping customers won't be patient enough to listen to the other side of the story or may even assume there is no other side of the story. Customers should recognize such situations are possible and allow the "accused" vendor time to provide their response.

---

inside the storage system, pointing out the benefit that such a function can work with any storage system. It can be useful to get the competitor's perspective on how to support the desired result rather than necessarily requiring a specific function be supported inside the storage system.

System Specifications

When questioning witnesses to a crime, an investigator on an old U.S. television drama series, Dragnet, was famous for saying "All we want are the facts." Customers sometimes want just the technical facts about a storage system, not marketing or pricing information. A published overview of system technical attributes is called a "specification sheet" or "spec sheet." Specification sheets are often in tabular form and typically a few pages long at most.

Landscape

- <u>Content</u>. Published specification information for a given storage system model or family may identify major hardware features (e.g., maximum supported physical capacity), major software features (e.g., supported replication functions), supported hosts, floor space requirements (e.g., area, weight, and height), and energy usage. An informal term sometimes used to refer to this kind of technical information is "speeds and feeds." This term originated in the machine tool industry, but is used by many in IT as meaning computer system specifications.

  Tip: Technical storage system specifications identify selected attributes of a particular system model. A spec sheet may be just a list of hardware components and selected quantitative attributes of those components. It does not describe qualitative details such as how all the components work together or how easy (or difficult) the system is to manage. As a comparison, a spec sheet for a car might specify major parts and estimated mileage; it can't describe what it is like to actually drive or ride in the car.

  Tip: Comparing different storage systems based solely on their specifications can be challenging because there are no industry standards specifying the form in which system specifications should be published or what information should be included or excluded. Each vendor makes their own decisions.

  The challenge is compounded because different vendors may use different names for features providing similar functions. There are no industry standards for feature names and vendors may invent names to not only provide some idea about what a feature does but to also add marketing pizzazz.[134] A vendor may use the same name for similar features

---

[134] Consider an example. A *controller* is an electronic component that supports a function and directs the flow of data between other components. An example of a controller in a storage system is a board of electronic (sub)components that connects to cables from servers, accepts I/O commands from those

among the vendor's multiple storage system families; however, that can create the misleading impression that the features provide identical function across those families which is not always the case. Customers need to drill down to determine what a feature really does and how it compares across different storage system models including different models from the same vendor.

In addition to a spec sheet, a vendor may publish a related document called a "data sheet." Data sheets are usually more prose-oriented than specification sheets; they often include marketing messages, but may also include system specifications.

- <u>Minimums, maximums, and increments</u>. Storage system hardware specifications generally include the maximum numbers or sizes of components such as host ports, physical drives, and cache. It's helpful if specifications also include minimum values and the component increments (aka granularity) a customer can install or add as upgrades.

  Tip: Minimum, maximum, and incremental values are important because they can impact cost. For example, host ports of a given type may be packaged on adapters each of which supports 4 or 8 or 16 ports. That may be more ports than needed, but an adapter with fewer ports may not be offered. (Customers are not obligated to use all ports, just to pay for them.) Or, there may be fewer ports than needed in which case an entire additional adapter must be installed. (Host adapters are typically configured in pairs with at least two paths from different adapters connected to a given host for redundancy.)

- <u>Nominal attributes</u>. Storage system specifications often cite the nominal capabilities of a component. Nominal means in name only, not necessarily in fact. A nominal specification of a component does not indicate how well the component actually supports the capability because that depends on factors such as how the component is implemented in the system and how the component is managed by system software. Here are some examples:

  1) A drive's (physical or raw) capacity may be cited in published specifications as a nominal value (such as 1TB), but after the drive is formatted by the storage system to hold data the usable capacity will be less than the nominal capacity. (Additional formatting by host and application software can further reduce storage capacity available to hold customer-generated data.)

  2) One of the industry-standard nominal speeds for Fibre Channel host-to-storage connections is 16Gb/s. A given storage system's specifications may state that 16Gb/s Fibre Channel ports are supported, while not stating that the system design is such that it is not possible for every Fibre Channel port in the storage system, or even every Fibre Channel port on the same multi-port adapter card, to perform at 16Gb/s at the same time.

---

servers, and sends those commands to internal drives that attach to the controller using another type of path. Many vendors call such controllers *adapters* (because they adapt host I/O connections to support the connections to internal drives), but some vendors call them *directors*, for no apparent reason other than to imply their controllers are somehow better than adapters.

3) Some storage systems have a limit on the maximum amount of data that can be stored, a limit that may be unexpectedly below the maximum physical (raw) capacity of the system even after accounting for RAID and formatting overheads. That kind of restriction may not be easy to identify other than by carefully comparing maximum physical vs. usable capacities.

- Performance specifications. Overall system performance capability (as opposed to the speed of individual components) is clearly an important specification, but is not always included in specification sheets. One reason may be due to the inherent complexity of performance; as discussed in the *Performance* chapter there are multiple relevant measurements and "it depends" factors.

Tip: Specifications may document the (nominal) speeds of selected individual components. That may not provide a useful indication of overall storage system performance. Overall system performance depends on the interplay of all components used to satisfy I/O requests or system commands, including the performance implications of the system software that manages those components. Consider the following examples:

1) A cache size specification has limited usefulness as an indicator of performance in one storage system or when comparing different storage systems. Consider:

o Many storage systems have a single cache to hold both user (application) data and storage system internal data. The specifications for those systems generally do not indicate the amount of cache available to hold user data. Some storage system specifications use the terms processor memory *or* raw cache, *indications that only a subset of cache capacity may be available to hold user data.*

o How efficiently cache is managed by storage system software can be more important than its size, and that information is typically not described in spec sheets.

Because of these issues, customers should generally not define a requirement for a specific cache size, especially when soliciting proposals from multiple vendors who sell different storage system models. (Exceptions include when a customer is upgrading an installed system in-place or has done a lot of research into the matter.) Instead, customers should define requirements for externally measurable storage system performance (e.g., required random I/O average response time) or a requirement for a specific minimum cache hit ratio, and let the vendors determine system configurations that support required performance.

2) A storage system's specification sheet may cite the number of internal processors and the speed of processors in gigahertz (GHz). A storage system supporting larger values may appear to support higher performance than storage systems with smaller numbers of processors or processors with lower GHz. However, those numbers alone are of little if any value as an indication of system performance for several reasons: They do not indicate whether the processors are using 32-bit or 64-bit architecture, they do not indicate how processor performance compares for differently designed processors, they do not indicate whether the processors are dedicated to specific system tasks (meaning that, even when those processors are idle they cannot be dynamically reassigned to tasks that could benefit from additional processing power), and, importantly, they do not indicate the degree of efficiency of the programming that runs on and manages the processors and other system resources.

3) *Some storage system spec sheets identify a value that may be called "internal bandwidth" or "data bandwidth" or some other type of bandwidth. There is no industry-standard definition for this value. It is usually a measure of sequential throughput of selected (not all) components (e.g., the maximum data flow through cache or the maximum data flow across the connections between certain internal components often expressed in gigabytes per second). This is a measure of internal system activity; it does not indicate performance applications can attain. In addition, it provides no information about the response time of random I/Os which are typically the most common type of I/Os in commercial applications.*

- <u>Software feature specifications</u>. Storage system software features often require relatively long explanations to describe their capabilities. That information is often documented separately from system specification sheets that focus on hardware attributes (e.g., software feature specifications may be published in brochures or user guides).

Tip: In some storage systems, not every software-based feature may be able to operate at the same time. That could complicate system management. For example, which replication features can run against a given volume at the same time is sometimes restricted. Such detail, though important, is typically not included in system specification sheets even if they provide a brief summary of software features. That kind of detail may be included in documents such as user guides.

Additional Tips

- *As a starting point to help identify storage system requirements, customers can review the specifications of the storage systems they currently have installed or want to replace.*

- *When comparing the specifications of different storage system models, it can be tempting to favor a particular model if the list of named features on its specification sheet is longer than similar lists on other vendors' specification sheets. However, the lengths of such lists can be misleading. Not every vendor names every feature. Some features have different names in different storage systems where some names sound more impressive than others that basically do the same thing. Some vendors implement a given capability as a storage system feature while others implement it via a separate appliance that may have its own specification sheet.*

- *The total number of supported ports for attachment to servers or Storage Area Networks (SANs) or other networks is sometimes ambiguous. For example, a specification like "up to 100 iSCSI or Fibre Channel host ports" could potentially mean up to 100 of only one type of port, or it could mean some combination of the two types up to a combined total of 100 which prompts the question of what combinations are supported.*

- *Some storage system specification items may apply only to models shipped after a specific date and not apply to previously installed systems of the same model. That may not be clearly documented. This situation can lead to confusion because a customer may be looking at a spec sheet that appears to apply to a particular model but actually does not apply to all instances of the model.*

  Here are two examples where this can occur:

  1) *Specification sheets for a given model may be updated to indicate changes in supported drives. Perhaps different capacity drives are now supported. Perhaps some older, slower drives can no longer be acquired (though a manufacturer may keep a warehoused supply to replace failed drives of that same type).*

  2) *System support for some new or planned capability may require internal hardware changes that the manufacturer decided not to retrofit to previously shipped systems of the same model. In such a case it may be serial number ranges that indicate which systems have which versions of hardware components.*

Prices and Costs

Customers are always attentive to what they are asked to pay for storage systems (and other IT assets). That stems from matters such as budgets, organization plans, local and global economic conditions, a need to comply with internal organization directives such as the ubiquitous "we need to do more with less," and a common desire among buyers for a good deal.

The good news is that the price customers pay per unit of storage capacity continues to decline over time. Yet, the demand for ever more capacity and new storage system capabilities can lead to storage expenses increasing over time.

Understanding the total picture of enterprise storage system costs can seem as daunting as understanding the underlying technology. Nevertheless, understanding the cost picture is important for several reasons. The initial price can range from several thousand U.S. dollars for a relatively small-capacity/low-function system to millions of U.S. dollars for a relatively high-capacity/high-function system. Moreover, the total cost of operating even a single storage system can be much higher than the system's initial price, and it can impact an organization's finances for several years.

Landscape

- Terminology. The terms *price* and *cost*, though informally often used interchangeably, can help distinguish between significantly different financial considerations.

  Price is the amount of money a buyer pays to acquire a product or service from a seller. In the case of a storage system, a price appears in a proposal or invoice a vendor gives a customer to have a storage system delivered to a customer's site.

  Cost is the amount of money required to produce a product or service. In the case of a storage system, a manufacturer has a cost to develop, build, and ship storage systems to customers. In turn, customers incur costs to provide a system's capacity and function to users.[135]

---

[135] Normally, a price for a product or service that is greater than its cost represents profit. However, many data centers are operated as "cost centers": a necessary cost to an organization of running their business; an overhead not directly tied to an organization's profits. In that case there may be no direct

Those definitions are behind the adage: "Beware the cost of the lowest price." An insightful way to analyze what customers pay for storage (as well as other IT) assets is to consider the cost of initially acquiring that storage and the ongoing cost of owning/operating that storage.

A customer's *Total Cost of Acquisition (TCA)* refers to the price paid for a storage system and other payments necessary to ready the system to serve its intended purpose. Examples of such other payments include payments to contractors to modify a data center to accommodate the floor space, power, and cooling requirements of a new storage system, shipping charges, installation charges, vendor services to help with migration from older systems being replaced, and administrator education.

A customer's *Total Cost of Ownership (TCO)* refers to the overall costs to acquire, manage, use, and eventually dispose of a storage system. The TCO of a storage system is essentially all costs incurred by a customer during the life of that system. TCO includes TCA, post-warranty maintenance charges, post-warranty system upgrades, electricity charges from the local power company, and other costs a customer may incur related to owning and operating a storage system.[136]

Tip: Both customers and vendors have motivations that may inhibit determining the comprehensive cost implications of TCA and TCO.

When a customer asks a vendor what a given storage system will cost, the vendor may not give a comprehensive response for various reasons. A vendor may mention only the price for the customer to acquire the physical system, hoping to avoid customer attention to other costs (such as high upgrade prices) that can make the system seem more expensive. It could be that the vendor is offering a low price to win the business while planning to gain compensating revenue via high post-warranty maintenance charges.

A customer department evaluating storage systems may limit their cost analysis to only certain areas for various reasons. A customer may consider only the most easily identifiable costs (e.g., a vendor's stated price for a storage system), ignoring costs that would take more time and effort to quantify. Some organizations do not separately charge a data center for energy use so that is not part of a CIO's budget concerns (though someone has

---

price users (e.g., departments) in an organization pay to use the data center. Some data centers employ *chargeback* schemes so that each user must pay a price for the data center resources they use; users treat that payment as a cost of achieving their goals.

[136] This chapter discusses the financial picture mainly from TCA and TCO perspectives. There are other possible ways to view the topic. One other way is to consider one-time capital expenses (CAPEX) and ongoing operational expenses (OPEX). For example, purchasing the original hardware and later hardware upgrades are CAPEX expenses, while ongoing lease charges and utility company charges are OPEX expenses. Another way to look at the financial picture is to consider Return on Investment (ROI). For example, the expense of a new storage system might be justified by projecting that the resulting increase in the organization's profit will be greater than the TCO of the system. Another view is to distinguish hard costs from soft costs (discussed later in this chapter). Yet another consideration is time-to-value, i.e., once all needed products and features are ordered, how long it takes before productive use can begin.

to pay that bill). A data center manager may be focused on staying within this year's budget and ignore budget implications for subsequent years. Moreover, estimating future expenses as part of a TCO estimate, such as what system upgrades might be needed and when and at what price, can be difficult.

Many customers likely never review the financial history of a storage system to determine the actual incurred TCA and TCO so that they might be able to refine their methods of estimating these values for future acquisitions.

For all these reasons it can be challenging for customers to accurately estimate their total cost of ownership. TCA, because it involves near-term costs, is easier to determine than TCO; that may motivate some customers to limit financial requirements and comparisons to TCA and ignore TCO. However, prudent customers should at least consider TCO because a vendor appearing to have the lowest TCA may not have the lowest TCO. And TCO is what a customer ultimately pays.

- Price and system capability. The smallest (aka entry-level or low-end) enterprise storage systems tend to compete mainly on price because there is often little differentiation in terms of other capabilities. Higher-end (aka midrange-class and enterprise-class) systems, while price is also a competitive differentiator, also compete on other attributes such as maximum usable capacity, maximum performance, data management functions, and ease-of-management.

Other factors influence the TCO story. Consider an aspect of ease-of-management. It's generally easier for customers to manage one storage system and share its resources than to manage multiple systems. It's also more efficient because if one storage system is very busy and another is idle, the resources of the idle system can't be used to help the busy system. In an efficient single system, the resources can be dynamically assigned to where they are needed; even an ability to manually reassign resources within a single system is preferable to no ability to reassign resources among multiple systems.

Tip: Capabilities that just a few years ago were supported by only the highest-end storage systems are now supported by many systems considered to be midrange or even entry-level class. In some cases, customers who in the past needed a high-end system may today have their storage requirements satisfied by midrange systems.

- Price and system capacity. The price to acquire the initial capacity of any storage system can be relatively high compared to later adding additional capacity. That's because the initial acquisition includes system infrastructure (such as cabinets, controllers, cache, power supplies, and microcode) required to support holding and using that capacity. Capacity upgrades may need to add only more drives, though sometimes additional infrastructure components to support them may also be required.

Tip: Sometimes, someone in a customer's organization may question why an enterprise storage system is relatively expensive per unit of capacity when a nearby computer store may be selling 4TB drives to consumers for under $200 (U.S.).

The short answer is: There is much more to enterprise storage systems than just their drives. Consider the following attributes that contribute to the cost of capacity in enterprise storage systems. This list is not intended to be complete.

o *Enterprise-class HDDs are usually designed to handle more intense I/O workloads than consumer class drives. Compared to HDDs designed for consumer use (e.g., in personal computers), enterprise-class drives are generally designed for better reliability and to support 24x7 operation. They may have longer warranties. Some enterprise-class HDDs run at 10K RPM or 15K RPM, delivering faster performance than consumer HDDs which typically run at 7200 RPM.*

o *An enterprise storage system manages multiple drives, often thousands of drives, supporting much larger capacities than possible in an individual drive. The system requires sophisticated internal system components to support those drives such as specialized controllers.*

o *Most enterprise storage systems are designed to be shared among multiple hosts. That includes supporting components such as host adapters to attach to those hosts, even hundreds of hosts in some cases. Capacity can often be reassigned among hosts via an administrator's command without requiring manually relocating individual drives.*

o *Enterprise storage systems may include large solid-state (DRAM) caches to improve performance compared to I/O requests going directly to drives.*

o *Enterprise storage systems include extensive infrastructure in the form of cabinets, internal enclosures, controllers, power supplies, and fans.*

o *Enterprise storage systems may support facilities to provide higher levels of data availability than supported by individual drives. That can include many redundant components, including two paths to internal drives from different controllers. In particular, the use of RAID to protect against data loss in case of a drive failure requires extra software and extra drives beyond what is needed to satisfy capacity requirements. Enterprise systems often support automatic recovery of data from a failed or failing drive onto pre-installed spare drives.*

o *Enterprise storage systems are often designed to be upgraded and repaired in place nondisruptively.*

o *Enterprise storage systems often provide extensive software-based functions such as data replication, data relocation, auto-tiering, and functions to support specific types of hosts.*

o *Manufacturers incur the costs of designing, integrating, and testing the components in an enterprise storage system. Some manufacturers include in the system price the cost of one of storage professionals to install the system.*

- <u>List price and discounts</u>. Storage system customers almost never pay list price. A vendor's list prices for a storage system and its features are generally for reference purposes. List prices allow a vendor to cite an official price for a product if sold to a competitor. High list prices enable a vendor to offer high discounts that can sound appealing to a customer. Discounts of 50% and higher off of list price have been common in the storage system industry. The size of a discount can vary by product, by vendor, and by the importance and/or size of the opportunity (e.g., some vendors offer *volume discounts*).

- Best price. The lowest price a vendor is willing to offer can vary based on multiple factors. For example, an opportunity for a vendor to sell multiple storage systems together in one deal may justify a lower price per system than an opportunity to sell a single system. Another example is where a non-incumbent vendor, trying to sell their first system to a new customer, offers a relatively low price – perhaps even no initial charge or a very long trial – "to buy the business" or "get a foot in the door," hoping to eventually be profitable through upgrades, services, and additional business.

  Tip: Vendors rarely propose their lowest acceptable price in their initial offer, unless a customer explicitly asks for a "best and final" price. Vendors usually leave some "wiggle room" to lower their price, allowing them to better address competitors' offers or to appear accommodating to a customer. This leaves room for customers to negotiate a lower price than a vendor's initial bid.

  Tip: If a lower price than a vendor's sales representative is authorized to offer is needed to win an opportunity, the vendor may have a standard procedure allowing the representative to escalate the request to higher vendor management. Whether that management is willing to bid a lower price may depend on factors such as the amount of revenue and profit involved, current progress towards meeting quarterly and yearly revenue and profit goals, the chance of winning vs. a competitor, whether a competitor's installed storage system would be displaced, and the perceived opportunity for future revenue (e.g., system upgrades, follow-on system generations, and opportunities to replace other competitors' installed systems).

  Tip: Some vendors may be more aggressive at trying to win an opportunity based on price than many customers may be comfortable with. Here are two examples: (1) Customers may ask vendors to state their best and final price in their bids. Nevertheless, a vendor may come back later with a still lower price if they determine (perhaps through a customer insider who favors that vendor) they might lose to a competitor who bid a lower price. (2) Some vendors stop trying to compete for a given opportunity once the customer indicates they have awarded the business to a competitor and ordered the system. Some vendors, however, may continue competing at that point by offering a lower price.

  Customers should consider whether they can trust and want to do business with vendors who use those kinds of tactics.

  Tip: Some customers request bids from multiple vendors just to incite a "price war" among them to help ensure the customers are getting a good deal. Upon seeing the lowest bid, a customer might tell the other vendors their bids are too high, hoping the vendors will return with even lower bids. In some cases, a customer's hidden agenda may be to lower the price bid by the vendor they already secretly prefer; the ethics here are questionable if the customer has no intention of buying from other vendors.

Tip: To help a customer determine they aren't paying more than other customers for similar acquisitions, a customer might ask the vendor for assurance that no other customer has received a higher discount for comparable systems from that vendor within a recent time period such as the last few months. Another approach is to ask storage industry analysts if they have discount information shared with them by other customers. (Note: It is more useful to ask about discounts than prices since system configurations can vary a lot.)

- Licensed software.   Pricing policies for licensed software-based features can vary considerably by vendor system model and even by feature in the same system model. One feature may have a fixed charge per system regardless of system configuration, another feature may have a charge based on a system's physical capacity, another feature may have a charge based on the subset of a system's physical capacity for which the feature will be used (e.g., perhaps only a subset of capacity needs to be protected by a remote mirroring feature), and another feature may be included as standard at no additional charge.

One storage system may offer multiple functions bundled into one feature at one price, while another system may split those functions into separate features for "à la carte" pricing.

Other pricing variations exist. Some vendors offer one-time purchase of a software feature license, sometimes called a "perpetual software license," allowing a software feature to be ported to a compatible replacement storage system (e.g., a next-generation system within the same family when it replaces an installed system). Some vendors offer a "site license" that permits installing a software feature on multiple storage systems; a site license may be offered to a relatively large multi-system data center. Some vendors may offer a temporary license a customer may use for a limited period of time to evaluate a software feature.

Tip: The wide variety of licensed software pricing policies is a reason to focus on the overall TCA and TCO of storage systems, rather than spending a lot of time comparing the prices of individual features in isolation.

Tip: A customer may have significant negotiating power for the prices of software features. Unlike inventorying and shipping hardware, it costs a vendor little (beyond development costs) to let a customer download software or to ship a customer a CD or to give a customer a license key to let them enable a feature already installed in their storage system.

- Multi-product package deals. A vendor may propose bundling multiple products together as a *package deal* at a single price that is lower than if the customer buys the products separately. The package may include multiple storage systems or may include storage plus other IT products the vendor offers. A related financial offering applies to volume discounts: a lower price per system when a customer agrees to acquire at least a certain number of systems within a specified time period.

Tip: A proposal for a package deal can represent financial savings to a customer who needs all the products in the bundle. A storage system vendor unable or unwilling to propose a comparable bundled deal may try to persuade the customer to require each product be priced separately, hoping to raise the price of the storage component. But that may not be in the customer's best interest. For example, assume a vendor offering a *package deal is asked by the customer to price each product separately. That can raise the total offering price of each product because of a vendor's pricing policies; or, perhaps one vendor division that is part of the overall deal may have agreed to accept a lower than usual profit, or even no profit, to help the entire deal – an offer they would not make when pricing an individual product independently.*

- Warranties. Warranty terms and conditions (T&C) can vary by vendor and by storage system model. Examples of warranty (and maintenance contract) T&C that can impact TCO:

  o The beginning and end dates

  o The system components covered

  o The days of the week and times of day a vendor will respond to a customer request (e.g., 24x7 or 9x5 Monday through Friday)

  o The maximum time before a vendor will respond to a customer after being notified of a problem (e.g., next business day or within n hours – and that time may be only an objective, not a guarantee)

  o Whether repair (parts replacement) is done by the vendor or the customer

  o Whether new parts that replace failed parts get their own full duration warranty or inherit the remaining warranty duration of the failed part (even if only one more day)

  o Whether new parts added as upgrades get their own full duration warranty or some other duration

Some vendors offer standard warranties and also enhanced warranties that provide better coverage for a higher price.

The longer the duration of a warranty, the more it costs the vendor to offer it. That's because the vendor has to cover the potential cost of repairing/replacing system components over the longer time period and, in general, the more time that passes, the higher the probability a given component may fail.[137] Whether the projected cost of a longer duration warranty is reflected in a higher system price for the customer or lower profit for the vendor is up to the vendor. (Note that hardware repair/replace can require new hardware parts and potentially on-site visits by a vendor representative. For software, fixes for defects are usually handled by transmitting new software over a network.)

Tip: Some vendors' warranties apply to both system hardware and software and last for the same period of time. Some vendors have separate warranties for hardware and software that last for different periods of time. For example, some vendors have a standard warranty for licensed software with a duration of only 90 days and even then the warranty may cover

---

[137] There may be higher rates of hardware failures in the first days and weeks after installation as defective components (not found by vendor tests) are discovered, then a period of relatively few failures, then increased failures as components age. A graph depicting this pattern is sometimes called a "bathtub curve." See https://en.wikipedia.org/wiki/Bathtub_curve.

only failure of the media on which the software ships (e.g., a CD), not any software defects (i.e., bugs). Customers may view such a software warranty as requiring they pay for a software maintenance plan that takes effect as soon as the storage system is installed.

Tip: Some vendors offer warranties where the customer can choose from selected durations (e.g., 1 year, 2 years, etc., up to some limit). There are benefits and drawbacks to customers of different warranty durations.

Benefits to customers of a longer warranty duration include delayed or avoided charges for maintenance including unanticipated future increases in maintenance pricing. Drawbacks include a likely higher system acquisition price. There's also the potential of having wasting money if the system's useful life ends before the warranty expires; for example, it may not make sense for a customer to sign up for a five year warranty if they generally replace their storage systems every four years..

Benefits to customers of a shorter duration warranty include a likely lower system acquisition price. Another benefit is the flexibility, when the warranty expires, to arrange for post-warranty maintenance with a third party maintainer who may charge less than the vendor/manufacturer responsible for supporting the original warranty. A drawback is an earlier impact to future budgets for maintenance charges that may not be known today.

In a competitive situation a vendor offering a selection of warranty durations may propose a relatively short warranty to keep their bid lower than it would otherwise be. It is certainly reasonable for a customer to accept a shorter warranty period to reduce TCA if they understand the implications.

Tip: To meet a customer's requirement for a storage system hardware warranty duration longer than a vendor's standard warranty, or to match the warranty terms of a competitor, a vendor may propose a customer buy a prepaid maintenance plan to cover the difference.

That prepaid maintenance would cover only the hardware components in the initially installed configuration, not any hardware upgrades installed later. Paying today for a maintenance plan that takes effect in the future can help lock in maintenance pricing, simplifying budget planning. Whether prepaid maintenance is as valuable as a true warranty depends on how their terms and conditions compare. Customers should also consider whether paying today for a future maintenance plan is justified considering the time value of money; the same point applies to choosing among longer vs. shorter warranty periods if both are offered. Keep in mind that prepaid maintenance, like a longer-term warranty, may discourage a customer from switching maintainers while the old coverage remains in effect.

Tip: Near the end of the hardware warranty period, a vendor may propose a new maintenance plan that would last longer than the likely remaining useful life of the storage system. Such a contract might be appealing to a customer if it reduces monthly payments compared to a shorter duration maintenance contract. However, the contract might be especially appealing to the vendor because it can later be used to motivate the customer to stay with that vendor when the customer decides to replace the storage system. The logic is this: When a customer replaces the system the maintenance charges already contracted for would continue, a situation the customer may not have been foreseen or budgeted for. The vendor may offer to "forgive" (i.e., dismiss) the future maintenance charges on the old system, but only if the customer acquires the replacement system from that vendor.

- Useful system life. The expected life (aka economically useful life) of a storage system clearly impacts the total cost of ownership of that system.

Customers can acquire a storage system that scales in capacity, performance, and function to address anticipated (and, perhaps, some unanticipated) future requirements and to support growth through upgrades. That may be less expensive than replacing an installed system with a more capable newer system or adding an additional system.

However, many factors that can impact the expected life of a storage system may be difficult or impossible to anticipate. Examples include: Whether the installed system will support future technology advances a customer decides they want, unanticipated circumstances (e.g., higher than expected need for capacity, or an unexpected need to migrate to a new data center along with a decision to acquire new equipment at that time), higher than anticipated failure rates as hardware components age, mergers and acquisitions by the customer, and mergers and acquisitions by the manufacturer.

A related consideration that often gets attention is the expected useful life of internal drives. It is quite reasonable for customers to be concerned about the reliability of the media that holds their data. In particular, solid-state drives (SSDs) based on flash technology have received scrutiny due to the nature of flash technology limiting each drive to a somewhat predictable number of write I/Os before the flash drive can no longer reliably process writes. That number, called *write endurance* generally exceeds customers' needs except in perhaps the most stressful I/O environments.[138]

Storage system vendors typically assign a single hardware warranty duration to an entire system (i.e., all its components) at the time the system is installed. The drive warranty durations received by a storage system manufacturer from its drive suppliers may be more or less than the warranty duration a manufacturer assigns to the entire storage system.

Tip: Vendors generally won't guarantee an "expected useful life" value to customers. Insights into the possible expected useful life of a system can include warranty duration; the historical durations from when the vendor announced comparable storage systems, later withdrew them from sale, and finally withdrew them from maintenance; a vendor's plans for

---

[138] A manufacturer's spec sheet for a given flash SSD model may identify the drive's write endurance in terms of total bytes that can be written over its useful life, or in terms of how long a drive can be expected to support writes if its nominal capacity is completely filled *n* times a day. A drive's warranty period may be an indirect indicator of write endurance and five year warranties are common for SSDs designed for enterprise storage systems.

The technical issue, in brief, is that the way flash technology processes write I/Os causes deterioration of the media. An analogy is that each use of a pencil's eraser removes part of it. After a large number of write I/Os to a flash SSD the media can no longer maintain data integrity. That number is substantially larger for flash SSDs designed for enterprise use rather than for consumer use due to facilities enterprise SSD designers include in those devices.

the timing of future system capabilities and generations (potentially shared via a non-disclosure agreement); whether the vendor normally supports (or plans to support) in-place upgrades to newer generation systems along with whether any associated disruption is acceptable to the customer, and any residual value a lessor assigns today to a system planned to be returned to the lessor after n years.

- Residual value. The monetary value a storage system has when a customer disposes of the system is called its *residual value (RV)*. A customer may be able to sell a used storage system to another customer on the secondary market.[139] Or, a customer may be able to return the system to the original vendor, or give it to another vendor, as a trade-in towards a new storage system. (Some vendors sometimes run programs that lower the price of a new storage system if the customer trades-in a system from a competitor.)

A storage system that has been upgraded with newer technology or that continues to support such upgrades will likely have a higher residual value than otherwise.

Tip: *When a lender financing a lease of a storage system determines the lease rate, higher anticipated residual values may result in a lower rate.*

Tip: *Customers who want the flexibility to resell a purchased storage system to whomever they want should ask their vendor about the terms and conditions for resale. Some vendors permit a customer to resell the storage system hardware but not any licensed software features needed to operate the system – a new customer would need to buy that software from the vendor.*

- Migration. Newer storage systems are often acquired to replace older storage systems. Reasons include increased capacity, higher performance, enhanced availability, desired new function, reduced energy requirements, and cost savings over time compared to post-warranty maintenance charges for older systems. (Removing an installed IT system and installing another system in its place is sometimes called *rip and replace* or a *forklift migration*.) The replacement process can require that data be migrated (i.e., moved) from the older storage system to the new system. (When new storage systems are acquired for new applications a data migration procedure is not needed.)

Storage system migration costs can include any or all of the following. This list is not necessarily complete: Personnel time diverted from other projects, priced host-based software to assist with migration, a business impact if the migration process makes data unavailable for some time (which can be due to the nature of some migration procedures or due to unforeseen problems during migration), the cost of any other IT equipment needed to support the new system (e.g., host ports or gateways), payments to vendors or consultants to assist with the migration, and costs to retain the old system if migration completion is delayed (e.g., maintenance charges; if the "from" and "to" systems are from the same vendor, that vendor may be more flexible in dealing with such charges).

---

[139] Used enterprise storage systems and individual hardware components have even been offered on eBay (http://www.ebay.com).

Tip: The cost of migration (in the broadest sense of "cost") should be compared to the cost of upgrading an installed system in-place to meet requirements if such an upgrade is possible. An upgrade may be less costly due to adding only needed components, compared to acquiring an entire system. An upgrade may require less time and effort than a migration. The upgrade process may support better system availability than a migration if, say, the upgrade is nondisruptive while the migration would be disruptive. Additional considerations include whether an upgrade significantly increases the useful life of the current system, budget factors, and the residual value or trade-in value of the current and upgraded system.

Tip: Ideally, a vendor will propose a method of migration at a low or no charge that is nondisruptive or minimally disruptive to applications. If migration is disruptive, business reasons may limit the time periods when migration is allowed to occur. Even if migration is nondisruptive, some customers may limit the calendar windows of time during which migrations can occur so migrations won't add a burden during important periods such as peak sales seasons.

Tip: A simple migration method some customers may be able to implement on their own is to use host-based volume mirroring to migrate data to the new system. (Create a mirror copy of production data on the new system; after the copy is complete the original data on the old system can be deleted.) A storage vendor may not mention this option since it does not result in additional revenue in contrast to selling offerings to assist with migration.

Tip: Sometimes migration is facilitated by storage system features designed for that purpose; such features may be standard or may be optional at extra cost. Some ISVs support priced host-based software to help manage migration, perhaps including the ability to consolidate volumes or to move only selected files, functions generally not supported by storage system-based migration features.

Tip: When one storage system in a remote mirroring configuration needs to be migrated, that may require migrating both the local and remote systems at the same time. One reason could be system interoperability requirements. Another reason is if a customer chooses to "cascade" the two systems by replacing the remote system with the local system and installing the new system locally. (That is, an A→B remote mirroring configuration migrates to a New→A configuration; B is disposed of or redeployed elsewhere.) In the case of leased systems, the practicality of replacing both systems at the same time may be facilitated if leases are coterminous.

- Service offerings. Vendors may offer or propose separately priced storage services (aka consulting or professional services) to help a customer implement or manage parts of a storage system. That may be especially attractive to customers for relatively complex features such as remote mirroring or for relatively complex procedures such as system migration. Benefits to a customer include education of their staff by experienced personnel and increased probability of a successful on-time implementation.

Tip: Customers may want to ask storage system vendors to include in their bids the prices of related services the customer wants in the near future. That avoids the customer needing to separately request funding for those services from internal approvers.

Tip: Some vendors have service offerings to manage some or all of a customer's storage systems or even entire data centers that may include equipment from multiple vendors. This is called outsourcing. Small organizations in particular may benefit by being able to focus on their core business and not have to also manage a data center.

- Physical environment. Physical environment constraints can influence storage system requirements in ways that can affect costs, e.g., by limiting which systems can meet requirements. Conversely, storage system constraints can require changes in the physical environment in ways that can affect costs.

  In some data centers, floor space or rack space may be so limited that the ability of a storage system to support high capacity densities per unit of floor space or rack space can be a high priority requirement. In some data centers, energy costs may be so high or available energy so limited that the ability of a storage system to help minimize energy use (for power and cooling) can be a high priority requirement. These topics are discussed in the *Physical (Hardware) Configuration Management* chapter.

  Additional costs can result when facilities in an existing data center cannot immediately accommodate a new storage system. Some data centers may need to rearrange equipment to accommodate floor space needed by a new system. Some data centers may require adjusting the floor to accommodate the weight of a storage system. Additional floor space may be needed to support auxiliary equipment such as network switches to connect storage to hosts. Additional energy resources may be needed to support the power and cooling requirements of a new system. Uninterruptible Power Supply (UPS) equipment may need to be upgraded. Customers implementing a remote mirroring configuration may need to acquire communication equipment and links; a remote data center might need to be constructed or a third party paid to provide a disaster recovery site.

Often overlooked costs and savings

Some costs, and potential ways to reduce costs, are sometimes neglected by customers when evaluating and comparing vendors and storage system models.

- Deal timing. Vendors as businesses, and individual sales representatives and their management, may be under increased pressure to achieve revenue and profit quotas during certain times of the year. In particular, there can be increased internal pressure in vendor companies to "make the numbers" or "make plan" as certain accounting periods approach, typically the end of a calendar quarter and the end of a fiscal year (which does not always coincide with the calendar year).

  This has two cost-related implications for customer: (1) Customers may have more negotiating leverage as those dates approach. (2) Customers may experience increased pressure from vendors to close deals as those deadlines near. For example, a vendor may say that the currently proposed discount expires at the end of a quarter to motivate a customer to close a deal in that time frame; however, if that discount provides a profit today, why wouldn't it provide a profit two weeks after the quarter ends? The vendor may still want the business then and on the same terms (rather than no business at all).

- Used storage. Used (i.e., pre-owned) storage equipment may be sold by vendors (or previous users) in what is called the *used market* or *secondary market* or *aftermarket*. For example, vendors that lease storage systems may offer them on the used market when the equipment returns after the leases end. Used storage can vary from complete systems to selected system hardware components such as drives.

  Used equipment generally has a lower acquisition cost than current generation equipment. That can be attractive to the most price-sensitive customers when their storage requirements do not require the latest technologies.

  Other used equipment cost-related issues to consider include: whether the seller provides a guarantee or certification for quality (e.g., whether the equipment is refurbished or sold as-is), whether any time is left on the original warranty or the seller provides a new warranty, whether installing used parts in a system violates a system's warranty or maintenance agreement, current and estimated future maintenance charges for hardware and software during the planned useful life of the system (because these charges often increase as hardware ages), how long announced hardware and software upgrades will continue to be offered, whether any future upgrades (such as new drive models) are planned to be offered by the manufacturer, whether licensed software features on the system must be relicensed (at full price) from the manufacturer even if originally installed by the previous owner, and the business implications of potential problems with aging hardware such as mechanical HDDs.

- Hardware upgrades. Adding additional hardware components to an installed system may entail unanticipated costs. For example:

  o A storage system may support installing and adding only specific increments of some hardware components. Host ports are often integrated into adapters (aka directors) that include multiple ports. Drives are usually configured in RAID groups of multiple drives, often eight or more at a time, and sometimes must be ordered in increments that match RAID group size.

  o Ancillary costs for hardware upgrades may include additional enclosures to hold added components, additional power supplies, and additional internal controllers.[140] The cost of additional floor/rack space and additional energy should also be considered.

---

[140] These kinds of granularity requirements are not necessarily a gimmick to get a customer to spend money for components they do not need. Rather, a set of components may share common parts to reduce manufacturing cost and customer prices compared to the higher cost of using dedicated parts for each component. For example, a single host port adapter card may support multiple host ports that share a common processor on the card to manage the ports; a multiport card also has the benefit of occupying only one internal adapter card slot which reduces the total number of slots a storage system would otherwise need to support. A multiport adapter card is priced higher than if it supported only one port, but the cost per port is reduced compared to multiple cards each supporting only one port.

o A given system model might have one or more of the following pricing policies for licensed software features: software features included as standard at no charge, software features charged based on the storage system's total physical (raw) capacity, software features charged based on the portion of physical capacity the feature applies to, and software features charged based on ranges of raw capacity. Increasing raw capacity in a storage system can thus result in increases in licensing charges and in post-warranty maintenance charges.[141]

o Vendors' pricing policies for storage system hardware upgrades vary. Some vendors price hardware so that ordering that hardware with the original system or adding it later as an upgrade has the same list price (assuming pricing has not changed since the time the storage system was installed). Many customers may not realize, however, that some vendors charge significantly more for at least some hardware upgrades than for the same hardware installed in the original system shipped from the factory. For example, the price may be much higher for a drive added as an upgrade than for the same drive included in the original system.

Tip: Customers should ask their vendors about their pricing policies for upgrades prior to an acquisition decision to better assess TCO and to avoid unexpected cost surprises.

Note that if a vendor has a policy that charges extra for hardware upgrades and the vendor promises to apply the same discount to any future upgrades as the discount they applied to the original system, there is still an increased charge for upgrades because the discount will be applied against the higher list price of the upgrade.

Customers who acquire storage system(s) from vendors who charge more for hardware upgrades than for the same components shipped as part of the original systems should consider including additional components in the original system, rather than adding them later as upgrades. Financial implications depend on factors such as customer confidence those additional components will truly be needed, component prices, when those prices have to be paid, and when those components' warranties would terminate and maintenance charges begin.

- Component bundling. Upgrading one storage system component may require paying for other components not needed if the system design bundles multiple types of components together (e.g., processors plus cache plus host ports plus back-end ports to drives). For example, if a new host port is needed in such a system, a customer may need to buy not only one or more additional ports (depending on the granularity of that particular component), but also additional cache, additional processors, and additional back-end paths to drives; even additional drives may be required if the resulting configuration has a requirement for a minimal number of drives. Because different applications can differ significantly in the storage resources they need, component bundling can raise costs

---

[141] It might seem software charges should be based on usable capacity. However, in many storage systems customers can choose the types of RAID used, can change types at any time, and can intermix different types. That would complicate assessing charges compared to charges based on physical capacity.

unexpectedly if a customer must pay for components they do not need just to get the components they do need.

- No-charge software features. Some vendors include software features "standard at no extra charge." That can simplify the configuration and ordering process. However, it does not indicate the total cost is necessarily less than a system where features are ordered "a la carte." And, it does not include the additional hardware that would be needed to actually use some software features such as the extra capacity needed to support intra-system data replication.

- RAID type. RAID (Redundant Array of Independent Drives) is a design technique that allows a storage system to store data in a group of physical drives such that data remains accessible even if one, or sometimes more than one, drive in the group fails. There are multiple RAID types the most common of which are RAID-1, RAID-5, RAID-6, and RAID-10.[142] Discussions comparing RAID types often focus on availability and performance attributes; however, different RAID types can also impact TCA and TCO.

  RAID-1 and RAID-10 are typically the most expensive types of RAID because they mirror data, meaning they require twice the number of drives compared to the number strictly needed just to hold data. Other RAID types also require more drives than strictly needed to hold data, but fewer than twice as many. For example, for storage systems where RAID-5 is supported and configured in groups of eight drives, only one additional drive for every seven drives, an increase of about 14%, is needed.

  Different RAID types can have cost implications beyond just the number of drives required. A larger number of drives, especially when considering multiple RAID groups in aggregate, can in turn require additional priced hardware such as enclosures and internal controllers. Energy requirements also increase. Moreover, many vendors charge for licensed software and post-warranty software maintenance based on the physical (aka raw) capacity of the storage system (or, sometimes, the subset of the storage system against which the feature will be used). Thus, RAID-1 and RAID-10 in particular can substantially increase charges for software-based features compared to other RAID types.

  Tip: Some customers configure storage systems as RAID-1 or RAID-10, even when other RAID types are supported, for less than solid reasons even though those are the most expensive types of RAID. For example: "We've always done it this way" or "I heard that RAID-10 is fastest."

  The point isn't that RAID-1 or RAID-10 is a bad choice. Rather, customers should be clear when determining their requirements for RAID and include cost in that determination as well as performance and availability. If efficiently designed, other RAID types (such as RAID-5) may more than "do the job" and cost much less than RAID-1 or RAID-10. Moreover, many storage systems support a mix of RAID types. In that case, even if it is determined that RAID-1 or RAID-10 is most appropriate for the drives used by one application, other drives

---

[142] RAID is discussed in more detail in the *Availability* chapter. Note that some storage systems have RAID-like designs but do not use the term RAID.

in the system could be protected by RAID-5 or RAID-6, lowering the total cost compared to configuring RAID-1 or RAID-10 for all drives.

- SSDs. SSDs offer significant advantages over HDDs including using much less power and delivering much faster performance (especially for random read I/Os, though write I/O and sequential I/O performance may also be superior). But SSDs typically cost more than HDDs for equivalent capacity.[143]

Some vendors selling all-SSD storage systems (aka all-flash arrays, AFAs) may claim that through capacity optimization techniques, such as thin provisioning and data compression, the price of SSD capacity is comparable to the price of HDD capacity. However, that claim often ignores that the same capacity optimization techniques can often be applied to HDDs. A "comparable price" claim by an all-SSD system vendor may ignore that some all-SSD storage systems are relatively new in the marketplace and may lack important data management functions found in more mature storage systems originally designed for HDDs and that now support SSDs. Finally, some storage systems can support a combination of SSDs and HDDs which can be less expensive than an all-SSD configuration.

That said, it's important to understand that a cost comparison focusing on only SSD vs. HDD price-per-unit-of-capacity may be oversimplified due to overlooking various financial benefits SSDs can provide:

- Because SSDs are supported by many storage systems originally designed for only HDDs, SSD benefits can often be obtained by adding SSDs to such systems. Even if SSD capacity is more costly, it often takes a relatively small number of SSDs in a mixed SSD+HDD configuration to provide a significant performance benefit.

- SSDs can provide a relatively straightforward way to support capacity growth in an installed storage system when HDD I/O performance becomes a bottleneck inhibiting further capacity growth. (For example, consider a need to support more orders from customers during peak buying season.)

- SSDs can improve storage system performance quickly, without modifying or redesigning applications. New (or modified) applications may be able to meet their performance goals without coding complexities sometimes implemented to compensate for the relatively slow performance of HDDs.

- The high performance of SSDs (compared to HDDs) provides opportunities for applications to access and analyze more data in real-time while still meeting response time goals. For example, SSDs can enable credit card transaction applications to analyze more information (such as recent card usage patterns) in the short time available to determine whether to approve or reject a purchase request, reducing approvals that shouldn't be made and increasing rejections that should be made.

---

[143] At the time this is written, most SSDs are based on flash memory technology. The industry is investigating other solid-state technologies that may someday compete with or supersede flash technology. However, the points made in this discussion of potential cost implications of SSDs compared to HDDs are largely independent of the particular underlying technology of SSDs.

o SSDs provide an increased ability to consolidate multiple storage systems into fewer systems due to their high performance. A single storage system with its shared resources and single management interface can be easier to manage than multiple systems.

o SSD high performance can reduce administrator time and effort spent on performance tuning, freeing administrators for other tasks.

o SSDs provide short time-to-value due to immediate performance and energy benefits.

o SSDs can provide possible rack and floor space savings when fewer SSDs can replace a larger number HDDs that are each limited by the customer to only being partially filled with data (i.e., short-stroked to minimize mechanical arm movement) to support a performance requirement.

That potential SSD benefit leads to a more important point. In cases where multiple HDDs have been provisioned for performance reasons, SSDs may be able to reduce or eliminate the price-per-unit-of-capacity advantage of HDDs. To illustrate how, assume three things: (1) An SSD costs five times more than an HDD of the same capacity. (2) An SSD supports ten times more IOPS than an HDD. And, (3) although an application needs only one HDD to meet its capacity needs, it needs five HDDs to support its IOPS and response time needs. Given those assumptions, just one SSD can meet the application's capacity requirement and exceed its performance requirement. The costs of the one SSD and the five HDDs are the same. Yet the SSD has performance capability to spare.

Compared to HDDs, the high performance of SSDs enables them to more easily be provisioned to satisfy both performance and capacity requirements. That prompts another way to compare the cost of HDDs and SSDs other than by price-per-unit-of-capacity: price-per-I/O.

o SSDs can sometimes be configured as in-host cache, providing even higher performance than storage system caches.

o SSDs can potentially (and perhaps unexpectedly) reduce host hardware and software costs. This is possible because the use of SSDs to dramatically reduce I/O response times (compared to HDDs) allows running host processors at higher utilizations than otherwise practical, while still meeting or beating application performance objectives.

Although increased host processor utilization by itself could potentially degrade application performance, lower I/O response time can offset that increase. Most commercial applications are I/O bound, meaning that I/O time is a larger component of response time for applications than processor time. Therefore, a reduction in I/O time can result in a significant reduction in end-user response time, offsetting any increase in end-user response time due to higher processor utilization.

This is illustrated in the diagram below showing major components of end user response time: processor time, I/O time, and network time. (1) illustrates the original end user response time when only HDDs are configured, (2) illustrates the reduced response time when SSDs are configured, and (3) illustrates that response time can remain the same or better than it was in (1) even if host processor utilization is increased somewhat. In practice, achievable changes in processor time and I/O time depend on the host/processor/network environment.

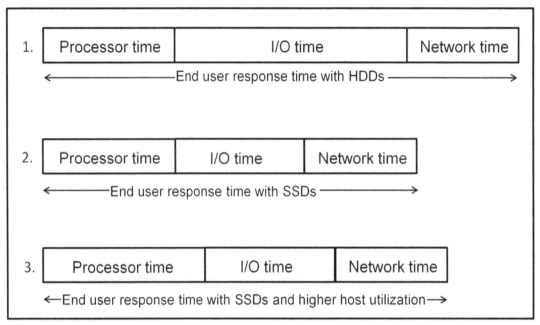

SSDs can reduce I/O time, enabling host processors to run at higher utilization. The degree of change shown is for illustration only.

A reduction in host cost resulting from an ability to run a host at increased processor utilization could be realized in one or more ways: (1) The useful life of a host might be elongated, delaying the costs of an upgrade or replacement. (2) Future hosts could be acquired with less processing power than otherwise needed. This can reduce hardware costs, reduce energy costs, reduce maintenance charges, and also reduce software license charges when those charges are based on the number of processor cores. (3) Multiple hosts might be consolidated into a fewer number of hosts; that in turn may result in floor or rack space savings and reduced network connections.

Tip: Some vendors support tools to help customers determine a mix of SSDs and HDDs to optimize price-performance. The reports generated by such tools can help avoid under-buying or over-buying SSDs. This is especially useful for storage systems that support automated storage tiering where the system periodically redistributes data among SSDs and HDDs to keep the most active data on SSDs.

- Multipath I/O drivers. Host software to manage multiple paths between a host and a storage system is called a *multipath I/O driver*. The key functions are driving an I/O request down an alternate path when one path fails, automatically reusing the failed path when it is again operational, and balancing I/O activity across the paths (using various algorithms) to help optimize performance. Other functions may also be supported.

Some storage system vendors provide multipath I/O drivers for selected hosts; these may be provided at no extra charge or may be priced. Some host operating systems and some ISV storage management software products include multipath I/O drivers.

When storage system vendors charge for host-based multipath drivers the charges may be based on the number of processors (aka CPUs) in a host in which the software is installed. The charges may be independent of the amount of I/O traffic that uses the drivers, so that a driver that is busy most of the time and one that is idle most of the time are priced the same. This pricing policy leads to additional charges when hosts are upgraded with new processors even if the upgraded hosts do not issue additional I/Os to the storage system supported by the multipath drivers.

- System consolidation. Consolidating multiple existing storage systems into a single, newer, more powerful storage system may increase acquisition costs, but may help lower the TCO over time. Various forms of storage consolidation are discussed in the *Logical (Software) Configuration Management* chapter.

- Soft costs. Some often overlooked storage system costs are sometimes said to be *soft costs* (or intangible costs, in contrast to hard (tangible) costs). While soft costs do not require financial payment to a vendor and may not be included as distinct items in budgets, they are associated with a real impact on an organization's internal resources such as staff time diverted from other, perhaps higher priority, projects. Here are examples of items often considered to be soft costs:

  o Time and effort is required for storage system migrations performed by customer personnel. That can include learning new terminology, new feature characteristics, and new management interfaces, all of which differ from familiar systems. It can also include time and effort to rewrite and test scripts (i.e., machine-executable customer-written procedures that manage system operations).

  o More storage administrators than otherwise necessary may be needed when multiple incompatible "islands" of storage are installed and require different skills to operate.

  o Some storage systems require (or may offer as an option) customer set-up (CSU) of a system, customer replaceable units (CRU), or both. That means it is a customer's responsibility, not the vendor's, to install a storage system or replace a failed hardware component with a new component the vendor ships to the customer, then return the failed component to the vendor. Those activities can require IT staff time and competence and could increase the chance for human error (due to tasks rarely performed). Vendors may offer to do the work at an additional charge.

- Pre-requisite features. A vendor may not identify all prerequisite products needed to enable all included storage system capabilities, then, after winning the business, inform the customer there are additional products they would need to pay for. Therefore, customers should ask vendors for assurance that all prerequisite features needed for the capabilities the customer wants are included in vendors' proposals.

Additional Tips

- *A vendor's proposal with the lowest acquisition price or lowest overall cost is not necessarily the best proposal. Price and cost are only some of the important attributes to consider when evaluating and comparing storage systems, as has been shown in this Guide.*

  The following quote is widely attributed to U.S. astronaut John Glenn: "As I hurtled through space, one thought kept crossing my mind - every part of this rocket was supplied by the lowest bidder."

- *Customers should question vendors about their rationale for proposed models and configurations – the answers may help reduce cost. Examples: Is a smaller, lower cost system model available that would satisfy requirements and be upgradable in-place to larger models (in case the I/O workload outgrows the smaller model)? If the proposed system is the high-end model in its family and is maximally configured, does the vendor have another family that would offer more room for growth? What would be the impact on I/O response time if a smaller, lower cost cache were configured? What would be the impact on performance if a smaller number of higher capacity drives were used instead of a larger number of smaller capacity drives? Would configuring a portion of storage system capacity as solid-state drives (SSDs) result in significant host hardware and software savings by allowing hosts to run at higher utilizations or with fewer CPUs while still maintaining or improving end user transaction response times?*

- *Historically, many customers used a price per megabyte (price/MB) measure to compare prices. With the significantly larger total capacities of today's storage systems, price/GB or even price/TB are more useful measures. (Consider that individual drives typically contain hundreds of gigabytes or even multiple terabytes.)*[144]

- *A vendor may try to win a sales opportunity by offering the lowest price, knowing the proposed configuration may not support a customer's performance requirements. (In contrast to components such as the number of host ports or specific software functions, the performance capabilities of a storage system are not a directly orderable feature. Unless a representative benchmark was run on the planned configuration prior to acquisition, system performance may not be determined until sometime after installation.)*

  A performance guarantee can help protect against this. If an effective guarantee is in place, once the customer provides evidence that the performance requirements specified in the guarantee are not being met, the vendor should meet the terms of the guarantee, e.g., to tune or upgrade the system at no extra charge. A low bidding vendor may have anticipated the customer action and determined they will still make a profit on the sale or that they will

---

[144] The price per megabyte for IBM's 1956 RAMAC 5MB disk storage system was about $10,000 (U.S.) in 1956 dollars. Today, a much faster, much smaller, and much higher capacity 4TB disk drive has a typical price under $200 (U.S.) for the entire drive, meaning about $.00005 per megabyte which is 200,000,000 times less than RAMAC. (Reference: http://en.wikipedia.org/wiki/Memory_storage_density.)

make a profit over time given expected upgrades during the life of the system and follow-on business with a replacement system. If there is no performance guarantee in place, the customer may have little recourse other than to pay to upgrade the system to the required level of performance. (Performance Guarantees are discussed in the Marketing Tactics *chapter.)*

- *A storage system vendor may attempt to* upsell *a customer by recommending various optional system features (particularly software-based features[145]) that sound good and perhaps do not appear to add much to what the customer will pay for the entire system. (They may also add post-warranty maintenance charges.) However, customers should consider whether there is a definite need for and a plan to use such features or whether they will just end up as "shelfware."*

- *Vendors may not identify potential alternatives to a priced storage system feature they want to sell. For example, many storage systems support priced software features that can make point-in-time copies of volumes. A vendor may not mention that many host operating systems and (ISV) volume managers support the ability to create volume copies (sometimes called* mirrors*), may work with any vendor's storage system, and even support making copies where the original volume and its copy reside in different storage systems. Such host-based copy functions may be acceptable alternatives to storage-based copy features in some customer environments.[146]*

- *A vendor may give a customer a customized analysis claiming their storage system will save the customer money during the years their system is installed. A customer should examine the analysis and not take the claimed bottom-line savings at face value. The potential savings may be exaggerated, may include "soft dollars," and may be savings competitors could also provide. The claimed potential savings are likely to be forgotten and not verified by a customer after the sale, and vendors know there is likely no penalty to them if the claimed savings are not realized.*

- *A vendor may state that a particular storage system feature is "free," a word that is always appealing to customers. What does "free" mean? A feature could be considered to be free if it was priced, but is now offered at zero price and no other prices were raised to compensate. A feature might also be considered to be free if it was added to the system without any other price increases (though perhaps the system price would have been lower if the feature wasn't offered).*

  A vendor may state that a particular storage system feature is "at no extra charge"; that may be a more accurate description than "free." The cost to the vendor of providing a particular

---

[145] *Upselling software features can be very profitable for a vendor since the incremental cost to the vendor for the feature may be merely the cost to ship a CD to the customer.*

[146] *This is an example of the tradeoffs resulting from locating a function in a storage system or in a host. Storage system-based functions can help offload work from hosts and may support any hosts attached to the storage system. Host-based functions can help offload work from storage systems and may support any storage systems attached to the host.*

system feature (e.g., the cost to design, develop, and test it) may be included in the base system price and just not visible as a separately priced line item.

Customers really have no way to determine how a vendor internally develops their storage system pricing policy.   The overall system price and the prices assigned to individual features may be based on factors such as the vendor's costs to provide the system or features, marketing tactics, and competitive pressures. What customers can determine, or at least estimate, is how a storage system acquisition will affect their financial picture including TCA, TCO, and the timing of cash flow.

Part IV.

Insights into
Making the Decision

With an understanding of its own business and applications, plus knowledge of storage system and vendor capabilities available in the market, an organization is positioned to determine its system and vendor requirements. The organization will then be ready to evaluate and compare alternatives to determine the system and vendor best able to address those requirements.

Determining System and Vendor Requirements

At this point, it might seem desirable for this Guide to directly recommend what any customers' enterprise storage system and vendor requirements should be. Customers could then use the recommended requirements as a standard to determine which storage systems and vendors best address them. Desirable, perhaps, but just not possible.

Knowing the potential value that enterprise storage systems and the vendors who sell them can offer, customers have information that is certainly critical to determining their storage and vendor requirements. That information is necessary, but not sufficient.

Different customers – and even different departments and applications within a customer's organization – differ in how they use (or want to use) storage and thus differ in their storage requirements. There can be differences in what technologies are needed and in what vendor capabilities are needed. Requirements are also impacted by budget constraints, whether a customer is willing to consider storage systems incompatible with currently installed systems, data center environmental constraints, organization plans such as anticipated mergers and acquisitions, and more.

All these factors mean each customer must determine their particular storage system and vendor requirements for themselves. That can even lead to different sets of requirements for different departments and applications within an organization. (In that case, customers can consider storage systems supporting a superset of all requirements, or separate systems for different applications, or some combination.)

So, much "homework" must be left to the customer. This chapter is intended to help with that by suggesting ways requirements can be defined, clarified, and organized.

Landscape

- <u>Requirements precede evaluation</u>. Enterprise storage systems use sophisticated technology to provide significant value to organizations through managing computer-generated data. Different system models can differ dramatically in many important attributes (such as availability, performance, capacity scalability, function, manageability, and so on). And, there is no single best storage system in an absolute sense, only the best system(s) to address a specific set of requirements. Different storage system models are definitely not readily interchangeable commodities.

There are many storage system vendors in the market, especially compared to the earliest days of commercial computers when there were only a handful of vertically integrated computer manufacturers, each offering storage for only their computers. Different vendors can differ dramatically in many important attributes (such as the portfolio of systems they sell, technical expertise, supported locations, service offerings, and financial offerings.) Like the storage systems they sell, vendors are definitely not commodities.

Therefore, customers should focus on clearly identifying their requirements for systems and vendors *before* attempting to evaluate and compare offerings available in the marketplace in detail. The requirements become the standard against which the evaluation and comparison take place. Using a variation of a popular adage: If you don't know what you need, any storage system (and vendor) will get you there. (But you might later realize it is not where you want to be.)

Tip: During the information gathering process, customers may gain insights into storage system and vendor capabilities in the market they had not previously been aware of. They can then determine whether any such capabilities should be included as requirements.

It can be helpful to realize the storage industry has evolved to the point that many of the "latest and greatest" storage system capabilities are often more advanced than the needs of many customers, especially smaller organizations. That is, not every system capability, no matter how wonderful a vendor may make it sound, is necessarily something every customer requires.

- Organizing technical requirements. Storage system technical requirements can be grouped into categories that make them easier to determine and organize.

  Tip: Below is a list of categories to consider based on earlier topics in this Guide. Customers can determine which categories matter to them and determine their system requirements within these categories. The list can also serve as a reference for organization management to use to verify these categories were considered when identifying specific requirements.

  o Host support. *(Requirements for supporting specific host models, operating system versions, connection types, and synergy functions.)*

  o Capacity for data. *(Requirements for usable data capacity.)*

  o Availability. *(Requirements for maintaining access to data and functions.)*

  o Performance. *(Requirements for the speed of processing I/O requests and function requests.)*

  o Intra-system data replication. *(Requirements for supporting internal point-in-time copies of data.)*

  o Inter-system data replication. *(Requirements for maintaining remote copies of data.)*

o Security. *(Requirements for limiting access to data and functions to authorized users only.)*

o Physical (Hardware) Configuration Management. *(Requirements for hardware flexibility.)*

o Logical (Software) Configuration Management. *(Requirements for administrators' controls.)*

- Organizing vendor requirements. Vendor requirements can be grouped into categories that make them easier to determine and organize.

Tip: Below is a list of categories to consider based on earlier topics in this Guide. Customers can determine which categories matter to them and determine their vendor requirements within these categories. The list can also serve as a reference for organization management to use to verify these categories were considered when identifying specific vendor requirements.

o Vendor viability. *(Requirements that a vendor would be a good partner to do business with for this acquisition.)*

o Sales role and qualifications. *(Requirements for the vendor as manufacturer or business partner or value-add reseller; requirements for certifications indicating a demonstrated degree of expertise.)*

o Product portfolio. *(Requirements for the kinds of offerings the vendor sells.)*

o Locations. *(Requirements for localities where the vendor does business.)*

o Product maintenance. *(Requirements for who would perform product maintenance.)*

o R & D access. *(Requirements for access to the manufacturer's researchers and developers (if appropriate).)*

o Technology currency. *(Requirements for the vendor to have a commitment to support new storage technologies, new host/OS versions, etc. in a timely manner.)*

o Local support personnel. *(Requirements for adequate vendor staffing to support the customer.)*

o Help desk support. *(Requirements for access to product experts by phone or email to get answers to installed product questions in a timely manner.)*

o Parts inventory. *(Requirements that a parts inventory be close enough to support a customer receiving replacement parts in a timely manner.)*

o Contract and warranty. *(Requirements a customer places on terms and conditions for these agreements.)*

o Guarantees. *(Requirements the customer has for vendor-supported guarantees.)*

o Financing. *(Requirements for financing offerings.)*

o IT Services. *(Requirements for vendor-provided services.)*

o References. *(Requirements for vendor-supplied customer references.)*

o User community. *(Requirements for the vendor fostering a community of users to share information.)*

o Vision. *(Requirements for the vendor's (and manufacturer's) vision for storage and for their business.)*

- <u>System viability</u>. Some customers may want to include a requirement that reflects what might be called "system viability," analogous to vendor viability. More risk adverse customers may want to require that vendors' proposals must be limited to system models with good track records, e.g., models with some minimum number of systems in production use for at least some minimum number of months. On the other hand, some customers may determine that a new storage system from a new vendor best meets their particular requirements; there is nothing wrong with that as long as the risks are understood and accepted. Below is a hierarchy of system risks defined based on principle (not evidence). In order of increasing risk:

o Current-generation models with a proven track record of productive use in many customer environments.

o Next-generation systems new to the market but based on previous models with a proven track record of productive use, where the systems have substantial changes to microcode or hardware, but not to both at the same time.

o Next-generation systems new to the market but based on previous models with a proven track record of productive use, where the systems have substantial changes to both microcode and hardware.

o New system models with little to no track record of productive use in customer environments. (A vendor selling a new storage system model with few customers using it may attempt to compensate for that in other ways such as a reduced price or extra technical support at the customer's site.)[147]

Tip: To help determine whether a proposed storage system or feature is already used successfully by other organizations, questions customers can ask vendors include: "How many systems of the proposed model are customers operating in production?" A more precise, but probably more difficult question for vendors to answer is: "How many of those systems are in environments similar to mine, e.g., supporting my server/OSs, my required performance, my required capacity, the microcode version my system would be running, and the system features I require?" A vendor may not be able to identify other customers

---

[147] The list could be augmented with additional considerations. Systems based on proven architectures may be less risky than systems using novel architectures. Systems using components from established manufacturers may be less risky than systems using other components.

with installed storage systems that precisely match a given customer's requirements, but even evidence of success in similar environments can help increase a customer's confidence in a proposed system.

Be careful when asking general questions such as "How many systems have been shipped?" or "How many systems shipped have software feature x?" The answers could include internal systems in vendors' labs and systems at customer locations not yet in production. The answers could include total licenses for a software feature acquired over the history of a storage system family or brand, not just current-generation models, and could include cases where the feature is no longer used or was never implemented by customers.

- <u>Constraints on requirements</u>.   Customers choose a storage system to support the requirements of their IT environment. Customers don't first choose a storage system they would like to have and then require that the surrounding environment must support that system.[148]

Customers acquire a storage system to support currently installed or planned hosts and applications, not the other way around. If an existing storage system is being replaced, many constraints on requirements may exist such as host-storage connection types and data access protocols. Similarly, if a new storage system is being acquired to support new applications, the needs of already-designed applications can constrain storage options, e.g., the applications may need storage systems that support a particular data access protocol the applications use.

Other constraints may also come into play. One constraint can be data center environmental issues such as available floor space and power. Budget can be another constraint. Some customers may have a constraint that major acquired assets must entirely or largely consist of components manufactured in a particular country.

Another potential constraint introduced in recent years is *converged systems* that combine servers and storage into one package. It is generally the server's capabilities that are the main focus of selecting such a system; if so, there may be limited choices for the integrated storage system.

Another potential constraint on requirements is service levels. Service levels refer to system goals to be achieved, especially for system availability and performance. Such goals are called *service level objectives (SLOs)*; SLOs may differ from application to application. Because an objective is not necessarily a commitment and may have no associated penalty if it is not attained, in some cases a service provider (whether in-house or external) and a user may forge a *service level agreement (SLA)* that codifies objectives as a contract. Requirements for a new storage system, then, are constrained to support the SLA.

---

[148] The difference between constraints and requirements is admittedly subtle. The idea behind this discussion is that constraints already exist before requirements for a particular storage system are defined. That is, constraints limit requirements. For example, available floor space is a constraint while usable capacity is a requirement.   A desire to install one larger storage system to simplify management rather than installing multiple smaller systems is a requirement, not a constraint.

For completeness, it's worth mentioning that a constraint of a different sort may occasionally be imposed on requirements by an organization's politics. For example, if a system model or vendor caused a serious problem for the customer, such as a loss of data or an unusually long outage of any kind, an overarching management decision may be made to eliminate that model or vendor from future consideration. The reason may only be to enable customer management to demonstrate they have done *something* to address the problem and punish the guilty party.

- <u>Prioritizing requirements</u>. It may be the case that no one storage system and vendor available in the marketplace will be able to perfectly satisfy all of a customer's requirements, e.g., performance level and availability level and vendor service offerings, all within budget. Therefore, it is important to prioritize requirements: What is essential? What is preferred? What is optional? What is irrelevant? Identifying requirement priorities helps manage the evaluation/comparison process (discussed in the next chapter).

Tip: Whether to share requirement priorities with the vendors when soliciting proposals is up to each customer. Sharing priorities has at least two benefits: (1) It informs the vendors which items they should focus on the most, especially if they are requested to provide their proposals in a short period of time. (2) It avoids discouraging vendors from submitting proposals just because they cannot support a capability the customer actually views as optional or preferred.

- <u>Projecting future requirements</u>. Enterprise storage system requirements should include both current requirements and, to whatever extent possible, projected requirements for the time period covering the expected useful life of storage systems to be acquired. Estimating such future requirements includes storage management disciplines such as capacity planning, performance planning, and data center floor space and energy planning.

Tip: Projected future requirements, such as an expected increase in required capacity some time after a system is installed, can impact the evaluation of systems to be acquired now because it is likely desirable they should be upgradeable in-place to support the projected requirements. Awareness of a projected capacity requirement can also prompt proactively implementing data management techniques to optimize capacity use such as archiving unused files or implementing data compression.

Additional Tips

- *Requirements should be documented, not just discussed. That provides a base for reference and modification by the customer, and fosters clear communication between a customer and vendors.*

- *Enterprise storage systems are amazing machines often taken for granted by users. Manufacturers and vendors of these marvelous feats of engineering certainly deserve the right to highlight the engineering work that has gone into them.*

However, it is recommended that, for the purpose of identifying requirements, customers pay the most attention to product attributes that make a visible/tangible/measurable difference to applications and users. That can include system attributes such as usable capacity, the number and types of host ports supported, the number of volumes or files or directories or objects that can be created, performance, and floor space. Visible attributes also include (software-based) functions such as point-in-time data replication including the required number of copies supported per data item and per system, and the impact of making copies on the performance of other work in the system.

(In contrast, many storage system attributes are invisible to applications and users and are often of little if any importance as requirements in an acquisition decision. For example, consider the number and speed of internal processors which are just one of many factors that contribute to performance users see. As another example, some vendors highlight their storage systems' internal hardware architectures; however, if there was such a thing as a single indisputably best storage system architecture, all manufacturers would likely be using it.)

Following this recommendation, it is generally best to specify requirements in terms of what is to be accomplished, rather than how. For example, a given level of performance might be achievable using any of several different combinations of cache size and drives that vary in type, capacity, and speed. Customers generally do not have the skill or time to model or run benchmarks to measure the performance of many alternative configurations of the same system model. That work is best left to a vendor, where a customer might reasonably ask for the lowest cost configuration that meets their performance needs. While it may not be feasible for a vendor to compare the performance of every possible configuration, they should be able to shed light on why they believe a proposed configuration is lower cost or otherwise preferred over (many) other configurations that deliver similar performance.

- *As important as storage system performance is, not every customer may need to identify explicit quantified storage system performance requirements. Many organizations, most likely organizations needing smaller (entry-level) storage systems, can and do accept the performance they get in these systems because it has always proven to be "good enough." A similar point applies to availability.*

- *Some requirements may be best expressed in the form of "supports at least x," such as "supports at least 3 copies per volume and at least 100 copies total per system." That allows a storage system to meet and potentially exceed a requirement, without a customer unintentionally implying a requirement must be met exactly and not exceeded.*

- *Beware of specifying requirements "because that's the way we've always done it." That could prohibit vendor recommendations that could reduce costs and/or improve operations. For example, some customers make RAID-1 or RAID-10 a requirement, perhaps without awareness that many of today's RAID-5 implementations can offer high levels of protection against data loss along with high levels of performance, all at substantial savings in the number of drives, floor space, and software license costs when those costs are based on physical (not usable) capacity. (RAID is discussed in the* Availability *chapter and the* Performance *chapter.)*

- *It is important that requirements be determined objectively. For example, a case where requirements are written by someone who has a pre-existing preference for a particular storage system or vendor can be counterproductive. Achieving objectivity in requirements and in the overall decision process is further discussed in the* Evaluating and Comparing Systems and Vendors *chapter.*

- *Requirements should be stated in a way that avoids terminology such as system feature names that are unique to one vendor or one storage system model. This supports the goal of objectivity and helps avoid any vendor getting an impression, whether accurate or not, that the requirements are biased towards a particular solution. This also avoids confusion on the part of vendors because not every vendor may be familiar with the feature names and capabilities of other vendors' storage systems. For example, it is better to have a requirement for a "point-in-time intra-system volume replication capability" than to have a requirement for "a capability like system XYZ's Galactic Data CopyItAll feature."*

- *Generally, the more precisely requirements are stated, the better. It can be a mistake to assume a storage system's function supports all needed capabilities without having required them explicitly.*

  For example, the briefly stated requirement "supports internal point-in-time volume replication" would be satisfied by a storage system that allows only one copy per volume, or allows only ten total copies of volumes in an entire storage system. Those limitations may not support a customer's real, but unstated, requirement.

  Here is a more detailed example. Consider three possible ways of stating requirements for storage system availability:

  1) *"The system should have a high level of availability."*

  2) *"The system should include redundant hardware."*

  3) *"All system hardware components should be redundant and support nondisruptive repair; all upgradable hardware components should be upgradable nondisruptively; the system should also support nondisruptive internal software (microcode) upgrades."*

  Of the three statements, (3) is clearly the most precise requirement. While (3) may initially sound comprehensive, consider yet another availability requirement that could be added: "The storage system should have a proven record of at least five nines availability (i.e., ≥99.999% uptime) over the last twelve months based on statistics of storage systems of the proposed model in production in customer environments using the version/release of internal software that would be installed on the proposed storage system."[149]

  The more precisely requirements are defined, the less chance there is that a vendor can validly reply "Yes, we support that," yet the nuances of what a customer really wants were not stated and may not be supported. Customers want to avoid post-installation surprises

---

[149] *A vendor should be able to show a customer detailed statistics to back up any availability claim; that may require a nondisclosure agreement with the customer.*

such as later hearing a vendor say "No, my system does not do that, but your requirements did not specifically ask for that."

Evaluating and Comparing Systems and Vendors

Once a decision to acquire a new storage system is made, and technical and vendor requirements are defined, the next steps are evaluating and comparing system and vendor candidates to determine which best address those requirements.

"Excellence is never an accident. It is always the result of high intention, sincere effort, and intelligent execution; it represents the wise choice of many alternatives – choice, not chance, determines your destiny."

> – Aristotle

Landscape

- Challenges. A storage system evaluation/comparison process is often far from easy. Challenges result from many factors such as: The time and effort it takes to do an evaluation/comparison; pressures to have the new system installed by a specific date, finding the participants with time and skills to support a quality evaluation/comparison, the number of different vendors and storage systems in the market, the large amount of information available about systems and vendors (see the *Sources of Product and Vendor Information* chapter), the need to separate often-impressive marketing claims from useful information, the lack of standard names and terminology for similar components and functions supported by different storage systems, the need to identify a given system's limitations and restrictions, and the need to reconcile vendors' claims about competitors and the competitors' defenses. In addition, consider an inability to accurately predict future storage requirements, future vendor developments, and future industry developments considering the useful life of an enterprise storage system is typically (hoped to be) at least four or five years.

- Asking vendors for general information: RFI (Request for Information). RFIs ask vendors for relatively high-level information about the vendors' offerings and about the vendors themselves. A vendor's response may consist largely of existing marketing information (e.g., brochures); that is, a vendor's response may contain little if any information customized to the customer's particular needs. A vendor may request the opportunity to meet one-on-one with the customer, especially if they have no prior relationship with the customer.

- <u>Asking vendors for proposals: RFP (Request for Proposal).</u> RFPs ask vendors to describe in detail how they would address a customer's specific requirements. Submitting an RFP to vendors may follow a customer's preliminary determination of which vendors seem able to potentially address the customer's needs; that determination may be   based on RFI responses or vendors' presentations or the customer's industry knowledge. (Appendix D contains a suggested outline for an RFP.)

A vendor's response to an RFP will normally be a customized proposal recommending specific products and configurations, describing how those products and how the vendor as a company address requirements specified in the RFP, along with the vendor's asking price. The customer analyzes received proposals to determine which vendor and product can best address the customer's requirements. The customer may discuss an RFP response with its vendor to clarify and perhaps negotiate items in the proposal.

Some vendors may respond "no bid" if they believe they cannot meet the customer's requirements or if they believe (perhaps based on how the RFP is written) the customer has already decided which vendor to award the business to and is not seriously considering other vendors. (Customers receiving "no bid" responses from vendors may find it insightful to ask those vendors why.)

Because so much product and vendor information is readily accessible on the Web and because many large organizations are familiar with many vendors' offerings, RFIs may be less common these days than RFPs.

Tip: An RFP for a storage system can be organized using the same categories suggested previously for organizing technical requirements and vendor requirements. Dividing an RFP into sections based on such categories helps structure the RFP. It also helps vendors in case the work to respond to related requirements (e.g., requirements about performance) needs to be distributed to particular specialists within the vendor's company.

Tip: Customers should allow sufficient time for creating an RFP and for letting vendors respond to an RFP. This facilitates each party being able to support a high quality decision process. In particular, customers should strive to be accurate, clear, and comprehensive when defining their requirements. Similarly, vendors should strive to be accurate, clear, and comprehensive when addressing requirements. Consider the following steps each of which takes time in an RFP process:

- o *Time to create the RFP. For a customer to identify and agree on requirements takes time and that time may not be easy to estimate.   There may be constraints on when a new storage system must be in production that in turn constrain the time available for the entire decision and acquisition process. Examples of constraints include upcoming end-of-lease dates or new applications that can begin production only when a new storage system is installed. If a customer takes too long to finalize an RFP and submit it to vendors, the time left for vendors' to do their work may be difficult to manage, or may result in a "rush job," or may result in the customer missing their self-imposed deadlines. (An adage posted on many office walls seems relevant: Failure to plan on your part does not constitute an emergency on my part.)*

o *Time for vendor questions.* Vendors sometimes need to ask questions about RFP items they find to be unclear or that might be addressed in ways other than those implied by the RFP. Customers need time to answer those questions and, normally, share those questions and replies with all vendors who received the RFP.

o *Time for vendors to develop their proposals.* Some RFP requirements or questions cannot always be answered quickly and easily. For example, vendors, like customers, have limited personnel who may not be immediately available to work on a given RFP response. Particularly complex requirements and questions may require extra time and expertise to address.

o *Time for customers to evaluate and compare proposals.* Proposals are sometimes lengthy. Customers may need to ask vendors to clarify various responses.

The right amount of time to allow for these steps, individually and together, is difficult to quantify. A few, perhaps obvious, general points can be made: More complex requirements and RFP responses naturally tend to need more time than simpler ones. A larger number of responses takes more time to evaluate than fewer responses. The time needed may be estimated by a customer based on their past experience or from the experiences of other customers.

Tip: An RFP may stipulate that vendors provide "best and final" prices. However, that may not stop an aggressive vendor from proposing a still lower price after submitting an RFP response if they think they are not going to win the business or have lost to a competitor. Customers may want to plan how they will handle such situations, considering what is fair to all vendors as well as what is best for the customer.

- Asking vendors only for price: Request for Quotation (RFQ). In the case where a customer knows the detailed specifications of a storage system they want to acquire – and that means knowing manufacturer, model, and features – they could submit a Request for Quotation (RFQ) asking for the price (and perhaps also for related items such as financing options and professional services). In the business world, an RFQ is most appropriate when asking vendors to bid on commodity offerings. For storage, an RFQ may be appropriate if a customer is acquiring an additional storage system that duplicates a system already installed and there are multiple vendors (e.g., the manufacturer and business partners) who can supply the system. Note that considering price only could overlook important differences among vendors who can ship the same product.

- Identifying vendors to contact. When customers want to solicit information from multiple vendors, identifying the vendors to contact is not always obvious.

It is likely neither necessary nor productive to send an RFI, RFP, or RFQ to each of the dozens of storage system vendors in the market. Fortunately, even knowing just a little about requirements and vendors can help identify which vendors are worthwhile considering for a given acquisition. For example, a conservative organization wanting a storage system for a new application critical to the business may want to focus on established vendors and system models with a proven track record in customer environments rather than consider industry startups.

Tip: Here are suggestions to help customers identify relevant vendors to contact. One or more of these suggestions may help in a given situation.

o If a customer has no other information to start from, the membership lists of industry standard organizations can be a useful resource for identifying storage system vendors, though those lists may have no information about vendors' particular offerings. For example, visit
http://www.snia.org/member_com/member_directory.

o Many customers know the names of many, if not all, storage system vendors who they wish to consider, perhaps based on past experience with those vendors.

o Some organizations (such as large organizations with multiple, globally located data centers) may have official internal lists of the vendors (and even the specific storage system models) organization departments are allowed to choose from. That limits the number of vendors and systems the organization deals with and reduces the total time and effort for evaluation.

o A customer may have contacts in other organizations or relevant industry groups, preferably those with storage needs similar to the customer's, who can be asked for recommendations.

o Storage industry consultants could be hired to recommend candidate vendors.

o As mentioned above, a criterion important to many customers is vendor viability. In particular, the length of time a vendor had been in the market can usually be determined from the vendor's website (e.g., from the history of press releases or from a section perhaps titled something like "About [company]").

o It can help narrow down a list of candidate vendors by identifying just those vendors that sell storage systems supporting the particular data access protocol(s) required because some vendors sell or specialize in only one kind of storage system, e.g., only block-access or file-access or object-access systems; unified systems may also be offered. Here are some sources of information that can help: (1) Some industry analysts publish papers identifying many storage industry vendors based on the type of data-access; these reports are often available by subscription, but are sometimes published on the public Web by the analysts or by other parties who have paid the analysts for the privilege. (2) Some websites publish the results of standardized performance benchmarks for storage systems from multiple vendors based on type of data access; consider http://www.storageperformance.org for block-access storage and http://www.spec.org for file-access storage. Note that not every relevant vendor may participate in these industry performance benchmark organizations.

o In some cases, a technical requirement is so specialized it may be satisfied only by particular storage system models from a few vendors. An example of that is storage system support for IBM z Systems z/OS hosts due to a unique host-storage connectivity protocol required called FICON. Such specialized requirements can help narrow down Web-based searches for relevant vendors and systems.

o *More generally, system specifications published on the Web generally include maximum physical (or, better, usable) capacity information that can be easily compared to a customer's minimum usable capacity requirement. That can quickly help narrow down a list of candidate vendors and systems.*

- High-level evaluation: SWOT. SWOT stands for **s**trengths, **w**eaknesses, **o**pportunities, and **t**hreats. A SWOT analysis can help evaluate the viability of products and vendors based on these four criteria. Though it does not support a quantified comparison in contrast to a weighted score analysis (discussed below), a SWOT analysis might be used along with a weighted score analysis as a form of cross-check. Some industry analysts publish reports with a SWOT analysis, perhaps available for a fee.

- Detailed evaluation/comparison: weighted score. Some customers evaluate each vendor's proposal by using a weighted score approach. Here is the basic idea: Two values are assigned by the customer to each item in an RFP response. The first value is a weight that reflects the item's importance to the customer and is constant across all proposals; a higher weight indicates higher importance. The second value is a score that reflects how well a given proposal addresses the item, perhaps on a scale from 0 (no support at all) to 10 (full support). The weighted score for each item in a particular proposal is calculated as its weight times its score. Highest consideration for awarding the business is given to the vendors' RFP responses that achieve the highest total weighted scores. The following table segment provides an example of a weighted score evaluation.

RFP Items	Weight	Vendor A score	Vendor A weighted score	Vendor B score	Vendor B weighted score
Item1 description	10	7	70	7	70
Item2 description	5	10	50	8	40
Total weighted scores			**120**		**110**

Example of a weighted score evaluation of two vendors' RFP responses. For Item1, vendors A and B are judged by the customer to have equivalent scores and thus equivalent weighted scores. For Item2, Vendor A is judged to provide better support than Vendor B. Vendor A has the highest total weighted score.

Tip: Searching the Web reveals more information about using a weighted score analysis.

Tip: A system supporting all required high priority items could potentially be out-scored by another system that did not support all absolutely required high priority items but supported a large number of preferred or optional items. A way to avoid that problem is to manage a separate table of just the absolutely required high priority items; only systems and vendors meeting those requirements would be further evaluated using a secondary table of only preferred/optional items.

- Participants. To help ensure the processes of developing requirements and evaluating and comparing proposals address all the aspects of an organization's storage needs, technical and non-technical, it can be important to involve a variety of organization personnel due to the different perspectives they will bring to the table and the different implications the decision may have on each party. While customer management and executives have a perspective on the broad needs of their organization as an enterprise, they may not understand the technical implications of a given storage system. On the other hand, while storage administrators, application designers, and their direct management may understand the technical issues, they may have limited awareness of overall enterprise considerations.

Thus, who decides what the decision criteria are, who influences the decision, who makes the final decision, and a way to potentially achieve consensus on the decision, should all be determined and agreed upon as early as possible. (It is usually critical to identify a single person to make (own) the final decision. Multiple participants in the process may not be able to reach a decision consensus. Even if they do, a high-level organization executive may choose to override that decision, potentially based on factors unknown to the participants.)

Broad participation doesn't necessarily require full-time participation by everyone involved. Some participants may just review work done by others or may be involved in only certain stages of the processes.

Tip: *Not all project participants may whole-heartedly agree with the decision maker's final choice. Management should consider having heart-to-heart discussions with participants to explain the reasons for the decision and help ensure everyone's support for successful system installation, migration, and ongoing operation.*

- <u>Project scheduling.</u> The time needed and allotted to complete a storage system acquisition project and phases within that project should be determined early. Scheduling when phases of a project are to be complete can address constraints such as the date by which a new storage system is required to be installed to support a major new application; earlier project phase dates can be set based on that key date.

Here is an example of a project plan showing major high-level milestones. An actual plan would/should be more detailed (e.g., by identifying who is responsible for each phase).

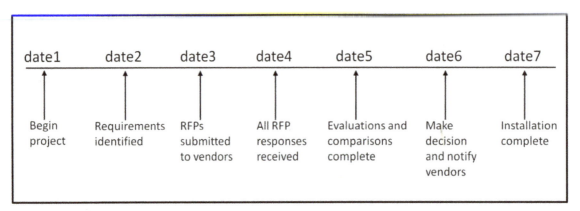

It can be useful to build in a buffer of extra time in case of unforeseen delays in project progress. For example, key participants may become ill or waylaid by organizational "emergencies"; some vendors may contest the decision. The acquisition project plan might be defined so that a new system will be ready for use a few weeks before it is expected to be needed; that may add some (hopefully small) additional cost but helps avoid the consequences of being late.

Regularly scheduled meetings of participants are recommended to assess project progress. Scheduled meetings help keep participants involved and foster participant communication. Organization management may request summary reports to keep them informed of project status.

If a schedule is too tight, there is a risk of making rushed decisions without prudent information and discussion. On the other hand, without calendar deadlines for project milestones there is the risk of a decision "never" being made. It's not difficult to come up with reasons to postpone a decision. Additional product and vendor attributes to consider might be identified resulting in *analysis paralysis*: an inability to make a decision because one can always think of more data to consider. Given the fast pace of the storage industry, additional products and vendors to consider may be announced during the project or may be reported in the press to likely be announced in the near future. Additional organization participants may ask (or be asked) to get involved as the project becomes more widely known within an organization. Some project participants may want to delay making a decision they anticipate will not be popular with everyone.

- Objectivity. Ideally, the requirement development process and the evaluation/comparison process should be in the best interests of the organization. This goal requires objectivity. Objectivity is also beneficial if it is necessary to later review and justify the acquisition process with higher management or to respond to any vendor objections to the processes. Objectivity does not happen automatically – it should be built into the processes.

Tip: Process participants can be cautioned to avoid personal agendas. For example, participants could potentially weave requirements into an RFP, or influence weights and scores, to favor a particular system or vendor even if those factors do not fairly represent an organization's needs. (Consider a requirement for a particular type of internal component supported by only one storage system even though it is not visible to users or applications.) Having the requirements and evaluation/comparison processes supported by a team of personnel rather than by only one person can help here. That said, even if intentional bias is absent it can still be difficult to be objective when assigning weights. Consider that without precise definitions, justifying assigning a weight to an item of 6 vs. 7 on a one-to-ten scale may not be possible.

Tip: Sometimes storage system decision makers and influencers have non-work-related relationships with vendors, perhaps personal friendships or relationships forged while previously working at other organizations. Such relationships might be positive or negative. Customer management should proactively advise decision makers and influencers to act in the best interest of the current organization and not let outside or past relationships unduly influence a recommendation or decision.

Tip: Some customers hire consultants to help in the requirement and evaluation/comparison process. That can be effective if the consultant has good knowledge of the customer's business and IT environment, good knowledge of storage system and vendor capabilities, and acts in the best interest of the customer, just as a loyal employee would.[150] However, some consultants may have preconceived views of what storage system or vendor they prefer and those views may work their way into the consultant's recommendations.)

Tip: Managing vendor contact during an RFP process can also be important to supporting objectivity. Objectivity is at risk if a vendor offers – or is asked – to help a customer write an RFP. Some customers prohibit vendor contact with organization personnel about RFP-related topics once an RFP has been submitted to the vendors; exceptions include questions a vendor can submit asking for clarifications of RFP items where answers are shared with all vendors.

Tip: The process of evaluating/comparing vendors' RFP responses likely cannot – and probably should not – be completely mechanical. Some subjective judgment on the part of proposal evaluators and the ultimate decision-maker may well be needed, though this is hopefully minimal and based solely on business considerations. For example, if it is determined that two vendors address RFP requirements equally well, an incumbent or well-known vendor and product may reasonably be judged as entailing less business risk than less familiar vendors and products. (Incumbency is likely not going to be an explicit RFP item since it could discourage non-incumbent vendors from responding.) Or, perhaps one vendor's proposed storage system supports a preferred but not absolutely required function while another vendor has proposed a significantly lower price to compensate for lacking that function. Or, perhaps one vendor's proposed storage system is claimed to support 1.05ms average I/O response time against a requirement of 1.0ms while offering other unique advantages. Sound business judgment, perhaps based on experience making such decisions, can help in such cases.

Additional Tips

- When customers need to replace an aging or inadequate storage system or need to add an additional system of similar characteristics, they often adopt the straightforward strategy of acquiring the latest generation storage system from the same vendor and system family.

  There are benefits and drawbacks to this strategy. It simplifies the acquisition decision process by avoiding the time and effort of an RFP process, avoiding having to deal with unfamiliar vendors, and minimizing the complexity of the system migration process. However, this strategy does not ensure the lowest overall cost which might be determined only by identifying what other vendors have to offer and are willing to bid to win the business. This strategy may also leave a customer unaware of valuable capabilities of other vendors' storage systems. These tradeoffs need to be weighed by a customer considering a straightforward acquisition strategy.

---

[150] As an analogy, consider "financial advisors." At least in the U.S., use of that title has historically been unregulated. Some financial advisors work for a firm and promote that firm's financial offerings. Some advisors may adhere to a "fiduciary duty": a legal duty to act solely in the customer's interests.

- *A customer's evaluation and comparison process should align with the customer's actual (and projected) needs. For example, a vendor might claim that their storage system is best because it supports higher maximum usable capacity than competing systems. That should prompt the question: So what? Assume a customer has a requirement for 100TB usable capacity where System A supports up to 500TB usable capacity and system B supports up to 5,000TB usable capacity. System B has much higher usable capacity scalability but no practical advantage over System A for this customer. (Otherwise, the requirement is likely not stated correctly.) Accordingly, if the customer conducts a weighted score analysis they may (or, perhaps should) reasonably decide to give System A and System B the same score for the usable capacity requirement. The point is, it is important that customers determine when exceeding requirements does not add value.*

- *When a storage system does not meet a particular requirement, the issue may sometimes be addressed by a vendor-supported process allowing the customer to request that support. Such a request is sometimes called an RPQ (Request for Price Quotation): a request for the vendor to quote a price for a hardware or software capability that is not currently available as a standard feature. A vendor may (offer to) implement a customer-initiated RPQ request to win a sales opportunity; then the questions are timing, cost, and how the vendor would support the capability. A vendor may even already support an RPQ for a desired non-standard capability; sales representatives may not always be aware of all existing RPQs so there is no harm in customers asking vendor representatives to look into it.*

- *When multiple business partners can sell a storage system model from the same manufacturer, one partner may do a detailed analysis of an RFP to develop a high-quality proposal, then another partner may suddenly appear and propose selling the same system configuration at a lower price they can afford to offer because they did not have to spend resources doing the upfront work. Awarding business based only on price in such a situation can be unfair to the partner initially involved. Some manufacturers avoid this situation by a process that lets the first business partner involved in an opportunity register for it with the manufacturer; however, this potentially results in the business partner best qualified to help the customer succeed in the acquisition not necessarily being the first business partner to register.*

- *It is useful to ask vendors to not necessarily limit RFP responses to only a simple Yes or No. Simple Yes or No responses may omit valuable information. Allowing for supplementary information or explanations also helps a customer assess a vendor's (or vendor representative's) product knowledge, product capability, trustworthiness, and helpfulness.*

  For example, assume some broad system characteristic, such as ease-of-management, is especially important due to limited administrator personnel, time, or skills. Ease-of-use is a characteristic that applies separately to many capabilities of a system – it is not a single simple Yes or No item. To deal with that a customer might request that vendors briefly summarize any noteworthy ease-of-management characteristics their systems have for technical RFP items supported by the vendor's proposal.

As another example, RFPs can request vendors to identify any exceptions, limitations, incompatibilities, and restrictions for relevant items. Consider that a customer may require two functions and a vendor may validly claim a given storage system supports each, but the storage system may not support using both functions against the same data at the same time. Or, a required function might not support volumes greater than a capacity that is less than volume capacities the customer plans to create. Or, the performance of a function may be such that using it is impractical in some circumstances.

- *Customers should ask their storage system vendors about plans for the next-generation system. Customers do not want to acquire a new storage system only to be caught by surprise the next day by the vendor's announcement of their next-generation system (at possibly the same or lower price for greater capability compared to current models, or possibly associated with a significant price decrease for current models). Customers should also ask their vendors about whether they plan to provide hardware and software upgrades to the current-generation system for any features planned to be introduced on the next-generation system (i.e., ask whether and which new features will be* backward-compatible*). These kinds of insights into vendor plans may require that a customer sign a non-disclosure agreement provided by the vendor.*

- *Customers should consider asking vendors for product demonstrations (aka "demos"). That can include at least a demonstration of the GUI administrator interface. A demo is most productive, however, if customers provide vendors a list of capabilities they want to see demonstrated. If the RFP is sent to only a very few vendors, a demo can be requested from each as part of the evaluation process. Otherwise, if the evaluation/comparison determines there are only a small number of systems and vendors able to meet requirements, demos can later be requested from just those vendors.*

- *When asking vendor sales representatives detailed questions about storage systems, whether in RFP items or in face-to-face meetings, customers should realize these representatives sometimes have limited knowledge about system technology, especially compared to product experts in the system's development and manufacturing organizations. That means answering questions may sometimes require the representatives to do some research. That is extra time and effort for the representatives who may already be under pressure to respond to an RFP on time.*

   While not always easy, customers should try to determine when answers to questions appear to provide official and accurate information rather than something a representative thinks is what the customer wants to hear or is an attempt to deflect the question so the representative does not have to spend more time on the matter or does not have to convey bad news.

- *If a customer determines that any of multiple storage systems meet their requirements, a potential tie breaker can be to choose the vendor or system that the customer is most familiar with, if that option exists. That choice can reduce time-and-effort and risks involved in migrating from more familiar to less familiar (or unfamiliar) systems and vendors. For example, when migrating from an installed system to an incompatible system, the incumbent vendor may have no incentive to help with the migration and the new vendor may have limited knowledge of the system being replaced.*

More generally, the greater the degree of change in any aspect of IT, the greater the chance of something going wrong including an increased chance for human error. Administrators may make mistakes due to differences between old and new systems in command syntax and semantics. New vendor service representatives may make mistakes due to being unfamiliar with a customer's IT environment.

Although it is common for customers to migrate between incompatible storage systems and even different vendors, they should be aware of the risks, ensure the reasons to switch are justified, and ensure thorough migration planning is done.

- *After a decision is made and business awarded to a vendor, a customer should hold an internal meeting to identify "lessons learned": what worked and what could be improved in the requirements/evaluation/comparison process. Lessons learned should be incorporated into documented procedures or at least preserved for future reference.*

Sources of Product and Vendor Information

Customers today have convenient access to an amazing amount of information about enterprise storage systems.

Sources of information that are generally readily accessible include: vendor/manufacturer press releases, vendor/manufacturer websites, specification sheets, data sheets, brochures, white papers, vendor Webcasts, product manuals (such as user guides), customer testimonials, social media (such as blogs, YouTube videos, LinkedIn discussions, and Twitter), fly-in briefings, presentations, conventions, roadshows, advertisements, and reports and opinions from analysts and commentators.

There is no readily accessible index that identifies all these sources or helps assess their value. Customers must identify available sources and select those they choose to rely on. Finding objective sources of information can be difficult. Customers are therefore advised to seek information from multiple sources and to use a critical eye when considering information ranging from product specifications to marketing claims to claims about competitors. Much of this Guide has been about providing insights to help customers do that. A brief review and a few additional comments are in order.

- <u>Information from vendors</u>. Vendors are the most direct sources of information about their own products. Vendor websites typically include information such as press releases (e.g., product announcements), product specifications, marketing collateral, white papers, and analysts' papers. (Business partners may publish less information about products, mainly to augment information published by the manufacturers.)

  Some vendor websites contain product manuals (such as user guides) and information on product software problems and fixes. It can be insightful to search this information (as opposed to marketing collateral) for terms such as *unsupported, not supported, can not, cannot, can't, must not, mustn't, should not, shouldn't, is not, isn't, are not, aren't, limitation(s), restriction(s), restricted, caution(s),* and *warning(s)*. Some vendors permit customer access to this information only by customers who have userid/password authorization; when that is the case, prospective customers are advised to request access from those vendors.

  Vendors' blogs, while often conveying marketing messages, may also provide insights into product capabilities. Note that while some vendors' blogs are published on the vendors' websites, others are published on other websites in which case it may not be clear the authors work for vendors. It is probably best to not assume material written by vendor employees about their employers and about competitors is always accurate and unbiased.

Keep in mind that most information published by vendors generally focuses on "good news" stories on their offerings, with little if any mention of weaknesses such as problems, limitations, restrictions, and unsupported capabilities.   In contrast, any mention of competitors typically focuses on weaknesses, not strengths. It is thus up to a customer to flush out a more complete story.   For example, any claims a vendor makes about competitors of interest to a customer warrant the customer asking the "accused" competitor for their side of the story.

- Information from customer references.   Customers can request vendors to provide references: the names of other customers who are using a storage system or feature being considered or, even better, who are willing to discuss their experiences with that system or feature.

  Realize that vendors will tell you about happy customers, but likely not about any unhappy customers.

  Some vendors may show customers a list of customer names or logos claimed to be using the vendors' storage system or feature. Customers should contact at least some referenced customers because such reference lists may be less than completely current or accurate. A customer may have uninstalled a system they are claimed to be using. A customer may have ordered a software feature but never implemented it. A vendor might cite a well-known company as using its storage system, but not indicate the system may be installed in only one subsidiary and the company also uses competitors' systems (and perhaps even more of them).

  Note that many companies, sometimes well-known companies in particular, do not support being cited as references for reasons such as the time it takes to respond to queries from other customers or not wanting to reveal the IT products they use.

- Information from analysts and industry watchers. Storage analysts' and industry watchers' opinions are often available in online articles and blogs at no charge.   Some analysts publish reports on storage vendors and their products and may be available for one-on-one consultations with customers; these offerings may be priced.

  Keep in mind, however, that some vendors hire analysts to write papers favorable to the vendor. Analysts may avoid criticizing a vendor in such papers or in other public forums due to fear of losing that vendor's business.

  It is important to realize that many industry analysts have little or no hands on experience with storage systems they comment on. They get much of their information from vendors and perhaps from some customers using those systems.

- Information from surveys. Some industry analysts publish the results of surveys they conduct that rate storage systems based on the answers to questions they ask of survey participants. The quality of such surveys can vary. Questions customers can ask about such surveys include: What storage system models were asked about? If ratings are by vendor name rather than by specific product, how useful is a particular vendor's rating if multiple and perhaps very different products are therefore lumped together? How many individuals were surveyed for each system included in the survey and what positions/titles did they hold? Did they have hands on experience or just buying authority? What countries were included in the survey? Were the questions asking for quantified answers (e.g., measurements of system uptime) or just subjective opinions (such as "Rate system reliability on a 1-to-5 scale")?

In Closing

This Guide has complemented the abundant information available on enterprise storage systems by focusing on information particularly relevant to the acquisition process. By helping customers understand potential capabilities of enterprise storage systems and vendors, helping customers be mindful of vendor marketing and selling activities, and helping customers determine the best systems and vendors for their environment, this Guide has hopefully contributed to a more successful and satisfying acquisition experience.

The storage industry has undergone incredible change since its inception in the mid-twentieth century. Storage has evolved from being "just a peripheral" to being a major area of specialization in its own right. Storage capabilities appear poised to continue to advance with no end in sight. Storage acquisition is an art as well as a science, and that keeps things very interesting for everyone in the industry.

Appendix A. Data Sharing

At first glance it may appear that all that is necessary to let multiple hosts share data is that those hosts are connected to the same storage system(s).[151] However, while that physical connectivity is necessary, it is not sufficient. There are two important considerations here.

A. Different hosts, and different applications may format storage differently. For example, volumes in a block-access storage system may be formatted differently by different host operating systems. Different word processing applications may format text files differently. In such cases, if software that does not support the way a volume or file is formatted tries to access it, results are unpredictable. This kind of obstacle to sharing data applies where sharing is done serially (i.e., different users but only one at a time) or done concurrently (i.e., multiple users at the same time).

B. Even assuming identical host software and formatting, the ability of multiple hosts to access the same data *at the same time* requires special handling to manage that access and protect data integrity. For example, applications that can concurrently run in multiple hosts can communicate to cooperatively manage how they share data. Without such cooperation, the following well known, but definitely undesirable, kind of scenario could occur.

1. Assume hosts A and B are attached to the same storage system in a bank. The hosts run the same database management system (DBMS) software and the same DBMS applications written by the bank. The storage system contains a database containing customers' accounts and a list of the day's deposits. Each night, each host accesses the list of the day's deposits in order to update the database records of account balances.

2. There are two deposits in the list that are to be applied to account X. The data for account X resides in record X in the database in storage. One deposit is for $2000 and the other is for $3000, for a total of $5000 in new deposits to account X. Record X shows an initial account X balance of $1000.

3. Host A accesses the $3000 deposit from the list and issues a read I/O to read record X into its memory in preparation to update it. Host A's in-memory copy of record X shows a balance of $1000.

---

[151] In contrast to multiple hosts sharing data by being cabled (directly or via a network) to the same external storage system(s), internal storage inside a host was historically limited to being accessed by only that host. Today, however, some vendors offer software that can be installed on hosts to make their internal storage accessible to other hosts.

308 Enterprise Storage Systems

4. Host B accesses the $2000 deposit from the list and reads the same record X into its memory in preparation to update it. Host B's in-memory copy of record X shows a balance of $1000.

5. Host A updates the copy of record X in its memory by adding the $3000 deposit to it. Host A's in-memory copy now shows a balance of $4000. Host A then issues a write I/O to write the updated record X back to the storage system. The storage system's record X now shows a balance of $4000.

6. Host B updates the copy of record X in its memory by adding $2000 to it. Host B's in-memory copy now shows a balance of $3000. Host B then writes the updated record X back to the storage system. The storage system's record X now shows a balance of $3000. Host B's update overlaid the previous update from Host A.

7. The result is that only one deposit ends up being credited to account X because only the last updater (Host B) had its update take effect.

The scenario is an example of what is called a *race condition:* the timing of interleaved changes affects the outcome of a computation.

One way the problem could be avoided is by only one host updating the account database and accessing only one entry from the list at a time. But perhaps two (or more) hosts are needed for performance reasons. In that case, a way the problem could be avoided is by the DBMS allowing an application in one host to indicate they are temporarily taking control of a particular record (a process called *locking*), so that no other host is allowed to access that record until the first host informs the DBMS it no longer needs control. Only one host at a time would be allowed to read and update record X. DBMSs generally work this way.

Different applications may use different ways of managing data sharing. For example, data sharing could be limited in granularity to a volume, to a file, or to a single record.

Appendix B. Load Balancing

Load balancing is an IT design principle to optimize performance by efficiently distributing work among multiple resources of the same type. Examples of storage system-related resources that can benefit from load balancing are host paths, internal drives, and internal processors.

The idea behind load balancing is that, if there are multiple resources in a system of the same type, it can often make sense to spread work around so each resource contributes to getting that work done. That helps work finish faster by helping to avoid situations where one resource is so busy it significantly degrades the performance of the work assigned to use it while another resource of the same type has little or no work to do. Load balancing helps the response time of work, such as I/O requests, to be more consistent.

The opposite of load balancing is where like resources are each dedicated to handling only certain work requests. For example, consider a system design where every file is assigned to its own dedicated HDD. Then all requests for a particular file are directed to the one and only HDD in which that file resides. Just due to the patterns of how files are accessed over time, one HDD could sometimes be very busy while at the same time other HDDs are much less busy or even idle. (In this case, an alternate way to store data to help balance the load would be having each HDD contain data from multiple files and every file's data distributed among multiple HDDs.)

Implementations of load balancing can be manual or dynamic. Manual load balancing requires administrators' time and effort to adjust what resources support what work requests. Dynamic load balancing means a storage system automatically adjusts what resources support what work requests. How often adjustment occurs in either case can vary, but dynamic load balancing can generally occur more often and more consistently than manual load balancing.

An example of manual load balancing is when administrators manually control how hosts are connected to a storage system so incoming I/O requests are balanced among host adapters; load balancing in that case can require moving cables coming in from some hosts to different adapters. An example of dynamic load balancing is a storage system automatically and nondisruptively relocating data among drives to reduce average drive performance utilization and, as a result, improve I/O response times.

An analogy may help. Consider a store (analogous to a storage system) with multiple cashiers (analogous to individual resources). A customer is analogous to an I/O request wanting to use one of those resources. A given customer doesn't care which cashier they use, they just want to finish shopping quickly. An arrangement with no load balancing means customers are pre-assigned (perhaps based on the first letter of their last name) to the cashier they must use whether or not that cashier is already busy. An arrangement with manual load balancing means a customer in a slow moving line can move to a different cashier only if and when someone in charge (an administrator) notices what is happening and directs the customer to make that change. A situation with dynamic load balancing means there is a single line (queue) of customers waiting for cashiers where the next customer in line is automatically assigned to the next available cashier. (Many stores implement a single queue for all cashiers because customers generally perceive it to be fair.)

Different load balancing algorithms are appropriate for different types of resources. Algorithms may vary in effectiveness and efficiency. Sometimes multiple algorithms are supported for a given type of resource and customers can choose which algorithm to implement.

Example 1: Prominent algorithms supported by host-based multipath I/O drivers to assign I/O requests to one of multiple paths to a storage system include: give the next I/O request to the next path in a circular list of paths (aka round-robin), give the next I/O request to the least busy path, and give the next I/O request to the path currently exhibiting the fastest average response time.

Example 2: A common algorithm to balance drive utilization is to balance the amount of data across drives (in the hope that will tend to balance the portion of I/O requests sent to each drive). A more effective approach is relocating data among drives based on a history of I/O patterns to specifically balance drive performance utilization even if that leaves capacity unbalanced.

The term "balance" notwithstanding, workload distribution across resources does not have to be precisely 50-50 or 25-25-25-25, or whatever, to be very effective at helping to optimize performance. Also, significant performance benefits can be gained by load balancing among subsets of all like resources; in a given system's architecture, load balancing among all like resources in an entire system may not be practical or desirable..

Appendix C. Intra-System Replication Consistency Groups

This discussion delves a bit deeper into consistency groups than the *Intra-System Data Replication* chapter. Some principles discussed here also apply to inter-system data replication (remote mirroring) consistency groups.

Many applications are designed to issue a series of write I/Os in a specific order; those writes are called *dependent writes*. The order is important because, if there is a failure before a series of writes completes (e.g., the application has a bug and terminates unexpectedly, or perhaps the entire host fails), when the application restarts, its awareness of the order in which writes were issued enables it to determine the point at which the series was interrupted. The application can then handle the situation. For such applications, it is important that the process of making a copy of data preserves the order of updates made by dependent writes because, at some future time, the application may be started against the copy.

A storage system cannot directly determine, as it receives write I/O requests, which ones are dependent on which other ones. But, why isn't write order naturally preserved when making a copy? After all, aren't write requests submitted by applications already in the right order (even if interleaved with I/Os arriving from unrelated applications)? They are, but problems arise when the dependent writes occur to more than one volume (or to more than one group of data of any type, but we'll use volumes in the following discussion).

When multiple volumes are copied individually rather than treated as a group to be copied all at once, the making of the copies inside the storage system, even if each appears to be made near-instantly, can potentially be interleaved with write I/Os to the volumes in an unpredictable way. An administrator cannot coordinate the timing of the copy commands with the times database transactions issue write I/Os (which may be issued only milliseconds apart). As a result, the data captured in the copy of the group of volumes may not contain all the dependent-write I/Os to volumes in the group.

How this can occur is illustrated by the following scenario. Assume volumes A, B, and L contain a database managed by a database management system (DBMS). Volumes A and B contain user data; volume L contains the database transaction log. A storage administrator quickly issues separate commands for each of the three volumes to be copied. (Or, the administrator might issue a single command with a list of the three volumes. It doesn't matter, because the storage system processes list entries one at a time.) The copies are made concurrently with I/O activity to the volumes.

Numbered events below occur in order of increasing time. "o" indicates the original contents of volumes. "u" indicates when a volume or a copy of a volume are updated. The original volume contents are shown in step (1); subsequent changes are shown in bold font in the step in which they occur.

	Data on volumes			Data on copies of		
	A	B	L	A	B	L
1. The original contents of A, B, and L. The copies are empty (-).	o	o	o	-	-	-
2. A user initiates transaction T.						
3. Transaction T updates a record on volume A.	**u**	o	o			
4. The command to copy volume A is received by the storage system. The update to volume A in (3) is captured in the copy of volume A.				**u**	-	-
5. The command to copy volume B is received by the storage system. Volume B has not yet been changed by transaction T.				u	**o**	-
6. Transaction T updates a record on volume B. The copy of volume B made in (5) is unchanged.	u	**u**	o			
7. Transaction T completes successfully. The DBMS writes a log entry to volume L indicating T completed normally.	u	u	**u**			
8. The command to copy volume L is received by the storage system. The log entry written in (7) is captured in the copy of volume L.				u	o	**u**

As a result, when the DBMS is (re)started against the *copies* of A, B, and L, the DBMS refers to the log and sees that transaction T completed normally. But the copy captured only the updates to A and L, not the update to B. The copy of the database has lost integrity.

If, instead of being copied independently, volumes A, B, and L had been defined by an administrator to be in a volume consistency group, the volumes in the group would have been copied together *as a group*. In that case, no dependent write (e.g., the update to volume B in the above scenario) would be omitted in the copies of the volumes in the consistency group. Depending on timing, the database copy would capture either the state of all three volumes before any updates were made, or would capture the original state of all three volumes plus the update to volume A, or would capture the original state of all three volumes plus the updates to volumes A and B, or would capture the updates to all three volumes. If the update to volume L, the log, was not captured, the DBMS would conclude that the transaction had not completed successfully and the DBMS would back out (undo) the changes made to A, or to A and B.

The basic methodology a storage system uses to make a copy of a consistency group is relatively straightforward, and is something like the following. In response to a request to make a point-in-time copy of a consistency group, a storage system temporarily "freezes" access to all data in the group at the same time (e.g., by signaling any host that sends an I/O request against that data to temporarily queue it inside host memory). During the time access is frozen, the storage system builds internal tables of information that identify the locations of the current (source) data.[152]   The copy is effectively (logically) complete.   Access is unfrozen and hosts are notified that I/Os against source and target data are now accepted.   If the storage system later receives a write I/O request to update any source data that had been frozen and the information tables indicate a physical copy had not yet been preserved for target use, the system takes action to preserve that data.

A request to make a copy of a single volume essentially treats that volume as a mini consistency group of one.   I/O requests to the volume are temporarily frozen while the system builds an information table about the current contents of the volume that represent the point-in-time data in the copy.   There is no need to explicitly create a consistency group in that case.

As an alternative to consistency group support, an administrator could halt all I/O activity to the database in a planned way so that a time-consistent copy of all volumes could be made without needing consistency group support in the storage system.   However, halting the database activity in that way means halting activity for seconds to minutes which is disruptive to users of the database.   Consistency groups allow time-consistent copies of multiple volumes to be made in a way such that users see no (or hopefully minimal) disruption.

---

[152] How long this takes could depend on the storage system, the number of volumes in the consistency group, their capacities, and other system activity.   For small groups, hosts may see only a small, temporary elongation of I/O response time while the system's information structures to support the copies are being established.   Vendors can be asked to provide insight into this time for particular system models.

Appendix D. RFP Outline

Below is a suggested outline for a storage system RFP. The formats of actual storage system RFPs created by customers vary, so there is some flexibility to tailor an RFP to meet customers' different needs. Searching the Web for *storage rfp sample* finds much information to look at.

1. Cover letter to vendors

This is an RFP; contents are to be kept confidential between *customer-name* and recipients; brief statement of objective; RFP proposal due date; how proposals are to be delivered to *customer-name*; the document type of the proposal (e.g., PDF); how and when submitters will be notified of the customer's decision; whether the intent is to award all business to one vendor or to potentially award parts of the business to different vendors; who vendors can contact to request clarification of RFP contents and whether answers will be distributed to all RFP participants.

2. Table of Contents

3. Introductory Material

Detailed statement of objective: The problem the proposed solution should address.

Customer background: About the customer's organization.

Overview of current IT environment and IT objectives.

4. Detailed Requirements

General: Description of how responses are to be formatted (see *Notes* below). Vendors are encouraged to include brief comments or explanations for responses to individual requirements; in particular, vendors should identify any and all exception cases to supported items. Vendors are encouraged to identify recommended alternatives to address any unsupported requirements. Responses should be factual and avoid "marketing prose."

This section can include questions in addition to requirements. For example, in addition to the section specifying a requirement for a 3-year warranty, vendors could be asked to provide the details of their warranty.

Technical requirements: Host support, availability, performance, etc.

Vendor requirements: How long the vendor has been in business, how long the proposed product(s) have been in the market, customer references for proposed offerings, parts supply locations, on-site customer support information, date by which the proposed solution must be installed, guarantees, etc.

Financial requirements: Contract requirements, warranty and maintenance requirements; purchase vs. lease requirements, whether proposed prices must be best-and-final, etc.

Notes

Individual requirements could be provided by the customer in a template to be filled in by each vendor. This promotes a consistent format for vendor responses and consistent, pre-numbered requirements. Here is an example:

ID	Description	Yes	No	Comments
1	**Technical requirements**			
1.1	**Host attachment items**			
1.1.1	The proposed system supports the following hosts/OSs: a, b, c,…			
1.1.2	The proposed system supports the following ISV host-based software: a, b, c,…			
1.2	**Availability items**			
1.2.1	All hardware components in the proposed solution are redundant			
1.2.2	The proposed system supports nondisruptive software upgrades			
…				
2	**Vendor requirements**			
…				
3	**Financial requirements**			

5. Appendices

This section contains ancillary information such as forms vendors may be asked to complete and sign (such as a confidentiality agreement or a form to be returned by a specified date indicating whether the vendor intends to submit a proposal).

Index

H

I

K

L

M

N